Beginning Java™ SE 6 Platform

Platform

From Novice to Professional

Jeff Friesen

Apress®

Beginning Java™ SE 6 Platform: From Novice to Professional

Copyright © 2007 by Jeff Friesen

ISBN-13 (paperback): 978-1-59059-830-6

ISBN-13 (electronic): 978-1-4302-0246-2

Printed and bound in the United States of America (POD)

Trademarked names may appear in this book. Rather than use a trademark symbol with every occurrence of a trademarked name, we use the names only in an editorial fashion and to the benefit of the trademark owner, with no intention of infringement of the trademark.

Java™ and all Java-based marks are trademarks or registered trademarks of Sun Microsystems, Inc., in the US and other countries. Apress, Inc., is not affiliated with Sun Microsystems, Inc., and this book was written without endorsement from Sun Microsystems, Inc.

Lead Editor: Steve Anglin
Technical Reviewers: Sumit Pal, John Zukowski
Editorial Board: Steve Anglin, Ewan Buckingham, Tony Campbell, Gary Cornell, Jonathan Gennick, Jason Gilmore, Kevin Goff, Jonathan Hassell, Matthew Moodie, Joseph Ottinger, Jeffrey Pepper, Ben Renow-Clarke, Dominic Shakeshaft, Matt Wade, Tom Welsh
Project Manager: Richard Dal Porto
Copy Editor: Marilyn Smith
Assistant Production Director: Kari Brooks-Copony
Production Editor: Elizabeth Berry
Compositor: Gina Rexrode
Proofreader: April Eddy
Indexer: Becky Hornyak
Artist: April Milne
Cover Designer: Kurt Krames
Manufacturing Director: Tom Debolski

Distributed to the book trade worldwide by Springer-Verlag New York, Inc., 233 Spring Street, 6th Floor, New York, NY 10013. Phone 1-800-SPRINGER, fax 201-348-4505, e-mail orders-ny@springer-sbm.com, or visit http://www.springeronline.com.

For information on translations, please contact Apress directly at 2855 Telegraph Avenue, Suite 600, Berkeley, CA 94705. Phone 510-549-5930, fax 510-549-5939, e-mail info@apress.com, or visit http://www.apress.com.

The source code for this book is available to readers at http://www.apress.com in the Source Code/Download section.

To my parents and my good friend Amaury

Contents at a Glance

Contents

Preface

In late 2005, I started to explore Java SE 6 by writing a JavaWorld article titled "Start saddling up for Mustang" (http://www.javaworld.com/javaworld/jw-01-2006/jw-0109-mustang.html). This article investigated Console I/O, partition-space methods, the Splash Screen API, and the System Tray API.

In mid-2006, I wrote "Mustang (Java SE 6) Gallops into Town" (http://www.informit.com/articles/article.asp?p=661371&rl=1) for informit.com. This article continued my earlier Java SE 6 exploration by focusing on access permissions control methods, the Desktop API, programmatic access to network parameters, and table sorting and filtering.

In late 2006, I completed my article-based coverage of Java SE 6 by writing a trilogy of articles for informit.com: "Taming Mustang, Part 1: Collections API" (http://www.informit.com/articles/article.asp?p=696620&rl=1), "Taming Mustang, Part 2: Scripting API Tour" (http://www.informit.com/articles/article.asp?p=696621&rl=1), and "Taming Mustang, Part 3: A New Script Engine" (http://www.informit.com/articles/article.asp?p=696622&rl=1).

This book continues my exploration of Java SE 6.

About the Author

JEFF FRIESEN has been actively involved with Java since the late 1990s. Jeff has worked with Java in various companies, including a health-care–oriented consulting firm, where he created his own Java/C++ software for working with smart cards. Jeff has written about Java in numerous articles for JavaWorld.com, informit.com, and java.net, and has authored *Java 2 by Example, Second Edition* (Que Publishing). Jeff has also taught Java in university and college continuing education classes. He has a Bachelor of Science degree in mathematics and computer science from Brandon University in Brandon, Manitoba, Canada.

About the Technical Reviewers

 **SUMIT PAL** has about 14 years of experience with software architecture, design, and development on a variety of platforms, including Java, J2EE. He has worked in the SQL Server Replication group while with Microsoft, and with Oracle's OLAP Server group while with Oracle. Apart from certifications such as IEEE-CSDP and J2EE Architect, Sumit has a Master of Science degree in Computer Science. Sumit has a keen interest in database internals, algorithms, and search engine technology. He currently works as an OLAP architect for LeapFrogRX. Sumit has invented some basic generalized algorithms to find divisibility between numbers, and also invented divisibility rules for prime numbers less than 100. Sumit has a fierce desire to work for Google some day.

JOHN ZUKOWSKI performs strategic Java consulting for JZ Ventures, Inc. He regularly contributes to Sun's monthly Tech Tips column and Java Technology Fundamentals newsletter. In addition, John monitors IBM's client-side Java programming forum at developerWorks. Since the beginning of Java time, John has authored ten books solo and contributed to several others. His best sellers include three editions each of the *Definitive Guide to Swing* (Apress) and *Mastering Java 2* (Sybex), and his latest, the predecessor to this book, *Java 6 Platform Revealed* (Apress).

Acknowledgments

I thank Steve Anglin for giving me the opportunity to continue my exploration of Java SE 6 via this book. I also thank Richard Dal Porto for guiding me through various aspects of the writing process. Thank you Sumit and John for your diligence in catching various flaws (including some embarrassing ones) that would otherwise have made it into this book. Finally, I thank Marilyn Smith, Elizabeth Berry, and April Eddy for making the book's content look good.

Introduction

Welcome to *Beginning Java SE 6 Platform*. Contrary to its title, this is not another beginner-oriented book on Java. You will not learn about classes, threads, file I/O, and other fundamental topics. If learning Java from scratch is your objective, you will need to find another book. But if you need to know (or if you just happen to be curious about) what makes Java SE 6 stand apart from its predecessors, this book is for you.

This book starts you on a journey of exploration into most of Java SE 6's new and improved features. Unfortunately, various constraints kept me from covering every feature, including the JavaBeans Activation Framework (<<sigh>>).

While you learn about these features, you'll also encounter exciting technologies, such as JRuby and JavaFX, and even catch a glimpse of Java SE 7. You'll also find numerous questions and exercises that challenge your understanding of Java SE 6, and numerous links to web resources for continuing this journey.

Beginning Java SE 6 Platform is a must-have resource if you want to quickly upgrade your skills. It is also the right choice if you need information about performance and other important topics before deciding if your company should upgrade to Java SE 6. This book will save you from wading through Java SE Development Kit (JDK) documentation and performing a lot of Internet searches.

Authors have idiosyncrasies; I am no different. For starters, although you'll often find links to various resources, I do not include links to entries in Sun's Bug Database. Rather than present individual links, I present bug identifiers and their names (Bug 6362451 "The string returned by toString() shows the bridge methods as having the volatile modificator," for example). If you want to find information about a bug, point your browser to `http://bugs.sun.com/bugdatabase/index.jsp`, enter the bug identifier in the appropriate field, and perform a search. In addition to the appropriate database entry appearing at the start of the search results, other results point you to related items that can enhance your understanding of a particular bug topic.

Other idiosyncrasies that you'll discover include my placing a `// filename.java` comment at the start of a source file (I forget the reason why I started to do this; old habits die hard), placing space characters between method names and their argument/parameter lists in source listings, importing everything from a package (`import java.awt.*;`, for example), limiting my comments in source listings, bolding certain parts of source listings to emphasize them, and adding the package name (unless the package is `java.lang`) to the first mention of a class or an interface in the text.

Who This Book Is For

This book assumes that you are a professional Java developer with a solid understanding of Java 2 Platform, Standard Edition 5 (J2SE 5). If you are new to Java, you'll probably feel overwhelmed by this book's content because it does not revisit basic Java concepts (such as classes and generics). It just is not possible to cover both the fundamentals and Java SE 6's new features in a single book.

For a version-agnostic treatment of Java and object-oriented fundamentals in general, refer to *Beginning Java Objects, Second Edition* (Apress, 2005; ISBN: 1-59059-457-6) by Jacquie Barker.

How This Book Is Structured

This book is organized into ten chapters and five appendixes. The first chapter introduces you to Java SE 6. The remaining chapters explore new and improved features in specific topic areas, in a tutorial style. The first three appendixes present additional features in a reference format. The penultimate appendix presents answers and solutions to the questions and exercises that are presented in Chapters 1 through 10. The final appendix gives you a preview of features that will most likely appear in Java SE 7. Here's a brief summary of the contents:

Chapter 1, Introducing Java SE 6: Every journey needs a beginning. Chapter 1 sets the stage for the remaining chapters by introducing you to Java SE 6. You'll learn the reason for the name change (it's not J2SE 6), the themes that define this release, and the big picture of what constitutes Java SE 6. You'll then get a taste of what is new and improved by exploring some Java SE 6 features not covered elsewhere in the book. Because Java SE 6 has evolved since build 105 (which is the build that I used to develop this book's code and examples), this chapter concludes with brief coverage of Java SE 6, update 1 and update 2.

Chapter 2, Core Libraries: Chapter 2 explores various core library topics. You'll learn about enhancements made to the BitSet class, the new Compiler API, I/O enhancements, mathematics enhancements, new and improved collections, new and improved concurrency, and the new ServiceLoader API. What are classpath wildcards? You'll find the answer in Chapter 2.

Chapter 3, GUI Toolkits: AWT: A lot of new stuff has been added to Java SE 6's Abstract Windowing Toolkit (or Abstract Window Toolkit, if you prefer). Chapter 3 explores the brand-new Desktop, Splash Screen, and System Tray APIs. It also looks at the new modality model and API. Various improvements have also been made to the existing infrastructure. This chapter briefly examines enhancements in the areas of dynamic layout, non-English locale input, and XAWT (the AWT for Solaris and Linux).

Chapter 4, GUI Toolkits: Swing: Not to be outdone, Swing has also benefited in Java SE 6. In Chapter 4, you'll learn how to add arbitrary components to JTabbedPane's tab headers. You'll also examine the improvements in the SpringLayout layout manager and in the area of dragging and dropping Swing components. Then you'll play with the new JTable class features for sorting and filtering table contents, learn about enhancements to the Windows and GTK look and feels, and explore the new SwingWorker class. Finally, you'll discover how to print text components.

Chapter 5, Internationalization: Chapter 5 introduces you to the Calendar class's support for the Japanese Imperial Era calendar, the locale-sensitive services, new locales, the Normalizer API, and ResourceBundle enhancements. Among other things, you'll learn how the locale-sensitive services are used to introduce an appropriate currency provider for a new locale.

Chapter 6, Java Database Connectivity: This chapter has a "split personality." The first half focuses on new Java Database Connectivity (JDBC) features ranging from automatic driver loading to wrapper pattern support. The second half explores Java DB (also known as Apache Derby), which happens to be a pure-Java database management system (DBMS) bundled with JDK 6. If you are unfamiliar with Java DB/Derby, this chapter will quickly get you up to speed on using this technology. This chapter's "Test Your Understanding" section provides an example of going beyond this book by challenging you to describe how to get MySQL Connector/J 5.1 to support automatic driver loading.

Chapter 7, Monitoring and Management: Java SE 6 brings important changes and additions to the area of monitoring and management. Chapter 7 first presents dynamic attach and the new Attach API. The dynamic attach mechanism allows JConsole to connect to and start the Java Management Extensions (JMX) agent in a target virtual machine, and the Attach API allows JConsole and other Java applications to take advantage of this mechanism. After having some fun with this feature, you'll explore the improved Instrumentation API, JVM Tool Interface, and Management and JMX APIs. Moving on, you'll learn about the JConsole tool's improved graphical user interface (GUI). Finally, you'll explore the concept of JConsole plugins and examine the JConsole API.

Chapter 8, Networking: Chapter 8 focuses on Java SE 6's networking enhancements. To complement Java 5's introduction of the abstract CookieHandler class, Java SE 6 provides a concrete CookieManager subclass, which makes it easy to list a web site's cookies. After examining this topic, Chapter 8 focuses on internationalized domain names; you'll learn something interesting about JEditorPane's setPage() methods. Then you'll be introduced to the new lightweight HTTP server and its API. (You'll discover this server's usefulness in Chapter 10.) Next, you'll learn about network parameters. Developers of networked games will find one of the new network parameter methods described in this chapter especially helpful. Finally, the chapter introduces the topic of SPNEGO-based HTTP authentication.

Chapter 9, Scripting: Chapter 9 introduces both the new Scripting API and the experimental jrunscript tool. You'll learn how your applications can benefit from having access to JavaScript. This is one of my favorite chapters because it also discusses JRuby and JavaFX, but only from a Scripting API perspective.

Chapter 10, Security and Web Services: Chapter 10 is another "split-personality" chapter. It begins with a look at two new security features: the Smart Card I/O and XML Digital Signature APIs. Then it explores the new support for web services, via a web services stack and assorted tools.

Appendix A, New Annotation Types: Appendix A provides a reference on the new annotation types introduced by Java SE 6. These types are organized into three categories: annotation types supported by annotation processors, Common Annotations 1.0, and additional annotation types for the Java Architecture for XML Binding (JAXB), Java API for XML Web Services (JAX-WS), Java Web Service (JWS), JMX, and JavaBeans APIs.

Appendix B, New and Improved Tools: Appendix B provides a reference to changes made to existing tools and the introduction of new tools. This tool-related information is organized into the categories of basic tools, command-line script shell, monitoring and management console, web services tools, Java Web Start, security tools, and troubleshooting tools. This appendix also reviews many of the enhancements to the virtual machine and runtime environment. Additional enhancements related to virtual machine performance are discussed in Appendix C.

Appendix C, Performance Enhancements: In addition to robustness, Java SE 6's performance enhancements are a good reason to upgrade to this version. Appendix C provides a reference on some of these enhancements: a fix to the gray-rect problem (this is more than just a perceived problem with performance), better-performing Image I/O, faster HotSpot virtual machines, and single-threaded rendering.

Appendix D, Test Your Understanding Answers: Each of Chapters 1 through 10 ends with a "Test Your Understanding" section. Appendix D provides my answers to these questions and my solutions to these exercises. I recommend giving each question/exercise a good try before looking up its answer/solution in this appendix.

Appendix E, A Preview of Java SE 7: Java SE 7 (assuming that Sun does not change the naming convention) will probably debut in mid-to-late 2008. As the Java community's focus shifts from Java SE 6 to Java SE 7, you'll want to know what you can expect from this upcoming release. In Appendix E, I "polish my crystal ball" and give you a glimpse of what will most likely be included in Java SE 7. As with Java 5 (I refer to Java 5 instead of J2SE 5 throughout the book), you can expect some sort of language changes (closures, I predict). You can also expect new APIs, such as the Swing Application Framework. You'll explore these and other items in Appendix E.

Prerequisites

This book assumes that you are using Java SE 6 build 105 or higher. The book's content and code have been tested against build 105.

Downloading the Code

The sample code associated with this book is available from the Source Code/Download area of the Apress web site (`http://www.apress.com`). After you have downloaded and unzipped the file that contains this book's code, you'll discover a `build.xml` file. This file conveniently lets you use Apache Ant 1.6.5 (and probably higher versions as well) to build most of the code. You will also find a `README.txt` file that contains instructions for building the code with Ant.

Contacting the Author

Feel free to contact me about the content of this book, the downloadable code, or any other related topic, at `jeff@javajeff.mb.ca`. Also, please visit my web site at `http://javajeff.mb.ca`.

■ ■ ■

Introducing Java SE 6

Java SE 6, the sixth generation of Java Standard Edition since version 1.0, officially arrived on December 11, 2006. This release offers many features that will benefit Java developers for years to come. This chapter introduces you to Java SE 6 and some of its features via the following topics:

- Name change for this Java edition

- Themes of Java SE 6

- Overview of Java SE 6

- Sampling of Java SE 6 new features

- Java SE 6, update 1 and update 2

Tip Meet the developers behind Java SE 6 by visiting the Planet JDK site (`http://planetjdk.org/`), which was created by Java SE Chief Engineer Mark Reinhold (see "Announcing planetjdk.org" at `http://weblogs.java.net/blog/mreinhold/archive/2005/11/announcing_plan.html`). You can learn a lot about Java SE 6 by reading the developers' blogs and articles. I present links to relevant blog and article entries throughout this book.

Name Change for This Java Edition

At different times during Java's 12-year history, Sun has introduced a new naming convention for its assorted Java editions, development kits, and runtime environments. For example, Java Development Kit (JDK) 1.2 became known as Java 2 Platform, Standard Edition 1.2 (J2SE 1.2). More recently, Sun announced that the fifth generation of its standard edition (since JDK 1.0) would be known as Java 2 Platform, Standard Edition 5.0 (J2SE 5.0), instead of the expected Java 2 Platform, Standard Edition 1.5.0 (J2SE 1.5.0).

The 5.0 is known as the external version number, and 1.5.0 is used as the internal version number.

Prior to releasing the latest generation, Sun's marketing team met with a group of its Java partners, and most agreed to simplify the Java 2 Platform's naming convention to build brand awareness. In addition to dropping the *2* from Java 2 Platform, Standard Edition, the "dot number" (the number following the period, as in 5.0) would be dropped, so that future updates to the Java platform would be noted as updates rather than dot numbers tacked onto the end of platform names. Hence, this latest Java release is known as *Java Platform, Standard Edition 6 (Java SE 6)*.

Similar to the 5.0 in J2SE 5.0 (which I refer to as Java 5 throughout this book), 6 is the external version number in the latest release. Also, 1.6.0 is the internal version number, which appears in the various places identified on Sun's Java SE 6, Platform Name and Version Numbers page (http://java.sun.com/javase/6/webnotes/version-6.html). This page also indicates that JDK (which now stands for Java SE Development Kit) continues to be the acronym for the development kit, and JRE continues to be the acronym for the Java Runtime Environment.

■**Note** Jon Byous discusses the new naming convention in more detail via his "Building and Strengthening the Java Brand" article (http://java.sun.com/developer/technicalArticles/JavaOne2005/naming.html). Also, check out Sun's "New! Java Naming Gets a Birthday Present" article (http://www.java.com/en/about/brand/naming.jsp).

The Themes of Java SE 6

Java SE 6 was developed under Java Specification Request (JSR) 270 (http://jcp.org/en/jsr/detail?id=270), which presents the themes listed in this section. The themes are also mentioned in Sun's official press release on Java SE 6, "Sun Announces Revolutionary Version of Java Technology – Java Platform Standard Edition 6" (http://www.sun.com/smi/Press/sunflash/2006-12/sunflash.20061211.1.xml).

Compatibility and stability: Many members of the Java community have invested heavily in Java technology. Because it is important that their investments are preserved, effort has been expended to ensure that the vast majority of programs that ran on previous versions of the Java platform continue to run on the latest platform. A few programs may need to be tinkered with to get them to run, but these should be rare. Stability is just as important as compatibility. Many bugs have been fixed, and the HotSpot virtual machines and their associated runtime environments are even more stable in this release.

Diagnosability, monitoring, and management: Because Java is widely used for mission-critical enterprise applications that must be kept running, it is important to have support for remote monitoring, management, and diagnosis. To this end, Java SE 6 improves the existing Java Management Extensions (JMX) API and infrastructure, as well as JVM Tool Interface. For example, you now have the ability to monitor applications not started with a special monitoring flag (you can look inside any running application to see what is happening under the hood).

Ease of development: Java SE 6 simplifies a developer's life by providing new annotation types, such as `@MXBean` for defining your own MBeans; a scripting framework that you can use to leverage the advantages offered by JavaScript, Ruby, and other scripting languages; redesigned Java Database Connectivity (JDBC) that benefits from automatic driver loading; and other features.

Enterprise desktop: As developers encounter the limitations of browser-based thin clients, they are once again considering rich client applications. To facilitate the migration to rich client applications, Java SE 6 provides better integration with native desktop facilities (such as the system tray, access to the default web browser and other desktop helper applications, and splash screens), the ability to print the contents of text components, the ability to sort and filter table rows, font anti-aliasing so that text is more readable on liquid crystal display (LCD) screens, and more.

XML and web services: Java SE 6 provides significant enhancements in the area of XML; XML digital signatures and Streaming API for XML (StAX) are two examples. Although Java 5 was supposed to include a web services client stack, work on this feature could not be finished in time for Java 5's release. Fortunately, Java SE 6 includes this stack—hello, Web 2.0!

Transparency: According to JSR 270, "Transparency is new and reflects Sun's ongoing effort to evolve the J2SE platform in a more open and transparent manner." This is in response to the desire of many developers to participate more fully in the development of the next generation of Java. Because of the positive reception to Sun's "experiment in openness"—making Java 5 (Tiger) snapshot releases available to the public, which allowed developers to collaborate with Sun on fixing problems—Sun enhanced this experiment for Java SE 6. This transparency has fully evolved into Sun open-sourcing the JDK. Developers now have more influence on the features to be made available in the next generation of Java.

■Note For more information about Java SE 6 transparency and open-sourcing, see Java SE Chief Engineer Mark Reinhold's "Mustang Snapshots: Another experiment in openness" blog entry (`http://weblogs.java.net/blog/mreinhold/archive/2004/11/index.html`) and the OpenJDK Community page (`http://community.java.net/openjdk/`).

Not every Java SE 6 feature is associated with a theme. For example, the class file specification update does not belong to any of the aforementioned themes. Also, not every theme corresponds to a set of features. For example, transparency reflects Sun's desire to be more open in how it interacts with the Java community while developing a platform specification and the associated reference implementation. Also, compatibility constrains how the platform evolves, because evolution is limited by the need to remain compatible with previous releases to support the existing base of Java software.

Overview of Java SE 6

Java SE 6 (which was formerly known by the code name Mustang during development) enhances the Java platform via improvements to the platform's performance and stability, by fixing assorted bugs, and even improvements to make graphical user interfaces (GUIs) look better (anti-aliasing LCD text is an example). Java SE 6 also enhances the Java platform by introducing a rich set of completely new features, some of which I've already mentioned. Many of these new features were developed by the various component JSRs of JSR 270, which serves as the "umbrella" JSR for Java SE 6:

- JSR 105: XML Digital Signature APIs (`http://jcp.org/en/jsr/detail?id=105`)

- JSR 199: Java Compiler API (`http://jcp.org/en/jsr/detail?id=199`)

- JSR 202: Java Class File Specification Update (`http://jcp.org/en/jsr/detail?id=202`)

- JSR 221: JDBC 4.0 API Specification (`http://jcp.org/en/jsr/detail?id=221`)

- JSR 222: Java Architecture for XML Binding (JAXB) 2.0 (`http://jcp.org/en/jsr/detail?id=222`)

- JSR 223: Scripting for the Java Platform (`http://jcp.org/en/jsr/detail?id=223`)

- JSR 224: Java API for XML-Based Web Services (JAX-WS) 2.0 (`http://jcp.org/en/jsr/detail?id=224`)

- JSR 268: Java Smart Card I/O API (`http://jcp.org/en/jsr/detail?id=268`)

- JSR 269: Pluggable Annotation Processing API (`http://jcp.org/en/jsr/detail?id=269`)

The one JSR specified in JSR 270's list of component JSRs that was not included in Java SE 6 is JSR 260: Javadoc Tag Technology Update (`http://jcp.org/en/jsr/detail?id=260`). Additional JSRs not specified in JSR 270's list, but that did make it into Java SE 6, are as follows:

- JSR 173: Streaming API for XML (`http://jcp.org/en/jsr/detail?id=173`)

- JSR 181: Web Services Metadata for the Java Platform (`http://jcp.org/en/jsr/detail?id=181`)

- JSR 250: Common Annotations for the Java Platform (`http://jcp.org/en/jsr/detail?id=250`)

Although these JSRs provide insight into what has been included in Java SE 6, "What's New in Java SE 6" (`http://java.sun.com/developer/technicalArticles/J2SE/Desktop/javase6/beta2.html`) offers a more complete picture. This article presents Danny Coward's "Top 10 Things You Need to Know" list of new Java SE 6 features (Danny Coward is the platform lead for Java SE), and Mark Reinhold's table of approved features. Of the table's listed features, internationalized resource identifiers (IRIs), the ability to highlight a `javax.swing.JTable`'s rows, and reflective access to parameter names did not make it into Java SE 6. IRIs, explained in RFC 3987: Internationalized Resource Identifiers (IRIs) (`http://www.ietf.org/rfc/rfc3987.txt`) were removed from the final release of Java SE 6 as part of `java.net.URI` being rolled back to the Java 5 version; see Bug 6394131 "Rollback URI class to Tiger version" in Sun's Bug Database").

Note The JDK 6 documentation's main page (`http://java.sun.com/javase/6/docs/`) presents a New Features and Enhancements link to the Features and Enhancements page (`http://java.sun.com/javase/6/webnotes/features.html`), which has more information about what is new and improved in Java SE 6.

Sampling of Java SE 6 New Features

As you will have noticed from the various feature references in the previous two sections, Java SE 6 has a lot to offer. This book explores most of Java SE 6's new and improved features, ranging from enhancements to the core libraries to a variety of performance enhancements. Before moving on, let's sample some of the features that set Java SE 6 apart from its predecessors.

A Trio of New Action Keys and a Method to Hide/Show Action Text

The `javax.swing.Action` interface extends the `java.awt.event.ActionListener` interface to bundle, in the same class, several component properties such as `toolTipText` and `icon` with common code. An instance of this class can be attached to multiple components (an Open menu item on a File menu and an Open button on a toolbar, for example), which then can be enabled/disabled from one place. Furthermore, selecting either component executes the common code. Java SE 6 lets you manipulate two new properties and a variation of `icon` via these new keys:

- `DISPLAYED_MNEMONIC_INDEX_KEY`: Identifies the index in the `text` property (accessed via the `NAME` key) where a mnemonic decoration should be rendered. This key corresponds to the new `displayedMnemonicIndex` property; the key's associated value is an `Integer` instance.

- `LARGE_ICON_KEY`: Identifies the `javax.swing.Icon` that appears on various kinds of Swing buttons, such as an instance of `javax.swing.JButton`. The `javax.swing.JMenuItem` subclasses, such as `javax.swing.JCheckBoxMenuItem`, use the `Icon` associated with the `SMALL_ICON` key. Unlike `LARGE_ICON_KEY`, there is no `SMALL_ICON_KEY` constant with a `_KEY` suffix.

- `SELECTED_KEY`: Initializes the selection state of a toggling component, such as an instance of `javax.swing.JCheckBox`, from an action and reflects this change in the component. This key corresponds to the new `selected` property; the key's associated value is a Boolean instance.

Java SE 6 also adds new action-related `public void setHideActionText(boolean hideActionText)` and `public boolean getHideActionText()` methods to the `javax.swing.AbstractButton` class. The former method sets the value of the `hideActionText` property, which determines whether (`true` passed to `hideActionText`) or not (`false` passed to `hideActionText`) a button displays an action's text; by default, a toolbar button does not display this text. The latter method returns this property's current setting. Listing 1-1 presents a notepad application that demonstrates these new action keys and methods.

Listing 1-1. *Notepad.java*

```
// Notepad.java

import java.awt.*;
import java.awt.event.*;

import javax.swing.*;
```

```java
import javax.swing.border.*;

public class Notepad extends JFrame
{
   private JTextArea document = new JTextArea (10, 40);

   public Notepad ()
   {
      super ("Notepad 1.0");
      setDefaultCloseOperation (EXIT_ON_CLOSE);

      JMenuBar menuBar = new JMenuBar ();

      JToolBar toolBar = new JToolBar ();

      JMenu menu = new JMenu ("File");
      menu.setMnemonic (KeyEvent.VK_F);

      Action newAction = new NewAction (document);
      menu.add (new JMenuItem (newAction));
      toolBar.add (newAction);

      // Java SE 6 introduces a setHideActionText() method to determine
      // whether or not a button displays text originating from an action. To
      // demonstrate this method, the code below makes it possible for a
      // toolbar button to display the action's text -- a toolbar button does
      // not display this text in its default state.

      JButton button = (JButton) toolBar.getComponentAtIndex (0);
      button.setHideActionText (false);

      menuBar.add (menu);

      menu = new JMenu ("View");
      menu.setMnemonic (KeyEvent.VK_V);

      Action statAction = new StatAction (this);
      menu.add (new JCheckBoxMenuItem (statAction));

      menuBar.add (menu);

      setJMenuBar (menuBar);
```

```
        getContentPane ().add (toolBar, BorderLayout.NORTH);
        getContentPane ().add (document, BorderLayout.CENTER);

        pack ();
        setVisible (true);
    }

    public static void main (String [] args)
    {
        Runnable r = new Runnable ()
                     {
                         public void run ()
                         {
                            new Notepad ();
                         }
                     };
        EventQueue.invokeLater (r);
    }
}

class NewAction extends AbstractAction
{
    JTextArea document;

    NewAction (JTextArea document)
    {
        this.document = document;

        putValue (NAME, "New");
        putValue (MNEMONIC_KEY, KeyEvent.VK_N);
        putValue (SMALL_ICON, new ImageIcon ("newicon_16x16.gif"));

        // Before Java SE 6, an action's SMALL_ICON key was used to assign the
        // same icon to a button and a menu item. Java SE 6 now makes it
        // possible to assign different icons to these components. If an icon
        // is added via LARGE_ICON_KEY, this icon appears on buttons, whereas
        // an icon added via SMALL_ICON appears on menu items. However, if there
        // is no LARGE_ICON_KEY-based icon, the SMALL_ICON-based icon is
        // assigned to a toolbar's button (for example), in addition to a menu
        // item.
```

```
      putValue (LARGE_ICON_KEY, new ImageIcon ("newicon_32x32.gif"));
   }

   public void actionPerformed (ActionEvent e)
   {
      document.setText ("");
   }
}

class StatAction extends AbstractAction
{
   private JFrame frame;
   private JLabel labelStatus = new JLabel ("Notepad 1.0");

   StatAction (JFrame frame)
   {
      this.frame = frame;

      putValue (NAME, "Status Bar");
      putValue (MNEMONIC_KEY, KeyEvent.VK_A);

      // By default, a mnemonic decoration is presented under the leftmost
      // character in a string having multiple occurrences of this character.
      // For example, the previous putValue (MNEMONIC_KEY, KeyEvent.VK_A);
      // results in the "a" in "Status" being decorated. If you prefer to
      // decorate a different occurrence of a letter (such as the "a" in
      // "Bar"), you can now do this thanks to Java SE 6's
      // displayedMnemonicIndex property and DISPLAYED_MNEMONIC_INDEX_KEY. In
      // the code below, the zero-based index (8) of the "a" appearing in
      // "Bar" is chosen as the occurrence of "a" to receive the decoration.

      putValue (DISPLAYED_MNEMONIC_INDEX_KEY, 8);

      // Java SE 6 now makes it possible to choose the initial selection state
      // of a toggling component. In this application, the component is a
      // JCheckBoxMenuItem that is responsible for determining whether or not
      // to display a status bar. Initially, the status bar will not be shown,
      // which is why false is assigned to the selected property in the method
      // call below.
```

```
        putValue (SELECTED_KEY, false);

        labelStatus = new JLabel ("Notepad 1.0");
        labelStatus.setBorder (new EtchedBorder ());
    }

    public void actionPerformed (ActionEvent e)
    {
        // Because a component updates the selected property, it is easy to find
        // out the current selection setting, and then use this setting to
        // either add or remove the status bar.

        Boolean selection = (Boolean) getValue (SELECTED_KEY);
        if (selection)
            frame.getContentPane ().add (labelStatus, BorderLayout.SOUTH);
        else
            frame.getContentPane ().remove (labelStatus);

        frame.getRootPane ().revalidate ();
    }
}
```

The numerous comments in the source code explain the new action keys and the
setHideActionText() method. However, you might be curious about my deferring the
creation of a Swing application's GUI to the event-dispatching thread, via a Runnable
instance and the EventQueue.invokeLater (r); method call. I do this here (and elsewhere
in the book) because creating a Swing GUI on any thread other than the event-dispatching
thread—such as an application's main thread or the thread that invokes an applet's public
void init() method—is unsafe.

Note Although you could invoke SwingUtilities.invokeLater() to ensure that an application's
Swing-based GUI is created on the event-dispatching thread, it is somewhat more efficient to invoke
EventQueue.invokeLater(), because the former method contains a single line of code that calls the
latter method. It is also somewhat more efficient to invoke EventQueue.invokeAndWait(), rather than
SwingUtilities.invokeAndWait(), to create an applet's Swing-based GUI on the event-dispatching
thread.

Creating a Swing GUI on a thread other than the event-dispatching thread is unsafe because the Swing GUI toolkit is not multithreaded. (Check out Graham Hamilton's "Multithreaded toolkits: A failed dream?" blog entry at `http://weblogs.java.net/blog/kgh/archive/2004/10/multithreaded_t.html` to find out why Swing is not multithreaded.) As a result, creating the GUI on the main thread while the event-dispatching thread is also running potentially leads to problems that might or might not be difficult to solve.

For example, suppose you create the GUI on the main thread, and part of the GUI-creation code indirectly creates a `javax.swing.text.JTextComponent` via some subclass, such as `javax.swing.JEditorPane`. `JTextComponent` includes several methods that call `invokeLater();` the `public void insertUpdate(DocumentEvent e)` event-handling method is an example. If this method should somehow be invoked during GUI creation, its call to `invokeLater()` would result in the event-dispatching thread starting (unless that thread is already running). The application would then be in a position where the integrity of the Swing GUI toolkit is violated.

According to older versions of *The Java Tutorial*, Swing GUIs could be created on threads other than the event-dispatching thread. This advice is also detailed in Hans Muller's and Kathy Walrath's older "Threads and Swing" article (`http://java.sun.com/products/jfc/tsc/articles/threads/threads1.html`). In contrast, the latest version of *The Java Tutorial* insists on creating the GUI on the event-dispatching thread (see `http://java.sun.com/docs/books/tutorial/uiswing/concurrency/initial.html`).

Note Tech writer Cay Horstmann's "The Single Thread Rule in Swing" blog entry (`http://weblogs.java.net/blog/cayhorstmann/archive/2007/06/the_single_thre.html`) provides an interesting read (especially in the comments section) of the create-Swing-GUI-on-event-dispatching-thread topic.

The notepad application in Listing 1-1 requires more work to turn it into something useful. However, it does serve the purpose of demonstrating these new action keys and methods. For example, after compiling `Notepad.java` and running this application, you'll notice the result of the `setHideActionText()` method: *New* on the toolbar icon. Also, when you open the File menu, you'll notice a different (and smaller) icon appearing beside the New menu item. Figure 1-1 shows the application's GUI with these enhancements. In the figure, I've moved the toolbar to the right so that you can easily see the two different icons. Of course, you will typically not display text on toolbar buttons that also present images.

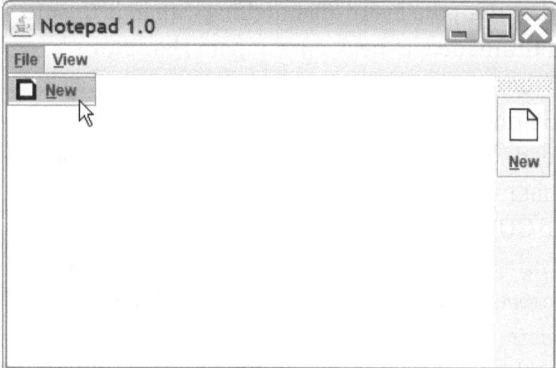

Figure 1-1. *The setHideActionText() method made it possible for New to appear with the icon on the toolbar button.*

Note DISPLAYED_MNEMONIC_INDEX_KEY, LARGE_ICON_KEY, SELECTED_KEY, and the setHideActionText() method are discussed in Scott Violet's "Changes to Actions in 1.6" blog entry (http://weblogs.java.net/blog/zixle/archive/2005/11/changes_to_acti.html). Scott's blog entry also discusses the swing.actions.reconfigureOnNull system property.

Clearing a ButtonGroup's Selection

You create a form-based GUI that includes a group of radio buttons, with none of these buttons initially selected. When the user clicks the form's Reset button, you want to clear any selected radio button in this group (no radio button should be selected). According to Java 5's JDK documentation for javax.swing.ButtonGroup:

> *There is no way to turn a button programmatically to "off," in order to clear the button group. To give the appearance of "none selected," add an invisible radio button to the group and then programmatically select that button to turn off all the displayed radio buttons. For example, a normal button with the label "none" could be wired to select the invisible radio button.*

The documentation's advice results in extra code that complicates the GUI design, and probably leads to GUI logic that is difficult to follow. Although it seems that passing false to ButtonGroup's public void setSelected(ButtonModel m, boolean b) method should do the trick, the method's source code recognizes only a true value. Fortunately, Java SE 6 comes to the rescue. In response to Bug 4066394 "ButtonGroup – cannot reset the model to the initial unselected state," Java SE 6 adds a new `public void clearSelection()` method to `ButtonGroup`. According to the JDK 6 documentation, this method "clears the selection such that none of the buttons in the `ButtonGroup` are selected."

Enhancements to Reflection

Java SE 6 enhances Java's support for reflection as follows:

- By fixing the `public String toGenericString()` and `public string toString()` methods in the `java.lang.reflect.Method` and `java.lang.reflect.Constructor` classes to correctly display modifiers

- By modifying the final parameter in Java 5's `public static Object newInstance(Class<?> componentType, int[] dimensions)` method to use variable arguments; the new method signature is `public static Object newInstance(Class<?> componentType, int... dimensions)`

- By generifying the following methods of `Class`:

    - `public Class<?>[] getClasses()`

    - `public Constructor<T> getConstructor(Class<?>... parameterTypes)`

    - `public Constructor<?>[] getConstructors()`

    - `public Class<?>[] getDeclaredClasses()`

    - `public Constructor<T> getDeclaredConstructor(Class<?>... parameterTypes)`

    - `public Constructor<?>[] getDeclaredConstructors()`

    - `public Method getDeclaredMethod(String name, Class<?>... parameterTypes)`

    - `public Class<?>[] getInterfaces()`

    - `public Method getMethod(String name, Class<?>... parameterTypes)`

The problems with the `toGenericString()` and `toString()` methods in Java 5's `Method` and `Constructor` classes are documented by Bug 6261502 (reflect) "Add the functionality to screen out the 'inappropriate' modifier bits," Bug 6316717 (reflect) "Method.toGenericString prints out inappropriate modifiers," Bug 6354476 (reflect) "{Method, Constructor}.toString prints out inappropriate modifiers," and Bug 6362451 "The string returned by toString() shows the bridge methods as having the volatile modificator."

Note During Java SE 6's development, consideration was given to enhancing Java's reflection capability by supporting reflective access to constructor and method parameter names. Although this feature did not make it into Java SE 6, it could make it into the next release. If you are curious about this feature, check out Andy Hedges' "Reflective Access to Parameter Names" blog entry (`http://hedges.net/archives/2006/04/07/reflective-access-to-parameter-names/`).

GroupLayout Layout Manager

Java SE 6 adds *GroupLayout* to its suite of layout managers. GroupLayout hierarchically groups components in order to position them within a container. It consists of the `javax.swing.GroupLayout` class (and inner classes) and the `GroupLayout.Alignment` enumeration. The `GroupLayout` class works with the new `javax.swing.LayoutStyle` class to obtain component-positioning information, as well as the `java.awt.Component` class's new `public Component.BaselineResizeBehavior getBaselineResizeBehavior()` and `public int getBaseline(int width, int height)` methods.

Note According to its JDK documentation, the `BaselineResizeBehavior` enumeration enumerates "the common ways the baseline of a component can change as the size changes." For example, the baseline remains a fixed distance from the component's center as the component is resized. GroupLayout invokes the `getBaselineResizeBehavior()` method when it needs to know the specific resize behavior. When it needs to identify the baseline from the top of the component, GroupLayout invokes `getBaseline()`.

Although this layout manager is intended for use with GUI builders (such as the Matisse GUI builder in NetBeans 5.5), GroupLayout also can be used to manually code layouts. If you are interested in learning how to do this, you should check out the "How to Use GroupLayout" section (`http://java.sun.com/docs/books/tutorial/uiswing/layout/group.html`) in *The Java Tutorial*'s "Laying Out Components Within a Container" lesson. You should also check out the `GroupLayout` class's JDK documentation.

Note GroupLayout originated as an open-source project at java.net's swing-layout project site (`http://swing-layout.dev.java.net`). Because of its success with NetBeans 5.0, GroupLayout was merged into Java SE 6 (with various changes, primarily in the area of package and method names). Although NetBeans 5.0 supports only the swing-layout version, NetBeans 5.5 supports the swing-layout version for pre-Java SE 6 and the Java SE 6 version for Java SE 6.

Image I/O GIF Writer Plug-in

For years, developers have wanted the Image I/O framework to provide a plug-in for writing images in the GIF file format—see Bug 4339415 "Provide a writer plug-in for the GIF file format." However, it was not possible to provide this plug-in as long as any Unisys patents on the Lempel-Ziv-Welch data compression algorithm used in writing GIF files remained in effect. Because Unisys's final international patents (Japanese patents 2,123,602 and 2,610,084) expired on June 20, 2004 (see "Sad day . . . GIF patent dead at 20," http://www.kuro5hin.org/story/2003/6/19/35919/4079), it finally became possible to add this plug-in to Image I/O. Java SE 6 includes a GIF writer plug-in. Listing 1-2 presents an application that uses this plug-in to write a simple image to image.gif.

Listing 1-2. *SaveToGIF.java*

```
// SaveToGIF.java

import java.awt.*;
import java.awt.image.*;

import java.io.*;

import javax.imageio.*;

public class SaveToGIF
{
   final static int WIDTH = 50;
   final static int HEIGHT = 50;
   final static int NUM_ITER = 1500;

   public static void main (String [] args)
   {
      // Create a sample image consisting of randomly colored pixels in
      // randomly colored positions.

      BufferedImage bi;
      bi = new BufferedImage (WIDTH, HEIGHT, BufferedImage.TYPE_INT_RGB);
      Graphics g = bi.getGraphics ();
      for (int i = 0; i < NUM_ITER; i++)
      {
          int x = rnd (WIDTH);
          int y = rnd (HEIGHT);
          g.setColor (new Color (rnd (256), rnd (256), rnd (256)));
```

```
            g.drawLine (x, y, x, y);
      }
      g.dispose ();

      // Save the image to image.gif.

      try
      {
          ImageIO.write (bi, "gif", new File ("image.gif"));
      }
      catch (IOException ioe)
      {
          System.err.println ("Unable to save image to file");
      }
   }

   static int rnd (int limit)
   {
      return (int) (Math.random ()*limit);
   }
}
```

Beyond the GIF writer plug-in, Java SE 6 improves Image I/O performance. Appendix C provides the details.

Incremental Improvements to String

The String class has slightly improved in Java SE 6. New public String(byte[] bytes, int offset, int length, Charset charset) and public String(byte[] bytes, Charset charset) constructors have been added as alternatives to the equivalent public String(byte[] bytes, int offset, int length, String charsetName) and public String(byte[] bytes, Charset charset) constructors. As pointed out in Bug 5005831 "String constructors and method which take Charset rather than String as argument," these older constructors were found to be inefficient at converting from bytes to strings, which is a common operation in I/O-bound applications, especially in a server-side environment. To complement these constructors, a new public byte[] getBytes(Charset charset) method has been introduced as a more efficient alternative to the public byte[] getBytes(String charsetName) method.

Finally, a new public boolean isEmpty() method has been added, in response to Bug 6189137 "New String convenience methods isEmpty() and contains(String)." This method returns true if the String's length equals 0.

Note Contrary to what appears in Sun's *Java SE 6 – In Depth Overview* PDF-based document (`https://java-champions.dev.java.net/pdfs/SE6-in-depth-overview.pdf`), String's `indexOf()` and `lastIndexOf()` methods have not been enhanced to support the Boyer-Moore algorithm for faster searching. The Java SE 6 source code for these methods is the same as the Java 5 source code. For the rationale in not supporting Boyer-Moore, check out Bug 4362107 "String.indexOf(String) needlessly inefficient."

LCD Text Support

The "LCD Text" section of tech writer Robert Eckstein's "New and Updated Desktop Features in Java SE 6, Part 1" article (`http://java.sun.com/developer/technicalArticles/javase/6_desktop_features/index.html`) describes a new Java SE 6 feature for improving text resolution on LCDs. This feature is an LCD text algorithm that anti-aliases text (to smooth edges) for presentation on LCDs. The anti-aliased text looks better and is easier to read, as evidenced by the article's screenshots. (You will need an appropriate display configuration, as explained in the article, to see the improvement offered by these images.) Because the Metal, GTK, and Windows look and feels automatically support LCD text, applications that use these look and feels benefit from this feature.

Note Chet Haase provides an excellent introduction to LCD text in his "LCD Text: Anti-Aliasing on the Fringe" article (`http://today.java.net/pub/a/today/2005/07/26/lcdtext.html`).

If you are developing a custom look and feel, and want it to take advantage of LCD text, you will need to acquaint yourself with the `java.awt.RenderingHints` class's `KEY_TEXT_ANTIALIASING` key constant, and its `VALUE_TEXT_ANTIALIAS_LCD_HRGB`, `VALUE_TEXT_ANTIALIAS_LCD_HBGR`, `VALUE_TEXT_ANTIALIAS_LCD_VRGB`, `VALUE_TEXT_ANTIALIAS_LCD_VBGR`, and `VALUE_TEXT_ANTIALIAS_GASP` value constants (which are described in Robert Eckstein's article). According to Bug 6274842 "RFE: Provide a means for a custom look and feel to use desktop font antialiasing settings," however, it may be a while before Java provides the API that custom look and feels need to automatically detect changes to and use the underlying desktop's settings for text anti-aliasing.

NumberFormat and Rounding Modes

The java.text.NumberFormat and java.txt.DecimalFormat classes are used to format numeric values. As evidenced by Bug 4092330 "RFE: Precision, rounding in NumberFormat," it has long been desired for these classes to support the specification of a rounding mode other than the half-even default.

Java SE 6 satisfies this desire by introducing new public void setRoundingMode (RoundingMode roundingMode) and public RoundingMode getRoundingMode() methods into NumberFormat and DecimalFormat. Each class's setRoundingMode() method throws a NullPointerException if you pass null to roundingMode. NumberFormat's setRoundingMode() and getRoundingMode() methods throw UnsupportedOperationException if you attempt to invoke these methods from another NumberFormat subclass that does not override them (java.text.ChoiceFormat, for example). The application shown in Listing 1-3 demonstrates these methods.

Listing 1-3. *NumberFormatRounding.java*

```
// NumberFormatRounding.java

import java.math.*;

import java.text.*;

public class NumberFormatRounding
{
   public static void main (String [] args)
   {
      NumberFormat nf = NumberFormat.getNumberInstance ();
      nf.setMaximumFractionDigits (2);

      System.out.println ("Default rounding mode: "+nf.getRoundingMode ());
      System.out.println ("123.454 rounds to "+nf.format (123.454));
      System.out.println ("123.455 rounds to "+nf.format (123.455));
      System.out.println ("123.456 rounds to "+nf.format (123.456));
      System.out.println ();

      nf.setRoundingMode (RoundingMode.HALF_DOWN);
      System.out.println ("Rounding mode: "+nf.getRoundingMode ());
      System.out.println ("123.454 rounds to "+nf.format (123.454));
      System.out.println ("123.455 rounds to "+nf.format (123.455));
      System.out.println ("123.456 rounds to "+nf.format (123.456));
      System.out.println ();
```

```
    nf.setRoundingMode (RoundingMode.FLOOR);
    System.out.println ("Rounding mode: "+nf.getRoundingMode ());
    System.out.println ("123.454 rounds to "+nf.format (123.454));
    System.out.println ("123.455 rounds to "+nf.format (123.455));
    System.out.println ("123.456 rounds to "+nf.format (123.456));
    System.out.println ();

    nf.setRoundingMode (RoundingMode.CEILING);
    System.out.println ("Rounding mode: "+nf.getRoundingMode ());
    System.out.println ("123.454 rounds to "+nf.format (123.454));
    System.out.println ("123.455 rounds to "+nf.format (123.455));
    System.out.println ("123.456 rounds to "+nf.format (123.456));
  }
}
```

The source code uses three values: 123.454, 123.455, and 123.456. The first example uses the default half-even rounding mode, which rounds toward the nearest neighbor, or rounds toward the even neighbor if both neighbors are equidistant. Assuming that these values represent 123 dollars and 45.4, 45.5, or 45.6 cents, the default mode is appropriate because it minimizes cumulative errors (statistically) when repeatedly applied to a sequence of calculations. For this reason, half-even is known as *bankers' rounding* (it is used mainly in the United States). However, you might prefer a different rounding mode for your application if the value to be formatted represents something other than currency.

For example, you could work with half-down rounding, which is similar to half-even, except that it rounds down instead of to the even neighbor when both neighbors are equidistant. You could also work with floor and ceiling rounding, to round toward negative and positive infinity, respectively. To see these rounding modes in action, compile NumberFormatRounding.java and run the application. You will see the following output:

```
Default rounding mode: HALF_EVEN
123.454 rounds to 123.45
123.455 rounds to 123.46
123.456 rounds to 123.46

Rounding mode: HALF_DOWN
123.454 rounds to 123.45
123.455 rounds to 123.45
123.456 rounds to 123.46
```

```
Rounding mode: FLOOR
123.454 rounds to 123.45
123.455 rounds to 123.45
123.456 rounds to 123.45

Rounding mode: CEILING
123.454 rounds to 123.46
123.455 rounds to 123.46
123.456 rounds to 123.46
```

Note In addition to the `NumberFormat` and `DecimalFormat` enhancements, Java SE 6 adds new `public static Locale[] getAvailableLocales()`, `public static final DecimalFormatSymbols getInstance()`, `public static final DecimalFormatSymbols getInstance(Locale locale)`, `public String getExponentSeparator()`, and `public void setExponentSeparator(String exp)` methods to the `java.text.DecimalFormatSymbols` class.

Improved File Infrastructure

Java SE 6 extends the `java.io.File` class with several new methods, which Chapter 2 explores. It also improves `File`'s infrastructure on Microsoft Windows platforms.

One improvement is that Windows devices (such as NUL, AUX, and CON) are no longer considered to be files, which results in `File`'s `public boolean isFile()` method returning false when confronted with a device name. For example, `System.out.println (new File ("CON").isFile ());` outputs true under Java 5 and false under Java SE 6.

Another improvement involves the critical message dialog box. Prior to Java SE 6, a `File` method's attempt to access a drive whose removable media (a CD or a floppy disk, for example) was absent resulted in Windows presenting a critical message dialog box, which provided the option to retry the operation, after the media was presumably inserted into the drive. If you were remotely monitoring this program, you obviously had a problem when confronted by the dialog box: you were not present to insert the disk and click the dialog box's Continue button. For this reason, Java SE 6 prevents this dialog box from appearing, and fails the operation by having the method return a suitable value. For example, if you try to execute `System.out.println (new File ("A:\\someFile.txt").exists ());` without a floppy disk in the A: drive, a dialog box will not appear, and `exists()` will return false.

Note File's infrastructure now supports long pathnames on Windows platforms, where each pathname element is Windows-limited to 260 characters. Check out Bug 4403166 "File does not support long paths on Windows NT."

Continuing with improvements to File's infrastructure, Bug 6198547 "File.create-NewFile() on an existing directory incorrectly throws IOException (win)" points out that invoking File's public boolean createNewFile() method with the name of the file to be created matching the name of an existing directory results in a thrown java.io.IOException, instead of false being returned (as stated in the JDK documentation). Java SE 6 corrects this discrepancy by having this method return false.

Note Java SE 6 also improves Mac Mac OS X's File infrastructure by addressing Bug 6395581 "File.listFiles() is unable to read nfs-mounted directory (Mac OS X)." File's listFiles() methods now reads Mac OS X's NFS-mounted directories.

As a final Windows-specific improvement, File's public long length() method no longer returns 0 for special files, such as pagefile.sys. Bug 6348207 "File.length() reports a length of 0 for special files hiberfil.sys and pagefile.sys (win)" documents this improvement. Although you might not find this improvement helpful, you will probably benefit from the platform-independent improvement offered by Bug 4809375 "File.deleteOnExit() should be implemented with shutdown hooks."

Note In addition to introducing new methods and making the aforementioned improvements to File, Java SE 6 has also deprecated this class's public URL toURL() method. The JDK documentation offers this explanation: "This method does not automatically escape characters that are illegal in URLs. It is recommended that new code convert an abstract pathname into a URL by first converting it into a URI via the toURI method, and then converting the URI into a URL via the URI.toURL method."

Window Icon Images

The java.awt.Frame class has always had a public void setIconImage(Image image) method to specify a frame window's icon image, which appears on the left side of the frame window's title bar, and a companion public Image getIconImage() method to return this image. Although these methods are also available to Frame's javax.swing. JFrame subclass, which overrides setIconImage() to invoke its superclass version and then fire a property change event in pre-Java SE 6, they are not available to javax.swing.JDialog. An application whose frame window displays a custom icon, but whose dialogs do not, gives the impression that the dialogs do not belong to the application.

Bug 4913618 "Dialog doesn't inherit icon from its parent frame" documents this problem. Java SE 6 provides a solution that results in a dialog window now inheriting the icon from its parent frame window. Because this might be problematic if you want to supply a different icon for some specific dialog, Java SE 6 also adds a new public void setIconImage(Image image) method to the java.awt.Window class. This method allows you to specify a custom icon for a dialog window.

Modern operating systems typically display an application's icon in multiple places. In addition to a window's title bar, an icon can appear on the taskbar, on a task switcher (such as the Windows XP task switcher), beside a task name in a list of running tasks (such as the Applications tab of the Windows XP Windows Task Manager), and so on. In some places, the icon will appear at a different size. For example, the icon on the Windows XP task switcher is larger than the icon on the window's title bar. Prior to Java SE 6, the icon image assigned to the frame window via setIconImage() was scaled to appear larger on the taskbar; the result often looked terrible. This problem is documented by Bug 4721400 "Allow to specify 32x32 icon for JFrame (or Window)."

Java SE 6 provides a solution by adding new public void setIconImages(List<? extends Image> icons) and public List<Image> getIconImages() methods to Window. The former method lets you specify a list of icon images for display on the window's title bar and in other contexts, such as the taskbar or a task switcher. Prior to an icon being selected for a specific context, the icons list is scanned from the beginning for the first icon that has appropriate dimensions.

To demonstrate solutions to the dialog-does-not-inherit-icon and one-icon-for-all-contexts problems, I've created an application that creates a small solid icon and a big striped icon, assigns them to a frame window, and displays the frame window and a dialog. Listing 1-4 presents the source code.

Listing 1-4. *WindowIcons.java*

```
// WindowIcons.java

import java.awt.*;
import java.awt.image.*;

import java.util.*;

import javax.swing.*;

public class WindowIcons extends JFrame
{
```

```java
final static int BIG_ICON_WIDTH = 32;
final static int BIG_ICON_HEIGHT = 32;
final static int BIG_ICON_RENDER_WIDTH = 20;

final static int SMALL_ICON_WIDTH = 16;
final static int SMALL_ICON_HEIGHT = 16;
final static int SMALL_ICON_RENDER_WIDTH = 10;

public WindowIcons ()
{
   super ("Window Icons");
   setDefaultCloseOperation (EXIT_ON_CLOSE);

   ArrayList<BufferedImage> images = new ArrayList<BufferedImage> ();

   BufferedImage bi;
   bi = new BufferedImage (SMALL_ICON_WIDTH, SMALL_ICON_HEIGHT,
                           BufferedImage.TYPE_INT_ARGB);
   Graphics g = bi.getGraphics ();
   g.setColor (Color.black);
   g.fillRect (0, 0, SMALL_ICON_RENDER_WIDTH, SMALL_ICON_HEIGHT);
   g.dispose ();
   images.add (bi);

   bi = new BufferedImage (BIG_ICON_WIDTH, BIG_ICON_HEIGHT,
                           BufferedImage.TYPE_INT_ARGB);
   g = bi.getGraphics ();
   for (int i = 0; i < BIG_ICON_HEIGHT; i++)
   {
       g.setColor (((i & 1) == 0) ? Color.black : Color.white);
       g.fillRect (0, i, BIG_ICON_RENDER_WIDTH, 1);
   }
   g.dispose ();
   images.add (bi);

   setIconImages (images);

   setSize (250, 100);
   setVisible (true);

   // Create and display a modeless Swing dialog via an anonymous inner
   // class.

   new JDialog (this, "Arbitrary Dialog")
```

```
      {
        {
          setSize (200, 100);
          setVisible (true);
        }
      };
  }

  public static void main (String [] args)
  {
     Runnable r = new Runnable ()
                {
                   public void run ()
                   {
                      new WindowIcons ();
                   }
                };
     EventQueue.invokeLater (r);
  }
}
```

In response to Bug 6339074 "Improve icon support," which states that icons should support transparency, the application renders only part of each icon in an ARGB buffer, to see if transparency is honored under Windows XP Service Pack (SP) 2. According to Figure 1-2, transparency is honored.

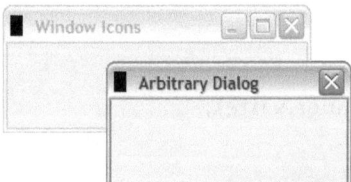

Figure 1-2. *The small icon appears on the title bar of the frame and dialog windows, and on the taskbar, but not on the task switcher. The big icon appears on the task switcher.*

Window Minimum Size

Bug 4320050 "Minimum size for java.awt.Frame is not being enforced" describes a long-standing GUI problem where it is not possible to establish a window's minimum size. If the minimum size could be set, you could then prevent your application's users from resizing the main window below the minimum size (and avoid phone calls from inexperienced and panicked users who can no longer access the GUI).

Java SE 6 adds a new `public void setMinimumSize(Dimension minimumSize)` method to `Window`, to let you enforce a minimum size. A subsequent call to `Window`'s inherited `public Dimension getMinimumSize()` method returns the new minimum size. If the window's size prior to this call is smaller than the minimum size, the window is automatically enlarged to honor the minimum. The following code fragment sets a frame window's minimum size to 400-by-300 pixels:

```
Frame frame = new Frame ("Some window title");

// Do not allow the user to resize the frame below 400
// pixels horizontally and 300 pixels vertically.

frame.setMinimumSize (new Dimension (400, 300));
```

Note `Window` overrides the `Component` class's `public void setSize(Dimension d)`, `public void setSize(int width, int height)`, `public void setBounds(int x, int y, int width, int height)`, and `public void setBounds(Rectangle r)` methods to prevent a window from being sized below its minimum size. If a method is called with a width or height that is less than the current minimum size, the method enlarges the width or height.

Interruptible I/O Switch for Solaris

Solaris native-thread implementations of the virtual machine take advantage of the Solaris operating system's support for interruptible I/O. As a result, a thread that is blocked on an I/O operation can be interrupted via a call to the `Thread` class's `public void interrupt()` method on the blocked thread's `Thread` object; a `java.io.InterruptedIOException` is thrown from the interrupted thread.

Bug 4154947 "JDK 1.1.6, 1.2/Windows NT: Interrupting a thread blocked does not unblock IO" explains the difficulty in trying to implement interruptible I/O on the Windows platform. Because it could prove impossible to provide this feature on Windows, and because having interruptible I/O support available to Solaris virtual machines but not available to Windows virtual machines violates Java's cross-platform nature, Java SE 6 introduces a new `UseVMInterruptibleIO` HotSpot option switch to turn off interruptible I/O on the Solaris virtual machine. Interruptible I/O is still enabled by default (it might be disabled by default in Java SE 7). You can explicitly disable interruptible I/O by specifying -XX:-UseVMInterruptibleIO when starting the Solaris virtual machine. For more information, check out Bug 4385444 "(spec) InterruptedIOException should not be required by platform specification (sol)."

ZIP and JAR Files

Java SE 6 introduces various enhancements in the context of ZIP and JAR files. From the API perspective, the java.util.zip package has new DeflaterInputStream and InflaterOutputStream classes. These classes allow an application to send compressed data over a network. Data is compressed into packets via DeflaterInputStream, and the packets are sent over the network to a destination, where they are then decompressed via InflaterOutputStream.

Non-API enhancements include allowing ZIP files to contain more than 64,000 entries on all platforms. For Windows platforms, the upper limit of 2,036 concurrently open ZIP files has been removed, and the limit is now determined by the platform; see Bug 6423026 "Java.util.zip doesn't allow more than 2036 zip files to be concurrently open on Windows." Also, filenames longer than 256 characters are supported; see Bug 6374379 "ZipFile class cannot open zip files with long filenames."

Regarding JAR files, the jar tool has been enhanced so that the timestamps of extracted files match the timestamps that appear in the archive. Prior to Java SE 6, an extracted file's timestamp was set to the current time. Check out Appendix B to see what else has changed for the jar tool.

Ownerless Windows

Chapter 3 introduces Java SE 6's new modality model and API. To work properly, this model depends on *ownerless windows*, which are windows without parent windows; a frame window created by the public JFrame() constructor is an example of an owner-less window.

It turns out that early attempts to support ownerless windows were problematic. For example, Bug 4256840 "Exception when using the no-argument Window() constructor on win32," and Bug 4262946 "API Change: remove constructors for ownerless Windows in java.awt.Window" revealed that the introduction of ownerless windows into Java 1.3 (Kestrel) via public Window() and public Window(GraphicsConfiguration gc) constructors led to ownerless Windows not showing up in the array returned by Frame's public static Frame[] getFrames() method. Suddenly, an automation tool could not access an application's entire tree of GUI components.

To address this problem, the JDialog class includes constructors such as public JDialog(Frame owner). If you pass null to owner, a shared hidden frame window is chosen as the owner of the dialog. Automation tools can get access to this frame window. Unfortunately, as pointed out in Bug 6300062 "JDialog need to support true parent-less mode," this frame window causes problems for the new modality model. You might want to read Chapter 3's modality model/API introduction before reading this bug report to first grasp the basics.

Java SE 6 solves both the modality problem and the automation tool problem as follows:

- By allowing you to pass null to the owner parameter in any of Window's constructors, so that these windows can be ownerless

- By allowing you to pass null to the owner parameter in any of java.awt.Dialog's constructors, so that these dialog windows can be ownerless

- By introducing several new JDialog constructors—the first parameter is of type Window (public JDialog(Window owner), for example)—that let you pass null to owner for true ownerless Swing dialog windows

- By introducing two new methods into the Window class: public static Window[] getWindows(), which lets an automation tool obtain an array of all ownerless and owned windows, and public static Window[] getOwnerlessWindows(), which lets this tool obtain an array of ownerless windows only

Listing 1-5 presents an application that demonstrates the public static Window[] getWindows() and public static Window[] getOwnerlessWindows() methods.

Listing 1-5. *Windows.java*

```
// Windows.java

import java.awt.*;

import javax.swing.*;

public class Windows
{
   public static void main (String [] args)
   {
      // Create a pseudo-ownerless Swing dialog (its owner is a hidden shared
      // frame window).

      JDialog d1 = new JDialog ((JFrame) null, "Dialog 1");
      d1.setName ("Dialog 1");
```

```
        // Create a true ownerless Swing dialog.

        JDialog d2 = new JDialog ((Window) null, "Dialog 2");
        d2.setName ("Dialog 2");

        // Create an ownerless frame.

        Frame f = new Frame ();
        f.setName ("Frame 1");

        // Create a window owned by the frame.

        Window w1 = new Window (f);
        w1.setName ("Window 1");

        // Create an ownerless window.

        Window w2 = new Window (null);
        w2.setName ("Window 2");

        // Output lists of all windows, ownerless windows, and frame windows.

        System.out.println ("ALL WINDOWS");
        Window [] windows = Window.getWindows ();
        for (Window window: windows)
            System.out.println (window.getName ()+": "+window.getClass ());
        System.out.println ();

        System.out.println ("OWNERLESS WINDOWS");
        Window [] ownerlessWindows = Window.getOwnerlessWindows ();
        for (Window window: ownerlessWindows)
            System.out.println (window.getName ()+": "+window.getClass ());
        System.out.println ();

        System.out.println ("FRAME WINDOWS");
        Frame [] frames = Frame.getFrames ();
        for (Frame frame: frames)
            System.out.println (frame.getName ()+": "+frame.getClass ());
    }
}
```

After compiling the source code and running this application, you'll discover the following output, which reveals that Dialog 1 is not a true ownerless window:

```
ALL WINDOWS
frame0: class javax.swing.SwingUtilities$SharedOwnerFrame
Dialog 1: class javax.swing.JDialog
Dialog 2: class javax.swing.JDialog
Frame 1: class java.awt.Frame
Window 1: class java.awt.Window
Window 2: class java.awt.Window

OWNERLESS WINDOWS
frame0: class javax.swing.SwingUtilities$SharedOwnerFrame
Dialog 2: class javax.swing.JDialog
Frame 1: class java.awt.Frame
Window 2: class java.awt.Window

FRAME WINDOWS
frame0: class javax.swing.SwingUtilities$SharedOwnerFrame
Frame 1: class java.awt.Frame
```

Navigable Sets

Chapter 2 introduces Java SE 6's enhanced collections framework. One enhancement worth mentioning here is a new java.util.NavigableSet<E> interface, which extends the older java.util.SortedSet<E> interface and facilitates navigating through an ordered set-based collection.

A navigable set can be accessed and traversed in ascending order via the Iterator<E> iterator() method, and in descending order via the Iterator<E> descendingIterator() method. It can return the closest matches for given search targets via methods public E ceiling(E e), public E floor(E e), public E higher(E e), and public E lower(E e). By default, these closest-match methods find the closest match in ascending order. To find a closest match in descending order, first obtain a reverse-order view of the set via the NavigableSet<E> descendingSet() method. Listing 1-6 presents an application that demonstrates descendingSet() and the four closest-match methods, with comments that describe each closest-match method in detail.

Listing 1-6. *CityNavigator.java*

```java
// CityNavigator.java

import java.util.*;

public class CityNavigator
{
    static NavigableSet<String> citiesSet;

    public static void main (String [] args)
    {
        String [] cities =
        {
            "Beijing",
            "Berlin",
            "Baghdad",
            "Buenos Aires",
            "Bangkok",
            "Belgrade"
        };

        // Create and populate a navigable set of cities.

        citiesSet = new TreeSet<String> ();
        for (String city: cities)
            citiesSet.add (city);

        // Dump the city names in ascending order. Behind the scenes, the
        // following code is implemented in terms of
        //
        // Iterator iter = citiesSet.iterator ();
        // while (iter.hasNext ())
        //     System.out.println (iter.next ());

        System.out.println ("CITIES IN ASCENDING ORDER");
        for (String city: citiesSet)
            System.out.println ("  "+city);
        System.out.println ();

        // Dump the city names in descending order. Behind the scenes, the
        // following code is implemented in terms of
```

```
   //
   // Iterator iter = citiesSet.descendingSet.iterator ();
   // while (iter.hasNext ())
   //    System.out.println (iter.next ());

   System.out.println ("CITIES IN DESCENDING ORDER");
   for (String city: citiesSet.descendingSet ())
       System.out.println ("  "+city);
   System.out.println ();

   // Demonstrate the closest-match methods in ascending order set.

   System.out.println ("CLOSEST-MATCH METHODS/ASCENDING ORDER DEMO");
   outputMatches ("Berlin");
   System.out.println ();

   outputMatches ("C");
   System.out.println ();

   outputMatches ("A");
   System.out.println ();

   // Demonstrate closest-match methods in descending order set.

   citiesSet = citiesSet.descendingSet ();
   System.out.println ("CLOSEST-MATCH METHODS/DESCENDING ORDER DEMO");
   outputMatches ("Berlin");
   System.out.println ();

   outputMatches ("C");
   System.out.println ();

   outputMatches ("A");
   System.out.println ();
}

static void outputMatches (String city)
{
   // ceiling() returns the least element in the set greater than or equal
   // to the given element (or null if the element does not exist).

   System.out.println ("  ceiling('"+city+"'): "+citiesSet.ceiling (city));
```

```
    // floor() returns the greatest element in the set less than or equal to
    // the given element (or null if the element does not exist).

    System.out.println ("  floor('"+city+"'): "+citiesSet.floor (city));

    // higher() returns the least element in the set strictly greater than
    // the given element (or null if the element does not exist).

    System.out.println ("  higher('"+city+"'): "+citiesSet.higher (city));

    // lower() returns the greatest element in the set strictly less than
    // the given element (or null if the element does not exist).

    System.out.println ("  lower('"+city+"'): "+citiesSet.lower (city));
  }
}
```

As shown in the source code, the closest-match methods return set elements that satisfy various conditions. For example, lower() returns the element that is greater than all other set elements, except for the element described by lower()'s argument; the method returns null if there is no such element. Although this description is intuitive when you consider a set that is ordered in ascending order, intuition fails somewhat when you consider the set ordered in descending order. For example, in the following output, Belgrade is lower than Berlin in ascending order, and Buenos Aires is lower than Berlin in descending order:

```
CITIES IN ASCENDING ORDER
  Baghdad
  Bangkok
  Beijing
  Belgrade
  Berlin
  Buenos Aires
```

```
CITIES IN DESCENDING ORDER
  Buenos Aires
  Berlin
  Belgrade
  Beijing
  Bangkok
  Baghdad

CLOSEST-MATCH METHODS/ASCENDING ORDER DEMO
  ceiling('Berlin'): Berlin
  floor('Berlin'): Berlin
  higher('Berlin'): Buenos Aires
  lower('Berlin'): Belgrade

  ceiling('C'): null
  floor('C'): Buenos Aires
  higher('C'): null
  lower('C'): Buenos Aires

  ceiling('A'): Baghdad
  floor('A'): null
  higher('A'): Baghdad
  lower('A'): null

CLOSEST-MATCH METHODS/DESCENDING ORDER DEMO
  ceiling('Berlin'): Berlin
  floor('Berlin'): Berlin
  higher('Berlin'): Belgrade
  lower('Berlin'): Buenos Aires

  ceiling('C'): Buenos Aires
  floor('C'): null
  higher('C'): Buenos Aires
  lower('C'): null

  ceiling('A'): null
  floor('A'): Baghdad
  higher('A'): null
  lower('A'): Baghdad
```

> **Note** Here are a few other interesting changes in Java SE 6:
>
> - Java SE 6 changes the class file version number to 50.0 because it supports split verification (see Appendix B).
>
> - Java SE 6's `jarsigner`, `keytool`, and `kinit` security tools no longer echo passwords to the screen.
>
> - The `javax.swing.text.Segment` class, which allows fast access to a segment of text, now implements the `CharSequence` interface. You can use `Segment` in regular-expression contexts, for example.

Java SE 6, Update 1 and Update 2

Following the initial release of Java SE 6 (which is the focus of this book), Sun released its first Java SE 6 update to introduce a number of bug fixes. This update release specifies 6u01 as its external version number, and 1.6.0_01-b06 (where *b* stands for build) as its internal version number.

One bug that has been fixed in 6u01 concerns memory leak problems with several methods. For example, the `Thread` class specifies a `public static Map<Thread, StackTraceElement[]> getAllStackTraces()` method that returns a map of stack traces for all live threads. Also, the `java.lang.management.ThreadMXBean` interface specifies several `getThreadInfo()` methods that return thread information. According to Bug 6434648 "Native memory leak when use Thread.getAllStackTraces()," all of these methods have a memory leak that leads to an `OutOfMemoryError`. You can reproduce this problem, which has been solved in this update release, by running the following application (which might run for a considerable period of time before `OutOfMemoryError` is thrown) on the initial release of Java SE 6:

```
public class TestMemoryLeak
{
    public static void main(String[] args)
    {
        while (true)
        {
            Thread.getAllStackTraces();
        }

    }
}
```

Another bug that has been fixed in 6u01 is Bug 6481004 "SplashScreen.getSplashScreen() fails in Web Start context." According to this bug, migrating a stand-alone application that uses the Splash Screen API to Java Web Start results in a `java.security.` `AccessControlException` being thrown. This exception is thrown as a result of the `System.loadLibrary("splashscreen")` method call in the `public static synchronized` `SplashScreen getSplashScreen()` method not being placed inside a `doPrivileged()` block.

The Java SE 6 Update Release Notes page (`http://java.sun.com/javase/6/webnotes/` `ReleaseNotes.html`) provides a complete list of all the bugs that have disappeared in the 6u01 update.

While this chapter was being written, a second Java SE 6 update was released. Although this update was rumored to contain a slimmed-down JRE, as pointed out by the posting on TheServerSide.com titled "Rumor: Java 6 update 2 will be 2-4MB?" (`http://www.theserverside.com/news/thread.tss?thread_id=45377`), the second update offered nothing quite so dramatic. This rumor was most likely based on the much-discussed Consumer JRE, which Chet Haase discusses in his "Consumer JRE: Leaner, Meaner Java Technology" article (`http://java.sun.com/developer/technicalArticles/` `javase/consumerjre/`).

To see what the second update has to offer, check out Sun's Java SE 6 Update Release Notes page.

Summary

Java SE 6 (formerly known as Mustang) officially arrived on December 11, 2006. This release contains many new and improved features that will benefit Java developers for years to come.

Java SE 6 was developed under JSR 270, which presents various themes. These themes include compatibility and stability; diagnosability, monitoring, and management; ease of development; enterprise desktop; XML and web services; and transparency.

JSR 270 identifies various component JSRs. These JSRs include JSR 105 XML Digital Signature APIs, JSR 199 Java Compiler API, JSR 202 Java Class File Specification Update, JSR 221 JDBC 4.0 API Specification, JSR 222 Java Architecture for XML Binding (JAXB) 2.0, JSR 223 Scripting for the Java Platform, JSR 224 Java API for XML-Based Web Services (JAX-WS) 2.0, JSR 268 Java Smart Card I/O API, and JSR 269 Pluggable Annotation Processing API. Although not identified by JSR 270, JSR 173 Streaming API for XML, JSR 181 Web Services Metadata for the Java Platform, and JSR 250 Common Annotations for the Java Platform are also component JSRs.

Java SE 6 provides many features that set it apart from its predecessors. Some of these features were explored in this chapter, and include a trio of new action keys and a method to hide/show action text, the ability to clear a button group's selection, reflection enhancements, the GroupLayout layout manager, an Image I/O GIF writer plug-in, incremental improvements to the String class, LCD text support, new NumberFormat methods for working with rounding modes, an improved File class infrastructure, window icon images, the ability to specify a minimum window size, an interruptible I/O switch for Solaris, DeflatorInputStream and InflatorOutputStream classes added to the java.util.zip package, ownerless windows, and navigable sets.

Following the initial release of Java SE 6 (which is the focus of this book), Sun released a pair of updates that primarily fix bugs.

Test Your Understanding

How well do you understand Java SE 6 thus far? Test your understanding by answering the following questions and performing the following exercises. (The answers are presented in Appendix D.)

1. Why does Sun refer to Java SE 6 instead of J2SE 6.0?

2. Identify the themes of Java SE 6.

3. Does Java SE 6 include internationalized resource identifiers (IRIs)?

4. What is the purpose of Action's new DISPLAYED_MNEMONIC_INDEX_KEY constant?

5. Why should you create a Swing program's GUI only on the event-dispatching thread?

6. How do you establish a window's minimum size?

7. Describe each of NavigableSet<E>'s closest-match methods.

8. Does public JDialog(Frame owner) create a true ownerless window when owner is null?

CHAPTER 2

∎∎∎

Core Libraries

Java's core libraries support mathematics, input/output (I/O), collections, and more. Java SE 6 updates existing core libraries and integrates new libraries into the core. This chapter explores the following core library topics:

- BitSet enhancements

- Compiler API

- I/O enhancements

- Mathematics enhancements

- New and improved collections

- New and improved concurrency

- Extension mechanism and ServiceLoader API

BitSet Enhancements

The java.util.BitSet class implements a growable vector of bits. Because of its compactness and other advantages, this data structure is often used to implement an operating system's priority queues and facilitate memory page allocation. Unix-oriented file systems also use bitsets to facilitate the allocation of inodes (information nodes) and disk sectors. And bitsets are useful in Huffman coding, a data-compression algorithm for achieving lossless data compression.

Although no new features have been added to BitSet, Java SE 6 has improved this class in the following ways:

- According to Bug 4963875 "Reduction of space used by instances of java.util.BitSet," the clone() method now returns a clone that can be smaller than the original bitset; bs.size() == bs.clone().size() is no longer guaranteed to be true. Also, a serialized bitset can be smaller. These optimizations reduce wasted space. However, a cloned or serialized bitset is not trimmed if the bitset was created via BitSet(int nbits), and its implementation size has not changed since creation.

- The equals(Object obj) method is now speed-optimized for sparse bitsets (only a few bits are set). It returns false when the number of words in the logical lengths of the bitsets being compared differ. Please consult Bug 4979017 "java.util.BitSet.equals(Object) can be optimized" for more information.

- The hashCode() method has been speed-optimized to hash only the used part of a bitset (the bitset's logical length), as opposed to the entire bitset (its implementation size). You can find more information about this optimization by reading Bug 4979028 "BitSet.hashCode() unnecessarily slow due to extra scanning of zero bits."

- The toString() method has been speed-optimized for large sparse bitsets. Check out Bug 4979031 "BitSet.toString() is too slow on sparse large bitsets" for more information.

- Some of BitSet's methods now call various methods in the Long class instead of implementing equivalent methods. For example, the BitSet class's public int nextSetBit(int fromIndex) method invokes the Long class's public static int numberOfTrailingZeroes(long i) method. This results in a simpler, faster, and smaller BitSet implementation. Bug 5030267 "Use new static methods Long.highestOneBit/Long.bitCount in java.util.BitSet" provides more information. Also, you might want to check out the BitSet.java source file.

- Previous violations of BitSet's internal invariants are no longer tolerated. For example, given bs.set(64,64);, bs.length() now returns 0 (instead of 64) and isEmpty() returns true (instead of false). More information can be found by reviewing Bug 6222207 "BitSet internal invariants may be violated."

Compiler API

The ability to dynamically compile Java source code is needed in many situations. For example, the first time a web browser requests a JavaServer Pages (JSP)-based document, the JSP container generates a servlet and compiles the servlet's code.

Prior to Java 1.2, you could achieve dynamic compilation only by creating a temporary .java file and invoking javac via Runtime.exec(). Alternatively, you could access javac internals. The first approach was problematic because of platform-specific process behavior and applet security restrictions. The latter approach suffered from being undocumented and compiler-specific.

Java 1.2 let you programmatically access the compiler via the JDK's tools.jar file. This access remained undocumented until Java 5 debuted. The following static methods in tools.jar's com.sun.tools.javac.Main class let you access the compiler:

- public static int compile(String[] args)

- public static int compile(String[] args, PrintWriter out)

The args parameter identifies the command-line arguments normally passed to javac. The out parameter specifies the location of compiler diagnostic output (error and warning messages). Each method returns the same value as javac's exit code.

As useful as these methods are, they are limited in the way they interact with their environment. For starters, they input source code from files and output compiled code to files. Also, they report errors to a single output stream—no mechanism exists to return diagnostics as structured data. I refer you to JSR 199 (http://jcp.org/en/jsr/detail?id=199) for more information.

To address this limitation, Sun has integrated the Compiler API into Java SE 6's core libraries. This API offers the following:

- Programmatic access to the compiler

- Ability to override the manner in which the compiler reads and writes source and class files

- Access to structured diagnostic information

Access to the Compiler and Other Tools

The Compiler API is hosted by the javax.tools package, which is designed to let programs invoke various tools, beginning with compilers. This package consists of six classes, eleven interfaces, and three enumerations. The entry point into javax.tools is the ToolProvider class, from which you can access the default Java compiler:

```
JavaCompiler compiler = ToolProvider.getSystemJavaCompiler();
```

The getSystemJavaCompiler() method returns an object that represents the default Java compiler. If a compiler is not available (tools.jar must be in the classpath), this method returns null.

The returned object is created from a class that implements the JavaCompiler interface. Using this interface, you can do the following:

- Identify the source versions of the Java language that are supported by the compiler.

- Determine if a compiler option is supported.

- Run the compiler with specific I/O streams and arguments.

- Obtain the standard file manager.

- Create a *future* (a java.util.concurrent.Future object that stores the result of an asynchronous computation) for a compilation task.

Identifying the Java language source versions that are supported by the compiler is important because a Java compiler cannot compile future source code that includes new language features and new/enhanced APIs. To determine the supported versions, call the JavaCompiler interface's inherited Set<SourceVersion> getSourceVersions() method. This method returns a java.util.Set<E> of SourceVersion enumeration constants whose methods provide the desired information.

Certain compiler options (such as -g, to generate all debugging information) can be specified when programmatically running the compiler. Before specifying an option, you must determine if the option is supported. Accomplish this task by calling the JavaCompiler interface's inherited int isSupportedOption(String option) method. If the option is not supported, this method returns -1; the number of required arguments for the option is returned if the option is supported. Listing 2-1 demonstrates isSupportedOption() and getSourceVersions().

Listing 2-1. *CompilerInfo.java*

```
// CompilerInfo.java

import java.util.*;

import javax.lang.model.*;

import javax.tools.*;

public class CompilerInfo
{
   public static void main (String [] args)
   {
```

```java
        if (args.length != 1)
        {
            System.err.println ("usage: java CompilerInfo option");
            return;
        }

        JavaCompiler compiler = ToolProvider.getSystemJavaCompiler ();
        if (compiler == null)
        {
            System.err.println ("compiler not available");
            return;
        }

        System.out.println ("Supported source versions:");
        Set<SourceVersion> srcVer = compiler.getSourceVersions ();
        for (SourceVersion sv: srcVer)
            System.out.println ("  " + sv.name ());

        int nargs = compiler.isSupportedOption (args [0]);
        if (nargs == -1)
            System.out.println ("Option "+args [0]+" is not supported");
        else
            System.out.println ("Option "+args [0]+" takes "+nargs+
                                " arguments");
    }
}
```

After compiling CompilerInfo.java (javac CompilerInfo.java), run the application with -g as the single command-line argument (as in java -g CompilerInfo). In response, you should observe the following output:

```
Supported source versions:
  RELEASE_3
  RELEASE_4
  RELEASE_5
  RELEASE_6
Option -g takes 0 arguments
```

The simplest way to run the compiler is to invoke the JavaCompiler interface's inherited int run(InputStream in, OutputStream out, OutputStream err, String... arguments) method. This method lets you specify the input, output, and error I/O streams (null arguments refer to System.in, System.out, and System.err), and a variable list of String arguments to pass to the compiler. This method returns zero on success and a nonzero value on failure. If any of the elements in the arguments array are null references, this method throws a NullPointerException. Listing 2-2 demonstrates the run() method.

Listing 2-2. *CompileFiles1.java*

```
// CompileFiles1.java

import javax.tools.*;

public class CompileFiles1
{
   public static void main (String [] args)
   {
      if (args.length == 0)
      {
         System.err.println ("usage: java CompileFiles1 srcFile [srcFile]+");
         return;
      }

      JavaCompiler compiler = ToolProvider.getSystemJavaCompiler ();
      if (compiler == null)
      {
         System.err.println ("compiler not available");
         return;
      }

      compiler.run (null, null, null, args);
   }
}
```

When you execute CompileFiles1, you can specify filename and compiler option arguments in any order. For example, java CompileFiles1 -g x.java y.java compiles x.java and y.java. Furthermore, all debugging information is generated and stored in each resulting class file.

Although the run() method is easy to use, there is not much you can do in the way of customization. For example, you cannot specify a listener that is invoked with diagnostic information when a problem is discovered in the source code. For more advanced customization, you need to work with the standard (or some other) file manager, and a future for a compilation task.

The Standard File Manager

The compiler tool is associated with the standard file manager, which is responsible for creating file objects—objects whose classes implement the JavaFileObject interface. These file objects represent regular files, entries in ZIP files, or entries in other kinds of containers. Invoke the following method of JavaCompiler to obtain the standard file manager:

```
StandardJavaFileManager getStandardFileManager
  (DiagnosticListener<? super JavaFileObject>diagnosticListener,
   Locale locale, Charset charset)
```

where:

- diagnosticListener identifies a listener that will be notified with nonfatal diagnostic information. A null argument implies that the compiler's default diagnostic-reporting mechanism is used.

- locale identifies the locale in which diagnostic messages are formatted. null indicates the default locale.

- charset identifies the character set for decoding bytes. null indicates the platform's default character set.

Continuing from this section's earlier example, the following example retrieves the compiler's standard file manager, choosing the default diagnostic listener, locale, and character set:

```
StandardJavaFileManager sjfm;
sjfm = compiler.getStandardFileManager (null, null, null);
```

Compilation Task Futures

After obtaining the standard file manager, you can invoke one of various StandardJavaFileManager methods to retrieve an Iterable of JavaFileObjects. Each JavaFileObject abstracts one file, which might or might not be a regular file. For example, assuming that args is an array of command-line arguments, the following example creates a JavaFileObject for each argument and returns these objects via an Iterable:

```
Iterable<? extends JavaFileObject> fileObjects;
fileObjects = sjfm.getJavaFileObjects (args);
```

This `Iterable` is then passed as an argument to the following method of `JavaCompiler` to return a compilation task future:

```
JavaCompiler.CompilationTask getTask
  (Writer out,
   JavaFileManager fileManager,
   DiagnosticListener<? super JavaFileObject> diagnosticListener,
   Iterable<String> options, Iterable<String> classes,
   Iterable<? Extends JavaFileObject> compilationUnits)
```

where:

- `out` identifies a `java.io.Writer` to which additional compiler output is sent. A `null` argument implies `System.err`.

- `fileManager` identifies a file manager for abstracting files. A `null` argument implies the standard file manager.

- `diagnosticListener` identifies a listener for receiving diagnostics. A `null` argument implies that the compiler's default diagnostic-reporting mechanism is used.

- `options` identifies compiler options. Pass `null` if there are none.

- `classes` identifies the names of classes for annotation processing. Pass `null` if there are none.

- `compilationUnits` identifies what will be compiled. A `null` argument implies no compilation units. An `IllegalArgumentException` is thrown from `getTask()` if any of these compilation units are of a kind other than `JavaFileObject.Kind.SOURCE`.

Continuing from the previous example, the following example invokes `getTask()` to return a compilation task future object that ultimately holds the compilation result. This future object's `call()` method is invoked to perform the compilation task:

```
compiler.getTask (null, sjfm, null, null, null, fileObjects).call ();
```

The example does not accomplish anything more than the previous `run()` method. To increase its usefulness, you can create a diagnostic listener (an object whose class implements the `DiagnosticListener<S>` interface) and pass this listener to `getStandardFileManager()` and `getTask()`. Whenever a problem occurs during compilation, this listener will be invoked to report the problem.

Diagnostic Information

Instead of implementing DiagnosticListener<S>, you can create an instance of the more convenient DiagnosticCollector<S> class, which collects diagnostics as a java.util.List<E> of Diagnostic<S>s. Following compilation, call the DiagnosticCollector<S> class's getDiagnostics() method to return this list. For each Diagnostic<S> in the list, you would then call various Diagnostic<S> methods to output diagnostic information. This is demonstrated in Listing 2-3.

Listing 2-3. *CompileFiles2.java*

```java
// CompileFiles2.java

import javax.tools.*;

public class CompileFiles2
{
   public static void main (String [] args)
   {
      if (args.length == 0)
      {
          System.err.println ("usage: java CompileFiles2 srcFile [srcFile]+");
          return;
      }

      JavaCompiler compiler = ToolProvider.getSystemJavaCompiler ();
      if (compiler == null)
      {
          System.err.println ("compiler not available");
          return;
      }

      DiagnosticCollector<JavaFileObject> dc;
      dc = new DiagnosticCollector<JavaFileObject>();

      StandardJavaFileManager sjfm;
      sjfm = compiler.getStandardFileManager (dc, null, null);

      Iterable<? extends JavaFileObject> fileObjects;
      fileObjects = sjfm.getJavaFileObjects (args);

      compiler.getTask (null, sjfm, dc, null, null, fileObjects).call ();
```

```
        for (Diagnostic d: dc.getDiagnostics ())
        {
            System.out.println (d.getMessage (null));
            System.out.printf ("Line number = %d\n", d.getLineNumber ());
            System.out.printf ("File = %s\n", d.getSource ());
        }
    }
  }
}
```

The CompileFiles1 and CompileFiles2 applications focus on compiling Java source code stored in files. File-based compilation is not helpful if you want to compile source code stored in a String.

String-Based Compilation

Although JavaCompiler's JDK documentation presents a JavaSourceFromString example that demonstrates how to subclass SimpleJavaFileObject (an implementation of JavaFileObject) to define a file object representing string-based source code, this example does not go far enough to show you how to actually compile the string. In contrast, Listing 2-4 shows you how to work with this class to describe a string-based application to the Compiler API. After compilation, this application's Test class is loaded and its main() method is run.

Listing 2-4. *CompileString.java*

```
// CompileString.java

import java.lang.reflect.*;

import java.net.*;

import java.util.*;

import javax.tools.*;

public class CompileString
{
    public static void main (String [] args)
    {
        JavaCompiler compiler = ToolProvider.getSystemJavaCompiler ();
        if (compiler == null)
```

```
    {
        System.err.println ("compiler not available");
        return;
    }

    String program =
    "class Test"+
    "{"+
    "    public static void main (String [] args)"+
    "    {"+
    "        System.out.println (\"Hello, World\");"+
    "        System.out.println (args.length);"+
    "    }"+
    "}";

    Iterable<? extends JavaFileObject> fileObjects;
    fileObjects = getJavaSourceFromString (program);

    compiler.getTask (null, null, null, null, null, fileObjects).call ();

    try
    {
        Class<?> clazz = Class.forName ("Test");
        Method m = clazz.getMethod ("main", new Class [] { String [].class });
        Object [] _args = new Object [] { new String [0] };
        m.invoke (null, _args);
    }
    catch (Exception e)
    {
        System.err.println ("unable to load and run Test");
    }
}

static Iterable<JavaSourceFromString> getJavaSourceFromString (String code)
{
    final JavaSourceFromString jsfs;
    jsfs = new JavaSourceFromString ("code", code);

    return new Iterable<JavaSourceFromString> ()
                {
                    public Iterator<JavaSourceFromString> iterator ()
                    {
                        return new Iterator<JavaSourceFromString> ()
                        {
```

```
                            boolean isNext = true;

                            public boolean hasNext ()
                            {
                                return isNext;
                            }

                            public JavaSourceFromString next ()
                            {
                                if (!isNext)
                                    throw new NoSuchElementException ();

                                isNext = false;

                                return jsfs;
                            }

                            public void remove ()
                            {
                                throw new UnsupportedOperationException ();
                            }
                        };
                    }
                };
        }
    }

class JavaSourceFromString extends SimpleJavaFileObject
{
    final String code;

    JavaSourceFromString (String name, String code)
    {
        super (URI.create ("string:///"+name.replace ('.', '/')+
                Kind.SOURCE.extension), Kind.SOURCE);
        this.code = code;
    }

    public CharSequence getCharContent (boolean ignoreEncodingErrors)
    {
        return code;
    }
}
```

Although I've shown you how to use the Compiler API to overcome the "Java source code must be stored in files" limitation, there is still the limitation of relying on tools.jar. Fortunately, this limitation can be overcome by taking advantage of Java SE 6's Service-Loader API to access an alternate compiler, as you will learn in the "Extension Mechanism and ServiceLoader API" section later in this chapter.

I/O Enhancements

Little things often mean a lot. Judging from the amount of comments to Bug 4050435 "Improved interactive console I/O (password prompting, line editing)" and Bug 4057701 "Need way to find free disk space," many developers will be thrilled to discover that Java SE 6 fixes these two long-standing bugs. The first fix lets you safely prompt for passwords without echoing them to the console (and more). The second fix lets you determine the amount of free disk space (and more). Furthermore, Sun has also addressed a need for setting a java.io.File object's read, write, and execute permissions by responding to Bug 6216563 "Need capability to manipulate more file access attributes in File class."

Note Java SE 6 has also fixed the I/O-related Bug 4403166 "File does not support long paths on Windows NT."

Console I/O

You are writing a console-based application that runs on the server. This application needs to prompt the user for a username and password before granting access. Obviously, you do not want the password to be echoed to the console. Prior to Java SE 6, you had no way to accomplish this task without resorting to the Java Native Interface (JNI). java.awt.TextField provides a public void setEchoChar(char c) method to accomplish this task, but this method is only appropriate for GUI-based applications.

Java SE 6's response to this need is a new java.io.Console class. This class provides methods that access the character-based console device, but only if that device is associated with the current Java virtual machine (JVM). To determine if this device is available, you need to call the System class's public static Console console() method:

```
Console console = System.console ();
if (console == null)
{
    System.err.println ("No console device is present");
    return;
}
```

This method returns a Console reference if a console is present; otherwise, it returns null. After verifying that the method did not return null, you can use the reference to call the Console class's methods, which Table 2-1 describes.

Table 2-1. *Console Class Methods*

Method	Description
public void flush()	Immediately writes all buffered output to the console.
public Console format(String fmt, Object... args)	Writes a formatted string to the console's output stream. The Console reference is returned so that you can chain method calls together (for convenience). Throws java.util.IllegalFormatException if the format string contains illegal syntax.
public Console printf(String format, Object... args)	An alias for format().
public Reader reader()	Returns the java.io.Reader associated with the console. This Reader can be passed to a java.util.Scanner constructor for more sophisticated scanning/parsing.
public String readLine()	Reads a single line of text from the console's input stream. The line (minus line-termination characters) is returned in a String. However, if the end of the stream has been reached, it returns null. Throws java.io.IOError if an error occurs during I/O.
public String readLine(String fmt, Object... args)	Writes a formatted string to the console's output stream, and then reads a single line of text from its input stream. The line (minus line-termination characters) is returned in a String. However, if the end of the stream has been reached, it returns null. Throws IllegalFormatException if the format string contains illegal syntax. Throws IOError if an error occurs during I/O.
public char[] readPassword()	Reads a password from the console's input stream with echoing disabled. The password (minus line-termination characters) is returned in a char array. However, if the end of the stream has been reached, it returns null. Throws IOError if an error occurs during I/O.
public char[] readPassword(String fmt, Object... args)	Writes a formatted string to the console's output stream, and then reads a password from its input stream with echoing disabled. The password (minus line-termination characters) is returned in a char array. However, if the end of the stream has been reached, it returns null. Throws IllegalFormatException if the format string contains illegal syntax. Throws IOError if an error occurs during I/O.
public PrintWriter writer()	Returns the java.io.PrintWriter associated with the console.

I have created an application that invokes Console methods to obtain a username and password. Check out Listing 2-5 for the application's source code.

Listing 2-5. *Login.java*

```java
// Login.java

import java.io.*;

public class Login
{
    public static void main (String [] args)
    {
        Console console = System.console ();
        if (console == null)
        {
            System.err.println ("No console device is present");
            return;
        }

        try
        {
            String username = console.readLine ("Username:");
            char [] pwd = console.readPassword ("Password:");

            // Do something useful with the username and password. For something
            // to do, this program just prints out these values.

            System.out.println ("Username = " + username);
            System.out.println ("Password = " + new String (pwd));

            // Prepare username String for garbage collection. More importantly,
            // destroy the password.

            username = "";
            for (int i = 0; i < pwd.length; i++)
                pwd [i] = 0;
        }
        catch (IOError ioe)
        {
            console.printf ("I/O problem: %s\n", ioe.getMessage ());
        }
    }
}
```

After obtaining and (presumably) doing something useful with the username and password, it is important to get rid of these items for security reasons. Most important, you will want to remove the password by zeroing out the char array.

If you have worked with the C language, you will notice the similarity between Console's printf() method and C's printf() function. Both take a format string argument, which specifies format specifiers (such as %s), and follow this argument with a variable list of arguments (one argument per specifier). To learn about the printf() method's format specifiers, check out the java.util.Formatter class's JDK documentation.

Disk Free Space and Other Partition-Space Methods

Obtaining the amount of free space on a disk is important to installers and other programs. Until Java SE 6 arrived, the only portable way to accomplish this task was to guess by creating files of different sizes. Java SE 6 remedied this situation by adding three partition-space methods to File. These methods are described in Table 2-2.

Table 2-2. *File Class Partition-Space Methods*

Method	Description
public long getFreeSpace()	Returns the number of unallocated bytes in the partition identified by this File object's abstract pathname. Returns zero if the abstract pathname does not name a partition.
public long getTotalSpace()	Returns the size (in bytes) of the partition identified by this File object's abstract pathname. Returns zero if the abstract pathname does not name a partition.
public long getUsableSpace()	Returns the number of bytes available to the current JVM on the partition identified by this File object's abstract pathname. Returns zero if the abstract pathname does not name a partition.

Although getFreeSpace() and getUsableSpace() appear to be equivalent, they differ in the following respect: unlike getFreeSpace(), getUsableSpace() checks for write permissions and other platform restrictions, resulting in a more accurate estimate.

Note The getFreeSpace() and getUsableSpace() methods return a hint (not a guarantee) that a Java program can use all (or most) of the unallocated or available bytes. These values are a hint because a program running outside the JVM can allocate partition space, resulting in actual unallocated and available values being lower than the values returned by these methods.

Listing 2-6 presents the source code for an application that demonstrates these methods. After obtaining an array of all available file-system roots, this application obtains and outputs the free, total, and usable space for each partition identified by the array.

Listing 2-6. *PartitionSpace.java*

```
// PartitionSpace.java

import java.io.*;

public class PartitionSpace
{
   public static void main (String [] args)
   {
      File [] roots = File.listRoots ();
      for (int i = 0; i < roots.length; i++)
      {
          System.out.println ("Partition: "+roots [i]);
          System.out.println ("Free space on this partition = "+
                              roots [i].getFreeSpace ());
          System.out.println ("Usable space on this partition = "+
                              roots [i].getUsableSpace ());
          System.out.println ("Total space on this partition = "+
                              roots [i].getTotalSpace ());
          System.out.println ("***");
      }
   }
}
```

I ran this application on a Windows XP machine with a read-only DVD inserted into the D: drive and no floppy disk in the A: drive, and observed the following output:

```
Partition: A:\
Free space on this partition = 0
Usable space on this partition = 0
Total space on this partition = 0
***
Partition: C:\
Free space on this partition = 134556323840
Usable space on this partition = 134556323840
Total space on this partition = 160031014912
***
```

```
Partition: D:\
Free space on this partition = 0
Usable space on this partition = 0
Total space on this partition = 4490307584
```

File-Access Permissions Methods

Java 1.2 added a `public boolean setReadOnly()` method to the `File` class, to mark a file or directory as read-only. However, a method to revert the file or directory to the writable state was not added. More important, until Java SE 6's arrival, `File` offered no way to manage an abstract pathname's read, write, and execute permissions. As described in Table 2-3, six new methods have been added to `File` to manage these permissions.

Table 2-3. *File Class Access-Permission Methods*

Method	Description
`public boolean setExecutable(boolean executable, boolean ownerOnly)`	Enables (pass true to executable) or disables (pass false to executable) this abstract pathname's execute permission for its owner (pass true to ownerOnly) or everyone (pass false to ownerOnly). If the file system does not differentiate between the owner and everyone, this permission always applies to everyone. It returns true if the operation succeeds. It returns false if the user does not have permission to change this abstract pathname's access permissions, or if executable is false and the file system does not implement an execute permission.
`public boolean setExecutable(boolean executable)`	A convenience method that invokes the previous method to set the execute permission for the owner.
`public boolean setReadable(boolean readable, boolean ownerOnly)`	Enables (pass true to readable) or disables (pass false to readable) this abstract pathname's read permission for its owner (pass true to ownerOnly) or everyone (pass false to ownerOnly). If the file system does not differentiate between the owner and everyone, this permission always applies to everyone. It returns true if the operation succeeds. It returns false if the user does not have permission to change this abstract pathname's access permissions, or if readable is false and the file system does not implement a read permission.
`public boolean setReadable(boolean readable)`	A convenience method that invokes the previous method to set the read permission for the owner.
`public boolean setWritable(boolean writable, boolean ownerOnly)`	Enables (pass true to writable) or disables (pass false to writable) this abstract pathname's write permission for its owner (pass true to ownerOnly) or everyone (pass false to ownerOnly). If the file system does not differentiate between the owner and everyone, this permission always applies to everyone. It returns true if the operation succeeds. It returns false if the user does not have permission to change this abstract pathname's access permissions.
`public boolean setWritable(boolean writable)`	A convenience method that invokes the previous method to set the write permission for the owner.

In addition to these methods, Java SE 6 has retrofitted the File class's public boolean canRead() and public boolean canWrite() methods, and introduced a public boolean canExecute() method to return an abstract pathname's access permissions. These methods return true if the file system object identified by the abstract pathname exists and if the appropriate permission is in effect. For example, canWrite() returns true if the abstract pathname exists and if the application has permission to write to the file.

Note Each of canRead(), canWrite(), canExecute(), and the methods listed in Table 2-3 throws a SecurityException if a security manager is present and denies access to the file-system object represented by the abstract pathname.

The canRead(), canWrite(), and canExecute() methods can be used to implement a simple utility that identifies which permissions have been assigned to an arbitrary file-system object. This utility's source code is presented in Listing 2-7.

Listing 2-7. *Permissions.java*

```java
// Permissions.java

import java.io.*;

public class Permissions
{
   public static void main (String [] args)
   {
      if (args.length != 1)
      {
         System.err.println ("usage: java Permissions filespec");
         return;
      }

      File file = new File (args [0]);

      System.out.println ("Checking permissions for "+args [0]);
      System.out.println ("   Execute = "+file.canExecute ());
      System.out.println ("   Read = "+file.canRead ());
      System.out.println ("   Write = "+file.canWrite ());
   }
}
```

Assuming the existence of a file named x (in the current directory), which is only readable and executable, java `Permissions` x generates the following output:

```
Checking permissions for x
  Execute = true
  Read = true
  Write = false
```

Mathematics Enhancements

Java SE 6 enhances java.math.BigDecimal in two main ways:

- By fixing bugs; see Bug 6337226 "BigDecimal.divideToIntegralValue(BigDecimal, MathContext) does not behave to spec"

- By making optimizations, such as caching the first toString() result and returning the cached value on subsequent calls to toString()

Java SE 6 also introduces new Math and StrictMath methods that support IEEE 754/854 recommended functions, as listed in Table 2-4.

Table 2-4. *New Math and StrictMath Methods*

Method	Description
public static double copySign(double magnitude, double sign)	Returns the first double-precision floating-point argument with the sign of the second double-precision floating-point argument.
public static float copySign(float magnitude, float sign)	Returns the first floating-point argument with the sign of the second floating-point argument.
public static int getExponent(double d)	Returns the unbiased exponent used in representing the double-precision floating-point argument.
public static int getExponent(float f)	Returns the unbiased exponent used in representing the floating-point argument.
public static double nextAfter(double start, double direction)	Returns the double-precision floating-point number adjacent to the first argument in the direction of the second argument.
public static float nextAfter(float start, double direction)	Returns the floating-point number adjacent to the first argument in the direction of the second argument.

Method	Description
`public static double nextUp(double d)`	Returns the double-precision floating-point number that is adjacent to the argument in the direction of positive infinity.
`public static float nextUp(float f)`	Returns the floating-point number that is adjacent to the argument in the direction of positive infinity.
`public static double scalb(double d, int scaleFactor)`	Returns the first argument multiplied by 2 to the power of the second argument. The result is rounded to a member of the double value set.
`public static float scalb(float f, int scaleFactor)`	Returns the first argument multiplied by 2 to the power of the second argument. The result is rounded to a member of the float value set.

The `getExponent()` methods are similar to IEEE 754/854's `logb` function family. Also, `nextUp()` is semantically equivalent to `nextAfter(d, Double.POSITIVE_INFINITY)`, but might run faster.

Note Check out Joseph D. Darcy's "Writing robust IEEE recommended functions in '100% Pure Java'" (`http://www.eecs.berkeley.edu/Pubs/TechRpts/1998/CSD-98-1009.pdf`) for more information about the recommended functions that prompted the new methods in `Math` and `StrictMath`.

New and Improved Collections

Java SE 6 has significantly enhanced the collections framework. In addition to fixing the framework's JDK documentation and source code in several places, Java SE 6 introduces several new interfaces and classes, and several new utility methods.

More Collections Interfaces and Classes

The `java.util` package provides the interfaces and classes that form the collections framework. I introduce collections-oriented interfaces and classes that also support concurrency later in this chapter, in the "New and Improved Concurrency" section. Table 2-5 describes the six new interfaces and classes that Java SE 6 integrates into this package.

Table 2-5. *New java.util Package Interfaces and Classes*

Interface/Class	Description
Deque<E>	An interface that describes a *double-ended queue*, a linear collection that supports the insertion and removal of elements at either end.
NavigableMap<K, V>	An interface that describes an extended SortedMap<K, V> with navigation methods that return the closest matches for specific search targets.
NavigableSet<E>	An interface that describes an extended SortedSet<E> with navigation methods that return the closest matches for specific search targets.
AbstractMap.SimpleEntry<K, V>	A class that implements a mutable Map.Entry<K, V>, maintaining a key and a value.
AbstractMap.SimpleImmutableEntry<K, V>	A class that implements an immutable Map.Entry<K, V>, maintaining a key and a value.
ArrayDeque<E>	A class that implements Deque<E> as a resizable array. It allows efficient insertion and removal of elements at both ends, and is a great choice for stacks or queues.

The Deque<E> interface and ArrayDeque<E> implementation class are preferable to the legacy java.util.Stack<E> class when introducing a stack data structure into source code. The fact that Stack<E> is implemented as a java.util.Vector<E> is one reason for this preference. This implementation makes it easy to access Vector<E> methods that can violate the integrity of the stack, such as public void add(int index, E element). To use a deque as a stack, Deque<E> provides void addFirst(E e), E removeFirst(), and E peekFirst() methods. These methods correspond to the Stack<E> class's E push(E item), E pop(), and E peek() methods.

One application that benefits from a stack is a postfix calculator, which requires an operator's operands to be specified before the operator. For example, 10.5 30.2 + is a postfix expression that sums 10.5 and 30.2. The source code for a postfix calculator application that uses Deque<E> and ArrayDeque<E> for its stack is presented in Listing 2-8.

Listing 2-8. *PostfixCalc.java*

```
// PostfixCalc.java

import java.io.*;

import java.util.*;
```

```java
public class PostfixCalc
{
    public static void main (String [] args) throws IOError
    {
        Console console = System.console ();
        if (console == null)
        {
            System.err.println ("unable to obtain console");
            return;
        }

        console.printf ("Postfix expression Calculator\n\n");
        console.printf ("Valid operators: + - * /\n");
        console.printf ("Valid commands: c/C (clear stack), "+
                        "t/t (view stack top)\n\n");

        Deque<Double> stack = new ArrayDeque<Double> ();

        loop:
        while (true)
        {
            String line = console.readLine (">").trim ();

            switch (line.charAt (0))
            {
                case 'Q':
                case 'q': break loop;

                case 'C':
                case 'c': while (stack.peekFirst () != null)
                            stack.removeFirst ();
                          break;

                case 'T':
                case 't': console.printf ("%f\n", stack.peekFirst ());
                          break;

                case '+': if (stack.size () < 2)
                          {
                              console.printf ("missing operand\n");
```

```
                                break;
                          }

                          double op2 = stack.removeFirst ();
                          double op1 = stack.removeFirst ();
                          double res = op1+op2;
                          console.printf ("%f+%f=%f\n", op1, op2, res);
                          stack.addFirst (res);
                          break;

            case '-': if (stack.size () < 2)
                          {
                                console.printf ("missing operand\n");
                                break;
                          }

                          op2 = stack.removeFirst ();
                          op1 = stack.removeFirst ();
                          res = op1-op2;
                          console.printf ("%f-%f=%f\n", op1, op2, res);
                          stack.addFirst (res);
                          break;

            case '*': if (stack.size () < 2)
                          {
                                console.printf ("missing operand\n");
                                break;
                          }

                          op2 = stack.removeFirst ();
                          op1 = stack.removeFirst ();
                          res = op1*op2;
                          console.printf ("%f*%f=%f\n", op1, op2, res);
                          stack.addFirst (res);
                          break;

            case '/': if (stack.size () < 2)
                          {
                                console.printf ("missing operand\n");
```

```
                           break;
                     }

             op2 = stack.removeFirst ();
             op1 = stack.removeFirst ();
             res = op1/op2;
             console.printf ("%f/%f=%f\n", op1, op2, res);
             stack.addFirst (res);
             break;

      default : try
                {
                    stack.addFirst (Double.parseDouble (line));
                }
                catch (NumberFormatException nfe)
                {
                    console.printf ("double value expected\n");
                }
          }
       }
    }
}
```

When you run this application, you will be prompted to enter a line of input. Enter an operator (+, -, *, or /), a number operand, or a command (c/C, t/T, or q/Q), but only one of these items. Before entering an operator, remember that you need at least two operands on the stack. Here is an example:

```
>10
>20
>+
10.000000+20.000000=30.000000
>q
```

Note The LinkedList<E> class has been reworked to implement Deque<E>.

The NavigableMap<K, V> and NavigableSet<E> interfaces provide methods that return a map view based on a range of keys and a set view based on a range of entries. For example, because the TreeMap<K, V> and TreeSet<E> classes have been retrofitted to implement these interfaces, the following TreeMap<K, V> method returns a TreeMap<K, V>-backed view that presents a range of the map's keys:

```
public NavigableMap<K,V> subMap(K fromKey, boolean fromInclusive,
                                K toKey, boolean toInclusive)
```

and the following TreeSet<E> method returns a TreeMap<E>-backed view that presents a range of the set's entries:

```
public NavigableSet<E> subSet(E fromElement, boolean fromInclusive,
                              E toElement, boolean toInclusive)
```

Listing 2-9 presents the source code to a product database application that demonstrates subMap() and two more new TreeMap<K, V> methods:

- SortedMap<K,V> headMap(K toKey), which returns a map view whose keys are less than toKey

- SortedMap<K,V> tailMap(K fromKey), which returns a map view whose keys are greater than or equal to fromKey

Listing 2-9. *ProductDB.java*

```java
//ProductDB.java

import java.util.*;
import java.util.Map;

public class ProductDB
{
    public static void build (Map<Integer, Product> map)
    {
        map.put (1000, new Product ("DVD player", 350));
        map.put (1011, new Product ("10 kilo bag of potatoes", 15.75));
        map.put (1102, new Product ("Magazine", 8.50));
        map.put (2023, new Product ("Automobile", 18500));
        map.put (2034, new Product ("Towel", 9.99));
    }
```

```
   public static void main(String[] args)
   {
      TreeMap<Integer, Product> db = new TreeMap<Integer, Product> ();
      build (db);

      System.out.println ("Database view of products ranging from 1000-1999");
      System.out.println (db.subMap (1000, 1999)+"\n");

      System.out.println ("Database view of products >= 1011");
      System.out.println (db.tailMap (1011)+"\n");

      System.out.println ("Database view of products < 2023");
      System.out.println (db.headMap (2023));
   }
}

class Product
{
   String desc;
   double price;

   Product (String desc, double price)
   {
      this.desc = desc;
      this.price = price;
   }

   public String toString ()
   {
      return "Description="+desc+", Price="+price;
   }
}
```

When you run this application, you will discover the following:

- db.subMap (1000, 1999) returns a view that identifies products whose keys are 1000, 1011, and 1102.

- db.tailMap (1011) returns a view that identifies products whose keys are 1011, 1102, 2023, and 2034.

- db.headMap (2023) returns a view that identifies products whose keys are 1000, 1011, and 1102.

> **Note** Check out Java Boutique's "SortedSet and SortedMap Made Easier with Two New Mustang Interfaces" article (`http://javaboutique.internet.com/tutorials/mustang/index.html`) for a complete look at the `NavigableMap<K,V>` and `NavigableSet<E>` methods.

More Utility Methods

The collections framework includes the `java.util.Collections` and `java.util.Arrays` utility classes. The former class provides utility methods for collections, and the latter class provides utility methods for arrays. Table 2-6 describes the two new methods that have been added to `Collections`.

Table 2-6. *New Collections Methods*

Method	Description
`public static <T>` `Queue<T> asLifoQueue(Deque<T> deque)`	Returns a last-in-first-out (LIFO) `Queue<E>` view of a `Deque<E>`. In contrast to the documentation, `Queue<E>`'s `boolean add(E e)` method is mapped to `Deque<E>`'s `void addFirst(E e)` method, and `Queue<E>`'s `E remove()` method is mapped to `Deque<E>`'s `E removeFirst()` method.
`public static <E> Set<E>` `newSetFromMap(Map<E,Boolean> map)`	Returns a `Set<E>` that is backed by a `Map<K, V>`. The `Map<K, V>`'s ordering, performance, and concurrency characteristics are reflected in the `Set<E>`. An `IllegalArgumentException` is thrown if the `Map<K, V>` is not empty when this method is invoked.

The view that is returned from `asLifoQueue()` is useful for those situations where you need to call a method that requires a `Queue<E>`, but you also need to achieve LIFO ordering. Also, you will find that `newSetFromMap()` makes it much easier to create `Set<E>` implementations for those `Map<K, V>` implementations that do not have corresponding `Set<E>` implementations. For example, the collections framework includes `WeakHashMap<K, V>`, but it does not include `WeakHashSet<E>`.

Not to be outdone, the `Arrays` class has been expanded with multiple overloaded versions of the `binarySearch()`, `copyOf()`, and `copyOfRange()` utility methods. Each overloaded method is described in Table 2-7.

Table 2-7. *New Arrays Methods*

Method	Description
`public static int binarySearch(byte[] a, int fromIndex, int toIndex, byte key)`	Uses the binary search algorithm to search the fromIndex (inclusive) to toIndex (exclusive) range of byte integer array a for the presence of key. Returns the position if found, or a negative value if not found. The range must be sorted prior to making this call. An `IllegalArgumentException` is thrown if `fromIndex` is greater than `toIndex`, and an `ArrayIndexOutOfBoundsException` is thrown if `fromIndex` is less than zero or `toIndex` is greater than a's length.
`public static int binarySearch(char[] a, int fromIndex, int toIndex, char key)`	Uses the binary search algorithm to search the fromIndex (inclusive) to toIndex (exclusive) range of character array a for the presence of key. Returns the position if found, or a negative value if not found. The range must be sorted prior to making this call. An `IllegalArgumentException` is thrown if `fromIndex` is greater than `toIndex`, and an `ArrayIndexOutOfBoundsException` is thrown if `fromIndex` is less than zero or `toIndex` is greater than a's length.
`public static int binarySearch(double[] a, int fromIndex, int toIndex, double key)`	Uses the binary search algorithm to search the fromIndex (inclusive) to toIndex (exclusive) range of double-precision floating-point array a for the presence of key. Returns the position if found, or a negative value if not found. The range must be sorted prior to making this call. An `IllegalArgumentException` is thrown if `fromIndex` is greater than `toIndex`, and an `ArrayIndexOutOfBoundsException` is thrown if `fromIndex` is less than zero or `toIndex` is greater than a's length.
`public static int binarySearch(float[] a, int fromIndex, int toIndex, float key)`	Uses the binary search algorithm to search the fromIndex (inclusive) to toIndex (exclusive) range of floating-point array a for the presence of key. Returns the position if found, or a negative value if not found. The range must be sorted prior to making this call. An `IllegalArgumentException` is thrown if `fromIndex` is greater than `toIndex`, and an `ArrayIndexOutOfBoundsException` is thrown if `fromIndex` is less than zero or `toIndex` is greater than a's length.
`public static int binarySearch(int[] a, int fromIndex, int toIndex, int key)`	Uses the binary search algorithm to search the fromIndex (inclusive) to toIndex (exclusive) range of integer array a for the presence of key. Returns the position if found, or a negative value if not found. The range must be sorted prior to making this call. An `IllegalArgumentException` is thrown if `fromIndex` is greater than `toIndex`, and an `ArrayIndexOutOfBoundsException` is thrown if `fromIndex` is less than zero or `toIndex` is greater than a's length.

Continued

Table 2-7. *Continued*

Method	Description

`public static int`
`binarySearch(long[] a,`
`int fromIndex, int toIndex,`
`long key)`
	Uses the binary search algorithm to search the fromIndex (inclusive) to toIndex (exclusive) range of long integer array a for the presence of key. Returns the position if found, or a negative value if not found. The range must be sorted prior to making this call. An `IllegalArgumentException` is thrown if `fromIndex` is greater than `toIndex`, and an `ArrayIndexOutOfBoundsException` is thrown if `fromIndex` is less than zero or `toIndex` is greater than a's length.

`public static int`
`binarySearch(Object[] a,`
`int fromIndex, int toIndex,`
`Object key)`
	Uses the binary search algorithm to search the fromIndex (inclusive) to toIndex (exclusive) range of object array a for the presence of key. Returns the position if found, or a negative value if not found. The range must be sorted into ascending order according to the natural ordering of its elements prior to making this call. An `IllegalArgumentException` is thrown if `fromIndex` is greater than `toIndex`, and an `ArrayIndexOutOfBoundsException` is thrown if `fromIndex` is less than zero or `toIndex` is greater than a's length.

`public static int`
`binarySearch(short[] a,`
`int fromIndex, int toIndex,`
`short key)`
	Uses the binary search algorithm to search the fromIndex (inclusive) to toIndex (exclusive) range of short integer array a for the presence of key. Returns the position if found, or a negative value if not found. The range must be sorted prior to making this call. An `IllegalArgumentException` is thrown if `fromIndex` is greater than `toIndex`, and an `ArrayIndexOutOfBoundsException` is thrown if `fromIndex` is less than zero or `toIndex` is greater than a's length.

`public static <T> int`
`binarySearch(T[] a,`
`int fromIndex, int toIndex,`
`T key, Comparator<? super T> c)`
	Uses the binary search algorithm to search the fromIndex (inclusive) to toIndex (exclusive) range of type array a for the presence of key. Returns the position if found, or a negative value if not found. The range must be sorted into ascending order according to the specified comparator prior to making this call. An `IllegalArgumentException` is thrown if `fromIndex` is greater than `toIndex`, an `ArrayIndexOutOfBoundsException` is thrown if `fromIndex` is less than zero or `toIndex` is greater than a's length, and a `ClassCastException` is thrown if the range contains elements that are not mutually comparable using the specified comparator (or the search key is not comparable to the range's elements using the comparator).

Method	Description

`public static boolean[]`
`copyOf(boolean[] original,`
`int newLength)`
	Creates and returns a copy of the original Boolean array. The copy is truncated or padded with zeros representing false so that it has exactly newLength elements. A NegativeArraySizeException is thrown if newLength is negative, and a NullPointerException is thrown if original is null.

`public static byte[]`
`copyOf(byte[] original,`
`int newLength)`
	Creates and returns a copy of the original byte integer array. The copy is truncated or padded with zeros so that it has exactly newLength elements. A NegativeArraySizeException is thrown if newLength is negative, and a NullPointerException is thrown if original is null.

`public static char[]`
`copyOf(char[] original,`
`int newLength)`
	Creates and returns a copy of the original character array. The copy is truncated or padded with zeros so that it has exactly newLength elements. A NegativeArraySizeException is thrown if newLength is negative, and a NullPointerException is thrown if original is null.

`public static double[]`
`copyOf(double[] original,`
`int newLength)`
	Creates and returns a copy of the original double-precision floating-point array. The copy is truncated or padded with zeros so that it has exactly newLength elements. A NegativeArraySizeException is thrown if newLength is negative, and a NullPointerException is thrown if original is null.

`public static float[]`
`copyOf(float[] original,`
`int newLength)`
	Creates and returns a copy of the original floating-point array. The copy is truncated or padded with zeros so that it has exactly newLength elements. A NegativeArraySizeException is thrown if newLength is negative, and a NullPointerException is thrown if original is null.

`public static int[]`
`copyOf(int[] original,`
`int newLength)`
	Creates and returns a copy of the original integer array. The copy is truncated or padded with zeros so that it has exactly newLength elements. A NegativeArraySizeException is thrown if newLength is negative, and a NullPointerException is thrown if original is null.

`public static long[]`
`copyOf(long[] original,`
`int newLength)`
	Creates and returns a copy of the original long integer array. The copy is truncated or padded with zeros so that it has exactly newLength elements. A NegativeArraySizeException is thrown if newLength is negative, and a NullPointerException is thrown if original is null.

`public static short[]`
`copyOf(short[] original,`
`int newLength)`
	Creates and returns a copy of the original short integer array. The copy is truncated or padded with zeros so that it has exactly newLength elements. A NegativeArraySizeException is thrown if newLength is negative, and a NullPointerException is thrown if original is null.

Continued

Table 2-7. *Continued*

Method	Description

`public static <T> T[]`
`copyOf(T[] original,`
`int newLength)`
	Creates and returns a copy of the original type array. The copy is truncated or padded with zeros representing null references so that it has exactly `newLength` elements. A `NegativeArraySizeException` is thrown if `newLength` is negative, and a `NullPointerException` is thrown if `original` is null.

`public static <T,U>`
`T[] copyOf(U[] original,`
`int newLength, Class<?`
`extends T[]> newType)`
	Creates and returns a copy of the original type array with the copy's type specified by `newType`. The copy is truncated or padded with zeros representing null references so that it has exactly `newLength` elements. A `NegativeArraySizeException` is thrown if `newLength` is negative, a `NullPointerException` is thrown if `original` is null, and an `ArrayStoreException` is thrown if there is a type conflict such that elements from the original array are not type-compatible with the new array.

`public static boolean[]`
`copyOfRange(boolean[] original,`
`int from, int to)`
	Creates and returns a copy, ranging from index `from` (inclusive) to index `to` (exclusive), of the original Boolean array. An `ArrayIndexOutOfBoundsException` is thrown if `from` is less than zero or greater than or equal to `original`'s length, an `IllegalArgumentException` is thrown if `from` is greater than `to`, and a `NullPointerException` is thrown if `original` is null.

`public static byte[]`
`copyOfRange(byte[] original,`
`int from, int to)`
	Creates and returns a copy, ranging from index `from` (inclusive) to index `to` (exclusive), of the original byte integer array. An `ArrayIndexOutOfBoundsException` is thrown if `from` is less than zero or greater than or equal to `original`'s length, an `IllegalArgumentException` is thrown if `from` is greater than `to`, and a `NullPointerException` is thrown if `original` is null.

`public static char[]`
`copyOfRange(char[] original,`
`int from, int to)`
	Creates and returns a copy, ranging from index `from` (inclusive) to index `to` (exclusive), of the original character array. An `ArrayIndexOutOfBoundsException` is thrown if `from` is less than zero or greater than or equal to `original`'s length, an `IllegalArgumentException` is thrown if `from` is greater than `to`, and a `NullPointerException` is thrown if `original` is null.

`public static double[]`
`copyOfRange(double[] original,`
`int from, int to)`
	Creates and returns a copy, ranging from index `from` (inclusive) to index `to` (exclusive), of the original double-precision floating-point array. An `ArrayIndexOutOfBoundsException` is thrown if `from` is less than zero or greater than or equal to `original`'s length, an `IllegalArgumentException` is thrown if `from` is greater than `to`, and a `NullPointerException` is thrown if `original` is null.

Method	Description

`public static float[]`
`copyOfRange(float[]`
`original, int from, int to)`
	Creates and returns a copy, ranging from index `from` (inclusive) to index `to` (exclusive), of the original floating-point array. An `ArrayIndexOutOfBoundsException` is thrown if `from` is less than zero or greater than or equal to `original`'s length, an `IllegalArgumentException` is thrown if `from` is greater than `to`, and a `NullPointerException` is thrown if `original` is null.

`public static int[]`
`copyOfRange(int[] original,`
`int from, int to)`
	Creates and returns a copy, ranging from index `from` (inclusive) to index `to` (exclusive), of the original integer array. An `ArrayIndexOutOfBoundsException` is thrown if `from` is less than zero or greater than or equal to `original`'s length, an `IllegalArgumentException` is thrown if `from` is greater than `to`, and a `NullPointerException` is thrown if `original` is null.

`public static long[]`
`copyOfRange(long[] original,`
`int from, int to)`
	Creates and returns a copy, ranging from index `from` (inclusive) to index `to` (exclusive), of the original long integer array. An `ArrayIndexOutOfBoundsException` is thrown if `from` is less than zero or greater than or equal to `original`'s length, an `IllegalArgumentException` is thrown if `from` is greater than `to`, and a `NullPointerException` is thrown if `original` is null.

`public static short[]`
`copyOfRange(short[]`
`original, int from, int to)`
	Creates and returns a copy, ranging from index `from` (inclusive) to index `to` (exclusive), of the original short integer array. An `ArrayIndexOutOfBoundsException` is thrown if `from` is less than zero or greater than or equal to `original`'s length, an `IllegalArgumentException` is thrown if `from` is greater than `to`, and a `NullPointerException` is thrown if `original` is null.

`public static <T> T[]`
`copyOfRange(T[] original,`
`int from, int to)`
	Creates and returns a copy, ranging from index `from` (inclusive) to index `to` (exclusive), of the original type array. An `ArrayIndexOutOfBoundsException` is thrown if `from` is less than zero or greater than or equal to `original`'s length, an `IllegalArgumentException` is thrown if `from` is greater than `to`, and a `NullPointerException` is thrown if `original` is null.

`public static <T,U> T[]`
`copyOfRange(U[] original,`
`int from, int to, Class<?`
`extends T[]> newType)`
	Creates and returns a copy, ranging from index `from` (inclusive) to index `to` (exclusive), of the original type array such that the copy's type is newType. An `ArrayIndexOutOfBoundsException` is thrown if `from` is less than zero or greater than or equal to `original`'s length, an `IllegalArgumentException` is thrown if `from` is greater than `to`, a `NullPointerException` is thrown if `original` is null, and an `ArrayStoreException` is thrown if there is a type conflict.

For performance reasons, the `Arrays` class contains a variety of pre-Java SE 6 `sort()` methods that sort only a portion of an array. Java SE 6's new `binarySearch()` methods complement their sorting counterparts by making it possible to search only part of the array. As a result, you can slowly fill an array, sort just the filled section, and search the filled section without first needing to copy this section to a new array (which has memory usage and performance implications, notably garbage collection's impact on performance).

The `Collection<E>` interface's `<T> T[] toArray(T[] a)` method lets you flexibly copy a collection to an array. The type of the returned array matches the type of the array argument. Also, if the size of this argument is less than the collection's size, reflection is used to dynamically create an array of the appropriate size. Java SE 6's new `copyOf()` and `copyOfRange()` methods implement the equivalent for copying all or part of an array to another array.

Note For more insight into `toArray()`, `copyOf()`, and `copyOfRange()`, read R. J. Lorimer's "Java 6: Copying Typed Arrays" tutorial (`http://www.javalobby.org/java/forums/t87043.html`).

New and Improved Concurrency

The concurrency framework, which was first introduced in Java 5, provides a higher level of support for concurrent programming. Java SE 6 enhances this support by making improvements to the existing infrastructure, and by integrating new interfaces and classes into the framework.

More Concurrent Interfaces and Classes

The `java.util.concurrent` package provides utility interfaces, classes, and enumerations for executors, synchronizers, and other high-level concurrency constructs. Java SE 6 integrates seven new interfaces and classes into this package, as described in Table 2-8.

Table 2-8. *New java.util.concurrent Interfaces and Classes*

Interface/Class	Description
`BlockingDeque<E>`	An interface that describes an extended `Deque<E>` with blocking operations that wait for the deque to become nonempty during element retrieval, and wait for the deque to become nonfull during element storage.
`ConcurrentNavigableMap<K, V>`	An interface that describes an extended `ConcurrentMap<K, V>` and `NavigableMap<K, V>`.

Interface/Class	Description
RunnableFuture<V>	An interface that describes an extended Future<V> and Runnable. The Future<V> completes if the run() method succeeds.
RunnableScheduledFuture<V>	An interface that describes an extended RunnableFuture<V> and ScheduledFuture<V>.
ConcurrentSkipListMap<K, V>	A class that implements ConcurrentNavigableMap<K, V> and provides a concurrent variant of the skip list data structure.
ConcurrentSkipListSet<E>	A class that implements NavigableSet<E> and provides a concurrent variant of the skip list data structure.
LinkedBlockingDeque<E>	A class that implements an optionally bounded BlockingDeque<E> via linked nodes.

Note To learn more about skip lists, check out Wikipedia's Skip list entry (http://en.wikipedia.org/wiki/Skip_list).

The BlockingDeque<E> interface and its LinkedBlockingDeque<E> implementation class complement the BlockingQueue<E> interface and LinkedBlockingQueue<E> class (introduced in Java 5) by supporting a LIFO blocking queue. You will find this LIFO behavior useful in concurrent situations that require a stack data structure.

The RunnableFuture<V> interface, which combines the functionality of Future<V> and Runnable, helps you create customized task classes that are similar to FutureTask<V> for representing cancelable asynchronous computations. Although you can subclass FutureTask<V>, any kind of useful customization is practically impossible because FutureTask<V> is not designed for extension. The javax.swing.SwingWorker<T, V> class, which implements RunnableFuture<V>, is an excellent example of a customized task class, as you'll learn in Chapter 4.

Because the AbstractExecutorService class, which provides default implementations of the ExecutorService interface's execution methods, no longer hardwires these methods to FutureTask<V>, you can easily couple these methods to your own custom task class. Accomplish this objective by overriding either or both of the following new methods of the AbstractExecutorService class:

```
protected <T> RunnableFuture<T> newTaskFor(Callable<T> callable)
protected <T> RunnableFuture<T> newTaskFor(Runnable runnable, T value)
```

Override the method in a custom executor class that directly or indirectly subclasses AbstractExecutorService, to return an instance of your custom task class, which must implement RunnableFuture<V>. AbstractExecutorService's JDK documentation provides an example.

Ownable and Queued Long Synchronizers

The java.util.concurrent.locks package provides interfaces and classes that create a framework for locking and waiting for conditions. As described in Table 2-9, Java SE 6 integrates two new classes into this package.

Table 2-9. *New java.util.concurrent.locks Classes*

Class	Description
AbstractOwnableSynchronizer	Describes a synchronizer that can be exclusively owned by a single thread. It provides the foundation for creating locks and synchronizers that support the concept of thread ownership.
AbstractQueuedLongSynchronizer	Describes an extended AbstractQueuedSynchronizer that maintains its synchronization state via a 64-bit long integer, instead of the 32-bit integer used by AbstractQueuedSynchronizer.

Detecting and recovering from deadlocked threads is important to all applications, especially mission-critical applications that run for extended periods of time. Java 5's java.lang.management.ThreadMXBean interface provides a findMonitorDeadlockedThreads() method whose goal is to find cycles of threads that are deadlocked as they wait to acquire object monitors. Because this method is limited to finding these cycles at the level of Object.wait(), it cannot find cycles arising from higher-level synchronizers, such as semaphores and countdown latches.

Java SE 6 rectifies this situation by providing the AbstractOwnableSynchronizer class. The requirement is that a synchronizer base its synchronization on this class, and both the Semaphore and CountDownLatch classes indirectly accomplish this via AbstractQueuedSynchronizer, which extends AbstractOwnableSynchronizer. In that case, the ThreadMXBean class's new long[] findDeadlockedThreads() method can include a thread waiting on this ownable synchronizer (in addition to including threads waiting to acquire object monitors) in its checks for thread cycles that lead to deadlock.

Java 5 introduced the AbstractQueuedSynchronizer class to provide a framework for implementing blocking locks and related synchronizers that rely on first-in-first-out (FIFO) wait queues. This class represents state information as an atomic 32-bit integer. Because you will probably want to represent state information as an atomic 64-bit integer on 64-bit machines (where 64 bits is the natural size of an integer), Java SE 6 introduces the AbstractQueuedLongSynchronizer class, which also subclasses AbstractOwnableSynchronizer.

Extension Mechanism and ServiceLoader API

While not technically a library, Java's extension mechanism is closely related to the ServiceLoader API. Java SE 6 improves the extension mechanism, and also introduces ServiceLoader as a replacement for the older undocumented `sun.misc.Service` and `sun.misc.ServiceConfigurationError` classes.

Extension Mechanism

Java 1.2 introduced the extension mechanism to provide a standard and scalable way to extend the Java platform via *standard extensions*. These are custom APIs packaged in Java Archive (JAR) files that are stored in the JRE's lib/ext (Solaris/Linux) or lib\ext (Windows) directory. When you start an application that requires a standard extension, the runtime environment locates and loads the extension from this directory, without requiring a classpath environment variable. Starting with Java 1.3, standard extensions are also known as *optional packages*.

The `java.ext.dirs` system property specifies the locations for installed optional packages. The default setting is the JRE's lib/ext (or lib\ext) directory. Beginning with Java SE 6, you can append to this system property the path to a platform-specific directory that is shared by all installed (Java SE 6 or higher) JREs. However, as Java SE 6's JDK documentation on the extension mechanism architecture specifies, this path must be one of the following:

- Windows: `%SystemRoot%\Sun\Java\lib\ext`

- Linux: `/usr/java/packages/lib/ext`

- Solaris: `/usr/jdk/packages/lib/ext`

ServiceLoader API

According to Bug 4640520 "java.util.Service," Java 1.3 extended the JAR file format to support a standard way to specify pluggable service providers, by placing a *provider configuration file* into the JAR file's `META-INF/services` directory. This configuration file is a text file that identifies concrete provider classes. This way, it is possible to extend Image I/O, Java Sound, and other Java subsystems via the following:

- *Services*, which are interfaces and abstract classes that identify tasks to be accomplished; read image data that is stored in a new image file format, for example

- *Service providers*, which are implementations of services

Many subsystems use sun.misc.Service to look up services and instantiate service providers. For example, after registering standard image reader/writer (and other) service providers, Image I/O works with Service to parse the provider configuration file and load installed providers from lib/ext (or lib\ext), which are subsequently registered. Because applications can benefit from services and service providers, it seems natural for them to use Service. However, its undocumented status means that Sun could change or remove this class in the future. For this reason, Java SE 6's ServiceLoader API is preferable.

Note In addition to being referenced as installed optional packages, which inhabit the JRE's lib/ext, lib\ext, or an additional directory specified by the java.ext.dirs system property, service/service provider plug-ins may be referenced via the classpath.

The ServiceLoader API consists of the java.util.ServiceLoader<S> and java.util. ServiceConfigurationError classes. The former class loads service providers via classloaders; the latter class describes an error that is thrown when a problem (such as a java.io.IOException while reading the provider configuration file) occurs while a service provider is being loaded.

ServiceLoader<S> is a simple class that consists of only six methods, which are described in Table 2-10.

Table 2-10. *ServiceLoader Class Methods*

Method	Description
public Iterator<S> iterator()	Lazily loads the available service providers for this service loader's service. The iterator first returns providers from an internal cache. Then it lazily loads and instantiates remaining providers, storing them in the cache.
public static <S> ServiceLoader<S> load(Class<S> service)	Creates a new service loader for the given service type. Uses the current thread's context classloader to load provider configuration files and service provider classes.
public static <S> ServiceLoader<S> load(Class<S> service, ClassLoader loader)	Creates a new service loader for the given service type. Uses the specified loader to load service provider configuration files and service provider classes. Pass null to use the system classloader. If there is no system classloader, use the bootstrap classloader.
public static <S> ServiceLoader<S> loadInstalled(Class<S> service)	Creates a new service loader for the given service type. Uses the extension classloader to load service provider configuration files and service provider classes. If the extension classloader cannot be found, use the system classloader. If there is no system classloader, use the bootstrap classloader.

Method	Description
public void reload()	Clears the cache so that all providers will be reloaded. Subsequent invocations lazily look up and instantiate providers. Use this method if providers are dynamically installed while the JVM is running.
public String toString()	Returns a string that contains the fully qualified package name of the service passed to one of the "load" methods.

One practical use for ServiceLoader<S> is to obtain an alternate Java compiler. For example, instead of executing JavaCompiler compiler = ToolProvider. getSystemJavaCompiler(); to use the default compiler, you might use Listing 2-10 to select one of the alternate Java compilers available on your platform.

Listing 2-10. *EnumAlternateJavaCompilers.java*

```java
// EnumAlternateJavaCompilers.java

import java.util.*;

import javax.tools.*;

public class EnumAlternateJavaCompilers
{
   public static void main (String [] args)
   {
      ServiceLoader<JavaCompiler> compilers;
      compilers = ServiceLoader.load (JavaCompiler.class);
      System.out.println (compilers.toString ());

      for (JavaCompiler compiler: compilers)
          System.out.println (compiler);
   }
}
```

When you run this application, its first line of output is always java.util. ServiceLoader[javax.tools.JavaCompiler], which describes the JavaCompiler service. Assuming that alternate Java compilers exist, you will see additional lines of output. If this output indicates multiple alternate compilers, you can always invoke JavaCompiler's getSourceVersions() and other inherited methods to narrow your choice to a specific compiler.

CLASSPATH WILDCARDS

Java SE 6 introduces classpath wildcards, which simplify classpaths. Instead of listing all JAR files individually, you can now specify an asterisk (*) to indicate all JAR files. The asterisk must be in quotation marks to prevent it from being interpreted by the shell. Here's an example:

```
java -cp "*"; Test
```

Notice the absence of the period character that represents the current directory; this appears to be another Java SE 6 feature. This example loads the first JAR file that contains the necessary class (or classes) that a hypothetical Test class references.

When a classpath wildcard is present, you cannot rely on the order in which a service loader returns service providers. As a result, you are forced to rely on a secondary mechanism to target a specific service provider. For example, you can specify a MIME type, a file extension, or some other criterion (with the appropriate method) when choosing an Image I/O reader/writer plug-in. Learn more about classpath wildcards by reading Mark Reinhold's "Class-Path Wildcards in Mustang" blog entry (http://blogs.sun.com/mr/entry/class_path_wildcards_in_mustang).

Summary

Java SE 6 introduces various improvements to existing core libraries. It also integrates new libraries into the core.

One of the improved libraries is the BitSet class. Most of the improvements made to this class are optimizations for speeding up various methods or reducing the size of BitSet objects.

The Compiler API is a new library that provides programmatic access to the compiler, lets you override the manner in which the compiler reads and writes source and class files, and provides access to structured diagnostic information. This API is hosted by the javax.tools package, which is designed to let programs invoke various tools, beginning with compilers.

A variety of minor, but important, I/O enhancements have been introduced via a new Console I/O library and an improved File class. The new Console I/O library lets you safely prompt for passwords without echoing them to the console. The improved File class provides new methods that let you easily determine the amount of free disk space, as well as set a file's read, write, and execute permissions.

The Java platform also benefits from improvements to various mathematics libraries. For example, the BigDecimal class has been improved through bug fixes and optimizations. Also, new methods that support IEEE 754/854-recommended functions have been added to the Math and StrictMath classes.

The collections framework has been significantly enhanced via fixes to the framework's JDK documentation and source code in several places, the addition of several new interfaces (such as NavigableMap<K, V>) and classes (such as ArrayDeque<E>), and the addition of several new utility methods (such as asLifoQueue() and copyOf()) to the Collections and Arrays classes.

Java's concurrency framework (first introduced in Java 5) has also been enhanced through improvements to existing infrastructure, and the integration of new interfaces (such as BlockingDeque<E>) and classes (such as AbstractOwnableSynchronizer) into the framework.

Finally, Java SE 6 improves Java's extension mechanism and introduces Service-Loader. This library provides a way for applications to look up services and instantiate service providers, without having to rely on the previously undocumented sun.misc.Service and sun.misc.ServiceConfigurationError classes.

Test Your Understanding

How well do you understand the changes to Java's core libraries? Test your understanding by answering the following questions and performing the following exercises. (The answers are presented in Appendix D.)

1. Under what condition is a cloned or serialized bitset not trimmed?

2. When you invoke close() on the Reader/PrintWriter objects returned by the Console class's reader()/writer() methods, is the underlying stream closed?

3. Create a command-line utility that lets you make a file or directory read-only or writable.

4. What is the difference between the Deque<E> interface's void addFirst(E e) and boolean offerFirst(E e) methods?

5. The NavigableMap<K, V> interface's K higherKey(K key) and K lowerKey(K key) closest-match methods return the least key strictly greater than key (or null if there is no key) and the greatest key strictly less than key (or null if there is no key), respectively. Extend ProductDB.java (Listing 2-9) to output the key higher than 2034 and the key lower than 2034.

6. Use a copyOf() method to copy an array of Strings to a new CharSequence array.

7. The ServiceLoader<S> class's iterator() method returns an Iterator<E> whose hasNext() and next() methods are capable of throwing ServiceConfigurationError. Why throw an error instead of an exception?

8. Some time ago, I created an Image I/O reader plug-in that reads images in the PCX image file format from files. Consider an EnumIO application whose main() method contains the following code:

```
ServiceLoader<ImageReaderSpi> imageReaders;
imageReaders = ServiceLoader.load (ImageReaderSpi.class);
for (ImageReaderSpi imageReader: imageReaders)
    System.out.println (imageReader.getClass ());
```

Whenever I execute java -cp pcx.jar; EnumIO, this application outputs ca.mb.javajeff.pcx.PCXImageReaderSpi. However, if I modify the code by passing null to load(), as in ServiceLoader.load (ImageReaderSpi.class, null), and then try to run the program, a ServiceConfigurationError is thrown. Why?

CHAPTER 3

■■■

GUI Toolkits: AWT

The Abstract Windowing Toolkit (AWT) is the foundation for both AWT-based and Swing-based GUIs. This chapter explores most of the new and improved features that Java SE 6 brings to the AWT:

- Desktop API

- Dynamic layout

- Improved support for non-English locale input

- New modality model and API

- Splash Screen API

- System Tray API

- XAWT support on Solaris

Desktop API

Java has traditionally faired better on servers and gadgets than on desktops. Sun's desire to improve Java's fortunes on the desktop is evidenced by three major new APIs: Desktop, Splash Screen, and System Tray. This section explores the Desktop API. You will learn about the Splash Screen and System Tray APIs later in this chapter.

The Desktop API helps to bridge the gap between Java and native applications that run on the desktop in two ways:

- It enables Java applications to launch applications associated with specific file types for the purposes of opening, editing, and printing documents based on those types. For example, the .wmv file extension is often associated with Windows Media Player on Windows platforms. A Java application could use the Desktop API to launch Windows Media Player (or whatever application associates with .wmv) to open (play) WMV-based movies.

- It enables Java applications to launch the default web browser with specific Uniform Resource Identifiers (URIs), and launch the default e-mail client.

Note The Desktop API originated with the JDesktop Integration Components (JDIC) project (`https://jdic.dev.java.net/`). According to its FAQ, JDIC's mission is "to make Java technology-based applications (Java applications) first-class citizens of current desktop platforms without sacrificing platform independence."

The `java.awt.Desktop` class implements the Desktop API. This class provides a `public static Desktop getDesktop()` method that your Java application calls to return a `Desktop` instance. Using this instance, the application invokes methods to launch the default mail client, launch the default browser, and so on. `getDesktop()` throws an `UnsupportedOperationException` if the API is not available on the current platform; for example, the Desktop API is available on the Linux platform only if GNOME libraries are present. Therefore, you should call the `Desktop` class's `public static boolean isDesktopSupported()` method first. If this method returns true, you can then call `getDesktop()`, as follows:

```
Desktop desktop = null;
if (Desktop.isDesktopSupported ())
    desktop = Desktop.getDesktop ();
```

Even if you successfully retrieve a `Desktop` instance, you might not be able to perform a browse, mail, open, edit, or print action via the appropriate method, because the `Desktop` instance might not support one or more of these actions. Therefore, you should first check for the action's availability by calling the `public boolean isSupported(Desktop.Action action)` method, where `action` is one of the following `Desktop.Action` enumeration instances:

- `BROWSE` represents a browse action that the current platform's default browser performs.

- `MAIL` represents a mail action that the current platform's default mail client performs.

- `OPEN` represents an open action that the application associated with a specific file type performs.

- `EDIT` represents an edit action that the application associated with a specific file type performs.

- PRINT represents a print action that the application associated with a specific file type performs.

After invoking isSupported() with one of these enumeration instances as its argument, check the return value. If this value is true, the appropriate action method can be invoked, as follows:

```
String uri = "http://www.javalobby.org";
if (desktop.isSupported(Desktop.Action.BROWSE))
    try
    {
        desktop.browse (new URI (uri)); // Invoke the default browser with this URI.
    }
    catch (Exception e)
    {
        // Do whatever is appropriate.
    }
```

The code fragment invokes the Desktop class's browse() action method to launch the default browser and present Javalobby's main web page. This method is one of Desktop's six action methods, which are described in Table 3-1.

Table 3-1. *Desktop Class Action Methods*

Method	Description
public void browse(URI uri)	Launches the default browser to display the specified uri. If the browser cannot handle this kind of URI (the URI begins with ftp://, for example), another application that is registered to handle the URI is launched.
public void edit(File file)	Launches the application registered with file's type for the purpose of editing this file.
public void mail()	Launches the default mail client with its mail-composing window open, so that the user can compose an e-mail.
public void mail(URI mailtoURI)	Launches the default mail client with its mail-composing window open, filling in message fields as specified by mailtoURI. These fields include cc, subject, and body.
public void open(File file)	Launches the application registered with file's type for the purpose of opening the file (run an executable, play a movie, preview a text file, and so on).
public void print(File file)	Launches the application registered with file's type for the purpose of printing this file.

All of the Desktop class's methods throw exceptions:

- UnsupportedOperationException, when the action is not supported on the current platform. Unless you are extremely concerned about your application's robustness, you do not need to catch this unchecked exception when you have previously verified this action's support via the isSupported() method (and the appropriate Desktop.Action enumeration instance).

- SecurityException, if a security manager exists and does not grant permission to perform the appropriate action.

- NullPointerException, when you have passed a null URI argument to browse(), for example.

- java.io.IOException, when an I/O problem has arisen while attempting to launch the application.

- IllegalArgumentException, when a file does not exist for printing, for example.

Check out Desktop's JDK documentation for more information about these exceptions.

The Desktop class's action methods are useful in a variety of situations. Consider an About dialog that presents a link (via a javax.swing.JButton subclass) to some web site. When the user clicks the link, the browse() method is called (with the web site's URI) to launch the default web browser and display the web site's main page.

Another example is a file manager. In Windows, when the user right-clicks while the mouse pointer hovers over a file/directory name, a context-sensitive pop-up menu appears and presents a combination of open/edit/print/mail options (as appropriate to the file type). Listing 3-1 presents the source code for a trivial file manager application that demonstrates open, edit, and print options.

Listing 3-1. *FileManager.java*

```
// FileManager.java

import java.awt.*;
import java.awt.event.*;

import java.io.*;

import java.net.*;

import javax.swing.*;
```

```java
import javax.swing.event.*;
import javax.swing.tree.*;

public class FileManager extends JFrame
{
    private Desktop desktop;

    private int x, y;

    public FileManager (String title, final File rootDir)
    {
        super (title);
        setDefaultCloseOperation (EXIT_ON_CLOSE);

        if (Desktop.isDesktopSupported ())
            desktop = Desktop.getDesktop ();

        DefaultMutableTreeNode rootNode;
        rootNode = new DefaultMutableTreeNode (rootDir);
        createNodes (rootDir, rootNode);
        final JTree tree = new JTree (rootNode);

        final JPopupMenu popup = new JPopupMenu ();
        PopupMenuListener pml;
        pml = new PopupMenuListener ()
            {
                public void popupMenuCanceled (PopupMenuEvent pme)
                {
                }

                public void popupMenuWillBecomeInvisible (PopupMenuEvent pme)
                {
                   int nc = popup.getComponentCount ();
                   for (int i = 0; i < nc; i++)
                       popup.remove (0);
                }

                public void popupMenuWillBecomeVisible (PopupMenuEvent pme)
                {
                   final Desktop.Action [] actions =
                   {
                      Desktop.Action.OPEN,
```

```
        Desktop.Action.EDIT,
        Desktop.Action.PRINT
    };

    ActionListener al;
    al = new ActionListener ()
        {
            public void actionPerformed (ActionEvent ae)
            {
                try
                {
                    TreePath tp;
                    tp = tree.getPathForLocation (x, y);
                    if (tp != null)
                    {
                        int pc = tp.getPathCount ();
                        Object o = tp.getPathComponent (pc-1);

                        DefaultMutableTreeNode n;
                        n = (DefaultMutableTreeNode) o;

                        File file = (File) n.getUserObject ();

                        JMenuItem mi;
                        mi = (JMenuItem) ae.getSource ();
                        String s = mi.getText ();

                        if (s.equals (actions [0].name ()))
                            desktop.open (file);
                        else
                        if (s.equals (actions [1].name ()))
                            desktop.edit (file);
                        else
                        if (s.equals (actions [2].name ()))
                            desktop.print (file);
                    }
                }
                catch (Exception e)
                {
                }
            }
        };
```

```
           for (Desktop.Action action: actions)
               if (desktop.isSupported (action))
               {
                   TreePath tp = tree.getPathForLocation (x, y);
                   if (tp != null)
                   {
                       int pc = tp.getPathCount ();
                       Object o = tp.getPathComponent (pc-1);

                       DefaultMutableTreeNode n;
                       n = (DefaultMutableTreeNode) o;

                       File file = (File) n.getUserObject ();
                       if (!file.isDirectory () ||
                           file.isDirectory () &&
                           action == Desktop.Action.OPEN)
                       {
                           JMenuItem mi;
                           mi = new JMenuItem (action.name ());
                           mi.addActionListener (al);
                           popup.add (mi);
                       }
                   }
               }
       };
if (desktop != null)
    popup.addPopupMenuListener (pml);

tree.addMouseListener (new MouseAdapter ()
                      {
                          public void mousePressed (MouseEvent e)
                          {
                              probablyShowPopup (e);
                          }

                          public void mouseReleased (MouseEvent e)
                          {
                              probablyShowPopup (e);
                          }
```

```
                                    void probablyShowPopup (MouseEvent e)
                                    {
                                        if (e.isPopupTrigger ())
                                        {
                                            x = e.getX ();
                                            y = e.getY ();
                                            popup.show (e.getComponent (),
                                                        e.getX (),
                                                        e.getY ());}
                                    }
                                });

        getContentPane ().add (new JScrollPane (tree));

        setSize (400, 300);
        setVisible (true);
    }

    private void createNodes (File rootDir, DefaultMutableTreeNode rootNode)
    {
        File [] files = rootDir.listFiles ();
        for (int i = 0; i < files.length; i++)
        {
            DefaultMutableTreeNode node;
            node = new DefaultMutableTreeNode (files [i]);
            rootNode.add (node);

            if (files [i].isDirectory ())
                createNodes (files [i], node);
        }
    }

    public static void main (String [] args)
    {
        String rootDir = ".";
        if (args.length > 0)
        {
            rootDir = args [0];
            if (!rootDir.endsWith ("\\"))
                rootDir += "\\";
        }
```

```
    final String _rootDir = rootDir;
    Runnable r - new Runnable ()
                {
                    public void run ()
                    {
                        new FileManager ("File Manager",
                                        new File (_rootDir));
                    }
                };
    EventQueue.invokeLater (r);
  }
}
```

Listing 3-1 recursively enumerates all files and directories that are located in either the current directory or the directory specified by the application's first command-line argument, and presents this tree via a tree component. When you trigger the pop-up menu that is attached to the tree component, this menu presents an Open menu item for directories and files, and Edit and Print menu items for files only.

Note I originally wanted to add a Mail menu item to the pop-up menu (for files), to activate the mail-composing window with the file whose name was clicked when activating the pop-up menu as an attachment. However, Desktop's mail(URI mailtoURI) method does not support attachments. This deficiency will probably be addressed in a future version of Desktop.

Dynamic Layout

Live resizing is a visual enhancement feature where a window's content is dynamically laid out as the window is resized. The content is continually redisplayed at the latest current size until resizing completes. In contrast, non-live resizing results in the window's content being laid out only after resizing completes. Platforms such as Mac OS X and Windows XP support live resizing. Java refers to live resizing as *dynamic layout*.

Java 1.4 introduced support for dynamic layout via the awt.dynamicLayoutSupported desktop property. To determine if dynamic layout is supported (and enabled) by the platform, invoke the java.awt.Toolkit class's public final Object getDesktopProperty(String propertyName) method with propertyName set to "awt. dynamicLayoutSupported". This method returns a Boolean object containing the value true if dynamic layout is supported and enabled; this object contains false if dynamic layout is not supported or has been disabled. Java 1.4 also introduced support for dynamic layout by adding dynamic layout methods to the Toolkit class, as listed in Table 3-2.

(Java versions subsequent to 1.4 also support awt.dynamicLayoutSupported in addition to the methods listed in Table 3-2.)

Table 3-2. *Toolkit Class Dynamic Layout Methods*

Method	Description
public void setDynamicLayout(boolean dynamic)	Programmatically determines whether container layouts should be dynamically validated during resizing (pass true to dynamic), or validated only after resizing finishes (pass false to dynamic). Calling this method with dynamic set to true has no effect on platforms that do not support dynamic layout. Calling this method with dynamic set to false has no effect on platforms that always support dynamic layout. Prior to Java SE 6, setDynamicLayout(false) was the default. Beginning with Java SE 6, this default has changed to setDynamicLayout(true).
public boolean isDynamicLayoutActive()	Returns true if dynamic layout is supported by the platform and is also enabled at the platform level. Also returns true if dynamic layout has been programmatically enabled, either by default or by previously invoking setDynamicLayout() with true as the argument.

I have created a demonstration application that lets you experiment with awt.dynamicLayoutSupported, setDynamicLayout(), and isDynamicLayoutActive(). This application's source code appears in Listing 3-2.

Listing 3-2. *DynamicLayout.java*

```
// DynamicLayout.java

import java.awt.*;
import java.awt.event.*;

import javax.swing.*;

public class DynamicLayout extends JFrame
{
```

```
public DynamicLayout (String title)
{
   super (title);
   setDefaultCloseOperation (EXIT_ON_CLOSE);

   getContentPane ().setLayout (new GridLayout (3, 1));

   final Toolkit tk = Toolkit.getDefaultToolkit ();
   Object prop = tk.getDesktopProperty ("awt.dynamicLayoutSupported");

   JPanel pnl = new JPanel ();
   pnl.add (new JLabel ("awt.DynamicLayoutSupported:"));
   JLabel lblSetting1;
   lblSetting1 = new JLabel (prop.toString ());
   pnl.add (lblSetting1);

   getContentPane ().add (pnl);

   pnl = new JPanel ();
   pnl.add (new JLabel ("Dynamic layout active:"));
   final JLabel lblSetting2;
   lblSetting2 = new JLabel (tk.isDynamicLayoutActive () ? "yes" : "no");
   pnl.add (lblSetting2);

   getContentPane ().add (pnl);

   pnl = new JPanel ();
   pnl.add (new JLabel ("Toggle dynamic layout"));
   JCheckBox ckbSet = new JCheckBox ();
   ckbSet.addItemListener (new ItemListener ()
                      {
                          public void itemStateChanged (ItemEvent ie)
                          {
                              if (tk.isDynamicLayoutActive ())
                                  tk.setDynamicLayout (false);
                              else
                                  tk.setDynamicLayout (true);

                              boolean active;
                              active = tk.isDynamicLayoutActive ();
                              lblSetting2.setText (active ? "yes"
                                                         : "no");
```

```
                                 }
                              });

     pnl.add (ckbSet);

     getContentPane ().add (pnl);

     pack ();
     setVisible (true);
   }


   public static void main (String [] args)
   {
     Runnable r = new Runnable ()
                  {
                      public void run ()
                      {
                         new DynamicLayout ("Dynamic Layout");
                      }
                  };
     EventQueue.invokeLater (r);
   }
}
```

The DynamicLayout application presents a GUI with five labels and a check box. The top two labels identify and report the value of the awt.dynamicLayoutSupported variable. If false is displayed, you will need to enable dynamic layout on your platform (if possible) to see its effect. The middle two labels identify and report the value of the isDynamicLayoutActive() method. If yes is displayed and you resize the window, the labels and check box will move during the resize. However, if no is displayed, the labels and check box will move only after resizing completes. The bottom label and check box let you toggle between active and inactive dynamic layout. However, this toggling action has no effect if the awt.dynamicLayoutSupported label reports false.

Tip Windows XP enables live resizing by default. If XP is your platform, you can disable and reenable live resizing (possibly to test your Java code) through the System Properties dialog box. Open this dialog box by starting the Control Panel and selecting the System icon. Then select the Advanced tab and click the Settings button in the Performance section to open the Performance Options dialog box. Select the Visual Effects tab and check (to enable live resizing) or uncheck (to disable live resizing) the "Show window contents while dragging" option in this tab's scrollable list.

Improved Support for Non-English Locale Input

If you are working with Java in the context of a non-English locale, and on a Solaris or Linux platform, you will be happy to know that Java SE 6 fixes a number of bugs related to keyboard input in non-English locales on those platforms. These bugs include the following:

- 2107667: "KP_Separator handled wrong in KeyEvents"

- 4360364: "Cyrillic input isn't supported under JRE 1.2.2 & 1.3 for Linux"

- 4935357: "Linux X cannot generate {}[] characters on Danish keyboards (remote display)"

- 4957565: "Character '|', '~' and more cannot be entered on Danish keyboard"

- 5014911: "b32c, b40, b42 input Arabic and Hebrew characters fail in JTextComponents"

- 6195851: "As XKB extension is ubiquitous now, #ifdef linux should be removed from awt_GraphicsEnv code"

Other non-English keyboard bugs have been addressed as well. You can find complete information in Sun's Bug Database (`http://bugs.sun.com/bugdatabase/index.jsp`).

Note If you would like to learn about keyboard layouts and the X keyboard extension (XKB), I recommend reading the Wikipedia articles on keyboard layout (`http://en.wikipedia.org/wiki/Keyboard_layout`), the AltGr key (`http://en.wikipedia.org/wiki/AltGr_key`), and XKB (`http://en.wikipedia.org/wiki/X_keyboard_extension`).

New Modality Model and API

The AWT's *modality model* supports modal and modeless dialogs. A *modal* dialog blocks input to various top-level windows. A *modeless* dialog does not block any windows. Prior to Java SE 6, this model was flawed in various ways. For example, Bug 4080029 "Modal Dialog block input to all frame windows not just its parent" states that a modal dialog can block all of an application's frame windows, not just the frame window that serves as the dialog's owner. You can prove this to yourself by compiling and running this bug's accompanying `ModalDialogTest` demo application.

To fix these flaws, Java SE 6 introduces a new modality model. This model lets you limit a dialog's blocking scope. It does this (in part) by introducing four modality types:

- *Modeless*: No windows are blocked while a modeless dialog is visible.

- *Document-modal*: All windows created from the same document as a document-modal dialog, except for the dialog's child windows, are blocked. A *document* is a hierarchy of windows that share a common ancestor, the *document root*, which is the closest ownerless ancestor.

- *Application-modal*: All windows created in the same application as the application-modal dialog, except for the dialog's child windows, are blocked.

- *Toolkit-modal*: All windows created in the same toolkit as the toolkit-modal dialog, except for the dialog's child windows, are blocked.

The problem with `ModalDialogTest` can be fixed by creating the dialog as document-modal. This works because each frame is a document root. Accomplish this task by calling the `java.awt.Dialog` class's new `public Dialog(Window owner, String title, Dialog.ModalityType modalityType)` constructor, where `Dialog.ModalityType` is an enumeration of the previously listed modality types. Set `modalityType` to `Dialog.ModalityType.DOCUMENT_MODAL`. So, instead of specifying this:

```
d1 = new Dialog(f1, "Modal Dialog", true);
```

you would specify this:

```
d1 = new Dialog(f1, "Modal Dialog", Dialog.ModalityType.DOCUMENT_MODAL);
```

Perhaps the most famous flaw involved JavaHelp, an API that makes it possible to display a Java application's help content in a separate dialog window. While the Help dialog was displayed, you could easily switch back and forth between the application's main window and this Help dialog window, unless a modal dialog (such as a file-open dialog) was presented. In this situation, the modal dialog prevented the user from interacting with the Help dialog.

The JavaHelp problem can be solved with the `java.awt.Window` class's new `public void setModalExclusionType(Dialog.ModalExclusionType exclusionType)` method, where `Dialog.ModalExclusionType` is an enumeration of exclusion types. The idea is to mark a window for exclusion so that it will not be blocked by a modal dialog. To demonstrate this concept, I have created an application that converts a few units, such as kilograms to pounds and vice versa. Take a look at Listing 3-3 for the source code.

Listing 3-3. *UnitsConverter.java*

```java
// UnitsConverter.java

import java.awt.*;
import java.awt.event.*;

import java.io.*;

import javax.swing.*;

public class UnitsConverter extends JFrame
{
   Converter [] converters =
   {
      new Converter ("Acres", "Square meters", "Area", 4046.8564224),
      new Converter ("Square meters", "Acres", "Area", 1.0/4046.8564224),
      new Converter ("Pounds", "Kilograms", "Mass or Weight", 0.45359237),
      new Converter ("Kilograms", "Pounds", "Mass or Weight", 1.0/0.45359237),
      new Converter ("Miles/gallon (US)", "Miles/liter", "Fuel Consumption",
                     0.2642),
      new Converter ("Miles/liter", "Miles/gallon (US)", "Fuel Consumption",
                     1.0/0.2642),
      new Converter ("Inches/second", "Meters/second", "Speed", 0.0254),
      new Converter ("Meters/second", "Inches/second", "Speed", 1.0/0.0254),
      new Converter ("Grains", "Ounces", "Mass (Avoirdupois)/UK", 1.0/437.5),
      new Converter ("Ounces", "Grains", "Mass (Avoirdupois)/UK", 437.5)
   };

   public UnitsConverter (String title)
   {
      super (title);
      setDefaultCloseOperation (EXIT_ON_CLOSE);
      getRootPane ().setBorder (BorderFactory.createEmptyBorder (10, 10, 10,
                                                                 10));

      JPanel pnlLeft = new JPanel ();
      pnlLeft.setLayout (new BorderLayout ());

      pnlLeft.add (new JLabel ("Converters"), BorderLayout.CENTER);

      final JList lstConverters = new JList (converters);
      lstConverters.setSelectionMode (ListSelectionModel.SINGLE_SELECTION);
```

```java
        lstConverters.setSelectedIndex (0);
        pnlLeft.add (new JScrollPane (lstConverters), BorderLayout.SOUTH);

        JPanel pnlRight = new JPanel ();
        pnlRight.setLayout (new BorderLayout ());

        JPanel pnlTemp = new JPanel ();
        pnlTemp.add (new JLabel ("Units:"));
        final JTextField txtUnits = new JTextField (20);
        pnlTemp.add (txtUnits);
        pnlRight.add (pnlTemp, BorderLayout.NORTH);

        pnlTemp = new JPanel ();
        JButton btnConvert = new JButton ("Convert");
        ActionListener al;
        al = new ActionListener ()
            {
                public void actionPerformed (ActionEvent ae)
                {
                  try
                  {
                      double value = Double.parseDouble (txtUnits.getText ());
                      int index = lstConverters.getSelectedIndex ();
                      txtUnits.setText (""+converters [index].convert (value));
                  }
                  catch (NumberFormatException e)
                  {
                      JOptionPane.showMessageDialog (null, "Invalid input "+
                                                "-- please re-enter");
                  }
                }

            };
        btnConvert.addActionListener (al);
        pnlTemp.add (btnConvert);
        JButton btnClear = new JButton ("Clear");
        al = new ActionListener ()
            {
                public void actionPerformed (ActionEvent ae)
                {
                  txtUnits.setText ("");
                }
            };
```

```java
        btnClear.addActionListener (al);
        pnlTemp.add (btnClear);
        JButton btnHelp = new JButton ("Help");
        al = new ActionListener ()
            {
                public void actionPerformed (ActionEvent ae)
                {
                    new Help (UnitsConverter.this, "Units Converter Help");
                }
            };
        btnHelp.addActionListener (al);
        pnlTemp.add (btnHelp);
        JButton btnAbout = new JButton ("About");
        al = new ActionListener ()
            {
                public void actionPerformed (ActionEvent ae)
                {
                    new About (UnitsConverter.this, "Units Converter");
                }
            };
        btnAbout.addActionListener (al);
        pnlTemp.add (btnAbout);

        pnlRight.add (pnlTemp, BorderLayout.CENTER);

        getContentPane ().add (pnlLeft, BorderLayout.WEST);
        getContentPane ().add (pnlRight, BorderLayout.EAST);

        pack ();
        setResizable (false);
        setVisible (true);
    }

    public static void main (String [] args)
    {
        Runnable r = new Runnable ()
                    {
                        public void run ()
                        {
                            new UnitsConverter ("Units Converter 1.0");
                        }
                    };
        EventQueue.invokeLater (r);
```

```java
      }
   }


class About extends JDialog
{
   About (Frame frame, String title)
   {
      super (frame, "About", true);

      JLabel lbl = new JLabel ("Units Converter 1.0");
      getContentPane ().add (lbl, BorderLayout.NORTH);

      JPanel pnl = new JPanel ();
      JButton btnOk = new JButton ("Ok");
      btnOk.addActionListener (new ActionListener ()
                        {
                              public void actionPerformed (ActionEvent e)
                              {
                                 dispose ();
                              }
                        });
      pnl.add (btnOk);
      getContentPane ().add (pnl, BorderLayout.SOUTH);

      pack ();
      setResizable (false);
      setLocationRelativeTo (frame);
      setVisible (true);
   }
}

class Converter
{
   private double multiplier;

   private String srcUnits, dstUnits, cat;

   Converter (String srcUnits, String dstUnits, String cat, double multiplier)
   {
      this.srcUnits = srcUnits;
      this.dstUnits = dstUnits;
```

```java
      this.cat = cat;
      this.multiplier = multiplier;
   }

   double convert (double value)
   {
      return value*multiplier;
   }

   public String toString ()
   {
      return srcUnits+" to "+dstUnits+" -- "+cat;
   }
}

class Help extends JDialog
{
   Help (Frame frame, String title)
   {
      super (frame, title);
      setModalExclusionType (Dialog.ModalExclusionType.APPLICATION_EXCLUDE);

      try
      {
         JEditorPane ep = new JEditorPane ("file:///"+new File ("").
                                            getAbsolutePath ()+"/uchelp.html");
         ep.setEnabled (false);
         getContentPane ().add (ep);
      }
      catch (IOException ioe)
      {
         JOptionPane.showMessageDialog (frame,
                                     "Unable to install editor pane");
         return;
      }

      setSize (200, 200);
      setLocationRelativeTo (frame);
      setVisible (true);
   }
}
```

This unit conversion application's user interface includes Help and About buttons. Click the Help button to create and present a modeless dialog for displaying help information. To create and present a modal dialog that presents information about the application, click the About button. If you click the Help button and then click the About button, you can easily switch back to the Help dialog (without closing the About dialog) because of `setModalExclusionType` (`Dialog.ModalExclusionType.APPLICATION_EXCLUDE`), which effectively states that the Help dialog will not be blocked by any application-modal dialogs. If you comment out this method call, you can no longer switch back to the Help dialog while the About dialog is present.

Note For more information and examples on the new modality model and API, check out the Sun Developer Network article "The New Modality API in Java SE 6" (`http://java.sun.com/developer/technicalArticles/J2SE/Desktop/javase6/modality/`).

Splash Screen API

Java SE 6 introduces support for application-specific splash screens. A *splash screen* can occupy the user's attention while the application performs lengthy startup initialization tasks, such as image loading.

This splash screen is implemented as an undecorated *splash window* that can display a GIF (including an animated GIF), JPEG, or PNG image. The new Splash Screen API lets you customize the splash screen.

Making a Splash

In response to the `-splash` command-line option, the `java` application launcher creates a splash window that displays the option's image argument. For example, the following command creates a splash window that displays the `logo.gif` file's image:

```
java -splash:logo.gif Application
```

Alternatively, you can create the splash window and display an image via an application JAR file's `SplashScreen-Image` manifest entry. For example, assume that the manifest contains the following:

```
Manifest-Version: 1.0
Main-Class: Application
SplashScreen-Image: logo.gif
```

Furthermore, assume that logo.gif and all other necessary files have been packaged into Application.jar. The following command line:

```
java -jar Application.jar
```

creates the splash window, which displays the logo.gif file's image.

Note If you specify both the -splash command-line option and the SplashScreen-Image manifest entry, as in java -splash:logo2.gif -jar Application.jar, the -splash command-line option takes precedence. In the example, the splash window displays logo2.gif's image.

Customizing the Splash Screen

A splash window is associated with an overlay image that can be drawn on and alpha-blended with the window's image, letting you customize the splash screen. Customization requires you to work with the java.awt.SplashScreen class. Table 3-3 describes this class's methods.

Table 3-3. *SplashScreen Class Methods*

Method	Description
public void close()	Hides and closes the splash window, and releases all resources. An IllegalStateException is thrown if the splash window is already closed.
public Graphics2D createGraphics()	Creates and returns a graphics context for drawing on the overlay image. Because drawing on this image doesn't necessarily update the splash window, you should call update() when you want to immediately update the splash window with the overlay image. An IllegalStateException is thrown if the splash window has been closed.
public Rectangle getBounds()	Returns the splash window's bounds. These bounds are important for replacing the splash window with your own window. An IllegalStateException is thrown if the splash window has been closed.
public URL getImageURL()	Returns the displayed splash image. An IllegalStateException is thrown if the splash window has been closed.
public Dimension getSize()	Returns the splash window size. This size is important for replacing the splash window with your own window. An IllegalStateException is thrown if the splash window has been closed.

Continued

Table 3-3. *Continued*

Method	Description
public static SplashScreen getSplashScreen()	Returns the SplashScreen object that is used to control the startup splash window. If there is no splash window (or if the window has been closed), this method returns null. An UnsupportedOperationException is thrown if the current AWT toolkit implementation does not support splash screens. A java.awt.HeadlessException is thrown if there is no display device.
public boolean isVisible()	Returns true if the splash window is visible. Returns false if the window has been hidden via a call to close() or when the first AWT/Swing window is made visible.
public void setImageURL(URL imageURL)	Changes the splash image to the image that is loaded from imageURL. GIF, JPEG, and PNG image formats are supported. This method returns after the image has been loaded and the splash window has been updated. The window is resized to the image's size and centered on the screen. A NullPointerException is thrown if you pass null to imageURL; an IOException is thrown if an error occurs while loading the image; and an IllegalStateException is thrown if the splash window has been closed.
public void update()	Updates the splash window with the current contents of the overlay image. An IllegalStateException is thrown if the overlay image does not exist (createGraphics() was never called) or if the splash window has been closed.

You cannot directly instantiate a SplashScreen object, because this object is meaningless if a splash window has not been created (in response to -splash or SplashScreen-Image). Instead, you must call the getSplashScreen() method to retrieve this object. Because this method returns null if a splash window does not exist, you need to test the return value prior to performing customization:

```
SplashScreen splashScreen = SplashScreen.getSplashScreen ();
if (splashScreen != null)
{
    // Perform appropriate customization.
}
```

I've created a skeletal document viewer application (you supply the document viewer code) that demonstrates how to customize a splash screen. Listing 3-4 presents this application's source code.

Listing 3-4. *DocViewer.java*

```java
// DocViewer.java

import java.awt.*;

public class DocViewer
{
    public static void main (String [] args)
    {
        SplashScreen splashScreen = SplashScreen.getSplashScreen ();
        if (splashScreen != null)
        {
            // Surround the image with a border that occupies 5% of the smaller
            // of the width and height.

            Dimension size = splashScreen.getSize ();
            int borderDim;
            if (size.width < size.height)
                borderDim = (int) (size.width * 0.05);
            else
                borderDim = (int) (size.height * 0.05);

            Graphics g = splashScreen.createGraphics ();
            g.setColor (Color.blue);
            for (int i = 0; i < borderDim; i++)
                g.drawRect (i, i, size.width-1-i*2, size.height-1-i*2);

            // Make sure the text fits the splash window before drawing -- the
            // text is centered in the lower part of the splash window.

            FontMetrics fm = g.getFontMetrics ();
            int sWidth = fm.stringWidth ("Initializing...");
            int sHeight = fm.getHeight ();
            if (sWidth < size.width && 2*sHeight < size.height)
            {
                g.setColor (Color.blue);
                g.drawString ("Initializing...",
                              (size.width-sWidth)/2,
                              size.height-2*sHeight);
            }
```

```
        // Update the splash window with the overlay image.

        splashScreen.update ();

        // Pause for 5 seconds to simulate a lengthy initialization task,
        // and to view the image.
        try
        {
            Thread.sleep (5000);
        }
        catch (InterruptedException e)
        {
        }
    }

    // Continue with the DocViewer application.
  }
}
```

Run this application via java -splash:dvlogo.jpg DocViewer. After verifying that a splash window exists and an image is displayed, the DocViewer.java source code draws a blue frame and an initialization message (also in blue) on the overlay image. The splashScreen.update() method call alpha-blends this overlay image with the underlying dvlogo.jpg image. Figure 3-1 shows the resulting combined image.

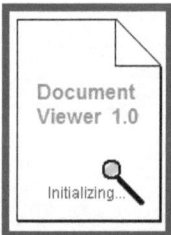

Figure 3-1. *Windows XP displays an hourglass mouse cursor when this cursor is moved over the splash window.*

■Note For more information about customizing splash screens, see the Sun Developer Network article "New Splash-Screen Functionality in Java SE 6" (http://java.sun.com/developer/ technicalArticles/J2SE/Desktop/javase6/splashscreen/index.html).

System Tray API

The new System Tray API makes it possible for an application to gain access to the desktop's *system tray*, which presents the system time and icons of applications that interact with the system tray. To access these applications, the user positions the mouse pointer over a tray icon and performs an appropriate mouse action. For example, right-clicking an icon might launch an application-specific pop-up menu, and double-clicking an icon might open the application's main window (if the platform supports these features).

The System Tray API consists of the `java.awt.SystemTray` and `java.awt.TrayIcon` classes. The former class lets you interact with the system tray, with emphasis on `TrayIcon` instances. The latter class lets you add listeners to and otherwise customize individual `TrayIcon`s.

Exploring the SystemTray and TrayIcon Classes

With `SystemTray`, you can add and remove tray icons, add property change listeners, and get information about the system tray. Table 3-4 describes the `SystemTray` class's methods.

Table 3-4. *SystemTray Class Methods*

Method	Description
`public void add(TrayIcon trayIcon)`	Adds the tray icon described by `trayIcon` to the system tray. This tray icon becomes visible after being added. The order in which tray icons appear in the system tray depends on the underlying platform. When this application exits, or whenever the system tray becomes unavailable, all of the application's tray icons are automatically removed. A `NullPointerException` is thrown if you pass `null` to `trayIcon`; an `IllegalArgumentException` is thrown if you try to add the same `trayIcon` more than once; and a `java.awt.AWTException` is thrown if there is no system tray.
`public void addPropertyChangeListener(String propertyName, PropertyChangeListener listener)`	Adds `listener` to the list of property change listeners for the `trayIcons` property (which must be the value of `propertyName`). This listener is invoked when this application adds a tray icon to or removes a tray icon from the system tray, or whenever the system tray becomes unavailable and all of the application's tray icons are automatically removed. If you pass `null` to `listener`, no exception is thrown and no action is taken.

Continued

Table 3-4. *Continued*

Method	Description
public PropertyChangeListener[] getPropertyChangeListeners(String propertyName)	Returns an array of all property change listeners that are associated with propertyName. Currently, only the trayIcons property is supported. An empty array is returned if you pass null to propertyName, if you pass something other than trayIcons to propertyName, or if no listeners are associated with the trayIcons property.
public static SystemTray getSystemTray()	Returns the SystemTray object that represents the desktop's system tray. Each application that calls this method obtains the same SystemTray instance. Because the system tray might not be supported on a specific platform, you should call the isSupported() method prior to invoking this method. The SystemTray instance is returned if the platform supports a system tray; otherwise, an UnsupportedOperationException is thrown. If there is no display device, this method throws a HeadlessException. Also, if a security manager has been installed and the accessSystemTray java.awt. AWTPermission has not been granted, this method throws a SecurityException.
public TrayIcon[] getTrayIcons()	Returns an array of all TrayIcons that represent tray icons added to the system tray by this application. To prevent modification to the actual array of TrayIcons, only a copy of the array is returned. This array is empty if the application has not added a tray icon to the system tray.
public Dimension getTrayIconSize()	Returns the horizontal and vertical size (in pixels) of the space occupied by a tray icon in the system tray as a java.awt.Dimension. This method is useful for obtaining a tray icon's preferred size before creating the icon.
public static boolean isSupported()	Returns true if there is minimal support for the system tray. In addition to displaying a tray icon, minimal support includes either a pop-up menu (which is displayed whenever you right-click a tray icon) or an action event (which is fired whenever you double-click a tray icon).
public void remove(TrayIcon trayIcon)	Removes the tray icon described by trayIcon from the system tray. No exception is thrown and no action is taken if you pass null to trayIcon. All tray icons added by this application are automatically removed from the system tray when the application exits or whenever the system tray becomes unavailable.

Method	Description
public void removePropertyChangeListener (String propertyName, PropertyChangeListener listener)	Removes listener from the list of property change listeners for the trayIcons property (which must be the value of propertyName). If you pass null to listener, no exception is thrown and no action is taken.

Just as you cannot instantiate a SplashScreen object, you also cannot instantiate a SystemTray object. Instead, you need to invoke getSystemTray() to retrieve the SystemTray singleton object. Because this method throws an UnsupportedOperationException if the platform does not support a system tray, it is best to first call isSupported():

```
if (SystemTray.isSupported ())
{
   SystemTray systemTray = SystemTray.getSystemTray ();


   // Work with the system tray.
}
```

Adding a property change listener is one of the things you can do with the SystemTray instance. This listener is invoked whenever you add or remove a system tray icon, or whenever the system tray becomes unavailable—all of the tray icons are automatically removed in this situation. The following example demonstrates how you would create a property change listener that outputs two arrays of TrayIcons (the first array itemizes TrayIcons before the addition/removal; the second array itemizes TrayIcons after the addition/removal), and attach this listener to the system tray:

```
PropertyChangeListener pcl;
pcl = new PropertyChangeListener ()
     {
         public void propertyChange (PropertyChangeEvent pce)
         {
            System.out.println (pce.getPropertyName ()+
                                " has changed\n");
            System.out.println ();

            TrayIcon [] tia = (TrayIcon []) pce.getOldValue ();
            if (tia != null)
            {
                System.out.println ("TrayIcon array before:");
                for (TrayIcon ti: tia)
                     System.out.println (ti);
```

```
                    System.out.println ();
            }

            tia = (TrayIcon []) pce.getNewValue ();
            if (tia != null)
            {
                System.out.println ("TrayIcon array after:");
                for (TrayIcon ti: tia)
                    System.out.println (ti);
                System.out.println ();
            }
        }
    };
systemTray.addPropertyChangeListener ("trayIcons", pcl);
```

You can also create TrayIcons and add them to the SystemTray. Table 3-5 describes the TrayIcon class's constructors for creating TrayIcons and methods for customizing these instances.

Table 3-5. *TrayIcon Class Constructors and Methods*

Method	Description
public TrayIcon(Image image)	Constructs a TrayIcon that displays the specified image. An IllegalArgumentException is thrown if you pass null to image; an UnsupportedOperationException is thrown if the platform does not support a system tray; a HeadlessException is thrown if there is no display device; and a SecurityException is thrown if the accessSystemTray AWTPermission has not been granted.
public TrayIcon(Image image, String tooltip)	Constructs a TrayIcon that displays the specified image and tooltip. An IllegalArgumentException is thrown if you pass null to image; an UnsupportedOperationException is thrown if the platform does not support a system tray; a HeadlessException is thrown if there is no display device; and a SecurityException is thrown if the accessSystemTray AWTPermission has not been granted.
public TrayIcon(Image image, String tooltip, PopupMenu popup)	Constructs a TrayIcon that displays the specified image and tooltip, and associates the specified popup menu with this object. An IllegalArgumentException is thrown if you pass null to image; an UnsupportedOperationException is thrown if

Method	Description
	the platform does not support a system tray; a HeadlessException is thrown if there is no display device; and a SecurityException is thrown if the accessSystemTray AWTPermission has not been granted.
public void addActionListener(ActionListener listener)	Adds an action listener to this TrayIcon. This listener is typically invoked with an action event when the user selects the tray icon via the mouse or keyboard. The circumstances by which action events are generated are platform dependent. Nothing happens if you pass null to listener.
public void addMouseListener(MouseListener listener)	Adds a mouse listener to this TrayIcon. This listener receives all mouse events for this TrayIcon, but does not recognize mouse entered and mouse exited. Mouse coordinates are relative to the screen. Nothing happens if you pass null to listener.
public void addMouseMotionListener(MouseMotionListener listener)	Adds a mouse-motion listener to this TrayIcon. This listener receives all mouse-motion events for this TrayIcon, but does not recognize mouse dragged. The mouse-moved event is sent to this listener as long as the mouse pointer moves over the related icon in the system tray. Mouse coordinates are relative to the screen. Nothing happens if you pass null to listener.
public void displayMessage(String caption, String text, TrayIcon.MessageType messageType)	Displays a pop-up message in the vicinity of the tray icon. The message disappears after a time interval expires (this interval is most likely platform dependent) or the user clicks the message (which might generate an action event). The message consists of an optional caption and optional text. If present, the caption is displayed (usually in bold) above the text. You can pass null to caption or text, but not both; a NullPointerException is thrown if you attempt this. The messageType enumeration identifies the type of message: error, information, warning, or simple. A message-type-specific icon is displayed alongside the caption; a system sound might also be generated. Some platforms might truncate the caption or text—the number of characters displayed is platform dependent. Some platforms might not even display the message.
public String getActionCommand()	Returns the (potentially null) command name of the action event fired by this TrayIcon.

Continued

Table 3-5. *Continued*

Method	Description
`public ActionListener[] getActionListeners()`	Returns an array of all action listeners that have been added to this `TrayIcon`. This array will be empty if no action listeners have been added.
`public Image getImage()`	Returns this `TrayIcon`'s image.
`public MouseListener[] getMouseListeners()`	Returns an array of all mouse listeners that have been added to this `TrayIcon`. This array will be empty if no mouse listeners have been added.
`public MouseMotionListener[] getMouseMotionListeners()`	Returns an array of all mouse-motion listeners that have been added to this `TrayIcon`. This array will be empty if no mouse-motion listeners have been added.
`public PopupMenu getPopupMenu()`	Returns the pop-up menu associated with this `TrayIcon`. Null is returned if a pop-up menu isn't associated with the icon.
`public Dimension getSize()`	Returns the horizontal and vertical size (in pixels) of the space occupied by a tray icon in the system tray as a `Dimension`. This method's source code reveals that it is implemented in terms of `SystemTray`'s `getTrayIconSize()` method.
`public String getToolTip()`	Returns this `TrayIcon`'s tool tip. Null is returned if this icon doesn't have a tool tip.
`public boolean isImageAutoSize()`	Returns the value of this `TrayIcon`'s autosize property (true indicates that the image is auto-sized). The `autosize` property determines if the tray icon is automatically resized to fit its available space in the system tray.
`public void removeActionListener(ActionListener listener)`	Removes `listener` from this `TrayIcon`'s list of action listeners. Nothing happens if you pass `null` to `listener`.
`public void removeMouseListener(MouseListener listener)`	Removes `listener` from this `TrayIcon`'s list of mouse listeners. Nothing happens if you pass `null` to `listener`.
`public void removeMouseMotionListener(MouseMotionListener listener)`	Removes `listener` from this `TrayIcon`'s list of mouse-motion listeners. Nothing happens if you pass `null` to `listener`.
`public void setActionCommand(String command)`	Sets the command name for this `TrayIcon`'s action events; the default setting is `null`. This

Method	Description
	method is handy for sharing the same action listener among multiple TrayIcons. In this situation, you want to know which TrayIcon is responsible for firing an action event and invoking the listener. If each TrayIcon has previously been assigned its own command name, the listener can quickly determine the originating TrayIcon via a string comparison.
public void setImage(Image image)	Sets this TrayIcon's image, which is handy for displaying an application status change. The previous image is discarded without calling java.awt.Image's public void flush() method; you need to manually call this method on the previous image. If the image is animated, it will appear animated in the system tray. Nothing happens if you call this method with the same image that is currently being displayed. A NullPointerException is thrown if you pass null to image.
public void setImageAutoSize(boolean autosize)	Sets this TrayIcon's autosize property, which determines if the tray icon is automatically resized to fit its available space in the system tray. A true value expands an image that is too small, or crops an image that is too large to fit the available space. This property defaults to false.
public void setPopupMenu(PopupMenu popup)	Sets this TrayIcon's pop-up menu. The pop-up menu can be associated with only this TrayIcon. An IllegalArgumentException is thrown if you attempt to share this pop-up menu with multiple TrayIcons. Some platforms might not support showing the pop-up menu after right-clicking the tray icon. In that case, either no menu or a native version of the menu will be displayed. Pass null to popup to remove this TrayIcon's current pop-up menu.
public void setToolTip(String tooltip)	Sets this TrayIcon's tool tip. The tool tip is automatically displayed (although it might be truncated, depending on the platform) when the mouse pointer hovers over the tray icon. Pass null to tooltip to remove this TrayIcon's current tool tip.

Continuing from the previous example, the following example creates a `TrayIcon` and adds it to the system tray (identified by `systemTray`):

```
Image image = Toolkit.getDefaultToolkit ().createImage ("image.gif");
systemTray.add (new TrayIcon (image));
```

Quickly Launching Programs via the System Tray

You can easily add icons to the system tray, but what kind of application is appropriate for the system tray? After all, the system tray is a finite resource, and you should not populate it with icons for just any old application. Types of applications that you might add to the system tray include battery-status indicator, print-job control, volume control, antivirus, QuickTime movie, and screen control programs. Another application that I believe is appropriate for the system tray is a program launcher. This application's source code is presented in Listing 3-5.

Listing 3-5. *QuickLaunch.java*

```
// QuickLaunch.java

import java.awt.*;
import java.awt.event.*;
import java.awt.geom.*;
import java.awt.image.*;

import java.io.*;

import javax.swing.*;

public class QuickLaunch
{
   static AboutBox aboutBox;
   static ChooseApplication chooseApplication;

   public static void main (String [] args)
   {
      if (!SystemTray.isSupported ())
      {
         JOptionPane.showMessageDialog (null, "System tray is not supported");
         System.exit (0);
      }
```

```java
SystemTray systemTray = SystemTray.getSystemTray ();

// Create the tray icon's image.

Dimension size = systemTray.getTrayIconSize ();
BufferedImage bi = new BufferedImage (size.width, size.height,
                                      BufferedImage.TYPE_INT_RGB);
Graphics g = bi.getGraphics ();
g.setColor (Color.black);
g.fillRect (0, 0, size.width, size.height);
g.setFont (new Font ("Arial", Font.BOLD, 10));
g.setColor (Color.yellow);
g.drawString ("QL", 1, 11);

try
{
    // Create and populate a popup menu with QuickLaunch menu items.
    // Attach an action listener to each menu item that does something
    // useful.

    PopupMenu popup = new PopupMenu ();

    MenuItem miAbout = new MenuItem ("About QuickLaunch");
    ActionListener al;
    al = new ActionListener ()
        {
            public void actionPerformed (ActionEvent e)
            {
                if (aboutBox == null)
                {
                    aboutBox = new AboutBox ();
                    aboutBox.setVisible (true);
                }
            }
        };
    miAbout.addActionListener (al);
    popup.add (miAbout);

    popup.addSeparator ();

    MenuItem miChoose = new MenuItem ("Choose Application");
```

```java
al = new ActionListener ()
    {
        public void actionPerformed (ActionEvent e)
        {
            if (chooseApplication == null)
                chooseApplication = new ChooseApplication ();
        }
    };
miChoose.addActionListener (al);
popup.add (miChoose);

MenuItem miLaunch = new MenuItem ("Launch Application");
ActionListener alLaunch;
alLaunch = new ActionListener ()
        {
            public void actionPerformed (ActionEvent e)
            {
                try
                {
                    JTextField txt;
                    txt = ChooseApplication.txtApp;
                    String cmd = txt.getText ().trim ();
                    Runtime r = Runtime.getRuntime ();
                    if (!cmd.equals (""))
                        r.exec (cmd);
                }
                catch (IOException ioe)
                {
                    JOptionPane.showMessageDialog (null,
                                            "Unable to "+
                                            "launch");
                }
            }
        };
miLaunch.addActionListener (alLaunch);
popup.add (miLaunch);

popup.addSeparator ();

MenuItem miExit = new MenuItem ("Exit");
al = new ActionListener ()
    {
```

```
                    public void actionPerformed (ActionEvent e)
                    {
                        System.exit (0);
                    }
                };
            miExit.addActionListener (al);
            popup.add (miExit);

            // Create and add a tray icon to the system tray. Use the previously
            // created image and popup, along with a Quick Launch tooltip.

            TrayIcon ti = new TrayIcon (bi, "Quick Launch", popup);
            ti.addActionListener (alLaunch);
            systemTray.add (ti);
        }
        catch (AWTException e)
        {
            JOptionPane.showMessageDialog (null, "Unable to create and/or "+
                                           "install tray icon");
            System.exit (0);
        }
    }
}

class AboutBox extends JDialog
{
    AboutBox ()
    {
        // Create an ownerless modal dialog. The cast is needed to differentiate
        // between the JDialog(Dialog, boolean) and JDialog(Frame, boolean)
        // constructors.

        super ((java.awt.Dialog) null, true);

        setDefaultCloseOperation (DO_NOTHING_ON_CLOSE);
        addWindowListener (new WindowAdapter ()
                        {
                            public void windowClosing (WindowEvent e)
                            {
                                dispose ();
                            }
```

```
                        public void windowClosed (WindowEvent e)
                        {
                            QuickLaunch.aboutBox = null;
                        }
                });

    JPanel pnl;
    pnl = new JPanel ()
        {
            {
                setPreferredSize (new Dimension (250, 100));
                setBorder (BorderFactory.createEtchedBorder ());
            }

            public void paintComponent (Graphics g)
            {
                Insets insets = getInsets ();
                g.setColor (Color.lightGray);
                g.fillRect (0, 0, getWidth ()-insets.left-insets.right,
                            getHeight ()-insets.top-insets.bottom);

                g.setFont (new Font ("Arial", Font.BOLD, 24));
                FontMetrics fm = g.getFontMetrics ();
                Rectangle2D r2d;
                r2d = fm.getStringBounds ("Quick Launch 1.0", g);
                int width = (int)((Rectangle2D.Float) r2d).width;

                g.setColor (Color.black);
                g.drawString ("Quick Launch 1.0", (getWidth()-width)/2,
                            insets.top+(getHeight ()-insets.bottom-
                            insets.top)/2);
            }
        };
    getContentPane ().add (pnl, BorderLayout.NORTH);

    final JButton btnOk = new JButton ("Ok");
    btnOk.addActionListener (new ActionListener ()
                    {
                        public void actionPerformed (ActionEvent e)
                        {
                            dispose ();
                        }
```

```
                                  });
      getContentPane ().add (new JPanel () {{ add (btnOk); }},
                           BorderLayout.SOUTH);

      pack ();
      setResizable (false);
      setLocationRelativeTo (null);
   }
}

class ChooseApplication extends JFrame
{
   static JTextField txtApp = new JTextField ("", 30);

   ChooseApplication ()
   {
      setDefaultCloseOperation (DO_NOTHING_ON_CLOSE);
      addWindowListener (new WindowAdapter ()
                      {
                            public void windowClosing (WindowEvent e)
                            {
                               dispose ();
                            }

                            public void windowClosed (WindowEvent e)
                            {
                               QuickLaunch.chooseApplication = null;
                            }
                      });

      JPanel pnl = new JPanel ();
      pnl.add (new JLabel ("Enter application"));
      pnl.add (txtApp);
      getContentPane ().add (pnl);

      pack ();
      setResizable (false);
      setLocationRelativeTo (null);
      setVisible (true);
   }
}
```

The QuickLauncher.java source code describes the architecture of a system tray application for choosing and quickly launching arbitrary applications. After determining that the system tray is supported, this application creates an appropriate tray icon image. It also creates a pop-up menu with About QuickLaunch, Choose Application, Launch Application, and Exit menu items. It then creates a TrayIcon associated with the tray icon image and pop-up menu, attaches an action listener that invokes the default Launch Application option's action listener (whenever the user performs the appropriate mouse action, such as double-clicking the tray icon under Windows XP), and adds the TrayIcon to the SystemTray. Figure 3-2 shows this application's tray icon and pop-up menu.

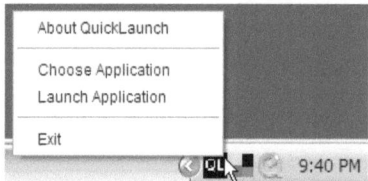

Figure 3-2. *QuickLaunch adds a program launcher icon to the system tray.*

The pop-up menu options work as follows:

- The About QuickLaunch option activates a Swing-based dialog that presents information about the program. This information is currently limited to the program title. Close this dialog via its Ok button or the system menu's Close menu item.

- The Choose Application option lets you select an application to launch. The dialog that appears presents a text field for entering the application name (for example, you might enter notepad.exe on a Windows XP system). Select the system menu's Close menu item to close this dialog.

- The Launch Application option launches the chosen application.

- The Exit option terminates this application and automatically removes the application's tray icon.

■**Note** The Sun Developer Network's article "New System Tray Functionality in Java SE 6" (http://java.sun.com/developer/technicalArticles/J2SE/Desktop/javase6/systemtray/) provides additional System Tray API information and examples.

XAWT Support on Solaris

Java 5.0 reimplemented the AWT for Solaris and Linux, to break its ties to the native Motif widget library and the native Xt (X toolkit) widget-support library. This was done to improve performance and correctness. The resulting X11 protocol-based XAWT toolkit is largely written in Java; minimal native code is used to communicate with Xlib (the X Window System protocol client library), which contains native functions for interacting with an X server.

Although XAWT became the default implementation of the AWT for Linux, Solaris still relied on Motif as its default AWT implementation. In Java SE 6, the Solaris AWT implementation now defaults to XAWT. This means that to select the XAWT implementation when running your Java applications on Solaris, you no longer need to set the AWT_TOOLKIT environment variable or the -Dawt.toolkit command-line parameter to sun.awt.X11.XToolkit.

Summary

The AWT is the foundation for both AWT-based and Swing-based GUIs. Java SE 6 enhances this foundation in various ways, beginning with the new Desktop API.

The Desktop API bridges the gap between Java and native applications that run on the desktop by enabling Java applications to launch applications associated with specific file types for the purposes of opening, editing, and printing documents based on those types. It also enables Java applications to launch the default web browser with specific URIs, and launch the default e-mail client.

Live resizing, which Java refers to as dynamic layout, is a visual enhancement feature where a window's content is dynamically laid out as the window is resized. In Java SE 6, the default behavior for Toolkit's setDynamicLayout(boolean dynamic) method has been changed to dynamically validate container layouts during resizing.

For developers who work with Java in the context of non-English locales, Java SE 6 fixes a number of bugs related to keyboard input on the Solaris and Linux platforms.

Prior to Java SE 6, the AWT's modality model was flawed in various ways. To fix these flaws, Java SE 6 introduces a new modality model, which lets you limit a dialog's blocking scope. This model also lets you mark a window for exclusion so that it will not be blocked by a modal dialog.

Java SE 6 supports splash screens, allowing you to present an undecorated splash window displaying a GIF, JPEG, or PNG image while an application is loading. You can accomplish this task via the -splash command-line option or an application JAR file's SplashScreen-Image manifest entry. The new Splash Screen API lets you customize the splash screen by providing the means to draw on the overlay image associated with the splash window.

Along with Desktop and Splash Screen, Java SE 6 provides the System Tray API for making Java applications first-class citizens of the desktop. The System Tray API allows an application to gain access to the desktop's system tray. You work with this API's `SystemTray` class to interact with the system tray. You also work with this API's `TrayIcon` class to add listeners to and otherwise customize individual tray icons.

Finally, Java SE 6 defaults the implementation of the AWT to XAWT on the Solaris platform.

Test Your Understanding

How well do you understand the changes to the AWT toolkit? Test your understanding by answering the following questions and performing the following exercises. (The answers are presented in Appendix D.)

1. Create a dialog with your own link component. When this link is clicked, invoke the `Desktop` class's `browse()` method to launch the default browser and display the page identified by the link.

2. In `UnitsConverter.java` (Listing 3-3), something strange happens when you change:

   ```
   setModalExclusionType (Dialog.ModalExclusionType.APPLICATION_EXCLUDE);
   ```

   to

   ```
   frame.setModalExclusionType (Dialog.ModalExclusionType.APPLICATION_EXCLUDE);
   ```

   After making this change, clicking the About button still prevents access to the underlying GUI as long as the resulting modal About dialog remains on the screen. However, if you click Help, close the Help dialog, and then click About to activate the About dialog, you can access the underlying GUI while the About dialog is still visible. Why?

3. Which takes precedence if specified together: the `-splash` command-line option or the `SplashScreen-Image` manifest entry?

4. The pop-up menus associated with tray icons typically display default menu items in bold type. Modify `QuickLaunch.java` (Listing 3-5) to boldface the default Launch Application menu item.

CHAPTER 4

■ ■ ■

GUI Toolkits: Swing

Swing, an extension to the Abstract Windowing Toolkit (AWT), is the preferred toolkit for building modern GUIs. This chapter explores most of the new and improved features that Java SE 6 brings to Swing:

- Arbitrary components for JTabbedPane tab headers

- Improved SpringLayout

- Improved Swing component drag-and-drop

- JTable sorting and filtering

- Look and feel enhancements

- New SwingWorker

- Text component printing

Arbitrary Components for JTabbedPane Tab Headers

The javax.swing.JTabbedPane class implements a component divided into tabs. Each tab contains one component. You can place more than one component on a tab by using a combination of layout managers and containers. The user clicks a tab's header to switch to that tab.

Prior to Java SE 6, the header was restricted to presenting some combination of a String label and a javax.swing.Icon (and a tool tip String). Many developers found this too limiting; for example, they wanted to be able to place a close button on the header, to allow users to close the tab. Java SE 6 now allows an arbitrary java.awt.Component to appear on the header.

Three methods have been added to JTabbedPane to support placing arbitrary components on tab headers. Check out their descriptions in Table 4-1.

Table 4-1. *JTabbedPane Class Tab-Component Methods*

Method	Description
public void setTabComponentAt(int index, Component component)	Specifies the component that renders the title for a specified tab. The tab is identified by the zero-based index. An IndexOutOfBoundsException is thrown if index is less than zero or greater than the final tab's index. An IllegalArgumentException is thrown if a component has already been specified.
public Component getTabComponentAt(int index)	Returns the component associated with the index tab. An IndexOutOfBoundsException is thrown if index is less than zero or greater than the final tab's index.
public int indexOfTabComponent(Component tabComponent)	Returns the index of the tab associated with tabComponent. Returns –1 if there is no tab.

To demonstrate the setTabComponentAt() and getTabComponentAt() methods, I've prepared a minimal web browser application. The application lets you enter a URL and display its web page on the current tab. You can add new tabs via the menu, switch between tabs, and click a tab header's close button to close the tab and remove the displayed page. Listing 4-1 shows the application's source code.

Listing 4-1. *Browser.java*

```
// Browser.java

import java.awt.*;
import java.awt.event.*;

import java.io.*;

import javax.swing.*;
import javax.swing.event.*;

public class Browser extends JFrame implements HyperlinkListener
{
   private JTextField txtURL;

   private JTabbedPane tp;
```

```java
private JLabel lblStatus;

private ImageIcon ii = new ImageIcon ("close.gif");

private Dimension iiSize = new Dimension (ii.getIconWidth (),
                                          ii.getIconHeight ());

private int tabCounter = 0;

public Browser ()
{
   super ("Browser");
   setDefaultCloseOperation (EXIT_ON_CLOSE);

   JMenuBar mb = new JMenuBar ();
   JMenu mFile = new JMenu ("File");
   JMenuItem mi = new JMenuItem ("Add Tab");
   ActionListener addTabl = new ActionListener ()
                     {
                         public void actionPerformed (ActionEvent e)
                         {
                            addTab ();
                         }
                     };
   mi.addActionListener (addTabl);
   mFile.add (mi);
   mb.add (mFile);
   setJMenuBar (mb);

   JPanel pnlURL = new JPanel ();
   pnlURL.setLayout (new BorderLayout ());
   pnlURL.add (new JLabel ("URL: "), BorderLayout.WEST);
   txtURL = new JTextField ("");
   pnlURL.add (txtURL, BorderLayout.CENTER);
   getContentPane ().add (pnlURL, BorderLayout.NORTH);

   tp = new JTabbedPane ();
   addTab ();
   getContentPane ().add (tp, BorderLayout.CENTER);

   lblStatus = new JLabel (" ");
```

```java
            getContentPane ().add (lblStatus, BorderLayout.SOUTH);

        ActionListener al;
        al = new ActionListener ()
            {
                public void actionPerformed (ActionEvent ae)
                {
                   try
                   {
                       Component c = tp.getSelectedComponent ();
                       JScrollPane sp = (JScrollPane) c;
                       c = sp.getViewport ().getView ();
                       JEditorPane ep = (JEditorPane) c;
                       ep.setPage (ae.getActionCommand ());
                   }
                   catch (Exception e)
                   {
                       lblStatus.setText ("Browser problem: "+e.getMessage ());
                   }
                }
            };
        txtURL.addActionListener (al);

        setSize (300, 300);
        setVisible (true);
    }

    void addTab ()
    {
        JEditorPane ep = new JEditorPane ();
        ep.setEditable (false);
        ep.addHyperlinkListener (this);
        tp.addTab (null, new JScrollPane (ep));

        JButton tabCloseButton = new JButton (ii);
        tabCloseButton.setActionCommand (""+tabCounter);
        tabCloseButton.setPreferredSize (iiSize);

        ActionListener al;
        al = new ActionListener ()
            {
                public void actionPerformed (ActionEvent ae)
```

```
                {
                    JButton btn = (JButton) ae.getSource ();
                    String s1 = btn.getActionCommand ();
                    for (int i = 1; i < tp.getTabCount (); i++)
                    {
                        JPanel pnl - (JPanel) tp.getTabComponentAt (i);
                        btn = (JButton) pnl.getComponent (0);
                        String s2 = btn.getActionCommand ();
                        if (s1.equals (s2))
                        {
                            tp.removeTabAt (i);
                            break;
                        }
                    }
                }
            };
        tabCloseButton.addActionListener (al);

        if (tabCounter != 0)
        {
            JPanel pnl = new JPanel ();
            pnl.setOpaque (false);
            pnl.add (tabCloseButton);
            tp.setTabComponentAt (tp.getTabCount ()-1, pnl);
            tp.setSelectedIndex (tp.getTabCount ()-1);
        }

        tabCounter++;
    }

    public void hyperlinkUpdate (HyperlinkEvent hle)
    {
        HyperlinkEvent.EventType evtype = hle.getEventType ();

        if (evtype == HyperlinkEvent.EventType.ENTERED)
            lblStatus.setText (hle.getURL ().toString ());
        else
        if (evtype == HyperlinkEvent.EventType.EXITED)
            lblStatus.setText (" ");
    }

    public static void main (String [] args)
```

```
    {
        Runnable r = new Runnable ()
                    {
                        public void run ()
                        {
                            new Browser ();
                        }
                    };
        EventQueue.invokeLater (r);
    }
}
```

In Listing 4-1, notice the use of tabCounter, setActionCommand(), and getActionCommand()
to uniquely identify each tab. I did this to identify the tab whose close button was clicked.
Although I could have attempted to use the JTabbedPane class's getSelectedIndex()
method to accomplish the same task, that method is useless if the tab is not selected
when its close button is clicked.

After compiling the source code, launch this application. As shown in Figure 4-1, the
GUI consists of a File menu (for adding tabs), a text field for entering URLs, a tabbed area
with a single starting tab for viewing a web page, and a status bar for viewing links and
error messages. The starting tab does not have a close button, because at least one tab
must be present for the button to be added.

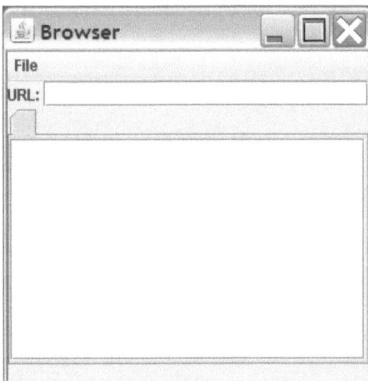

Figure 4-1. *The simple web browser application lets you add tabs, which will appear with
close buttons.*

Enter a complete URL in the text field (http://www.apress.com, for example), and the page will appear on the starting tab. (The status bar will present an error message if the page cannot be loaded.) From the File menu, choose the Add Tab menu item to add another tab. Then enter another complete URL. Notice the close button on this new tab's header. After toggling between these tabs, click this button to close the newly added tab.

■**Caution** The Browser application must be able to load close.gif, which presents the close button's graphic. If this file cannot be loaded, you will not see a close button on the tab headers (the starting tab header never displays a close button), and you will not be able to close these tabs.

Improved SpringLayout

The SpringLayout layout manager consists of the javax.swing.SpringLayout class and its nested SpringLayout.Constraints class. These classes work together to lay out components via *springs* (triplets containing different minimum, preferred, and maximum sizes) and *struts* (springs where the minimum, preferred, and maximum sizes are identical). The idea behind this layout manager is for a GUI's components to maintain their positions relative to container edges or the edges of other components after the GUI is resized.

SpringLayout officially debuted in version 1.4 of Java 2 Platform, Standard Edition. An early version of this layout manager existed in alpha and beta versions of Swing, but was not formally introduced prior to Java 1.4 because it was unfinished. Even after officially becoming part of Swing, SpringLayout required additional work. For example, SpringLayout does not always correctly resolve its constraints. This problem was brought to Sun's attention via Bug 4726194 "SpringLayout doesn't always resolve constraints correctly." As explained in this bug entry, the problem was subsequently resolved in Java SE 6 by basing the algorithm used to calculate springs on the last two specified springs, along each axis.

■**Note** Although you can hand-code GUIs that use this layout manager, SpringLayout was originally created for assisting GUI-building tools.

Improved Swing Component Drag-and-Drop

Java SE 6 has greatly improved drag-and-drop for Swing components. These improvements have to do with telling a component how to determine drop locations and having Swing provide all relevant transfer information during a transfer. Let's consider the first improvement in the context of Swing's text components—javax.swing.JTextComponent subclasses.

Text components move the *caret* (text-insertion point) to the location under the mouse during a drag-and-drop operation, to visually identify where selected text will be dropped. Prior to Java SE 6, this action temporarily cleared the selection, which caused the user to lose the context of the text being dragged.

Java SE 6 remedies this situation by introducing a public final void setDropMode(DropMode dropMode) method in the JTextComponent class, as well as a javax.swing.DropMode enumeration, whose constants identify the means by which a component tracks and indicates a drop location during drag-and-drop. Of the various constants provided by this enumeration, only DropMode.INSERT and DropMode.USE_SELECTION are valid for text components.

The DropMode.INSERT constant specifies that the drop location should be tracked in terms of the position where the data will be inserted. This implies that selected text is not cleared (even temporarily). In contrast, DropMode.USE_SELECTION specifies that a text component's caret will be used to track the drop location, so selected text will be temporarily deselected.

I have created an application that demonstrates the difference between these drop modes. This application's source code appears in Listing 4-2.

Listing 4-2. *TextDrop.java*

```
// TextDrop.java

import java.awt.*;
import java.awt.event.*;

import java.io.*;

import javax.swing.*;

public class TextDrop extends JFrame
{
    private JTextField txtField1, txtField2;

    public TextDrop (String title)
    {
```

```
super (title);
setDefaultCloseOperation (EXIT_ON_CLOSE);

getContentPane ().setLayout (new GridLayout (3, 1));

JPanel pnl = new JPanel ();
pnl.add (new JLabel ("Text field 1"));
txtField1 = new JTextField ("Text1", 25);
txtField1.setDragEnabled (true);
pnl.add (txtField1);
getContentPane ().add (pnl);

pnl = new JPanel ();
pnl.add (new JLabel ("Text field 2"));
txtField2 = new JTextField ("Text2", 25);
txtField2.setDragEnabled (true);
pnl.add (txtField2);
getContentPane ().add (pnl);

pnl = new JPanel ();
pnl.add (new JLabel ("Drop mode"));
JComboBox cb = new JComboBox (new String [] { "USE_SELECTION",
                                              "INSERT" });
cb.setSelectedIndex (0);
ActionListener al;
al = new ActionListener ()
    {
        public void actionPerformed (ActionEvent e)
        {
           JComboBox cb = (JComboBox) e.getSource ();
           int index = cb.getSelectedIndex ();
           if (index == 0)
           {
               txtField1.setDropMode (DropMode.USE_SELECTION);
               txtField2.setDropMode (DropMode.USE_SELECTION);
           }
           else
           {
               txtField1.setDropMode (DropMode.INSERT);
               txtField2.setDropMode (DropMode.INSERT);
           }
        }
```

```
                };
            cb.addActionListener (al);
            pnl.add (cb);
            getContentPane ().add (pnl);

            pack ();
            setVisible (true);
        }

        public static void main (String [] args)
        {
            Runnable r = new Runnable ()
                        {
                            public void run ()
                            {
                                new TextDrop ("Text Drop");
                            }
                        };
            EventQueue.invokeLater (r);
        }
    }
}
```

When you run this application, its GUI presents three labels, two text fields, and a combo box. The idea is to select text in either text field and drag the selected text to the other text field. By choosing the drop mode from the combo box, you can verify each drop mode's influence in terms of selected and deselected text.

Figure 4-2 shows a copy operation, where the top text field's text has previously been selected. The text copy is being dragged to the end of the top text field, where it will be dropped. Notice that the combo box indicates the INSERT drop mode. When you switch to USE_SELECTION drop mode, you will see the text but not the selection during the drag operation. (Don't forget to hold down the Ctrl key to drag a copy of the text.)

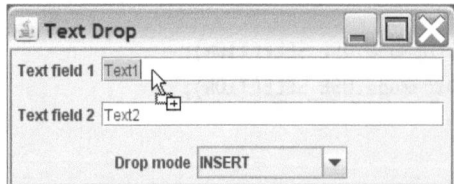

Figure 4-2. *The TextDrop application demonstrates the DropMode.INSERT and DropMode.USE_SELECTION drop modes.*

Shannon Hickey, a member of the Swing Team, has created a blog that outlines the work done to improve Swing component drag-and-drop. Rather than "reinvent the wheel" by reiterating Shannon's blog (which includes several Web Start-based demos), I refer you to these blog entries for complete coverage:

- "Improved Drag Gesture in Swing"
  (http://weblogs.java.net/blog/shan_man/archive/2005/06/improved_drag_g.html)

- "First Class Drag and Drop Support in Mustang"
  (http://weblogs.java.net/blog/shan_man/archive/2006/01/first_class_dra.html)

- "Location-Sensitive Drag and Drop in Mustang"
  (http://weblogs.java.net/blog/shan_man/archive/2006/01/location_sensit.html)

- "Enable Dropping into Empty JTables"
  (http://weblogs.java.net/blog/shan_man/archive/2006/01/enable_dropping.html)

- "Choosing the Drop Action, and Further Changes to Swing Drag and Drop"
  (http://weblogs.java.net/blog/shan_man/archive/2006/02/choosing_the_dr.html)

Note `JTextComponent` also provides a companion `public final DropMode getDropMode()` method to return the current drop mode. For backward compatibility, `DropMode.USE_SELECTION` is the default drop mode.

JTable Sorting and Filtering

The ability to sort and filter a `javax.swing.JTable`'s contents has been simplified by Java SE 6. By clicking a column header, you can sort rows according to the column's contents. You can also filter rows based on regular expressions and other criteria, and display only those rows that match the criteria.

Sorting the Table's Rows

Three classes provide the foundation for sorting and filtering a `JTable`'s content:

- The abstract `javax.swing.RowSorter<M>` class, which provides a mapping between a view and an underlying data source, such as a model

- Its abstract javax.swing.DefaultRowSorter<M, I> subclass, which supports sorting and filtering around a grid-based data model

- The DefaultRowSorter<M, I>'s javax.swing.table.TableRowSorter<M extends TableModel> subclass, which provides table component sorting and filtering via a javax.swing.table.TableModel

It is easy to introduce sorting to a table component. After creating the table's model and initializing the table component with this model, pass the model to TableRowSorter<M extends TableModel>'s constructor. Then pass the resulting RowSorter<M> to JTable's public void setRowSorter(RowSorter<? extends TableModel> sorter) method:

```
TableModel model = ...
JTable table = new JTable (model);
RowSorter<TableModel> sorter = new TableRowSorter<TableModel> (model);
table.setRowSorter (sorter);
```

To demonstrate how easy it is to add sorting to your tables, I have designed a simple application that itemizes some grocery items and their prices in a two-column table. Listing 4-3 presents the source code.

Listing 4-3. *PriceList1.java*

```
// PriceList1.java

import javax.swing.*;
import javax.swing.table.*;

public class PriceList1 extends JFrame
{
   public PriceList1 (String title)
   {
      super (title);
      setDefaultCloseOperation (EXIT_ON_CLOSE);

      String [] columns = { "Item", "Price" };

      Object [][] rows =
      {
         { "Bag of potatoes", 10.98 },
         { "Magazine", 7.99 },
```

```
            { "Can of soup", 0.89 },
            { "DVD movie", 39.99 }
        };

        TableModel model = new DefaultTableModel (rows, columns);
        JTable table = new JTable (model);
        RowSorter<TableModel> sorter = new TableRowSorter<TableModel> (model);
        table.setRowSorter (sorter);
        getContentPane ().add (new JScrollPane (table));

        setSize (200, 150);
        setVisible (true);
    }

    public static void main (String [] args)
    {
        Runnable r = new Runnable ()
                    {
                        public void run ()
                        {
                            new PriceList1 ("Price List #1");
                        }
                    };
        java.awt.EventQueue.invokeLater (r);
    }
}
}
```

Run this application, and you will see output similar to the table shown in Figure 4-3.

Figure 4-3. *Unsorted table*

Click the Item column's header, and the rows will sort in ascending order of this column's values. A small up triangle will appear beside the column name to identify the current sort direction, as shown in Figure 4-4.

Figure 4-4. *Sorted table based on the Item column*

Suppose that you decide to sort the items in ascending order of price (smallest price item first). After clicking the Price column's header, a small up triangle appears beside the column name. However, as Figure 4-5 indicates, the sort result is unexpected.

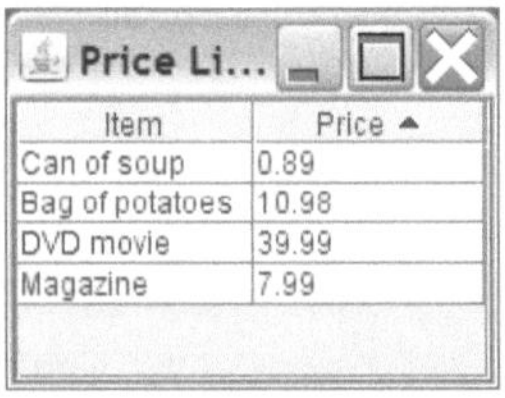

Figure 4-5. *Prices are sorted based on string comparisons.*

The prices are not sorted based on their numerical values. If they were, the row containing DVD movie and 39.99 would be the last row in the table. Instead, rows have been sorted based on the string representations of the price values.

According to the JDK documentation for the `TableRowSorter<M extends TableModel>` class, `java.util.Comparator<T>` comparators are used to compare objects during a sort. The `Comparator<T>` comparator that is chosen is based on five rules, which I have excerpted (with minor additions) from the documentation (in the top-down order in which the decision is made):

- If a `Comparator<T>` has been specified for the column by the `setComparator` method, use it.

- If the column class as returned by `getColumnClass` is `String`, use the `Comparator<T>` returned by `Collator.getInstance()`.

- If the column class implements `Comparable<T>`, use a `Comparator<T>` that invokes the `compareTo` method.

- If a javax.swing.table.TableStringConverter has been specified, use it to convert the values to Strings and then use the Comparator<T> returned by Collator.getInstance().

- Otherwise, use the Comparator<T> returned by Collator.getInstance() on the results from calling toString on the objects.

If you explicitly attach a Comparator<T> to a column via public void setComparator(int column, Comparator<?> comparator), this Comparator<T> will be used during the sort (as indicated by the first rule). In contrast, it is easier to subclass javax.swing.table.DefaultTableModel and override the public Class getColumnClass(int column) method, which is what Listing 4-4 accomplishes.

Listing 4-4. *PriceList2.java*

```java
// PriceList2.java

import javax.swing.*;
import javax.swing.table.*;

public class PriceList2 extends JFrame
{
   public PriceList2 (String title)
   {
      super (title);
      setDefaultCloseOperation (EXIT_ON_CLOSE);

      String [] columns = { "Item", "Price" };

      Object [][] rows =
      {
         { "Bag of potatoes", 10.98 },
         { "Magazine", 7.99 },
         { "Can of soup", 0.89 },
         { "DVD movie", 39.99 }
      };

      TableModel model = new DefaultTableModel (rows, columns)
                         {
                            public Class getColumnClass (int column)
                            {
                               if (column >= 0 &&
```

```
                                    column <= getColumnCount ())
                                return getValueAt (0, column).getClass ();
                            else
                                return Object.class;
                        }
                    };
        JTable table = new JTable (model);
        RowSorter<TableModel> sorter = new TableRowSorter<TableModel> (model);
        table.setRowSorter (sorter);
        getContentPane ().add (new JScrollPane (table));

        setSize (200, 150);
        setVisible (true);
    }

    public static void main (String [] args)
    {
        Runnable r = new Runnable ()
                    {
                        public void run ()
                        {
                            new PriceList2 ("Price List #2");
                        }
                    };
        java.awt.EventQueue.invokeLater (r);
    }
}
```

DefaultTableModel always returns Object.class from its getColumnClass() method. According to the fifth rule, this results in the toString() method being called during sorting (and the result shown previously in Figure 4-5). By overriding getColumnClass() and having the overridden method return the appropriate type, sorting takes advantage of the returned Class object's Comparable<T> (if there is one), according to the third rule. Figure 4-6 shows the properly sorted price list.

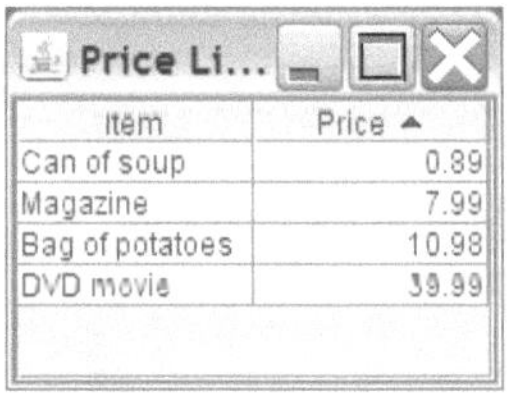

Figure 4-6. *The DVD movie item is now displayed in the last row, where it should be based on its price.*

Tip JTable's public void setAutoCreateRowSorter(boolean autoCreateRowSorter) method offers the simplest way to attach a row sorter to a table component. For more information about this method, check out "Mustang (Java SE 6) Gallops into Town" (http://www.informit.com/articles/article.asp?p=661371&rl=1).

Filtering the Table's Rows

The DefaultRowSorter<M, I> class provides a public void setRowFilter(RowFilter<? super M,? super I> filter) method for installing a filter that lets you determine which rows are displayed and which rows are hidden. You can pass to filter an instance of one of the filters returned from the static methods in the abstract javax.swing.RowFilter<M, I> class, or pass null to remove any installed filter and allow all rows to be displayed. Table 4-2 shows RowFilter's filter factory methods.

Table 4-2. *RowFilter Filter Factory Methods*

Method	Description
public static <M,I> RowFilter<M,I> andFilter(Iterable<? extends RowFilter<? super M,? super I>> filters)	Returns a row filter that includes a row if all of the specified row filters include the row.
public static <M,I> RowFilter<M,I> dateFilter(RowFilter.ComparisonType type, Date date, int... indices)	Returns a row filter that includes only those rows that have at least one java.util.Date value in the indices columns that meets the criteria specified by type. If the indices argument is not specified, all columns are checked.
public static <M,I> RowFilter<M,I> notFilter(RowFilter<M,I> filter)	Returns a row filter that includes a row if the specified row filter does not include the row.
public static <M,I> RowFilter<M,I> numberFilter(RowFilter.ComparisonType type, Number number, int... indices)	Returns a row filter that includes only those rows that have at least one Number value in the indices columns that meets the criteria specified by type. If the indices argument is not specified, all columns are checked.

Continued

Table 4-2. *Continued*

Method	Description
`public static <M,I> RowFilter<M,I> orFilter(Iterable<? extends RowFilter<? super M,? super I>> filters)`	Returns a row filter that includes a row if any of the specified row `filters` include the row.
`public static <M,I> RowFilter<M,I> regexFilter(String regex, int... indices)`	Returns a row filter that uses a regular expression to determine which rows to include. Each column identified by `indices` is checked. The row is returned if one of the column values matches the regex. If the `indices` argument is not specified, all columns are checked.

Row filtering is useful in the context of a database application. Rather than submit a potentially expensive SQL `SELECT` statement to the database management system to retrieve a subset of a table's rows based on some criteria, filtering rows via a table component and its row filter is bound to be much faster. For example, suppose your table component presents a log of bugs (bug identifier, description, date filed, and dated fixed) found while testing software. Furthermore, suppose that you want to present only those rows whose description matches some entered regular expression. Listing 4-5 presents an application that accomplishes this task.

Listing 4-5. *BugLog.java*

```
// BugLog.java

import java.awt.*;
import java.awt.event.*;

import java.text.*;

import java.util.*;

import javax.swing.*;
import javax.swing.table.*;

public class BugLog extends JFrame
{
   private static DateFormat df;

   public BugLog (String title) throws ParseException
```

```java
{
    super (title);
    setDefaultCloseOperation (EXIT_ON_CLOSE);

    String [] columns = { "Bug ID", "Description", "Date Filed",
                          "Date Fixed" };

    df = DateFormat.getDateTimeInstance (DateFormat.SHORT, DateFormat.SHORT,
                                         Locale.US);

    Object [][] rows =
    {
        { 1000, "Crash during file read", df.parse ("2/10/07 10:12 am"),
          df.parse ("2/11/07 11:15 pm") },
        { 1020, "GUI not repainted", df.parse ("3/5/07 6:00 pm"),
          df.parse ("3/8/07 3:00 am") },
        { 1025, "File not found exception", df.parse ("1/18/07 9:30 am"),
          df.parse ("1/22/07 4:13 pm") }
    };

    TableModel model = new DefaultTableModel (rows, columns);
    JTable table = new JTable (model);
    final TableRowSorter<TableModel> sorter;
    sorter = new TableRowSorter<TableModel> (model);
    table.setRowSorter (sorter);
    getContentPane ().add (new JScrollPane (table));

    JPanel pnl = new JPanel ();
    pnl.add (new JLabel ("Filter expression:"));
    final JTextField txtFE = new JTextField (25);
    pnl.add (txtFE);
    JButton btnSetFE = new JButton ("Set Filter Expression");
    ActionListener al;
    al = new ActionListener ()
        {
            public void actionPerformed (ActionEvent e)
            {
                String expr = txtFE.getText ();
                sorter.setRowFilter (RowFilter.regexFilter (expr));
                sorter.setSortKeys (null);
            }
        };
```

```
        btnSetFE.addActionListener (al);
        pnl.add (btnSetFE);
        getContentPane ().add (pnl, BorderLayout.SOUTH);

        setSize (750, 150);
        setVisible (true);
    }

    public static void main (String [] args)
    {
        Runnable r = new Runnable ()
                    {
                        public void run ()
                        {
                            try
                            {
                                new BugLog ("Bug Log");
                            }
                            catch (ParseException pe)
                            {
                                JOptionPane.showMessageDialog (null,
                                                        pe.getMessage ());
                                System.exit (1);
                            }
                        }
                    };
        EventQueue.invokeLater (r);
    }
}
```

Run this application, specify [F|f]ile as a regular expression, and click the Set Filter Expression button. In response, only the first and third rows will be displayed. To restore all rows, simply leave the text field blank and click the button.

Note The sorter.setSortKeys (null); method call unsorts the view of the underlying model after changing the row filter. In other words, if you have performed a sort by clicking some column header, the sorted view will revert to the unsorted view following this method call.

Look and Feel Enhancements

Unlike other Java-based GUI toolkits, Swing decouples its API from the underlying platform's windowing system toolkit. This decoupling has resulted in trade-offs between platform independence and the faithful reproduction of a native windowing system's look and feel. Because of user demand for the best possible fidelity of system look and feels, Java SE 6 improves the Windows look and feel and the GTK look and feel by allowing them to use the native widget rasterizer to render Swing's widgets (components, if you prefer).

Starting with Java SE 6, Sun engineers have reimplemented the Windows look and feel to use UxTheme, a Windows API hammered out between Microsoft and the author of the popular WindowBlinds (http://www.stardock.com/products/windowblinds/) theming engine. This API exposes the manner in which Windows controls are rendered. As a result, a Swing application running under Windows XP should look like XP; when this application runs under Windows Vista, it should look like Vista. For completeness, the original Windows look and feel is still available as the Windows Classic look and feel (com.sun.java.swing.plaf.windows.WindowsClassicLookAndFeel).

Sun engineers have also reimplemented the GTK look and feel to employ native calls to GIMP Toolkit (GTK) engines, which makes it possible to reuse any installed GTK engine to render Swing components. If you are running Linux or Solaris, you can now use all of your favorite GTK themes to render Swing applications and make these applications integrate (visually) nicely with the desktop.

New SwingWorker

Multithreaded Swing programs can include long-running tasks, such as a task that performs an exhaustive database search across a network. If these tasks are run on the *event-dispatching thread* (the thread that dispatches events to GUI listeners), the application will become unresponsive. For this reason, a task must run on a *worker thread*, which is also known as a *background thread*. When the task completes and the GUI needs to be updated, the worker thread must make sure that the GUI is updated on the event-dispatching thread, because most Swing methods are not thread-safe. Although the javax.swing.SwingUtilities public static void invokeLater(Runnable doRun) and public static void invokeAndWait(Runnable doRun) methods (or their java.awt. EventQueue counterparts) could be used for this purpose, it is easier to work with Java SE 6's new javax.swing.SwingWorker<T, V> class, because this class takes care of interthread communication.

Note Although the new `SwingWorker<T, V>` class shares the same name as an older `SwingWorker` class, which was widely used for some of the same purposes (but never officially part of Swing), the two classes are very different. For example, methods that perform the same functions have different names. Also, a separate instance of the new `SwingWorker<T, V>` class is required for each new background task, whereas old `SwingWorker` instances were reusable.

`SwingWorker<T, V>` is an abstract class that implements the `java.util.concurrent.RunnableFuture<T, V>` interface. A subclass must implement the `protected abstract T doInBackground()` method, which runs on a worker thread, to perform a long-running task. When this method finishes, the `protected void done()` method is invoked on the event-dispatching thread. By default, this method does nothing. However, you can override `done()` to safely update the GUI.

Type parameter `T` specifies `doInBackground()`'s return type, and is also the return type of the `SwingWorker<T, V>` class's `public final T get()` and `public final T get(long timeout, TimeUnit unit)` methods. These methods, which normally wait indefinitely or for a specific period of time for a task to complete, return immediately with the task's result when invoked from within the `done()` method.

Type parameter `V` specifies the type for interim results calculated by the worker thread. Specifically, this type parameter is used by the `protected final void publish(V... chunks)` method, which is designed to be called from within `doInBackground()`, to send intermediate results for processing to the event-dispatching thread. These results are retrieved by an overridden `protected void process(List<V> chunks)` method whose code runs on the event-dispatching thread. If there are no intermediate results to process, you can specify `Void` for `V` (and avoid using the `publish()` and `process()` methods).

Image loading is one example where `SwingWorker<T, V>` comes in handy. Without this class, you might consider loading all images before displaying the GUI, or loading them from the event-dispatching thread. If you load the images prior to displaying the GUI, there might be a significant delay before the GUI appears. Of course, the new splash-screen feature (see Chapter 3) obviates this concern. If you attempt to load the images from the event-dispatching thread, the GUI will be unresponsive for the amount of time it takes to finish loading all of the images. For an example of using `SwingWorker<T, V>` to load images, check out the "Simple Background Tasks" lesson in *The Java Tutorial* (`http://java.sun.com/docs/books/tutorial/uiswing/concurrency/simple.html`).

To demonstrate `SwingWorker<T, V>`, I've created a simple application that lets you enter an integer and click a button to find out if this integer is prime. This application's GUI consists of a labeled text field for entering a number, a button for checking if the number is prime, and another label that shows the result. Listing 4-6 presents the application's source code.

Listing 4-6. *PrimeCheck.java*

```java
// PrimeCheck.java

import java.awt.*;
import java.awt.event.*;

import java.math.*;

import java.util.concurrent.*;

import javax.swing.*;

public class PrimeCheck extends JFrame
{
    public PrimeCheck ()
    {
        super ("Prime Check");
        setDefaultCloseOperation (EXIT_ON_CLOSE);

        final JLabel lblResult = new JLabel (" ");

        JPanel pnl = new JPanel ();
        pnl.add (new JLabel ("Enter integer:"));
        final JTextField txtNumber = new JTextField (10);
        pnl.add (txtNumber);
        JButton btnCheck = new JButton ("Check");
        ActionListener al;
        al = new ActionListener ()
            {
                public void actionPerformed (ActionEvent ae)
                {
                    try
                    {
                        BigInteger bi = new BigInteger (txtNumber.getText ());
                        lblResult.setText ("One moment...");
                        new PrimeCheckTask (bi, lblResult).execute ();
                    }
                    catch (NumberFormatException nfe)
                    {
                        lblResult.setText ("Invalid input");
                    }
```

```java
            }
        };
    btnCheck.addActionListener (al);
    pnl.add (btnCheck);
    getContentPane ().add (pnl, BorderLayout.NORTH);

    pnl = new JPanel ();
    pnl.add (lblResult);
    getContentPane ().add (pnl, BorderLayout.SOUTH);

    pack ();
    setResizable (false);
    setVisible (true);
}

public static void main (String [] args)
{
    Runnable r = new Runnable ()
                {
                    public void run ()
                    {
                        new PrimeCheck ();
                    }
                };
    EventQueue.invokeLater (r);
}
}

class PrimeCheckTask extends SwingWorker<Boolean, Void>
{
    private BigInteger bi;
    private JLabel lblResult;

    PrimeCheckTask (BigInteger bi, JLabel lblResult)
    {
        this.bi = bi;
        this.lblResult = lblResult;
    }

    @Override
    public Boolean doInBackground ()
    {
```

```
        return bi.isProbablePrime (1000);
   }


   @Override
   public void done ()
   {
      try
      {
         try
         {
            boolean isPrime = get ();
            if (isPrime)
               lblResult.setText ("Integer is prime");
            else
               lblResult.setText ("Integer is not prime");
         }
         catch (InterruptedException ie)
         {
            lblResult.setText ("Interrupted");
         }
      }
      catch (ExecutionException ee)
      {
         String reason = null;
         Throwable cause = ee.getCause ();
         if (cause == null)
            reason = ee.getMessage ();
         else
            reason = cause.getMessage ();

         lblResult.setText ("Unable to determine primeness");
      }
   }
}
```

When the user clicks the button, its action listener invokes new PrimeCheckTask (bi, lblResult).execute () to instantiate and execute an instance of PrimeCheckTask, a SwingWorker<T, V> subclass. The bi parameter references a java.math.BigInteger argument that contains the integer to check. The lblResult parameter references a javax.swing.Jlabel, which shows the prime/not prime result (or an error message).

Execution results in a new worker thread starting and invoking the overridden doInBackground() method. When this method completes, it returns a value that is stored in a future. (A *future* is an object that stores the result of an asynchronous computation, as discussed in Chapter 2.) Furthermore, method completion results in a call to the overridden done() method on the event-dispatching thread. Within this method, the call to get() returns the value stored within the future, which is then used to set the label's text.

The doInBackground() method invokes bi.isProbablePrime (1000) to determine if the integer stored in bi is a prime number. It returns true if the probability that the integer is prime exceeds $1-1/2^{1000}$ (which is practically 100% certainty that the integer is prime). Because it takes longer to determine whether an integer with a lot of digits is a prime, the "One moment . . ." message will be displayed for longer periods when such a number is entered. As long as this message is displayed, the GUI remains responsive. You can easily close the application, or even click the Check button (although you should not click this button until you see the message stating whether or not the integer is prime).

Text Component Printing

Java 5 integrated printing support into JTable via several new print() methods and a new getPrintable() method. Java SE 6 does the same thing for javax.swing.JTextField, javax.swing.JTextArea, and javax.swing.JEditorPane by integrating new methods into their common JTextComponent superclass.

One new method is public Printable getPrintable(MessageFormat headerFormat, MessageFormat footerFormat). It returns a java.awt.print.Printable that prints the contents of this JTextComponent as it looks on the screen, but reformatted so that it fits on the printed page. You can wrap this Printable inside another Printable to create complex reports and other kinds of complex documents. Because Printable shares the document with the JTextComponent, this document must not be changed while the document is being printed. Otherwise, the printing behavior is undefined.

Another new method is public boolean print(MessageFormat headerFormat, MessageFormat footerFormat, boolean showPrintDialog, PrintService service, PrintRequestAttributeSet attributes, boolean interactive). This method prints this JTextComponent's content. Specify its parameters as follows:

- Specify page header and footer text via headerFormat and footerFormat. Each java.text.MessageFormat identifies a format pattern, which can contain only a single format item—an Integer that identifies the current page number—in addition to literal text. Pass null to headerFormat if there is no header; pass null to footerFormat if there is no footer.

- If you would like to display a print dialog (unless headless mode is in effect) that lets the user change printing attributes or cancel printing, pass true to showPrintDialog.

- Specify the initial `javax.print.PrintService` for the print dialog via `service`. Pass `null` to use the default print service.

- Specify a `javax.print.attribute.PrintRequestAttributeSet` containing an initial set of attributes for the print dialog via `attributes`. These attributes might be a number of copies to print or supply needed values when the dialog is not shown. Pass `null` if there are no print attributes.

- Determine if printing is performed in `interactive` mode. If headless mode is not in effect, passing `true` to `interactive` causes a modal (when called on the event-dispatching thread; otherwise, nonmodal) progress dialog with an abort option to be displayed for the duration of printing. If you call this method on the event-dispatching thread with `interactive` set to `false`, all events (including repaints) are blocked until printing completes. As a result, you should do this only if there is no visible GUI.

A `java.awt.print.PrinterException` is thrown if the print job is aborted because of a print system error. If the current thread is not allowed to initiate a print job request by an installed security manager, the `print()` method throws a `SecurityException`.

Two convenience methods are also provided. `public boolean print(MessageFormat headerFormat, MessageFormat footerFormat)` invokes the more general `print()` method via `print(headerFormat, footerFormat, true, null, null, true)`. The `public boolean print()` method invokes the more general `print()` method via `print(null, null, true, null, null, true)`.

I took advantage of `public boolean print()` to add a printing capability to the web browser application shown earlier (in Listing 4-1). The revised application's source code is shown in Listing 4-7.

Listing 4-7. *BrowserWithPrint.java*

```java
// BrowserWithPrint.java

import java.awt.*;
import java.awt.event.*;
import java.awt.print.*;

import java.io.*;

import javax.swing.*;
import javax.swing.event.*;

public class BrowserWithPrint extends JFrame implements HyperlinkListener
{
```

```java
private JTextField txtURL;

private JTabbedPane tp;

private JLabel lblStatus;

private ImageIcon ii = new ImageIcon ("close.gif");

private Dimension iiSize = new Dimension (ii.getIconWidth (),
                                          ii.getIconHeight ());

private int tabCounter = 0;

public BrowserWithPrint ()
{
   super ("Browser");
   setDefaultCloseOperation (EXIT_ON_CLOSE);

   JMenuBar mb = new JMenuBar ();
   JMenu mFile = new JMenu ("File");
   JMenuItem miFile = new JMenuItem ("Add Tab");
   ActionListener addTabl = new ActionListener ()
                   {
                       public void actionPerformed (ActionEvent e)
                       {
                           addTab ();
                       }
                   };
   miFile.addActionListener (addTabl);
   mFile.add (miFile);
   final JMenuItem miPrint = new JMenuItem ("Print...");
   miPrint.setEnabled (false);
   ActionListener printl = new ActionListener ()
                   {
                       public void actionPerformed (ActionEvent e)
                       {
                           Component c = tp.getSelectedComponent ();
                           JScrollPane sp = (JScrollPane) c;
                           c = sp.getViewport ().getView ();
                           JEditorPane ep = (JEditorPane) c;

                           try
```

```
                              {
                                  ep.print ();
                              }
                              catch (PrinterException pe)
                              {
                                  JOptionPane.showMessageDialog
                                    (BrowserWithPrint.this,
                                     "Print error: "+pe.getMessage ());
                              }
                          }
                      };
miPrint.addActionListener (printl);
mFile.add (miPrint);
mb.add (mFile);
setJMenuBar (mb);

JPanel pnlURL = new JPanel ();
pnlURL.setLayout (new BorderLayout ());
pnlURL.add (new JLabel ("URL: "), BorderLayout.WEST);
txtURL = new JTextField ("");
pnlURL.add (txtURL, BorderLayout.CENTER);
getContentPane ().add (pnlURL, BorderLayout.NORTH);

tp = new JTabbedPane ();
addTab ();
getContentPane ().add (tp, BorderLayout.CENTER);

lblStatus = new JLabel (" ");
getContentPane ().add (lblStatus, BorderLayout.SOUTH);

ActionListener al;
al = new ActionListener ()
    {
        public void actionPerformed (ActionEvent ae)
        {
          try
          {
              Component c = tp.getSelectedComponent ();
              JScrollPane sp = (JScrollPane) c;
              c = sp.getViewport ().getView ();
              JEditorPane ep = (JEditorPane) c;
              ep.setPage (ae.getActionCommand ());
```

```
                        miPrint.setEnabled (true);
                }
                catch (Exception e)
                {
                    lblStatus.setText ("Browser problem: "+e.getMessage ());
                }
            }
        };
    txtURL.addActionListener (al);

    setSize (300, 300);
    setVisible (true);
}


void addTab ()
{
    JEditorPane ep = new JEditorPane ();
    ep.setEditable (false);
    ep.addHyperlinkListener (this);
    tp.addTab (null, new JScrollPane (ep));

    JButton tabCloseButton = new JButton (ii);
    tabCloseButton.setActionCommand (""+tabCounter);
    tabCloseButton.setPreferredSize (iiSize);

    ActionListener al;
    al = new ActionListener ()
        {
            public void actionPerformed (ActionEvent ae)
            {
                JButton btn = (JButton) ae.getSource ();
                String s1 = btn.getActionCommand ();
                for (int i = 1; i < tp.getTabCount (); i++)
                {
                    JPanel pnl = (JPanel) tp.getTabComponentAt (i);
                    btn = (JButton) pnl.getComponent (0);
                    String s2 = btn.getActionCommand ();
                    if (s1.equals (s2))
                    {
                        tp.removeTabAt (i);
                        break;
                    }
```

```
                }
            }
        };
    tabCloseButton.addActionListener (al);

    if (tabCounter != 0)
    {
        JPanel pnl = new JPanel ();
        pnl.setOpaque (false);
        pnl.add (tabCloseButton);
        tp.setTabComponentAt (tp.getTabCount ()-1, pnl);
        tp.setSelectedIndex (tp.getTabCount ()-1);
    }

    tabCounter++;
}

public void hyperlinkUpdate (HyperlinkEvent hle)
{
    HyperlinkEvent.EventType evtype = hle.getEventType ();

    if (evtype == HyperlinkEvent.EventType.ENTERED)
        lblStatus.setText (hle.getURL ().toString ());
    else
    if (evtype == HyperlinkEvent.EventType.EXITED)
        lblStatus.setText (" ");
}

public static void main (String [] args)
{
    Runnable r = new Runnable ()
                {
                    public void run ()
                    {
                        new BrowserWithPrint ();
                    }
                };
    EventQueue.invokeLater (r);
}
}
```

After selecting the Print menu item, the current tab's editor pane is retrieved and its `print()` method is invoked to print the HTML content. Figure 4-7 shows the print dialog.

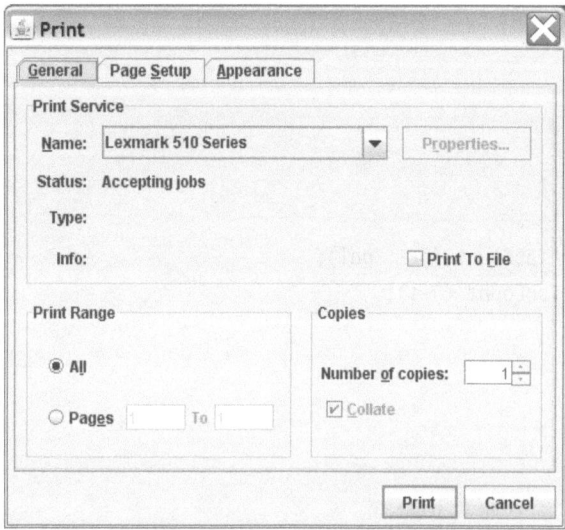

Figure 4-7. *The print dialog presents its own tabbed interface.*

Summary

Swing is the preferred toolkit for building modern GUIs. Java SE 6 enhances this toolkit in various ways.

For starters, Java SE 6 enhances JTabbedPane so that you can add arbitrary components to a tabbed pane's tab headers. You are no longer restricted to placing a combination of a string label and an icon on a tab header.

The SpringLayout layout manager makes it possible to lay out a GUI using springs and struts. Although this layout manager predates Java SE 6, it has suffered from bugs such as not always correctly resolving its constraints. Java SE 6 fixes this bug by basing the algorithm used to calculate springs on the last two specified springs, along each axis.

Java SE 6 has also greatly improved drag-and-drop for Swing components. These improvements have to do with telling a component how to determine drop locations and having Swing provide all relevant transfer information during a transfer.

The ability to sort and filter a JTable's contents has been simplified by Java SE 6. By clicking a column header, you can sort rows according to the column's contents. You can also filter rows based on regular expressions and other criteria, and display only those rows that match the criteria.

Java SE 6 improves the Windows look and feel and the GTK look and feel by allowing them to use the native widget rasterizer to render Swing's components. These improvements make it possible to faithfully reproduce a native windowing system's look and feel on Windows, Linux, and Solaris platforms.

A multithreaded Swing program can include a long-running task that needs to update the GUI when it completes. This task must not be run on the event-dispatching thread; otherwise, the GUI will be unresponsive. The GUI must not be updated on any thread other than the event-dispatching thread; otherwise, the program will violate the single-threaded nature of the Swing toolkit. Because it can be difficult to code for these requirements, Java SE 6 introduces a new SwingWorker<T, V> class. A subclass implements the doInBackground() method, which runs on a worker thread, to perform a long-running task. When this method finishes, the done() method (overridden by the subclass) is invoked on the event-dispatching thread, and the GUI can be safely updated from that method.

Finally, Java SE 6 integrates printing support into JTextComponent so that you can print the contents of various text components. This support consists of a getPrintable() method and three print() methods.

Test Your Understanding

How well do you understand the changes to the Swing toolkit? Test your understanding by answering the following questions and performing the following exercises. (The answers are presented in Appendix D.)

1. What does indexOfTabComponent() return if a tab is not associated with its Component argument?

2. Which of DropMode.INSERT and DropMode.USE_SELECTION causes selected text to be temporarily deselected?

3. JTable's public int convertRowIndexToModel(int viewRowIndex) method maps a row's index in terms of the view to the underlying model. The public int convertRowIndexToView(int modelRowIndex) method maps a row's index in terms of the model to the view. To better understand the relationship between the view and model indices, extend PriceList1 with a list selection listener that presents the selected row's (view) index and model index (via convertRowIndexToModel()) via an option pane dialog. As you sort this table via different column headers and select different rows (you might want to set the table's selection mode to single selection), you will notice that sorting affects only the view and not the model.

4. Why is it necessary to have SwingWorker<T, V>'s doInBackground() method return a value, and then retrieve this value from within the done() method?

5. Modify BrowseWithPrint.java (Listing 4-7) to work with PrintRequestAttributeSet.

CHAPTER 5

■ ■ ■

Internationalization

Java SE 6's internationalization (i18n) support ranges from Abstract Windowing Toolkit-oriented non-English locale input bug fixes (see Chapter 3), to network-oriented internationalized domain names (see Chapter 8), to these i18n-specific features:

- Japanese Imperial Era calendar

- Locale-sensitive services

- New locales

- Normalizer API

- ResourceBundle enhancements

Japanese Imperial Era Calendar

Many Japanese commonly use the Gregorian calendar. Because Japanese governments also use the Japanese Imperial Era calendar for various government documents, Java SE 6 introduces support for this calendar.

In the Japanese Imperial Era calendar, eras are based on the reigning periods of emperors; an era begins with an emperor's ascension. This calendar regards a year as a combination of a Japanese era name (Heisei, for example) and the one-based year number within this era. For example, Heisei 1 corresponds to 1989, and Heisei 19 corresponds to 2007. Other eras supported by Java's implementation of the Japanese Imperial Era calendar are Meiji, Taisho, and Showa. The calendar rules keep track of eras and years.

Date Handling

You can obtain an instance of the Japanese Imperial Era calendar by invoking the `java.util.Calendar` class's `public static Calendar getInstance(Locale aLocale)` method with ja_JP_JP as the locale. After obtaining this instance, you can set, fetch, and modify dates, as follows:

```
Calendar cal = Calendar.getInstance (new Locale ("ja", "JP", "JP"));
cal.setTime (new Date ());
System.out.println (cal.get (Calendar.ERA));
System.out.println (cal.get (Calendar.YEAR));
cal.add (Calendar.DAY_OF_MONTH, -120);
System.out.println (cal.get (Calendar.ERA));
System.out.println (cal.get (Calendar.YEAR));
```

If the current date were April 13, 2007, for example, the first two System.out.println() method calls would output 4 (which corresponds to the Heisei era) and 19, respectively. After subtracting 120 days from this date, the era would remain the same, but the year would change to 18.

■**Note** Sun's Supported Calendars documentation (http://java.sun.com/javase/6/docs/technotes/guides/intl/calendar.doc.html) provides a detailed look at its support for the Japanese Imperial Era calendar.

Calendar Page Display

Let's suppose you want to create a Swing program whose calendar page component presents a calendar page for the current month. This component will adapt to different calendars based on locale. For simplicity, let's limit this program to English Gregorian, Japanese Gregorian, and Japanese Imperial Era calendars. Let's also assume that you've installed appropriate fonts for rendering Japanese text. The requirements for this program are as follows:

Present the month and era using locale-specific text. Both requirements are accommodated by Calendar's new public String getDisplayName(int field, int style, Locale locale) method, which is used with Calendar's new LONG and SHORT style constants to obtain locale-specific display names with long and short styles (January versus Jan, for example) for certain calendar fields, such as Calendar.ERA. This method returns null if no string representation is applicable to the specific calendar field.

Display short weekday names using locale-specific text. For example, the calendar should display Fri as opposed to Friday. Although you could invoke getDisplayName(Calendar.DAY_OF_WEEK, Calendar.SHORT, locale) to obtain this text for the current weekday, you also need the remaining weekday names. These names can be obtained by calling the java.text.DateFormatSymbols class's public String[] getShortWeekdays() method. The resulting array must be indexed by Calendar. SUNDAY, Calendar.MONDAY, and Calendar's other weekday constants.

Show the current date. As part of the calendar page, the component will display the current date. In order to do this, the component invokes DateFormat. getDateInstance(DateFormat.FULL, locale) to return a locale-specific formatter, followed by this class's public final String format(Date date) method to format the current date according to this locale.

I have created a program that takes all of these requirements into account. For convenience, I've chosen to implement the program as a Swing-based applet. This applet's source code is presented in Listing 5-1.

Listing 5-1. *ShowCalPage.java*

```
// ShowCalPage.java

import java.applet.Applet;

import java.awt.*;
import java.awt.event.*;

import java.text.*;

import java.util.*;

import javax.swing.*;

public class ShowCalPage extends JApplet
{
   public void init ()
   {
      try
      {
         EventQueue.invokeAndWait (new Runnable ()
                                   {
```

```
                                      public void run ()
                                      {
                                         createGUI ();
                                      }
                              });
      }
      catch (Exception exc)
      {
         System.err.println (exc);
      }
   }

   private void createGUI ()
   {
      String [] localeDescriptions =
      {
         "English",
         "Japanese Gregorian",
         "Japanese Imperial Era"
      };

      final Locale [] locales =
      {
         Locale.ENGLISH,
         Locale.JAPANESE,
         CalPage.JAPAN_IMP_ERA
      };

      final CalPage cp = new CalPage (getWidth ()-50, getHeight ()-50,
                                      locales [0]);
      cp.setBorder (BorderFactory.createEtchedBorder ());
      JPanel pnl = new JPanel ();
      pnl.add (cp);
      getContentPane ().add (pnl, BorderLayout.NORTH);

      pnl = new JPanel ();
      pnl.add (new JLabel ("Locale:"));
      JComboBox cbLocales = new JComboBox (localeDescriptions);
      ItemListener il;
      il = new ItemListener ()
         {
            public void itemStateChanged (ItemEvent e)
            {
```

```
                    if (e.getStateChange () == ItemEvent.SELECTED)
                    {
                        JComboBox cb = (JComboBox) e.getSource ();
                        cp.setNewLocale (locales [cb.getSelectedIndex ()]);
                    }
                }
            };
        cbLocales.addItemListener (il);
        pnl.add (cbLocales);
        getContentPane ().add (pnl, BorderLayout.CENTER);
    }
}

class CalPage extends JPanel
{
    final static Locale JAPAN_IMP_ERA = new Locale ("ja", "JP", "JP");

    private Locale locale;

    CalPage (int width, int height, Locale initLocale)
    {
        setPreferredSize (new Dimension (width, height));

        locale = initLocale;
    }

    public void paintComponent (Graphics g)
    {
        int width = getWidth ();
        int height = getHeight ();

        g.setColor (Color.white);
        g.fillRect (0, 0, width, height);

        Calendar cal = Calendar.getInstance (locale);
        Date now = new Date ();
        cal.setTime (now);

        String header = cal.getDisplayName (Calendar.MONTH, Calendar.LONG,
                                            locale);
        if (locale.equals (JAPAN_IMP_ERA))
            header = cal.getDisplayName (Calendar.ERA, Calendar.LONG, locale)+
                    " "+cal.get (Calendar.YEAR)+" -- "+header;
```

```
        else
            header += " "+cal.get (Calendar.YEAR);

        FontMetrics fm = g.getFontMetrics ();
        Insets insets = getInsets ();
        g.setColor (Color.black);
        g.drawString (header, (width-fm.stringWidth (header))/2,
                    insets.top+fm.getHeight ());

        DateFormatSymbols dfs = new DateFormatSymbols (locale);
        String [] weekdayNames = dfs.getShortWeekdays ();
        int fieldWidth = (width-insets.left-insets.right)/7;
        g.drawString (weekdayNames [Calendar.SUNDAY], insets.left+
                    (fieldWidth-
                    fm.stringWidth (weekdayNames [Calendar.SUNDAY]))/2,
                    insets.top+3*fm.getHeight ());
        g.drawString (weekdayNames [Calendar.MONDAY], insets.left+fieldWidth+
                    (fieldWidth-
                    fm.stringWidth (weekdayNames [Calendar.MONDAY]))/2,
                    insets.top+3*fm.getHeight ());
        g.drawString (weekdayNames [Calendar.TUESDAY], insets.left+2*fieldWidth+
                    (fieldWidth-
                    fm.stringWidth (weekdayNames [Calendar.TUESDAY]))/2,
                    insets.top+3*fm.getHeight ());
        g.drawString (weekdayNames [Calendar.WEDNESDAY], insets.left+3*
                    fieldWidth+(fieldWidth-
                    fm.stringWidth (weekdayNames [Calendar.WEDNESDAY]))/2,
                    insets.top+3*fm.getHeight ());
        g.drawString (weekdayNames [Calendar.THURSDAY], insets.left+4*
                    fieldWidth+(fieldWidth-
                    fm.stringWidth (weekdayNames [Calendar.THURSDAY]))/2,
                    insets.top+3*fm.getHeight ());
        g.drawString (weekdayNames [Calendar.FRIDAY], insets.left+5*fieldWidth+
                    (fieldWidth-
                    fm.stringWidth (weekdayNames [Calendar.FRIDAY]))/2,
                    insets.top+3*fm.getHeight ());
        g.drawString (weekdayNames [Calendar.SATURDAY], insets.left+6*
                    fieldWidth+(fieldWidth-
                    fm.stringWidth (weekdayNames [Calendar.SATURDAY]))/2,
                    insets.top+3*fm.getHeight ());

        int dom = cal.get (Calendar.DAY_OF_MONTH);
        cal.set (Calendar.DAY_OF_MONTH, 1);
```

```
    int col = 0;
    switch (cal.get (Calendar.DAY_OF_WEEK))
    {
       case Calendar.MONDAY: col = 1; break;

       case Calendar.TUESDAY: col = 2; break;

       case Calendar.WEDNESDAY: col = 3; break;

       case Calendar.THURSDAY: col = 4; break;

       case Calendar.FRIDAY: col = 5; break;

       case Calendar.SATURDAY: col = 6;
    }
    cal.set (Calendar.DAY_OF_MONTH, dom);

    int row = 5*fm.getHeight ();
    for (int i = 1; i <= cal.getActualMaximum (Calendar.DAY_OF_MONTH); i++)
    {
        g.drawString (""+i, insets.left+fieldWidth*col+
                      (fieldWidth-fm.stringWidth (""+i))/2, row);
        if (++col > 6)
        {
            col = 0;
            row += fm.getHeight ();
        }
    }

    row += 2*fm.getHeight ();
    DateFormat df = DateFormat.getDateInstance (DateFormat.FULL, locale);
    g.drawString (df.format (now),
                  (width-fm.stringWidth (df.format (now)))/2, row);
  }

  void setNewLocale (Locale locale)
  {
    this.locale = locale;
    repaint ();
  }
}
```

In addition to the calendar page component, this applet's GUI includes a combo box component for selecting an appropriate calendar type: English, Japanese Gregorian, or Japanese Imperial Era. When you select a calendar type from the combo box, its item listener passes the associated locale to the calendar page component, which updates its display to reflect the new calendar type. The current date is presented at the bottom of the calendar page. Figure 5-1 shows this GUI for the Japanese Imperial Era calendar.

Figure 5-1. *The ShowCalendar applet displaying the Japanese Imperial Era calendar*

Locale-Sensitive Services

Are you tired of waiting for Sun to implement a specific locale that is important to your application? If so, you'll want to check out the locale-sensitive services. This new Java SE 6 feature consists of Service Provider Interface (SPI) classes that let you plug locale-dependent data and services into Java.

Service Provider Interface Classes

The SPI classes in the `java.text.spi` package focus on returning localized objects such as break iterators and number formats. Table 5-1 describes these SPI classes.

Table 5-1. *SPI Classes in the java.text.spi Package*

Service Provider Class	Description
BreakIteratorProvider	An abstract class whose subclasses provide concrete implementations of java.text.BreakIterator, by implementing the public abstract BreakIterator getCharacterInstance(Locale locale), public abstract BreakIterator getLineInstance(Locale locale), public abstract BreakIterator getSentenceInstance(Locale locale), and public abstract BreakIterator getWordInstance(Locale locale) methods.
CollatorProvider	An abstract class whose subclasses provide concrete implementations of java.text.Collator, by implementing public abstract Collator getInstance(Locale locale).
DateFormatProvider	An abstract class whose subclasses provide concrete implementations of java.text.DateFormat, by implementing the public abstract DateFormat getDateInstance(int style, Locale locale), public abstract DateFormat getDateTimeInstance(int dateStyle, int timeStyle, Locale locale), and public abstract DateFormat getTimeInstance(int style, Locale locale) methods.
DateFormatSymbolsProvider	An abstract class whose subclasses provide concrete implementations of java.text.DateFormatSymbols, by implementing public abstract DateFormatSymbols getInstance(Locale locale).
DecimalFormatSymbolsProvider	An abstract class whose subclasses provide concrete implementations of java.text.DecimalFormatSymbols, by implementing public abstract DecimalFormatSymbols getInstance(Locale locale).
NumberFormatProvider	An abstract class whose subclasses provide concrete implementations of java.text.NumberFormat, by implementing the public abstract NumberFormat getCurrencyInstance(Locale locale), public abstract NumberFormat getIntegerInstance(Locale locale), public abstract NumberFormat getNumberInstance(Locale locale), and public abstract NumberFormat getPercentInstance(Locale locale) methods.

The SPI classes in the java.util.spi package return localized currency symbols and other localized names. These classes are shown in Table 5-2.

Table 5-2. *SPI Classes in the java.util.spi Package*

Service Provider Class	Description
CurrencyNameProvider	An abstract class whose subclasses provide localized currency symbols for the java.util.Currency class, by providing concrete implementations of public abstract String getSymbol(String currencyCode, Locale locale).
LocaleNameProvider	An abstract class whose subclasses provide localized names for the java.util.Locale class, by providing concrete implementations of the public abstract String getDisplayCountry(String countryCode, Locale locale), public abstract String getDisplayLanguage(String languageCode, Locale locale), and public abstract String getDisplayVariant(String variant, Locale locale) methods.
LocaleServiceProvider	An abstract superclass for all SPI classes in the java.text.spi and java.util.spi packages. This superclass's public abstract Locale[] getAvailableLocales() method returns an array of all Locales for which this service provider will provide localized objects or names. These Locales are included in the array of Locales returned by BreakIterator's, Collator's, DateFormat's, DateFormatSymbols's, DecimalFormatSymbols's, NumberFormat's, and Locale's getAvailableLocales() method.
TimeZoneNameProvider	An abstract class whose subclasses provide localized time zone names for the java.util.TimeZone class, by providing concrete implementations of public abstract String getDisplayName(String ID, boolean daylight, int style, Locale locale).

To fully support a new locale, you need to implement all of Table 5-1's and Table 5-2's SPI classes. For partial support, you may need to implement only a few classes. After implementing the classes for a given locale, package them and a provider configuration file in a JAR file, and then place this JAR file in an extension directory (see Chapter 2's discussion of the new ServiceLoader API for more information).

A New Currency for Java

Eritrea is an independent African state situated between Sudan, Djibouti, Ethiopia, and the Red Sea. Its official currency is the Nafka (ISO 4217 code ERN; currency symbol Nfk), and one of its languages is Tigrinya (spoken by the Tigray-Tigrinya people in central Eritrea). Because Java does not yet officially support this locale, I've prepared a simple example that introduces a currency name provider for a new ti_ER locale. The new currency name provider class appears in Listing 5-2.

Listing 5-2. *CurrencyNameProviderImpl.java*

```java
// CurrencyNameProviderImpl.java

import java.util.*;
import java.util.spi.*;

public class CurrencyNameProviderImpl extends CurrencyNameProvider
{
   final static Locale [] locales = new Locale [] { new Locale ("ti", "ER") };

   public Locale [] getAvailableLocales ()
   {
      return locales;
   }

   public String getSymbol (String currencyCode, Locale locale)
   {
      if (currencyCode == null || locale == null)
          throw new NullPointerException ();

      if (currencyCode.length () != 3)
          throw new IllegalArgumentException ("currency code length not 3");

      for (int i = 0; i < 3; i++)
          if (!Character.isUpperCase (currencyCode.charAt (i)))
              throw new IllegalArgumentException ("bad currency code");

      if (!locale.equals (locales [0]))
          throw new IllegalArgumentException ("unsupported locale");

      if (currencyCode.equals ("ERN"))
          return "Nfk";
      else
          return null;
   }
}
```

The CurrencyNameProviderImpl class follows all rules set out by CurrencyNameProvider's JDK documentation. For example, the getSymbol() method must throw a NullPointerException if either of its currencyCode and locale arguments is null.

Let's introduce this currency name provider to Java. This task divides into two subtasks:

Create the JAR file. This JAR file must include CurrencyNameProviderImpl.class and a META-INF directory whose services subdirectory stores java.util.spi. CurrencyNameProvider. This file must contain a single line: CurrencyNameProviderImpl. Assuming that the current directory contains CurrencyNameProviderImpl.class and META-INF, the following creates a tiER.jar file:

```
jar cf tiER.jar -C META-INF/ services CurrencyNameProviderImpl.class
```

Install the JAR file as an optional package (standard extension). Copy the JAR to the extensions directory. For Windows XP platforms where both JDK 1.6.0 and JRE 1.6.0 are installed, make sure this file is placed in the JDK's jre\lib\ext directory when you run Java applications via the JDK's java.exe tool (located in the JDK's bin directory). If you run Java applications via the java.exe tool located in the windows\system32 directory, place this file in the JRE's lib\ext directory.)

If this currency name provider has been successfully installed, Locale. getAvailableLocales() will include ti_ER in its list of available locales. You can then obtain a Currency instance based on this locale, from which you can retrieve the Nafka currency code and symbol. Check out Listing 5-3.

Listing 5-3. *ShowCurrencies.java*

```
// ShowCurrencies.java

import java.awt.*;

import java.util.*;

import javax.swing.*;
import javax.swing.table.*;

public class ShowCurrencies extends JFrame
{
   public ShowCurrencies ()
   {
      super ("Show Currencies");
      setDefaultCloseOperation (EXIT_ON_CLOSE);

      final Locale [] locales = Locale.getAvailableLocales ();

      TableModel model = new AbstractTableModel ()
```

```
{
    public int getColumnCount ()
    {
        return 3;
    }

    public String getColumnName (int column)
    {
        if (column == 0)
            return "Locale";
        else
        if (column == 1)
            return "Currency Code";
        else
            return "Currency Symbol";
    }

    public int getRowCount ()
    {
        return locales.length;
    }

    public Object getValueAt (int row, int col)
    {
        if (col == 0)
            return locales [row];
        else
            try
            {
                if (col == 1)
                    return Currency.getInstance (locales [row])
                                    .getCurrencyCode ();
                else
                    return Currency.getInstance (locales [row])
                                    .getSymbol (locales [row]);
            }
            catch (IllegalArgumentException iae)
            {
                return null;
            }
    }
};
```

```
        JTable table = new JTable (model);
        JScrollPane sp = new JScrollPane (table);

        // Make sure that the table displays exactly 10 rows.

        Dimension size = sp.getViewport ().getPreferredSize ();
        size.height = 10*table.getRowHeight ();
        table.setPreferredScrollableViewportSize (size);

        getContentPane ().add (sp);

        pack ();
        setVisible (true);
    }

    public static void main (String [] args)
    {
        Runnable r = new Runnable ()
                     {
                         public void run ()
                         {
                             new ShowCurrencies ();
                         }
                     };
        EventQueue.invokeLater (r);
    }
}
```

Listing 5-3's Swing application presents a table of locale names, currency codes, and currency symbols. Unless you choose to resize the GUI, only ten rows of locale data are visible, as shown in Figure 5-2.

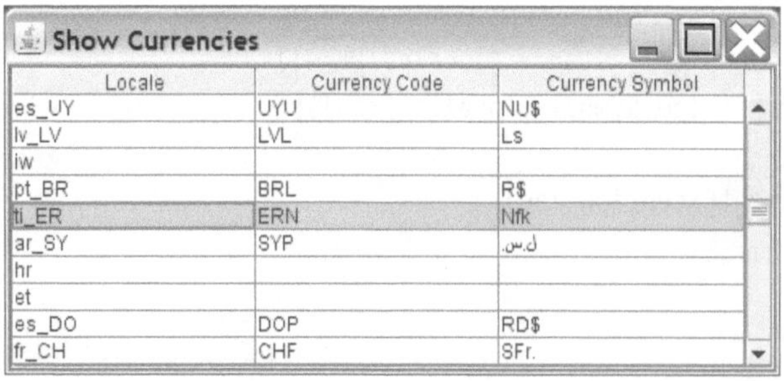

Figure 5-2. *The highlighted row shows the ti_ER locale with its ERN currency code and Nfk currency symbol.*

> ■**Note** If you are wondering why Sun created new SPI packages instead of documenting the resource bundle format used in implementing the appropriate `java.text` and `java.util` classes, check out the "Locale Sensitive Services SPI" blog entry (`http://blogs.sun.com/norbert/entry/locale_sensitive_services_spi`).

New Locales

Java SE 6 adds several new locales to the Java platform, which the locale-sensitive classes fully support. Table 5-3 lists these new locales.

Table 5-3. *New Locales*

Locale ID	Language	Country
el_CY	Greek	Cyprus
en_MT	English	Malta
en_PH	English	Philippines
en_SG	English	Singapore
es_US	Spanish	United States
ga_IE	Irish	Ireland
in_ID	Indonesian	Indonesia
ja_JP_JP	Japanese (Japanese Imperial Era calendar)	Japan
ms_MY	Malay	Malaysia
mt_MT	Maltese	Malta
sr_BA	Serbian	Bosnia and Herzegovina
sr_CS	Serbian	Serbia and Montenegro
zh_SG	Chinese (Simplified)	Singapore

In contrast to the handling of previous locales, Sun obtained data (such as currency symbols, locale names, and calendar data) for these new locales from the Unicode Consortium's Common Locale Data Repository (`http://unicode.org/cldr/`), and then converted this XML-based data into the JRE's locale data format.

Normalizer API

Text is often transformed prior to processing; this activity is known as *text normalization*. Examples of text-normalization tasks include converting lowercase letters to their uppercase equivalents, removing punctuation, and expanding abbreviations. One important text-normalization category is *Unicode normalization*, which transforms equivalent character sequences (or individual characters) into a consistent representation to facilitate comparison. This capability is important for searching and sorting.

The Unicode Consortium has put together Unicode Standard Annex (UAX) #15: Unicode Normalization Forms (http://www.unicode.org/reports/tr15/), a technical document describing four forms (or kinds) of Unicode normalization: Normalization Form Canonical Decomposition (NFD), Normalization Form Canonical Composition (NFC), Normalization Form Compatibility Decomposition (NFKD), and Normalization Form Compatibility Composition (NFKC). Underlying these forms are the following concepts:

- *Precomposed characters*: Characters that combine letters and diacritical marks. For example, the German vowel *ü* (U+00FC in Unicode) is a precomposed character consisting of base (nonaccented) letter *u* (U+0075) and diacritical mark (accent) *umlaut* (U+0308).

- *Composition*: Combining letters and diacritical marks into precomposed characters.

- *Decomposition*: Splitting precomposed characters into their base letters and diacritical marks.

- *Canonical equivalence*: Characters and character sequences that are visually indistinguishable and mean the same thing from the text-comparison and rendering perspectives. For example, the German vowel *ü* and character sequence *u* followed by the combining *umlaut* are canonically equivalent.

- *Compatibility equivalence*: Characters and character sequences that are visually distinguishable and have extra semantic information. For example, the digit *1*, superscript *¹*, and subscript *₁* are compatibility equivalent because they are all variations of the same basic character *1*.

The four forms of Unicode normalization and their Java SE 6 enumeration constants, defined by java.text.Normalizer.Form, are described in Table 5-4.

Table 5-4. *Unicode Normalization Forms and Their Enumeration Constants*

Normalization Form	Enumeration Constant	Description
NFD	Normalizer.Form.NFD	Canonical decomposition
NFC	Normalizer.Form.NFC	Canonical decomposition followed by canonical composition
NFKD	Normalizer.Form.NFKD	Compatibility decomposition
NFKC	Normalizer.Form.NFKC	Compatibility decomposition followed by canonical composition

The `Normalizer.Form` enumeration is only one part of the new `java.text.Normalizer` utility class. This class also includes a `public static String normalize(CharSequence src, Normalizer.Form form)` method for normalizing a `src` sequence of `char`s according to a specific Unicode normalization `form`, and a `public static boolean isNormalized(CharSequence src, Normalizer.Form form)` method that returns `true` if `src` is normalized according to the specific `form`. Each method throws `NullPointerException` if you pass `null` to `src` or `form`.

Interestingly, `Normalizer` is not really new. Prior to Java SE 6, a version of this class existed in a private package. It was used behind the scenes by the `java.text.RuleBasedCollator` class, a concrete subclass of `Collator`, to perform locale-sensitive `String` comparisons based on a variety of rules. Although you can use `Normalizer` in partnership with `String`'s `equals()` and `compareTo()` methods to perform more accurate string comparisons, you really should use `Collator/RuleBasedCollator` for comparing strings. This is because the `Collator` and `RuleBasedCollator` classes recognize that the sorting order for accented letters differs from language to language. Furthermore, when it comes to sorting, some languages place accented letters after all base letters, whereas other languages place accented letters immediately after their base letters.

You might consider using `Normalizer` when implementing additional `Collator` subclasses that need to handle more complex comparisons. Also, this class is handy for replacing a string's accented letters with unaccented equivalents; you can then use the resulting strings to name files, directories, database tables, URIs, and other entities on platforms that do not support accented letters in these names. Listing 5-4 presents the source code for a handy utility application for accomplishing this task.

Listing 5-4. *RemoveAccents.java*

```java
// RemoveAccents.java

import java.awt.*;
import java.awt.event.*;

import java.text.*;

import javax.swing.*;

public class RemoveAccents extends JFrame
{
   public RemoveAccents ()
   {
      super ("Remove Accents");
      setDefaultCloseOperation (EXIT_ON_CLOSE);
```

```java
        JPanel pnl = new JPanel ();
        pnl.add (new JLabel ("Enter text"));

        final JTextField txtText;
        txtText = new JTextField (" façade touché "+
            "Rindfleischetikettierungsüberwachungsaufgabenübertragungsgesetz ");
        pnl.add (txtText);

        JButton btnRemove = new JButton ("Remove");
        ActionListener al;
        al = new ActionListener ()
            {
                public void actionPerformed (ActionEvent e)
                {
                   String text = txtText.getText ();
                   text = Normalizer.normalize (text, Normalizer.Form.NFD);
                   txtText.setText (text.replaceAll ("[^\\p{ASCII}]", ""));
                }
            };
        btnRemove.addActionListener (al);
        pnl.add (btnRemove);

        getContentPane ().add (pnl);

        pack ();
        setVisible (true);
    }

    public static void main (String [] args)
    {
       Runnable r = new Runnable ()
                    {
                        public void run ()
                        {
                           new RemoveAccents ();
                        }
                    };
       EventQueue.invokeLater (r);
    }
}
```

This application's GUI consists of a labeled text field and a button. The text field contains some text with accented letters. (*Rindfleischetikettierungsüberwachungsaufgaben-übertragungsgesetz*, which literally translates to "cattle marking and beef labeling supervision duties delegation law," is the longest verified German word.) When you click this button, normalize() is invoked to perform canonical decomposition on the text's precomposed characters (*ç*, *é*, and *ü*). Because the normalized result contains base letters followed by the diacritical marks for these characters, a regular expression is used to throw away these marks.

Note For additional information about Unicode normalization and the Normalizer API, see Sergey Groznyh's "Text Normalization and Monitoring Image I/O Events" Tech Tip (http://java.sun.com/mailers/techtips/corejava/2007/tt0207.html#1). You should also check out the internationalization section of John O'Conner's blog (http://www.joconner.com/category/internationalization/) for entries like "Normalization: Canonical Decomposition." Sergey is a Swing Text developer at Sun. John has spent many years developing the i18n features at Sun.

ResourceBundle Enhancements

Resource bundles store locale-specific objects such as text, icons, measurements, and audio. They help you adapt an already internationalized program to new locales—a task known as *localization*. Because I address only what is new in the java.util.ResourceBundle class, check out John O'Conner's "Java Internationalization: Localization with ResourceBundles" article (http://java.sun.com/developer/technicalArticles/Intl/ResourceBundles/) if you need a refresher on resource bundles.

A review of ResourceBundle reveals a Control inner class and the eight new methods described in Table 5-5.

Table 5-5. *New ResourceBundle Methods*

Method	Description
public static final void clearCache()	Removes from the cache all resource bundles that have been loaded using the caller's classloader.
public static final void clearCache(ClassLoader loader)	Removes from the cache all resource bundles that have been loaded using the specified classloader. A NullPointerException is thrown if loader is null.
public boolean containsKey(String key)	Returns true if the specified key is contained in this resource bundle or any of its parent resource bundles. A NullPointerException is thrown if key is null.

Continued

Table 5-5. *Continued*

Method	Description
`public static ResourceBundle getBundle(String baseName, Locale targetLocale, ClassLoader loader, ResourceBundle.Control control)`	Returns a resource bundle using the specified baseName, targetLocale, loader, and control. ResourceBundle.Control exposes each step in the resource bundle loading process as a separate method. A NullPointerException is thrown if baseName, targetLocale, loader, or control is null. A java.util.MissingResourceException is thrown if baseName cannot be found. An IllegalArgumentException is thrown if control fails to work properly (control.getCandidateLocales() returns null, for example).
`public static final ResourceBundle getBundle(String baseName, Locale targetLocale, ResourceBundle.Control control)`	Returns a resource bundle using the specified baseName, specified targetLocale, caller's classloader, and specified control. A NullPointerException is thrown if baseName, targetLocale, or control is null. A MissingResourceException is thrown if baseName cannot be found. An IllegalArgumentException is thrown if control fails to work properly (control.getCandidateLocales() returns null, for example).
`public static final ResourceBundle getBundle(String baseName, ResourceBundle.Control control)`	Returns a resource bundle using the specified baseName, default locale, caller's classloader, and specified control. A NullPointerException is thrown if baseName or control is null. A MissingResourceException is thrown if baseName cannot be found. An IllegalArgumentException is thrown if control fails to work properly (control.getCandidateLocales() returns null, for example).
`protected Set<String> handleKeySet()`	Returns the set of string-based keys for this resource bundle only.
`public Set<String> keySet()`	Returns the set of string-based keys for this resource bundle and its parents.

To improve performance, ResourceBundle caches resource bundles; getBundle() methods are designed to return cached resource bundles. Because it has long been desirable to support reloadable resource bundles, especially in the context of a long-running server program (see Bug 4212439 "No way to reload a ResourceBundle for a long-running process"), ResourceBundle now includes a pair of clearCache() methods for removing cached resource bundles.

The containsKey() method was introduced in response to long-standing Bug 4286358 "RFE: Want ResourceBundle.hasKey()." Prior to containsKey(), the only way to determine if a key existed was to call ResourceBundle's public final Object getObject(String key) method and catch this method's thrown MissingResourceException for a nonexistent key.

However, throwing and catching an exception is too time consuming just to determine that a key does not exist.

Three new getBundle() methods have been added to give you control over the formats in which resource bundles are stored, the search strategy for locating resource bundles, caching, and more. These methods work with the ResourceBundle.Control class, which exposes each step in the resource bundle loading process as a separate method. Each method can be overridden and customized to obtain the desired behavior.

Prior to Java SE 6, ResourceBundle's public abstract Enumeration<String> getKeys() method was poorly documented. There was no way to tell if this method should return only this resource bundle's keys, or if it should return keys for this resource bundle and all of its parent resource bundles. Starting with Java SE 6, this method is documented to return keys for this resource bundle and all of its parents. As a result, ResourceBundle subclasses might implement getKeys() to return only the current resource bundle's keys or, via the protected parent field, walk the inheritance chain to retrieve all keys; see Bug 4095319 "ResourceBundle inheritance and getKeys()" for more information. This situation has led to the introduction of new handleKeySet() and keySet() methods. keySet() and containsKey() invoke handleKeySet().

If you examine handleKeySet()'s source code, you will discover that it invokes getKeys(). Because the returned enumeration might include parent resource bundle keys, handleKeySet() next filters out all keys where the current resource bundle's protected abstract Object handleGetObject(String key) method returns null. In other words, only the current resource bundle's keys are included in the set of strings that handleKeySet() returns. This is inefficient if getKeys() returns only the current resource bundle's keys. For this reason, you can override handleKeySet() to explicitly return only those keys supported by the current resource bundle, as demonstrated in ResourceBundle's JDK documentation.

Taking Advantage of Cache Clearing

Server programs are meant to run continuously; you'll probably lose customers and get a bad reputation if these programs fail often. As a result, it is preferable to change some aspect of their behavior interactively, rather than stop and restart them. Prior to Java SE 6, you could not dynamically update the resource bundles for a server program that obtains localized text from these bundles and sends this text to clients. Because resource bundles are cached, a change to a resource bundle properties file, for example, would never be reflected in the cache, and ultimately not seen by the client.

With Java SE 6's new clearCache() and clearCache(ClassLoader loader) methods, you can design a server program to clear out all cached resource bundles upon command. You would clear the cache after updating the appropriate resource bundle storage, which might be a file, a database table, or some other entity that stores resource data in some format. To demonstrate this cache clearing, I've created a date-server program that sends localized text and the current date (also localized) to clients. This application's source code is shown in Listing 5-5.

Listing 5-5. *DateServer.java*

```java
// DateServer.java

import java.io.*;

import java.net.*;

import java.text.*;

import java.util.*;

public class DateServer
{
   public final static int PORT = 5000;

   private ServerSocket ss;

   public DateServer (int port)
   {
      try
      {
          ss = new ServerSocket (port);
      }
      catch (IOException ioe)
      {
          System.err.println ("Unable to create server socket: "+ioe);
          System.exit (1);
      }
   }

   private void runServer ()
   {
      // This server application is console-based, as opposed to GUI-based.

      Console console = System.console ();
      if (console == null)
      {
```

```java
            System.err.println ("Unable to obtain system console");
            System.exit (1);
        }

        // This would be a good place to log in the system administrator. For
        // simplicity, I've omitted this section.

        // Start a thread for handling client requests.

        Handler h = new Handler (ss);
        h.start ();

        // Receive input from system administrator; respond to exit and clear
        // commands.

        while (true)
        {
            String cmd = console.readLine (">");
            if (cmd == null)
                continue;

            if (cmd.equals ("exit"))
                System.exit (0);

            if (cmd.equals ("clear"))
                h.clearRBCache ();
        }
    }

    public static void main (String [] args)
    {
        new DateServer (PORT).runServer ();
    }
}

class Handler extends Thread
{
    private ServerSocket ss;

    private volatile boolean doClear;

    Handler (ServerSocket ss)
```

```
   {
      this.ss = ss;
   }

   void clearRBCache ()
   {
      doClear = true;
   }

   public void run ()
   {
      ResourceBundle rb = null;

      while (true)
      {
         try
         {
            // Wait for a connection.

            Socket s = ss.accept ();

            // Obtain the client's locale object.

            ObjectInputStream ois;
            ois = new ObjectInputStream (s.getInputStream ());
            Locale l = (Locale) ois.readObject ();

            // Prepare to output message back to client.

            PrintWriter pw;
            pw = new PrintWriter (s.getOutputStream ());

            // Clear ResourceBundle's cache upon request.

            if (doClear && rb != null)
            {
               rb.clearCache ();
               doClear = false;
            }

            // Obtain a resource bundle for the specified locale. If resource
            // bundle cannot be found, the client is still waiting for
```

```
                  // something, so send a ?.

                  try
                  {
                      rb = ResourceBundle.getBundle ("datemsg", l);
                  }
                  catch (MissingResourceException mre)
                  {
                      pw.println ("?");
                      pw.close ();
                      continue;
                  }

                  // Prepare a MessageFormat to format a locale-specific template
                  // containing a reference to a locale-specific date.

                  MessageFormat mf;
                  mf = new MessageFormat (rb.getString ("datetemplate"), l);

                  Object [] args = { new Date () };

                  // Format locale-specific message and send to client.

                  pw.println (mf.format (args));

                  // It's important to close the PrintWriter so that message is
                  // flushed to the client socket's output stream.

                  pw.close ();
              }
          catch (Exception e)
          {
              System.err.println (e);
          }
      }
   }
}
```

After obtaining the console (check out the "Console I/O" section in Chapter 2 to learn about this new feature), the date server starts a handler thread to respond to clients requesting the current date formatted to their locale requirements. Following this thread's creation, you are repeatedly prompted to enter a command: clear to clear the cache and exit to exit the program are the only two possibilities. After changing a resource bundle, type clear to ensure that future getBundle() method calls initially retrieve their bundles from storage (and then the cache on subsequent method calls).

The date server relies on resource bundles whose base name is datetemplate. I've created two bundles, stored in files named datemsg_en.properties and datemsg_fr.properties. The contents of the former file appear in Listing 5-6.

Listing 5-6. *datemsg_en.properties*

```
datetemplate = The date is {0, date, long}.
```

After connecting to the date server, a date-client program sends the server a Locale object; the client receives a String object in response. If the date server does not support the locale (a resource bundle cannot be found), it returns a string consisting of a single question mark. Otherwise, the date server returns a string consisting of localized text. Listing 5-7 presents the source code for a simple date-client application.

Listing 5-7. *DateClient.java*

```java
// DateClient.java

import java.io.*;

import java.net.*;

import java.util.*;

public class DateClient
{
   final static int PORT = 5000;

   public static void main (String [] args)
   {
      try
      {
         // Establish a connection to the date server. For simplicity, the
         // server is assumed to run on the same machine as the client. The
         // PORT constants of both server and client must be the same.

         Socket s = new Socket ("localhost", PORT);

         // Send the default locale to the date server.
```

```
        ObjectOutputStream oos;
        oos = new ObjectOutputStream (s.getOutputStream ());
        oos.writeObject (Locale.getDefault ());

        // Obtain and output the server's response.

        InputStreamReader isr;
        isr = new InputStreamReader (s.getInputStream ());
        BufferedReader br = new BufferedReader (isr);
        System.out.println (br.readLine ());
    }
    catch (Exception e)
    {
        System.err.println (e);
    }
   }
}
```

For simplicity, the date client sends the default locale to the server. You can override this locale via the java program's -D option. For example, assuming that you've previously started the date server, java -Duser.language="fr" DateClient sends a Locale("fr", "") object to the server and receives a reply in French. (I obtained the French text via Babel Fish Translation, AltaVista's online translation tool at http://babelfish.altavista.com/tr.)

You can verify the usefulness of cache clearing by performing a simple experiment with the date server and date client programs. Before you begin this experiment, create a second copy of Listing 5-6, in which Thee replaces The. Make sure that the properties file containing Thee is in the same directory as the date server. Then follow these steps:

1. Start the date server.

2. Run the client using en as the locale (via java DateClient, if English is the default locale, or java -Duser.language="en" DateClient). You should see a message beginning with "Thee date is."

3. Copy the Listing 5-6 properties file to the server's directory.

4. Type clear at the server prompt.

5. Run the client using en as the locale. This time, you should see a message beginning with "The date is."

■**Caution** It is tempting to want to always invoke `clearCache()` before invoking `getBundle()`. However, this negates the performance benefit that caching brings to an application. For this reason, you should use `clearCache()` sparingly, as the date server program demonstrates.

Taking Control of the getBundle() Methods

Before Java SE 6, `ResourceBundle`'s `getBundle()` methods were hardwired to look for resource bundles as follows:

- Look for certain kinds of bundles: properties-based or class-based.

- Look in certain places: properties files or class files whose directory paths are indicated by fully qualified resource bundle base names.

- Use a specific search strategy: if a search based on a specified locale fails, perform the search using the default locale.

- Use a specific loading procedure: if a class and a properties file share the same candidate bundle name, the class is always loaded while the properties file remains hidden.

Furthermore, resource bundles were always cached.

Because this lack of flexibility prevents you from performing tasks such as obtaining resource data from sources other than properties files and class files (an XML file or a database, for example), Java SE 6 reworks `ResourceBundle` to depend on its `Control` inner class. This nested class provides several callback methods that are invoked during the resource bundle search-and-load process. By overriding specific callback methods, you can achieve the desired flexibility. If none of these methods are overridden, the `getBundle()` methods behave as they always have. Table 5-6 describes all of the methods in `ResourceBundle.Control`.

Table 5-6. *ResourceBundle.Control Methods*

Method	Description
`public List<Locale> getCandidateLocales(String baseName, Locale locale)`	Returns a list of candidate locales for the specified `baseName` and `locale`. A `NullPointerException` is thrown if `baseName` or `locale` is null.
`public static final ResourceBundle.Control getControl(List<String> formats)`	Returns a `ResourceBundle.Control` whose `getFormats()` method returns the specified formats. A `NullPointerException` is thrown if the `formats` list is null. An `IllegalArgumentException` is thrown if the list of `formats` is not known.

Method	Description
public Locale getFallbackLocale(String baseName, Locale locale)	Returns a fallback locale for further resource bundle searches (via ResourceBundle.getBundle()). A NullPointerException is thrown if baseName or locale is null.
public List<String> getFormats(String baseName)	Returns a list of strings that identify the formats to be used in loading resource bundles that share the given baseName. A NullPointerException is thrown if baseName is null.
public static final ResourceBundle.Control getNoFallbackControl(List<String> formats)	Returns a ResourceBundle.Control whose getFormats() method returns the specified formats, and whose getFallBackLocale() method returns null. A NullPointerException is thrown if the formats list is null. An IllegalArgumentException is thrown if the list of formats is not known.
public long getTimeToLive(String baseName, Locale locale)	Returns the time-to-live value for resource bundles loaded via this ResourceBundle.Control. A NullPointerException is thrown if baseName or locale is null.
public boolean needsReload(String baseName, Locale locale, String format, ClassLoader loader, ResourceBundle bundle, long loadTime)	Determines if the expired cached bundle needs to be reloaded by comparing the last modified time with loadTime. It returns a true value (the bundle needs to be reloaded) if the last modified time is more recent than the loadTime. A NullPointerException is thrown if baseName, locale, format, loader, or bundle is null.
public ResourceBundle newBundle(String baseName, Locale locale, String format, ClassLoader loader, boolean reload)	Creates a new resource bundle based on a combination of baseName and locale, and taking the format and loader into consideration. A NullPointerException is thrown if baseName, locale, format, or loader is null (or if toBundleName(), which is called by this method, returns null). An IllegalArgumentException is thrown if format is not known or if the resource identified by the given parameters contains malformed data. A ClassCastException is thrown if the loaded class cannot be cast to ResourceBundle. An IllegalAccessException is thrown if the class or its empty constructor is not accessible. An InstantiationException is thrown if the class cannot be instantiated for some other reason. An ExceptionInInitializerError is thrown if the class's static initializer fails. A SecurityException is thrown if a security manager is present and disallows instantiation of the resource bundle class.
public String toBundleName(String baseName, Locale locale)	Converts the specified baseName and locale into a bundle name whose components are separated by underscore characters. For example, if baseName is MyResources and locale is en, the resulting bundle name is MyResources_en. A NullPointerException is thrown if baseName or locale is null.

Continued

Table 5-6. *Continued*

Method	Description

`public final String`
`toResourceName(String bundleName,`
`String suffix)`
	Converts the specified `bundleName` to a resource name. Forward-slash separators replace package period separators; a period followed by `suffix` is appended to the resulting name. For example, if `bundleName` is `com.company.MyResources_en` and `suffix` is `properties`, the resulting resource name is `com/company/MyResources_en.properties`. A `NullPointerException` is thrown if `bundleName` or `suffix` is `null`.

The `getCandidateLocales()` method is called by a `ResourceBundle.getBundle()` factory method each time the factory method looks for a resource bundle for a target locale. You can override `getCandidateLocales()` to modify the target locale's parent chain. For example, if you want your Hong Kong resource bundles to share traditional Chinese strings, make Chinese/Taiwan resource bundles the parent bundles of Chinese/Hong Kong resource bundles. *The Java Tutorial*'s "Customizing Resource Bundle Loading" lesson (http://java.sun.com/docs/books/tutorial/i18n/resbundle/control.html) shows how to accomplish this task.

The `getFallbackLocale()` method is called by a `ResourceBundle.getBundle()` factory method each time the factory method cannot find a resource bundle based on `getFallbackLocale()`'s `baseName` and `locale` arguments. You can override this method to return null if you do not want to continue a search using the default locale.

The `getFormats()` method is called by a `ResourceBundle.getBundle()` factory method when it needs to load a resource bundle that is not found in the cache. This returned list of formats determines if the resource bundles being sought during the search are class files only, properties files only, both class files and properties files, or some other application-defined formats. When you override `getFormats()` to return application-defined formats, you will also need to override `newBundle()` to load bundles based on these formats. Check out Sun's "Customizing Resource Bundle Loading with ResourceBundle.Control" Tech Tip (http://java.sun.com/developer/JDCTechTips/2005/tt1018.html#2) for an example.

Earlier, I demonstrated using `clearCache()` to remove all resource bundles from `ResourceBundle`'s cache. Rather than explicitly clear the cache, you can control how long resource bundles remain in the cache before they need to be reloaded, by using the `getTimeToLive()` and `needsReload()` methods. The `getTimeToLive()` method returns one of the following:

- A positive value representing the number of milliseconds that resource bundles loaded under the current `ResourceBundle.Control` can remain in the cache without being validated against their source data

- 0 if the bundles must be validated each time they are retrieved from the cache

- `ResourceBundle.Control.TTL_DONT_CACHE` if the bundles are not cached

- The default `ResourceBundle.Control.TTL_NO_EXPIRATION_CONTROL` if the bundles are not to be removed from the cache under any circumstance (apart from low memory, or if you explicitly clear the cache)

If a `ResourceBundle.getBundle()` factory method finds an expired resource bundle in the cache, it calls `needsReload()` to determine if the resource bundle should be reloaded. If this method returns true, the factory method removes the expired resource bundle from the cache; a false return value updates the cached resource bundle with the time-to-live value returned from `getTimeToLive()`.

The `toBundleName()` method is called from the default implementations of `needsReload()` and `newBundle()` when they need to convert a base name and a locale to a bundle name. You can override this method to load resource bundles from different packages instead of the same package. For example, assume that `MyResources.properties` stores your application's default (base) resource bundle, and that you also have a `MyResources_de.properties` file for storing your application's German language resources. The default implementation of `ResourceBundle.Control` organizes these bundles in the same package. By overriding `toBundleName()` to change how these bundles are named, you can place them into different packages. For example, you could have a `com.company.app.i18n.base.MyResources` package corresponding to the `com/company/app/i18n/base/MyResources.properties` resource file, and a `com.company.app.i18n.de.MyResources` package corresponding to the `com/company/app/i18n/de/MyResources.properties` file. You can learn how to do this by exploring a similar example in Sun's "International Enhancements in Java SE 6" article (`http://java.sun.com/developer/technicalArticles/javase/i18n_enhance/`).

Although you will often subclass `ResourceBundle.Control` and override some combination of the callback methods, this isn't always necessary. For example, if you want to restrict resource bundles to class files only or to properties files only, you can invoke `getControl()` to return a ready-made `ResourceBundle.Control` (thread-safe singleton) object that takes care of this task. To get this object, you will need to pass one of the following `ResourceBundle.Control` constants to `getControl()`:

- `FORMAT_PROPERTIES`, which describes an unmodifiable `List<String>` containing `"java.properties"`

- `FORMAT_CLASS`, which describes an unmodifiable `List<String>` containing `"java.class"`

- `FORMAT_DEFAULT`, which describes an unmodifiable `List<String>` containing `"java.class"` followed by `"java.properties"`

The first example in ResourceBundle.Control's JDK documentation uses getControl() to return a ResourceBundle.Control that restricts resource bundles to properties files.

You can also invoke getNoFallbackControl() to return a ready-made ResourceBundle. Control that, in addition to restricting resource bundles to only class files or properties files, tells the new getBundle() methods to avoid falling back to the default locale when searching for a resource bundle. The getNoFallbackControl() method recognizes the same formats argument as getControl(); it returns a thread-safe singleton whose getFallbackLocale() method returns null.

Summary

Java SE 6 introduces several new i18n features to Java. For example, you can now obtain an instance of the Japanese Imperial Era calendar by invoking the Calendar class's public static Calendar getInstance(Locale aLocale) method with ja_JP_JP as the locale. You can then use this instance to set, fetch, and modify dates that correspond to imperial eras such as Heisei.

If you are tired of waiting for Sun to implement a specific locale that is important to your application, you'll want to check out locale-sensitive services. This new feature consists of SPI classes that let you plug locale-dependent data and services into Java. For example, you can introduce a new currency provider for a new locale.

A variety of new locales (in_ID, for Indonesian/Indonesia, for example) have been added. These locales are fully supported by Java's locale-sensitive classes.

Java SE 6's Normalizer API supports four forms of Unicode normalization. This API makes it possible to transform equivalent character sequences (or individual characters) into a consistent representation to facilitate comparison. This capability is important for searching and sorting.

Finally, Java SE 6 improves the ResourceBundle class by adding eight new methods and a new Control inner class. The new methods include a pair of clearCache() methods that are useful for removing loaded resource bundles from ResourceBundle's cache without having to stop a long-running program. The new ResourceBundle.Control class allows you to write applications that control the format in which resource bundles are stored (XML, for example), the search strategy for locating resource bundles, and more.

Test Your Understanding

How well do you understand the new i18n features? Test your understanding by answering the following questions and performing the following exercises. (The answers are presented in Appendix D.)

1. Which `Calendar` fields handle irregular rules in an imperial era's first year?

2. Is it true that all canonically equivalent characters are also compatibility equivalent?

3. Extend the example that introduced a currency name provider for a new `ti_ER` locale (see Listings 5-2 and 5-3) to also include a locale name provider. The `LocaleNameProviderImpl` subclass should implement `getDisplayCountry()` to return "Eritrea" for English locales, `"\u12a4\u122d\u1275\u122b"` as the localized text for the `ti_ER` locale, and null for other locales. Similarly, `getDisplayLanguage()` should return "Tigrinya" for English locales, `"\u1275\u130d\u122d\u129b"` as the localized text for the `ti_ER` locale, and null for other locales. Because there is no variant, `getDisplayVariant()` should always return null. After compiling `LocaleNameProviderImpl.java`, update the `tiER.jar` file to include the resulting class file. Furthermore, place a `java.util.spi.LocaleNameProvider` text file (containing `LocaleNameProviderImpl`) in this JAR file's `META-INF/services` directory. Replace the previously installed `tiER.jar` file with this new JAR file.

   To prove that the `tiER.jar` file's contents are correct, and that this JAR file has been installed successfully, create a `ShowLocaleInfo` application that invokes `getDisplayCountry()` and `getDisplayLanguage()` for the `ti_ER` locale. Make two calls to each method, passing `Locale.ENGLISH` as the argument in the first call and a `ti_ER` Locale object as the argument in the second call. For `ti_ER`, output the result in hexadecimal. Your program should generate the following output:

```
Eritrea
12a4 122d 1275 122b
Tigrinya
1275 130d 122d 129b
```

4. If you are up for a challenge, create a ShowLocales application that is similar to ShowCurrencies. Replace the Currency Code and Currency Symbol columns with Country (Default Locale), Language (Default Locale), Country (Localized), and Language (Localized) columns. The first two columns present the result of the no-argument getDisplayCountry() and getDisplayName() methods; the last two columns present the result of the getDisplayCountry() and getDisplayName() methods that take a Locale argument.

The Unicode strings for Eritrea and Tigrinya identify symbols from the Ge'ez alphabet. (See Wikipedia's Ge'ez alphabet entry at http://en.wikipedia.org/wiki/Ge%27ez_alphabet for more information about this alphabet.) Under the Windows XP version of ShowLocales, you will probably not see these symbols. However, you can correct this by downloading the gfzemenu.ttf TrueType font file from ftp://ftp.ethiopic.org/pub/fonts/TrueType/gfzemenu.ttf, placing this file in the windows/fonts directory, and installing a table cell renderer on the Country (Localized) and Language (Localized) columns. This renderer would extend javax.swing.JLabel and implement javax.swing.table.TableCellRenderer. Furthermore, TableCellRenderer's Component getTableCellRendererComponent(JTable table, Object value, boolean isSelected, boolean hasFocus, int row, int column) method would execute setFont (new Font ("GF Zemen Unicode", Font.PLAIN, 12)); whenever it detects that value contains "\u12a4\u122d\u1275\u122b" or "\u1275\u130d\u122d\u129b". You should end up with something similar to Figure 5-3. Feel free to modify getTableCellComponent() to extend the highlight bar over the last two columns.

Locale	Country (Default Locale)	Language (Default Locale)	Country (Localized)	Language (Localized)
ar_LB	Lebanon	Arabic	لبنان	العربية
ko		Korean		한국어
fr_CA	Canada	French	Canada	français
et_EE	Estonia	Estonian	Eesti	Eesti
ar_KW	Kuwait	Arabic	الكويت	العربية
es_US	United States	Spanish	Estados Unidos	español
es_MX	Mexico	Spanish	México	español
ar_SD	Sudan	Arabic	السودان	العربية
in_ID	Indonesia	Indonesian	Indonesia	Bahasa Indonesia
ru		Russian		русский
lv		Latvian		Latviešu
es_UY	Uruguay	Spanish	Uruguay	español
lv_LV	Latvia	Latvian	Latvija	Latviešu
iw		Hebrew		עברית
pt_BR	Brazil	Portuguese	Brasil	português
ti_ER	Eritrea	Tigrinya	ኤርትራ	ትግርኛ
ar_SY	Syria	Arabic	ᑌᑌᑌᑌᑌ	ᑌᑌᑌᑌᑌᑌᑌ
hr		Croatian		hrvatski
et		Estonian		Eesti

Figure 5-3. *The ShowLocales application shows the localized names for Eritrea and Tigrinya.*

CHAPTER 6

■■■

Java Database Connectivity

Databases are a critical part of many client-based and server-based Java applications. An application uses Java Database Connectivity (JDBC) to access a database in a database management system (DBMS)-agnostic manner. The following topics explore Java SE 6's improved JDBC feature set and its new JDBC-accessible DBMS:

- JDBC 4.0

- Java DB

JDBC 4.0

JDBC 4.0, the latest version of Java's database-access API, was developed under JSR 221: JDBC 4.0 API Specification (http://jcp.org/en/jsr/detail?id=221) and is part of Java SE 6. According to this JSR, JDBC 4.0 "seeks to improve Java application access to SQL data stores by the provision of ease-of-development focused features and improvements at both the utility and API level."

Note A document containing the JDBC 4.0 specification is available for download from the JDBC 4.0 API Specification Final Release section of Sun's JDBC Downloads page (http://java.sun.com/products/jdbc/download.html#corespec40). As stated in this document, one of JDBC 4.0's goals is to focus on the major components of the SQL:2003 specification that are likely to be widely supported by the industry; the SQL:2003 XML data type is an example. To learn more about SQL:2003's enhancements over its SQL:1999 predecessor, check out the SQL2003Features.pdf document available from Whitemarsh Information Systems Corporation (http://www.wiscorp.com/SQL2003Features.pdf). This document was created by IBM employee Krishna Kulkarni.

The JDBC 4.0 API includes the java.sql package's core API and the javax.sql package's API, which extends JDBC from the client side to the server side. JDBC 4.0 adds new classes and interfaces to these packages and extends existing types with new methods. This topic explores most of these additions.

Note Early Java SE 6 builds included JDBC 4.0 Annotations, which simplifies the creation of Data Access Objects (DAOs) by associating SQL queries with Java classes (saving you from having to write a lot of code). This feature did not make it into Java SE 6 because the JDBC 4.0 reference implementation had quality-control issues. However, because JDBC 4.0 Annotations will probably be included in a Java SE 6 update or Java SE 7, you can start to learn about this feature by reading the "Annotation-Based SQL Queries" section of Srini Penchikala's "JDBC 4.0 Enhancements in Java SE 6" article (http://www.onjava.com/pub/a/onjava/2006/08/02/jjdbc-4-enhancements-in-java-se-6.html?page=2).

Automatic Driver Loading

Prior to Java 1.4's introduction of javax.sql.DataSource, the java.sql.DriverManager class was the only way for JDBC to obtain connections to *data sources* (data-storage facilities ranging from simple files to complex databases managed by DBMSs). Before letting you obtain a data source connection, early versions of JDBC required you to explicitly load a suitable driver, by specifying Class.forName() with the name of the class that implements the java.sql.Driver interface. For example, the JDBC-ODBC Bridge driver (typically used only for development and testing or if no alternative driver is available) is loaded via Class.forName("sun.jdbc.odbc.JdbcOdbcDriver"). After creating an instance of itself, the driver class's static initializer registers this instance with DriverManager via DriverManager's public static void registerDriver(Driver driver) method. Later versions of JDBC relaxed this requirement by letting you specify a list of drivers to load via the jdbc.drivers system property. DriverManager would attempt to load all of these drivers during its initialization.

Beginning with Java SE 6, DriverManager uses the older sun.misc.Service-based service provider mechanism as a way to implicitly load drivers. (Chapter 2's discussion of the ServiceLoader API mentions sun.misc.Service.) You no longer need to remember driver class names. This mechanism requires a driver to be packaged in a JAR file that includes META-INF/services/java.sql.Driver. This JAR file must contain a single line that names the driver's implementation of the Driver interface. The first call to one of DriverManager's public static Driver getDriver(String url), public static Enumeration<Driver> getDrivers() or its various getConnection() methods results in a call to an internal method that loads all drivers from accessible driver JAR files, followed by drivers identified by the jdbc.drivers system property. Each loaded driver instantiates and registers itself with DriverManager via registerDriver(). When invoked, a getConnection() method walks through loaded drivers, returning a java.sql.Connection from the first driver that recognizes getConnection()'s JDBC URL. You might want to check out DriverManager's source code to see how this is done.

Note The JDK documentation for DataSource states that this interface is the preferred way to obtain data source connections. You can use logical names instead of hard-coding driver information. And you can benefit from connection pooling and distributed transactions. If you are not familiar with DataSource, *The Java Tutorial* provides an example that uses this interface to obtain a connection in its "Establishing a Connection" lesson (http://java.sun.com/docs/books/tutorial/jdbc/basics/connecting.html).

Enhanced BLOB and CLOB Support

SQL:1999 introduced the binary large object (BLOB) and character large object (CLOB) data types. BLOB is useful for storing large amounts of byte-oriented data, such as images, music, and videos. Similarly, CLOB is useful for storing large amounts of character-oriented data. JDBC 4.0 builds on previous support for BLOB and CLOB in the following ways:

- The Blob createBlob() method has been added to the Connection interface to create and return an empty object whose class implements interface java.sql.Blob, which represents a SQL BLOB type. Invoke a Blob method such as int setBytes(long pos, byte[] bytes) to add data to this object.

- The void free() and InputStream getBinaryStream(long pos, long length) methods have been added to the Blob interface to free a Blob object (releasing held resources) and make a stream from part of a BLOB.

- Four new updateBlob() methods have been added to java.sql.ResultSet for updating a BLOB column from an input stream.

- The void setBlob(int parameterIndex, InputStream inputStream) and void setBlob(int parameterIndex, InputStream inputStream, long length) methods have been added to the java.sql.PreparedStatement interface, to tell the driver that the inputStream parameter value should be sent to the data source as a SQL BLOB. You do not need to use PreparedStatement's setBinaryStream() methods, in which the driver might have to perform extra work to determine if this parameter value should be sent as a SQL LONGVARBINARY or as a SQL BLOB.

- The Clob createClob() method has been added to the Connection interface to create and return an empty object whose class implements interface java.sql.Clob, which represents a SQL CLOB type. Invoke a Clob method such as int setString(long pos, String str) to add data to this object.

- The void free() and Reader getCharacterStream(long pos, long length) methods have been added to the Clob interface to free a Clob object (releasing held resources) and make a stream from part of a CLOB.

- Four new updateClob() methods have been added to ResultSet for updating a CLOB column from an input stream.

- The void setClob(int parameterIndex, Reader reader) and void setClob(int parameterIndex, Reader reader, long length) methods have been added to the PreparedStatement interface, to tell the driver that the reader parameter value should be sent to the data source as a SQL CLOB. You do not need to use PreparedStatement's setCharacterStream() methods, in which the driver might need to perform extra work to determine if this parameter value should be sent as a SQL LONGVARCHAR or as a SQL CLOB.

Suppose you have an EMPLOYEE table with a NAME column of SQL VARCHAR type, and a PHOTO column of SQL BLOB type, and you want to insert a new employee into this table. The createBlob() method is handy for creating an initially empty BLOB that is then populated with an image icon used for the employee's photo, as demonstrated in the following code fragment:

```
Connection con = getConnection (); // Assume the existence of a getConnection ()
                                   // method.
PreparedStatement ps;
ps = con.prepareStatement ("INSERT INTO EMPLOYEE (NAME, PHOTO) VALUES (?, ?)");
ps.setString (1, "Duke");
Blob blob = con.createBlob ();
// Serialize an ImageIcon with duke.png image to blob.
...
ps.setBlob (2, blob);
ps.execute ();
blob.free ();
ps.close ();
```

The createBlob() and createClob() methods address the long-standing JDBC specification problem of being unable to efficiently and portably create new BLOB and/or CLOB items for insertion into a new table row. Check out "Insert with BLOB/CLOB - is this a hole in the JDBC spec?" (http://forum.java.sun.com/thread.jspa?threadID=425246) to learn more about this problem.

Enhanced Connection Management

Because Connection is central to accessing databases via JDBC, optimizing the performance of this interface's implementation is important to achieving better overall JDBC
performance, and also to achieving better performance for higher-level APIs built on top
of JDBC. Common optimization techniques are *connection pooling* and *statement pooling*, where application servers and web servers reuse database connections and, on a
per-connection basis, SQL statement objects.

When an application server or a web server provides connection pooling, a connection request from the application is sent to the server's connection pool manager instead
of the driver. Because the driver does not participate in the request, it cannot associate
an application with the connection. Therefore, it is not possible for a server-based monitoring tool to identify the application behind a JDBC connection that is hogging the CPU
or otherwise bogging down the server.

JDBC 4.0 alleviates this problem by adding new void setClientInfo(Properties
properties) and void setClientInfo(String name, String value) methods to Connection.
Following a successful connection, the application calls either method to associate
client-specific information (such as the application's name) with the JDBC connection
object. The driver executes these methods and passes the information to the database
server. The server invokes Connection's new Properties getClientInfo() and String
getClientInfo(String name) methods to retrieve this information for the monitoring tool.

Typically, applications execute certain statements many times during the application's life. They also execute other statements only a few times. Prior to JDBC 4.0, there
was no way to specify which statements should be placed in a statement pool. A statement might automatically be placed in a pool, displacing another statement that should
remain in the pool because of its frequent execution.

Beginning with JDBC 4.0, an application can hint to the connection pool manager
that a statement should be placed in (or removed from) a statement pool by invoking the
java.sql.Statement interface's new void setPoolable(boolean poolable) method. By
default, only PreparedStatements and java.sql.CallableStatements are eligible to be placed
into this pool. You need to call setPoolable(true) on a Statement to make the Statement
eligible for pool placement. The new boolean isPoolable() method indicates whether a
statement is eligible for a statement pool, returning true if the statement can be placed
in a pool.

Prior to JDBC 4.0, a connection pool manager could not identify a connection that
had become unusable. However, the pool manager could determine that something was
wrong with at least one of the pooled connections, as a result of the connection pool running out of resources or taking excessive time to communicate with a database. The pool
manager typically terminated all connections and reinitialized the pool with new connections, but this solution led to potential data loss, poor performance, and angry users.

Some connection pool managers erroneously used Connection's boolean isClosed()
method to identify an unusable connection. However, this method determines only if a

connection is open or closed. An unusable connection will probably be open (hogging resources). Fortunately, JDBC 4.0 addresses this problem by adding a new `boolean` `isValid(int timeout)` method to `Connection`. This method returns true if the connection object's connection has not been closed and is still valid. If both `isClosed()` and `isValid()` return false, the connection is unusable and can be closed.

■**Note** When `isValid()` is called, the driver submits a query on the connection or uses some other means to positively verify that the connection is still valid.

Finally, JDBC 4.0 provides an enhancement that allows a driver to inform the connection pool manager when an application closes a pooled prepared statement, or when the driver finds a pooled prepared statement to be invalid. When so informed, the connection pool manager can return the `PreparedStatement` object to the statement pool for reuse, or it can throw away the invalid statement. This enhancement consists of the following new items:

- `javax.sql.StatementEventListener`: This interface is implemented by the connection pool manager to listen for events that are related to the driver detecting closed and invalid prepared statements.

- `javax.sql.StatementEvent`: Instances of this class are passed to the listener's `void statementClosed(StatementEvent event)` and `void statementErrorOccurred(StatementEvent event)` methods. This class contains a `public PreparedStatement getStatement()` method that returns the `PreparedStatement` being closed or found to be invalid, and a `public SQLException getSQLException()` method that returns the `java.sql.SQLException` that the driver is about to throw (for an invalid `PreparedStatement`).

- `void addStatementEventListener(StatementEventListener listener)` and `void removeStatementEventListener(StatementEventListener listener)`: These methods are added to the `javax.sql.PooledConnection` interface.

A connection pool manager invokes `addStatementEventListener()` to register itself as a listener for notifications sent by the driver. When an application closes a *logical prepared statement* (a prepared statement that will be returned to the statement pool for reuse), the driver invokes the `statementClosed()` method for each `StatementEventListener` registered on the connection. If the driver detects an invalid prepared statement, it invokes each registered `StatementEventListener`'s `statementErrorOccurred()` method prior to throwing a `SQLException`.

Enhanced Exception Handling

Java 1.4 introduced *chained exceptions* (see http://java.sun.com/j2se/1.4.2/docs/guide/lang/chained-exceptions.html) as a standard mechanism for wrapping an exception inside another exception. JDBC 4.0 introduces this mechanism to SQLException via four new constructors. Each constructor takes a Throwable argument that identifies the SQLException's cause (which might be a non-SQLException).

The chained exception mechanism is not a replacement for SQLException's public SQLException getNextException() method. Because the SQL standard allows multiple SQLExceptions to be thrown during a statement's execution, you need to work with both getNextException() and the inherited public Throwable getCause() method to extract all exceptions and their causes, as follows:

```
public static void main (String [] args)
{
   try
   {
      throw new SQLException ("Unable to access database file",
                             new java.io.IOException ("File I/O problem"));
   }
   catch (SQLException sqlex)
   {
      /*
         This clause generates the following output:

         java.sql.SQLException: Unable to access database file
         Cause:java.io.IOException: File I/O problem
      */
      while (sqlex != null)
      {
         System.out.println (sqlex);

         Throwable t = sqlex.getCause ();
         while (t != null)
         {
            System.out.println ("Cause:"+t);
            t = t.getCause ();
         }

         sqlex = sqlex.getNextException ();
      }
   }
}
```

Note The `java.sql.BatchUpdateException` and `java.sql.DataTruncation` exception classes now support chained exceptions as well. Regarding `DataTruncation`, its `SQLState` is now set to `"22001"` if data is truncated during a write operation, or set to `"01004"` for data truncation during a read operation.

Under JDBC 4.0, `SQLException` implements the `Iterable<T>` interface so that you can use Java 5's for-each loop to iterate over the exception and its cause (if there is one). Behind the scenes, the for-each loop invokes `SQLException`'s `public Iterator<Throwable> iterator()` method to return an iterator for this task. The result is a much simpler `catch` clause, as shown in the following code fragment:

```
catch (SQLException sqlex)
{
   /*
      This clause generates the following output:

      java.sql.SQLException: Unable to access database file
      Cause:java.sql.SQLException: Unable to access database file
      Cause:java.io.IOException: File I/O problem
   */
   while (sqlex != null)
   {
      System.out.println (sqlex);

      for (Throwable t: sqlex)
         System.out.println ("Cause:"+t);

      sqlex = sqlex.getNextException ();
   }
}
```

When a `SQLException` is thrown, the reason for this exception is not readily apparent. The exception could be the result of a temporary failure, such as a database being rebooted or a deadlock occurring in a database. The exception might be the result of a permanent failure, such as a syntax error in a SQL statement or a constraint violation involving foreign keys.

Before JDBC 4.0, you needed to extract the exception's `SQLState` value to find out why it occurred. You also had to find out if this value followed (as determined by the driver) the X/Open (now known as Open Group) SQL Call Level Interface (CLI) convention or the SQL:2003 convention; the convention can be identified via `java.sql.DatabaseMetaData`'s `int getSQLStateType()` method.

JDBC 4.0 introduces two new `SQLException` subclass hierarchies that more conveniently describe the reason for the exception. The `java.sql.SQLTransientException` class is the root class for those exception classes describing failed operations that can be retried immediately. Table 6-1 describes these classes.

Table 6-1. *SQLTransientException Subclasses*

Subclass	Description
SQLTimeoutException	A Statement's timeout has expired. There is no SQLState value.
SQLTransactionRollbackException	The DBMS automatically rolled back the current statement because of deadlock or some other transaction serialization failure. The SQLState value is "40".
SQLTransientConnectionException	A failed connection operation might succeed if retried. No application-level changes are required. The SQLState value is "08".

In contrast to `SQLTransientException`, the `java.sql.SQLNonTransientException` class is the root class for those exception subclasses describing failed operations that cannot be retried without changing application source code or some aspect of the data source. Each of these subclasses is described in Table 6-2.

Table 6-2. *SQLNonTransientException Subclasses*

Subclass	Description
SQLDataException	An invalid function argument has been detected, an attempt has been made to divide by zero, or some other data-related problem has occurred. The SQLState value is "22".
SQLFeatureNotSupportedException	The driver does not support an optional JDBC feature such as an optional overloaded method. For example, this exception is thrown if the driver does not support Connection's optional overloaded Statement createStatement(int resultSetType, int resultSetConcurrency) method. The SQLState value is "0A".
SQLIntegrityConstraintViolationException	A foreign key or some other integrity constraint has been violated. The SQLState value is "23".

Continued

Table 6-2. *Continued*

Subclass	Description
SQLInvalidAuthorizationSpecException	The authorization credentials that were specified while trying to establish a connection are invalid. The SQLState value is "28".
SQLNonTransientConnectionException	A failed connection operation will not succeed if it is retried, unless the failure's cause has been corrected. The SQLState value is "08".
SQLSyntaxErrorException	An in-progress query has violated SQL syntax rules. The SQLState value is "42".

JDBC 4.0 also introduces the java.sql.SQLRecoverableException and java.sql.
SQLClientInfoException classes. An instance of SQLRecoverableException is thrown if a failed operation might succeed provided that the application performs recovery steps. At minimum, a recovery operation must close the current connection and obtain a new connection.

An instance of SQLClientInfoException is thrown when one or more client information properties cannot be set on a connection; for example, if you called one of Connection's setClientInfo() methods on a closed connection. This exception identifies a list of those client information properties that could not be set.

National Character Set Support

SQL:2003 introduced the NCHAR, NVARCHAR, LONGNVARCHAR, and NCLOB data types for supporting national character sets. These data types are analogous to the CHAR, VARCHAR, LONGVARCHAR, and CLOB data types, except that their values are encoded via a national character set.

JDBC 4.0 represents NCHAR, NVARCHAR, and LONGNVARCHAR data items as String objects. It automatically converts between Java's UTF-16 character encoding and the national character set encoding. In contrast, NCLOB is represented via a new java.sql.NClob interface, which mirrors Blob and Clob. JDBC 4.0 does not automatically convert between NClob and Clob.

In addition to providing NClob, JDBC 4.0 adds a variety of new methods to the PreparedStatement, CallableStatement (a subinterface of PreparedStatement), and ResultSet interfaces, to further support the NCHAR, NVARCHAR, LONGNVARCHAR, and NCLOB data types:

- Applications invoke PreparedStatement's new setNString(), setNClob(), setNCharacterStream(), and setObject() methods to tell the driver when parameter marker values correspond to national character set types. (setObject()'s targetSqlType argument must be java.sql.Types.NCHAR, Types.NCLOB,

Types.NVARCHAR, or Types.LONGNVARCHAR.) If this is not done and a driver detects a potential data-conversion error, the driver will throw a SQLException. The driver might also throw this exception if it does not support national character set types and one of the setNXXX() methods is called.

- Applications invoke CallableStatement's new getNString(), getNClob(), getNCharacterStream(), and getObject() methods to retrieve national character set values.

- In addition to new getNString(), getNClob(), and getNCharacterStream() methods, ResultSet also provides new updateNString(), updateNClob(), and updateNCharacterStream() methods for performing update operations that involve national character sets.

Note JDBC 4.0's national character set support extends to customized type mapping (see Chapter 17 in the JDBC 4.0 specification), where SQL structured and distinct types are mapped to Java classes. This support consists of new NClob readNClob() and String readNString() methods added to the java.sql.SQLInput interface, and new void writeNClob(NClob x) and void writeNString(String x) methods added to the java.sql.SQLOutput interface.

New Scalar Functions

Most data sources support numeric, string, date/time, conversion, and system functions that operate on scalar values. These functions may be used in SQL queries and are accessed via the portable {fn *function-name* (*argument list*)} escape syntax. For example, {fn now() } returns the current date and time as a TIMESTAMP value. Table 6-3 describes the JDBC 4.0 specification's eight new scalar functions.

Table 6-3. *New Scalar Functions*

Function	Description
CHAR_LENGTH(string)	Returns the length in characters of the string expression denoted by string, if this expression is a character data type. If the expression is not a character data type, this function returns its length in bytes such that the length is the smallest integer not less than the number of bits divided by 8.
CHARACTER_LENGTH(string)	A synonym for CHAR_LENGTH(string).
CURRENT_DATE()	A synonym for CURDATE(), which returns the current date as a DATE value.

Continued

Table 6-3. *Continued*

Function	Description
CURRENT_TIME()	A synonym for CURTIME(), which returns the current time as a TIME value.
CURRENT_TIMESTAMP()	A synonym for NOW(), which returns a TIMESTAMP value representing the current date and time.
EXTRACT(field FROM source)	Returns the YEAR, MONTH, DAY, HOUR, MINUTE, or SECOND field from the date-time source.
OCTET_LENGTH(string)	Returns the length in bytes of the string expression denoted by string such that the length is the smallest integer not less than the number of bits divided by 8.
POSITION(substring IN string)	Returns the position of the first substring occurrence in string as a NUMERIC. The precision is implementation-defined, and the scale is zero.

If a data source supports these new scalar functions, the driver should map their escape syntaxes to DBMS-specific syntaxes. An application can determine which scalar functions are supported by invoking DatabaseMetaData methods such as String getStringFunctions(), which returns a comma-separated list of the Open Group CLI names for all supported string functions.

To assist an application in discovering if a data source supports a specific scalar function, I've created a simple utility method that takes connection and function-name arguments, and returns a Boolean true value if the function name is supported by the data source. The following is this method's source code:

```
static boolean isSupported (Connection con, String func) throws SQLException
{
    DatabaseMetaData dbmd = con.getMetaData ();

    if (func.equalsIgnoreCase ("CONVERT"))
        return dbmd.supportsConvert ();

    func = func.toUpperCase ();

    if (dbmd.getNumericFunctions ().toUpperCase ().indexOf (func) != -1)
        return true;

    if (dbmd.getStringFunctions ().toUpperCase ().indexOf (func) != -1)
        return true;

    if (dbmd.getSystemFunctions ().toUpperCase ().indexOf (func) != -1)
        return true;
```

```
    if (dbmd.getTimeDateFunctions ().toUpperCase ().indexOf (func) != -1)
        return true;

    return false;
}
```

Suppose you want to find out if a data source supports the `CHAR_LENGTH` scalar function. After acquiring a connection to the data source, as identified by `Connection` variable `con`, you can execute this statement:

```
System.out.println (isSupported (con, "CHAR_LENGTH"));
```

This outputs `true` if `CHAR_LENGTH` is supported, or `false` if this scalar function is not supported.

When it comes to checking for `CONVERT` scalar function support, `isSupported()` tests for support in the general case of being able to convert an arbitrary JDBC type to another JDBC type. It does not test for support in the specific case of being able to convert an exact JDBC type (`Types.DECIMAL`, for example) to another exact JDBC type (such as `Types.DOUBLE`).

SQL ROWID Data Type Support

Although not defined in SQL:2003, the SQL ROWID data type is supported by Oracle, DB2, and other DBMSs. Its values can be thought of as logical or physical table row addresses (depending on the originating data source). According to Oracle, row identifiers are the fastest way to access table rows. You can also take advantage of their uniqueness when you need to store the rows of a query that are otherwise not unique in a hash table or another kind of collection that does not permit duplicates.

Note If you are not familiar with ROWID, the *Oracle Database SQL Reference* discusses Oracle's implementation of this data type (`http://download-east.oracle.com/docs/cd/B19306_01/server.102/b14200/pseudocolumns008.htm`).

JDBC 4.0 offers the following enhancements to support SQL ROWID:

- The `java.sql.RowId` interface to represent the SQL ROWID data type

- New `getRowId()` methods to `CallableStatement` and `ResultSet`

- New `updateRowId()` methods to `ResultSet`

- A new setRowId() method to CallableStatement and PreparedStatement

- A new RowIdLifetime getRowIdLifetime() method to DatabaseMetaData, which indicates a data source's support for ROWID and the lifetime of a row identifier via Table 6-4's enumeration constants

Table 6-4. *java.sql.RowIdLifetime Enumeration Constants*

Constant	Description
ROWID_UNSUPPORTED	This data source does not support the SQL ROWID data type.
ROWID_VALID_FOREVER	The lifetime of this data source's row identifiers is unlimited as long as these rows are not deleted.
ROWID_VALID_OTHER	The lifetime of this data source's row identifiers is indeterminate, but is not one of the lifetimes described by the other ROWID_VALID_*xxx* constants.
ROWID_VALID_SESSION	The lifetime of this data source's row identifiers is limited to at least the containing session as long as these rows are not deleted.
ROWID_VALID_TRANSACTION	The lifetime of this data source's row identifiers is limited to at least the containing transaction as long as these rows are not deleted.

Consider the EMPLOYEE table (with NAME and PHOTO columns) that I introduced earlier in the context of enhanced support for BLOBs and CLOBs. Suppose you want to store all rows in a hash table, where each key must be unique or you risk overwriting an entry. You cannot use the name as the key because two employees might have the same name. Instead, you use the row identifier as the key:

```
Connection con = getConnection (); // Assume agetConnection () method.
PreparedStatement ps;
ps = con.prepareStatement ("SELECT ROWID, NAME, PHOTO FROM EMPLOYEE");
ResultSet rs = ps.executeQuery ();
HashMap<RowId, Employee> emps = new HashMap<RowId, Employee> ();
while (rs.next ())
{
   RowId rowid = rs.getRowId (1);
   String name = rs.getString (2);
   Blob photo = rs.getBlob (3);
   Employee emp = new Employee (name, photo); // Assume an Employee class.
   emps.put (rowid, emp);
}
ps.close ();
```

Caution When working with row identifiers, keep in mind that they typically are not portable between data sources.

SQL XML Data Type Support

For years, many DBMSs have supported XML as one of their native data types. This ubiquity of support has been formalized in the SQL:2003 standard via a new SQL XML data type. Because SQL XML is supported in JDBC 4.0, applications no longer need to work with CLOBs and other SQL data types for storing and retrieving XML data elements.

JDBC's support for SQL XML begins with a new java.sql.SQLXML interface, which maps the SQL XML data type to Java. This interface specifies methods for retrieving XML values from and storing XML values to SQLXML objects. It also specifies a void free() method that closes a SQLXML object, releasing held resources. Once closed, the object becomes invalid and is not accessible.

Note Before an application starts to work with the SQLXML interface, it needs to verify that the data source associated with the current connection supports SQL XML. The application can accomplish this task by invoking the DatabaseMetaData class's ResultSet getTypeInfo() method. This method has been extended to include a result set row with the DATA_TYPE column set to Types.SQLXML if SQL XML is supported.

In addition to SQLXML, JDBC adds several new SQLXML-related methods to the Connection, PreparedStatement, CallableStatement, and ResultSet interfaces:

- A SQLXML createSQLXML() method has been added to Connection for creating an initially empty SQLXML object.

- A void setSQLXML(int parameterIndex, SQLXML xmlObject) method has been added to PreparedStatement for assigning a SQLXML object to a parameter.

- The void setSQLXML(String parameterName, SQLXML xmlObject), SQLXML getSQLXML(int parameterIndex), and SQLXML getSQLXML(String parameterName) methods have been added to CallableStatement.

- The SQLXML getSQLXML(int columnIndex), SQLXML getSQLXML(String columnLabel), void updateSQLXML(int columnIndex, SQLXML xmlObject), and void updateSQLXML(String columnLabel, SQLXML xmlObject) methods have been added to ResultSet.

Suppose the EMPLOYEE table has been modified to contain a FAV_RECIPE column that stores each employee's favorite recipe in XML format (perhaps the company's chef prepares these food items for an employee-appreciation day). The following code fragment uses SQLXML to associate a favorite recipe with a new employee:

```
Connection con = getConnection (); // Assume agetConnection () method.
PreparedStatement ps;
ps = con.prepareStatement ("INSERT INTO EMPLOYEE (NAME, PHOTO, FAV_RECIPE)"+
                           "VALUES (?, ?, ?)");
ps.setString (1, "Duke");
Blob blob = con.createBlob ();
// Serialize an ImageIcon with duke.png image to blob.
ps.setBlob (2, blob);
SQLXML xml = con.createSQLXML ();
xml.setString ("<recipe>…</recipe>");
ps.setSQLXML (3, xml);
ps.execute ();
xml.free ();
blob.free ();
ps.close ();
```

Note To learn more about working with SQLXML, check out Deepak Vohra's "Using the SQLXML data type" article (http://www-128.ibm.com/developerworks/xml/library/x-sqlxml/). While reading this article, keep in mind that the SQLXML interface has evolved since this article was written; this interface no longer specifies createXMLStreamReader() and createXMLStreamWriter() methods. To obtain this functionality, you need to first invoke appropriate SQLXML methods to obtain input (input stream, reader, or source) and output (output stream, writer, or result) objects. Then invoke the javax.xml.stream.XMLOutputFactory createXMLStreamWriter() method that takes the output object as an argument, and the javax.xml.stream.XMLInputFactory createXMLStreamReader() method that takes the input object as an argument.

Wrapper Pattern Support

The *wrapper pattern*, also known as the *adapter pattern*, is used in many JDBC driver implementations to wrap JDBC extensions that are more flexible or perform better than standard JDBC. (Wikipedia's Adapter pattern entry, http://en.wikipedia.org/wiki/Adapter_pattern, discusses this design pattern.) For example, Oracle's oracle.jdbc.OracleStatement interface provides performance-related extensions.

Note To discover more Oracle extensions, check out Chapter 6 in the *Oracle9i JDBC Developer's Guide and Reference* (http://www.stanford.edu/dept/itss/docs/oracle/9i/java.920/a96654/ oraint.htm).

JDBC 4.0 introduces the `java.sql.Wrapper` interface to access these vendor-specific resources. The wrapped objects are known as *resource delegates*. Because the `Connection`, `DatabaseMetaData`, `ParameterMetaData`, `ResultSet`, `ResultSetMetaData`, `Statement`, and `DataSource` interfaces extend `Wrapper`, implementations of these interfaces must include `Wrapper`'s two methods:

- The `boolean isWrapperFor(Class<?> iface)` method returns true if the caller implements the `iface` argument, or is directly or indirectly a wrapper for an object whose class implements the argument.

- The `<T> T unwrap(Class<T> iface)` method returns an object whose class implements the `iface` argument. Prior to invoking `unwrap()`, you should call `isWrapperFor()`, because `unwrap()` is a time-consuming operation—why waste time if `unwrap()` would fail?

The `OracleStatement` interface provides a `public synchronized void defineColumnType(int column_index, int type)` method for defining the type under which a column's data is fetched, saving the driver from making an extra round-trip to the Oracle data source to ask for the column's type. The following code fragment unwraps the `OracleStatement` resource delegate to access this method:

```
Connection con = ds.getConnection (); // Assume the existence of a data source.
Statement stmt = con.createStatement ();
Class clzz = Class.forName ("oracle.jdbc.OracleStatement");
OracleStatement os;
if (stmt.isWrapperFor (clzz))
{
    os = stmt.unwrap (clzz);
    // Assign Oracle's NUMBER type to column 1. Let's
    // assume that the OCI or Server-Side Internal driver,
    // which gets better performance with
    // defineColumnType(), is the connection's Oracle
    // driver. In contrast, Oracle's Thin driver achieves
    // better performance without defineColumnType().
    os.defineColumnType (1, OracleTypes.NUMBER);
}
stmt.close ();
```

JDBC 4.0's support for the wrapper pattern offers a portable way to access non-portable vendor-specific resource delegates. If having a portable way to access nonportable delegates seems strange to you, keep in mind that Wrapper lets you confine your nonportable code to delegates; you do not also need to introduce nonportable code that provides access to these delegates.

Java DB

Java DB is Sun's supported distribution of Apache's open-source Derby product, which is based on IBM's Cloudscape relational DBMS code base. This pure-Java DBMS is bundled with JDK 6 (not the JRE). It is secure, supports JDBC and SQL (including transactions, stored procedures, and concurrency), and has a small footprint—its core engine and JDBC driver occupy 2MB.

Java DB is capable of running in an embedded environment or in a client/server environment. In an embedded environment, where an application accesses the database engine via the Embedded JDBC driver, the database engine runs in the same virtual machine as the application. Figure 6-1 illustrates the embedded environment architecture, where the database engine is embedded in the application.

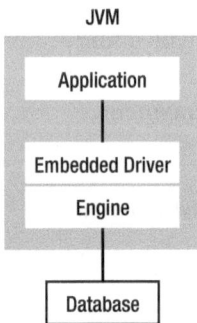

Figure 6-1. *No separate processes are required to start up or shut down an embedded database engine.*

In a client/server environment, client applications and the database engine run in separate virtual machines. A client application accesses the network server through the Client JDBC driver. The network server, which runs in the same virtual machine as the database engine, accesses the database engine through the Embedded JDBC driver. Figure 6-2 illustrates this architecture.

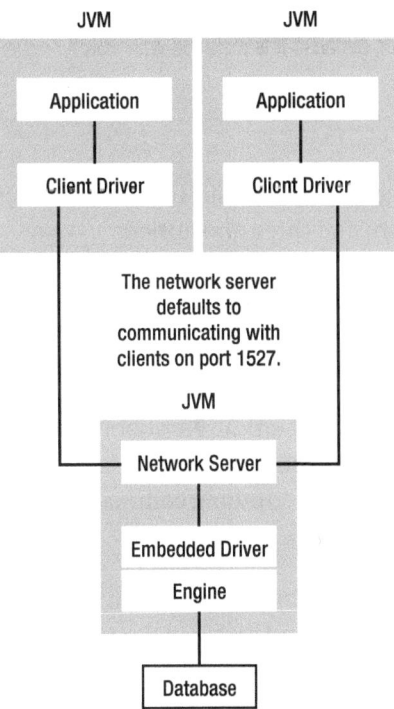

Figure 6-2. *Multiple clients communicate with the same database engine through the network server.*

Java DB implements the database portion of the architectures shown in Figures 6-1 and 6-2 as a directory with the same name as the database. Within this directory, Java DB creates a `log` directory to store transaction logs, a `seg0` directory to store the data files, and a `service.properties` file to store configuration parameters.

Note Java DB does not provide a SQL command to drop (destroy) a database. Destroying a database requires that you manually delete its directory structure.

Java DB Installation and Configuration

When you install JDK 6 build 1.6.0-b105 or later with the default settings, the bundled Java DB is installed into `%JAVA_HOME%\db` on Windows systems, or into the `db` subdirectory in the equivalent location on Unix systems.

> **Note** I focus on version 10.2.1.7 of the Java DB in this chapter, because it is included with JDK 6 build 1.6.0-b105, which is the build on which this book is based.

The db directory contains six files (although most of the files are license-oriented, RELEASE-NOTES.html contains a lot of useful information) and three directories:

- The demo directory is divided into databases and programs subdirectories. The databases directory contains a sample database packaged in a JAR file. The programs directory contains several examples that demonstrate various Java DB features.

- The frameworks directory is divided into embedded and NetworkServer subdirectories whose bin subdirectories contain scripts for setting up embedded and client/server environments (also known as *frameworks*), running command-line tools, and starting/stopping the network server.

- The lib directory contains various JAR files that house the engine library (derby. jar), the command-line tools libraries (derbytools.jar and derbyrun.jar), the network server library (derbynet.jar), the network client library (derbyclient.jar), and various locale libraries. You will also find a derby.war file in this directory. Because it is also possible to manage the Java DB network server remotely via the servlet interface (see http://db.apache.org/derby/docs/10.1/adminguide/ cadminservlet98430.html), derby.war is used to register the network server's servlet at the /derbynet relative path.

Before you can try out the examples and tools, and start/stop the network server, you must set the DERBY_HOME environment variable. Set this for Windows as follows:

```
set DERBY_HOME=%JAVA_HOME%\db
```

In Unix (Korn shell), set the environment variable with this command:

```
export DERBY_HOME=$JAVA_HOME/db
```

> **Note** The embedded and client/server framework setup scripts refer to a DERBY_INSTALL environment variable. According to the "Re: DERBY_INSTALL and DERBY_HOME" mail item (http://www.mail-archive. com/derby-dev@db.apache.org/msg22098.html), DERBY_HOME is equivalent to and replaces DERBY_ INSTALL for consistency with other Apache projects.

You must also set the classpath environment variable before trying out the examples. The easiest way to set the classpath environment variable is to run a script file included with Java DB. Windows and Unix versions of various "set*xxx*CP" script files (which extend the current classpath) are located in embedded's and NetworkServer's bin subdirectories. The script file(s) to run will depend on whether you work with the embedded or client/server framework:

- For the embedded framework, invoke setEmbeddedCP to add derby.jar and derbytools.jar to the classpath.

- For the client/server framework, invoke setNetworkServerCP to add derby.jar, derbytools.jar, and derbynet.jar to the classpath. In a separate command window, invoke setNetworkClientCP to add derbyclient.jar and derbytools.jar to the classpath.

Note From time to time, Sun will release an updated version of Java DB. At the time of this writing, the latest version is 10.2.2. Visit Sun's Java DB Downloads page (http://developers.sun.com/javadb/downloads/) and follow the instructions to download and install the latest version.

Java DB Examples

The programs subdirectory of the demo directory contains HTML documentation that describes the examples included with Java DB; the readme.html file is the entry point into this documentation. These examples include a simple JDBC application for working with Java DB, network server sample programs, and sample programs that are introduced in the *Working with Derby* manual.

Note The *Working with Derby* manual underscores Java DB's Derby heritage. You can download this manual and other Derby manuals from the documentation section (http://db.apache.org/derby/manuals/index.html) of Apache's Derby project site (http://db.apache.org/derby/index.html).

In this section, I focus on the simple JDBC application that is located in the programs subdirectory's simple subdirectory. This application runs in either the default embedded environment or the client/server environment. It creates and connects to a DERBYDB database, creates a table, performs insert/update/select operations on this table, drops the table, and disconnects from the database.

To run this application in the embedded environment, open a command-line window and make sure that the DERBY_HOME and classpath environment variables have been set properly; invoke setEmbeddedCP to set the classpath. Assuming that simple is the current directory, invoke java SimpleApp or java SimpleApp embedded to run this application. You should observe the following output:

```
SimpleApp starting in embedded mode.
Loaded the appropriate driver.
Connected to and created database derbyDB
Created table derbyDB
Inserted 1956 Webster
Inserted 1910 Union
Updated 1956 Webster to 180 Grand
Updated 180 Grand to 300 Lakeshore
Verified the rows
Dropped table derbyDB
Closed result set and statement
Committed transaction and closed connection
Database shut down normally
SimpleApp finished
```

Examining this output reveals that an application running in the embedded framework shuts down the database engine before exiting. This is done to perform a checkpoint and release resources. If this shutdown does not occur, Java DB notes the absence of the checkpoint, assumes a crash, and causes recovery code to run prior to the next database connection (which takes longer to complete).

To run this application in the client/server environment, you need to start the network server and run the application in separate command-line windows. In one command-line window, set DERBY_HOME. Start the network server via the startNetworkServer script (located in NetworkServer's bin subdirectory), which takes care of setting the classpath. You should see output similar to this:

```
Apache Derby Network Server - 10.2.1.7 - (453926)
started and ready to accept connections on port 1527 similar at 2007-05-30
19:30:43.140 GMT
```

In the other command-line window, set DERBY_HOME followed by the classpath (via setNetworkClientCP). Assuming that simple is the current directory, invoke java SimpleApp derbyClient to run this application. This time, you should observe the following output:

```
SimpleApp starting in derbyclient mode.
Loaded the appropriate driver.
Connected to and created database derbyDB
Created table derbyDB
Inserted 1956 Webster
Inserted 1910 Union
Updated 1956 Webster to 180 Grand
Updated 180 Grand to 300 Lakeshore
Verified the rows
Dropped table derbyDB
Closed result set and statement
Committed transaction and closed connection
SimpleApp finished
```

Notice that the database engine is not shut down in the client/server environment. Although not indicated in the output, there is a second difference between running SimpleApp in the embedded and client/server environments. In the embedded environment, the derbyDB database directory is created in the simple directory. In the client/server environment, this database directory is created in the directory identified by DERBY_HOME.

You can learn a lot about working with Java DB by examining SimpleApp.java. In addition to identifying and loading the appropriate driver (which is no longer necessary in JDBC 4.0), the source code shows how to connect to and create a Java DB database, and shows how to shut down the database engine for the embedded environment:

- The conn = DriverManager.getConnection(protocol + "derbyDB;create=true;", props); statement makes a connection to the database. For the embedded environment, protocol is set to "jdbc:derby:". For the client/server environment, protocol is set to "jdbc:derby://localhost:1527/". Regardless of the environment, protocol is followed by "derbyDB;create=true;", which names the database (and directory), and causes the database to be created. The props object contains this example's username and password connection properties.

- The DriverManager.getConnection("jdbc:derby:;shutdown=true"); statement shuts down the database engine for the embedded environment. This statement is placed in a try handler because it always throws a SQLException (which is normal) with SQLState set to "XJ015".

> **Note** When running SimpleApp (or any other Java DB application) in the embedded environment, you can determine where the database directory will be created by setting the derby.system.home property. For example, java -Dderby.system.home=c:\ SimpleApp causes derbyDB to be created in the root directory of the C: drive on a Windows platform.

When you are finished playing with SimpleApp in the client/server environment, you should shut down the network server and database engine. Accomplish this task by invoking the stopNetworkServer script (in NetworkServer's bin subdirectory). You can also shut down (or start and otherwise control) the network server by running the NetworkServerControl script (also located in NetworkServer's bin directory). For example, NetworkServerControl shutdown shuts down the network server and database engine.

Java DB Command-Line Tools

The bin subdirectories of the embedded and NetworkServer directories contain three Windows and Unix script files for launching command-line tools:

- Run sysinfo to view the Java environment/Java DB configuration.

- Run ij to run scripts that execute ad hoc SQL commands and perform repetitive tasks.

- Run dblook to view all or part of a database's Data Definition Language (DDL).

If you experience trouble with Java DB (such as not being able to connect to a database), you can run sysinfo to see if the problem is configuration related. The embedded version of this tool reports various settings under the Java Information, Derby Information, and Locale Information headings. It outputs the following information on my platform:

```
------------------ Java Information ------------------
Java Version:    1.6.0
Java Vendor:     Sun Microsystems Inc.
Java home:       c:\progra~1\java\jdk1.6.0\jre
Java classpath:  c:\PROGRA~1\Java\JDK16~1.0\db\lib\derby.jar;
c:\PROGRA~1\Java\JDK16~1.0\db\lib\derbytools.jar;
OS name:         Windows XP
OS architecture: x86
OS version:      5.1
Java user name:  Jeff Friesen
```

```
Java user home:  C:\Documents and Settings\Jeff Friesen
Java user dir:   C:\PROGRA~1\Java\JDK16~1.0\db\FRAMEW~1\NETWOR~1\bin
java.specification.name: Java Platform API Specification
java.specification.version: 1.6
--------- Derby Information --------
JRE - JDBC: Java SE 6 - JDBC 4.0
[C:\Program Files\Java\jdk1.6.0\db\lib\derby.jar] 10.2.1.7 - (453926)
[C:\Program Files\Java\jdk1.6.0\db\lib\derbytools.jar] 10.2.1.7 - (453926)
------------------------------------------------------
---------------- Locale Information -----------------
Current Locale :  [English/United States [en_US]]
Found support for locale: [de_DE]
        version: 10.2.1.7 - (453926)
Found support for locale: [es]
        version: 10.2.1.7 - (453926)
Found support for locale: [fr]
        version: 10.2.1.7 - (453926)
Found support for locale: [it]
        version: 10.2.1.7 - (453926)
Found support for locale: [ja_JP]
        version: 10.2.1.7 - (453926)
Found support for locale: [ko_KR]
        version: 10.2.1.7 - (453926)
Found support for locale: [pt_BR]
        version: 10.2.1.7 - (453926)
Found support for locale: [zh_CN]
        version: 10.2.1.7 - (453926)
Found support for locale: [zh_TW]
        version: 10.2.1.7 - (453926)
```

The client/server version of sysinfo has more information to report. Because the network server uses the Distributed Relational Database Architecture (DRDA) protocol to receive and reply to client queries, the output begins with a Derby Network Server Information section that lists the values of various DRDA properties:

```
--------- Derby Network Server Information --------
Version: CSS10020/10.2.1.7 - (453926)  Build: 453926  DRDA Product Id: CSS10020
-- listing properties --
derby.drda.maxThreads=0
derby.drda.keepAlive=true
derby.drda.minThreads=0
```

```
derby.drda.portNumber=1527
derby.drda.logConnections=false
derby.drda.timeSlice=0
derby.drda.startNetworkServer=false
derby.drda.host=localhost
derby.drda.traceAll=false
----------------- Java Information ------------------
Java Version:    1.6.0
Java Vendor:     Sun Microsystems Inc.
Java home:       c:\progra~1\java\jdk1.6.0\jre
Java classpath:  c:\progra~1\java\jdk1.6.0\db\lib\derby.jar;
c:\progra~1\java\jdk1.6.0\db\lib\derbytools.jar;
c:\progra~1\java\jdk1.6.0\db\lib\derbynet.jar;
c:\progra~1\java\jdk1.6.0\db\lib\derby.jar;
c:\progra~1\java\jdk1.6.0\db\lib\derbytools.jar;
c:\progra~1\java\jdk1.6.0\db\lib\derbynet.jar;
OS name:         Windows XP
OS architecture: x86
OS version:      5.1
Java user name:  Jeff Friesen
Java user home:  C:\Documents and Settings\Jeff Friesen
Java user dir:   C:\PROGRA~1\Java\jdk1.6.0\db\frameworks\NetworkServer\bin
java.specification.name: Java Platform API Specification
java.specification.version: 1.6
--------- Derby Information --------
JRE - JDBC: Java SE 6 - JDBC 4.0
[C:\Program Files\Java\jdk1.6.0\db\lib\derby.jar] 10.2.1.7 - (453926)
[C:\Program Files\Java\jdk1.6.0\db\lib\derbytools.jar] 10.2.1.7 - (453926)
[C:\Program Files\Java\jdk1.6.0\db\lib\derbynet.jar] 10.2.1.7 - (453926)
------------------------------------------------------
----------------- Locale Information -----------------
Current Locale :  [English/United States [en_US]]
Found support for locale: [de_DE]
                 version: 10.2.1.7 - (453926)
Found support for locale: [es]
                 version: 10.2.1.7 - (453926)
Found support for locale: [fr]
                 version: 10.2.1.7 - (453926)
Found support for locale: [it]
                 version: 10.2.1.7 - (453926)
Found support for locale: [ja_JP]
                 version: 10.2.1.7 - (453926)
```

```
Found support for locale: [ko_KR]
                version: 10.2.1.7 - (453926)
Found support for locale: [pt_BR]
                version: 10.2.1.7 - (453926)
Found support for locale: [zh_CN]
                version: 10.2.1.7 - (453926)
Found support for locale: [zh_TW]
                version: 10.2.1.7 - (453926)
```

Note The client/server version of `sysinfo` duplicates the classpath entry, which is most likely due to this version invoking `org.apache.derby.drda.NetworkServerControl sysinfo` instead of `org.apache.derby.tools.sysinfo` (which is invoked by the embedded version).

The `ij` script is useful for creating a database and initializing a user's *schema* (a namespace that logically organizes database objects) by running a script file that specifies appropriate DDL statements. For example, suppose that you want to create the EMPLOYEE table described earlier, with its NAME and PHOTO columns. The following embedded `ij` script session accomplishes this task:

```
C:\db>ij
ij version 10.2
ij> connect 'jdbc:derby:employee;create=true';
ij> run 'create_emp_schema.sql';
ij> CREATE TABLE EMPLOYEE(NAME VARCHAR(30), PHOTO BLOB);
0 rows inserted/updated/deleted
ij> disconnect;
ij> exit;
C:>\db>
```

As indicated in the script session, the contents of `create_emp_schema.sql` are `CREATE TABLE EMPLOYEE(NAME VARCHAR(30), PHOTO BLOB);`. After `run 'create_emp_schema.sql'` finishes, the specified EMPLOYEE table is added to the newly created EMPLOYEE database. To verify the table's existence, run `dblook` against the `employee` directory, as the following session demonstrates:

```
 C:\db>dblook -d jdbc:derby:employee
-- Timestamp: 2007-05-31 19:08:20.375
-- Source database is: employee
-- Connection URL is: jdbc:derby:employee
```

```
-- appendLogs: false


-- ----------------------------------------------
-- DDL Statements for tables
-- ----------------------------------------------


CREATE TABLE "APP"."EMPLOYEE" ("NAME" VARCHAR(30), "PHOTO" BLOB(2147483647));

C:\db>
```

All database objects (such as tables and indexes) are assigned to user and system schemas, which logically organize these objects in the same way that packages logically organize classes. When a user creates or accesses a database, Java DB uses the specified username as the namespace name for newly added database objects. In the absence of a username, Java DB chooses APP, as shown in the preceding example.

Play with the EMPLOYEE Database

Now that the EMPLOYEE database and its EMPLOYEE table have been created, you can start to play with JDBC 4.0 features. For example, you can use Connection's createBlob() method to create an initially empty BLOB, which you populate with an image, and then insert a row into the table with this BLOB and an employee name. Listing 6-1 presents an application that makes this happen.

Listing 6-1. *EmployeeInit.java*

```java
// EmployeeInit.java

import java.io.*;

import java.sql.*;

import javax.swing.*;

public class EmployeeInit
{
    public static void main (String [] args)
    {
        try
        {
            Connection con;
            con = DriverManager.getConnection ("jdbc:derby://localhost:1527/"+
```

```
                                        "c:\\db\\employee");

        PreparedStatement ps;
        ps = con.prepareStatement ("insert into employee(name,photo) "+
                                   "values(?,?)");
        ps.setString (1, "Duke");

        Blob blob = con.createBlob ();
        try
        {
            ImageIcon ii = new ImageIcon ("duke.png");

            ObjectOutputStream oos;
            oos = new ObjectOutputStream (blob.setBinaryStream (1));
            oos.writeObject (ii);
            oos.close ();
            ps.setBlob (2, blob);
            ps.execute ();
        }
        catch (Exception ex)
        {
            System.out.println (ex);
        }
        blob.free ();
        ps.close ();
    }
    catch (SQLException sqlex)
    {
        System.out.println (sqlex);
    }
  }
}
```

This application first attempts to connect to the EMPLOYEE database in the c:\db directory. It uses the Client JDBC driver (the network server must be running) instead of the Embedded JDBC driver (which would be requested via "jdbc:derby:c:\\db\\ employee"), because the latter driver results in a thrown SQLFeatureNotSupportedException.

Note Version 10.2.1.7 of the Embedded JDBC driver does not support Blob's java.io.OutputStream setBinaryStream(long pos) method.

If a connection is successfully made, a prepared statement is created to insert the name and image of Sun's Duke mascot into the EMPLOYEE table. The image is obtained from duke.png via a javax.swing.ImageIcon, which is then serialized to the BLOB (the starting offset to setBinaryStream() is 1, not 0). Finally, the prepared statement is executed to perform the insertion.

After invoking java EmployeeInit, you can be sure that the Duke employee was added to the EMPLOYEE table if there are no exception messages. However, let's verify that this employee's name and image were stored in the table. Accomplish this task by running the application whose source code is presented in Listing 6-2.

Listing 6-2. *EmployeeShow.java*

```java
// EmployeeShow.java

import java.io.*;

import java.sql.*;

import javax.swing.*;

public class EmployeeShow extends JFrame
{
   static ImageIcon image;

   public EmployeeShow ()
   {
      super ();

      setDefaultCloseOperation (EXIT_ON_CLOSE);

      ImageArea ia = new ImageArea ();
      ia.setImage (image.getImage ());

      getContentPane ().add (ia);

      pack ();

      setVisible (true);
   }

   public static void main (String [] args)
   {
```

```
try
{
    Connection con;
    con = DriverManager.getConnection ("jdbc:derby://localhost:1527/"+
                                        "c:\\db\\employee");

    Statement s = con.createStatement ();
    ResultSet rs = s.executeQuery ("select photo from employee where "+
                                    "name = 'Duke'");
    if (rs.next ())
    {
        Blob photo = rs.getBlob (1);

        ObjectInputStream ois = null;
        try
        {
            ois = new ObjectInputStream (photo.getBinaryStream ());
            image = (ImageIcon) ois.readObject ();
        }
        catch (Exception ex)
        {
            System.out.println (ex);
        }
        finally
        {
            try
            {
                ois.close ();
            }
            catch (IOException ioex)
            {
            }
        }
    }
    else
        JOptionPane.showMessageDialog (null, "No Duke employee");
    s.close ();

    if (con.getMetaData ().getDriverName ().equals ("Apache Derby "+
        "Embedded JDBC Driver"))
        try
        {
```

```
                    DriverManager.getConnection ("jdbc:derby:;shutdown=true");
                }
                catch (SQLException sqlex)
                {
                    System.out.println ("Database shut down normally");
                }

            if (image != null)
            {
                Runnable r = new Runnable ()
                            {
                                public void run ()
                                {
                                    new EmployeeShow ();
                                }
                            };
                java.awt.EventQueue.invokeLater (r);
            }
        }
        catch (SQLException sqlex)
        {
            System.out.println (sqlex);
        }
    }
}
```

After successfully connecting to the database, this application executes a query that returns one row containing Duke's name and photo. The photo BLOB is read, its ImageIcon is deserialized from the BLOB, and a GUI is created to display Duke's picture. (The GUI for the picture display was created with the help of a special ImageArea class whose source code is not shown here, but is included with this book's downloadable code.) Figure 6-3 shows a relaxed employee.

Figure 6-3. *Sun's Duke mascot has been open-sourced. The java.net Duke project (https://duke.dev.java.net/) provides details.*

Summary

JDBC 4.0 is the latest version of Java's database-access API. Version 4.0 introduces automatic driver loading, enhanced BLOBs and CLOBs, improved connection management, enhanced exception handling, national character set improvements, new scalar functions, SQL ROWID and SQL XML data type support, and support for the wrapper pattern.

Java DB is a pure-Java DBMS bundled with JDK 6 (not the JRE). It is secure, supports JDBC and SQL (including transactions, stored procedures, and concurrency), and has a small footprint—its core engine and JDBC driver occupy 2MB. You can take advantage of this DBMS to test your database-oriented applications.

Test Your Understanding

How well do you understand the new JDBC features? Test your understanding by answering the following questions and performing the following exercises. (The answers are presented in Appendix D.)

1. Suppose you have installed a copy of MySQL 5.1 DBMS and MySQL Connector/J 5.1, which connects MySQL 5.1 to JDBC. To use the connector, you need to add `mysql-connector-java-5.1.0-bin.jar` to the classpath environment variable. Because this version does not support JDBC 4.0's automatic driver-loading feature, you are required to specify `Class.forName ("com.mysql.jdbc.Driver");` to load the connector's JDBC driver. Describe what needs to be done to the connector/driver to take advantage of automatic driver loading.

2. When you are working with Blob's setBinaryStream() and new getBinaryStream() methods, and Clob's setCharacterStream() and new getCharacterStream() methods, you need to specify the position where you will start writing to or reading from the BLOB or CLOB. Is this starting position 0 or 1?

3. What benefit to connection management do Connection's new setClientInfo() and getClientInfo() methods provide?

4. What is the difference between a transient SQLException and a nontransient SQLException?

5. Create a FuncSupported application that employs the previously shown isSupported() method to determine if a scalar function is supported by a data source. This application takes two command-line arguments: the first argument is a JDBC URL to the data source, and the second argument is the name of a function. It outputs a message such as Function CHAR is supported or Function FOURIER is not supported. Run this application against a Java DB data source and determine if any of the scalar functions identified in Table 6-3 are supported.

   For example, assuming that DERBY_HOME has been set, setEmbeddedCP has been run, and the current directory contains a derbyDB database directory, java FuncSupported jdbc:derby:derbyDB CHAR_LENGTH will tell you if the new CHAR_LENGTH function is supported. If you have installed MySQL 5.1 (and have started the server; mysqld-nt --console, for example), execute java FuncSupported jdbc:mysql://localhost/test?user=root *funcname*, where test is the name of a MySQL database and *funcname* is the name of a new scalar function. Which of these functions does MySQL 5.1 not support?

6. Create a SQLROWIDSupported application that takes a single command-line argument, the JDBC URL to a data source, and outputs a message stating whether or not the data source supports the SQL ROWID data type. Does Java DB version 10.2.1.7 support this data type?

7. Create a SQLXMLSupported application that takes a single command-line argument, the JDBC URL to a data source, and outputs a message stating whether or not the data source supports the SQL XML data type. Does Java DB version 10.2.1.7 support this data type?

8. What is the purpose of dblook's -z, -t, and -td options?

9. Create a DumpSchemas application that takes a single command-line argument, the JDBC URL to a data source, and dumps the names of its schemas to the standard output. What schemas are identified when you run this application against the EMPLOYEE database?

CHAPTER 7

Monitoring and Management

Java's monitoring and management infrastructure combines virtual machine instrumentation with the Java Management Extensions (JMX) agent and JConsole to monitor an application's virtual machine resource usage, such as heap memory use. Java SE 6 enhances this infrastructure via these features:

- Dynamic attach and the Attach API

- Improved Instrumentation API

- Improved JVM Tool Interface

- Improved Management and JMX APIs

- JConsole GUI makeover

- JConsole plug-ins and the JConsole API

Dynamic Attach and the Attach API

HotSpot virtual machines contain instrumentation that JMX-compliant tools like JConsole access via the JMX agent to monitor memory consumption, class loading, and so on. Prior to Java SE 6, you needed to start an application with the com.sun.management.jmxremote system property, which was often specified on the command line, to locally monitor the virtual machine's instrumentation via JConsole (or a similar tool). This property caused the JMX agent and a connector server to start up in the application's virtual machine, so that JConsole could connect to this virtual machine without needing to prompt the user for connection details. This is known as *local monitoring*, because JConsole must run on the same machine (and belong to the same user) as the application. The following command line demonstrates running an application under Java 5 with com.sun.management.jmxremote:

```
java -Dcom.sun.management.jmxremote BuggyApp
```

Behind the scenes, JConsole uses a `javax.management.remote.JMXConnector`–based client to establish a connection to a `javax.management.remote.JMXConnectorServer`–based connector server running in the target virtual machine (the virtual machine in which the application runs). Before Java SE 6, if the application was not started with the JMX agent (because `com.sun.management.jmxremote` was not specified), a `JMXConnectorServer`–based connector server would not be running, and JConsole could not make a connection. Starting with Java SE 6, JConsole overcomes this problem by using a virtual machine mechanism to start the JMX agent in the target virtual machine. This mechanism, which is known as *dynamic attach*, is supported by Sun's new Attach API (`http://java.sun.com/javase/6/docs/technotes/guides/attach/index.html`).

The Attach API consists of two packages, which are stored in `tools.jar`:

- `com.sun.tools.attach`: This package provides six classes for use in attaching to virtual machines and loading tool agents. These classes are described in Table 7-1.

- `com.sun.tools.attach.spi`: This package provides the `AttachProvider` class, which virtual machine developers use to support dynamic attach and the Attach API on their machines.

Although Sun generally discourages working with its "`com.sun.*`" packages, you need to work with these packages to access the Attach API.

Table 7-1. *com.sun.tools.attach Classes*

Class	Description
AgentInitializationException	An agent did not initialize within a target virtual machine.
AgentLoadException	An agent could not be loaded into a target virtual machine.
AttachNotSupportedException	The target virtual machine does not have a compatible AttachProvider.
AttachPermission	The permission checked by a SecurityManager (if present) when attempting to attach to a target virtual machine.
VirtualMachine	A target virtual machine representation.
VirtualMachineDescriptor	A description of a target virtual machine. This description consists of an identifier (usually a target virtual machine's process identifier) returned via the public String id() method, an AttachProvider reference (for use in attaching to a target virtual machine) returned via the public AttachProvider provider() method, and a display name (a human-readable string that is useful in building a GUI-based list of virtual machine names) returned via the public String displayName() method.

The VirtualMachine class is the entry point into the Attach API. Its public static VirtualMachine attach(String id) method lets you attach the current virtual machine to a target virtual machine. The id parameter is an abstract identifier for the target virtual machine, usually its process identifier. This method returns a target VirtualMachine instance, or it throws one of the following exceptions:

- AttachNotSupportedException: The attach() method's argument does not identify a valid target virtual machine, or the target virtual machine does not have a compatible AttachProvider.

- java.io.IOException: An I/O-related problem has occurred.

- NullPointerException: The null argument was passed to id.

- SecurityException: A SecurityManager is present and denies AttachPermission or some other AttachProvider implementation-specific permission.

This attach() method is useful in those tools where users specify identifiers (perhaps obtained by the jps process status tool) on tool command lines. If you prefer to have the user choose a target machine from a GUI list, and then attach to the target, you will want to work with the public static List<VirtualMachineDescriptor> list() and public static VirtualMachine attach(VirtualMachineDescriptor vmd) methods. These methods also can throw the exceptions shown in the preceding list.

In addition to the attach() and list() methods, VirtualMachine specifies public abstract void detach(), to detach the current virtual machine from a target virtual machine; public final String id() to return the target virtual machine's identifier; and several other methods, such as those described in Table 7-2. I will demonstrate most of these methods in upcoming sample applications that interact with target virtual machines.

Table 7-2. *Additional VirtualMachine Methods*

Method	Description
public abstract Properties getAgentProperties()	Returns the target virtual machine's current agent properties, which are typically used to store communication end points and other configuration details. This method includes only those properties whose keys and values are Strings.
public abstract Properties getSystemProperties()	Returns the target virtual machine's system properties, which are useful for deciding which agent to load into the target virtual machine. Only properties with String-based keys and values are included.

Continued

Table 7-2. *Continued*

Method	Description
public abstract void loadAgent(String agent, String options)	Loads an agent into the target virtual machine. The argument passed to agent is the path and name of the agent's JAR file relative to the target virtual machine's file system. The JAR file is added to the target virtual machine's system classpath, and the agent class's agentmain() method is invoked with the specified options. The agent class is identified by the Agent-Class attribute in the JAR file's manifest. The loadAgent() method completes after agentmain() completes. An AgentLoadException is thrown if the agent does not exist or cannot be started. An AgentInitializationException is thrown if agentmain() throws an exception. An IOException is thrown if some I/O-related problem occurs. A NullPointerException is thrown if null is passed to agent.
public void loadAgent(String agent)	A convenience method that invokes the previous loadAgent() method by passing null to options.

Using the Attach API with the JMX Agent

A JMX client uses the Attach API to dynamically attach to a target virtual machine and load the JMX agent (if it is not already loaded) from the management-agent.jar file, which is located in the lib subdirectory of the target virtual machine's JRE home directory. Listing 7-1 presents a simple thread information viewer application that takes care of these tasks and communicates with the JMX agent.

Listing 7-1. *ThreadInfoViewer.java*

```
// ThreadInfoViewer.java;

// Unix compile    : javac -cp $JAVA_HOME/lib/tools.jar ThreadInfoViewer.java
//
// Windows compile: javac -cp %JAVA_HOME%/lib/tools.jar ThreadInfoViewer.java

import static java.lang.management.ManagementFactory.*;

import java.lang.management.*;

import java.io.*;

import java.util.*;

import javax.management.*;
```

```java
import javax.management.remote.*;

import com.sun.tools.attach.*;

public class ThreadInfoViewer
{
    static final String CON_ADDR =
      "com.sun.management.jmxremote.localConnectorAddress";

    public static void main (String [] args) throws Exception
    {
        if (args.length != 1)
        {
            System.err.println ("Unix usage    : "+
                            "java -cp $JAVA_HOME/lib/tools.jar:. "+
                            "ThreadInfoViewer pid");
            System.err.println ();
            System.err.println ("Windows usage: "+
                            "java -cp %JAVA_HOME%/lib/tools.jar;. "+
                            "ThreadInfoViewer pid");
            return;
        }

        // Attempt to attach to the target virtual machine whose identifier is
        // specified as a command-line argument.

        VirtualMachine vm = VirtualMachine.attach (args [0]);

        // Attempt to obtain the target virtual machine's connector address so
        // that this virtual machine can communicate with its connector server.

        String conAddr = vm.getAgentProperties ().getProperty (CON_ADDR);

        // If there is no connector address, a connector server and JMX agent
        // are not started in the target virtual machine. Therefore, load the
        // JMX agent into the target.

        if (conAddr == null)
        {
            // The JMX agent is stored in management-agent.jar. This JAR file
            // is located in the lib subdirectory of the JRE's home directory.

            String agent = vm.getSystemProperties ()
```

```
                        .getProperty ("java.home")+File.separator+
                        "lib"+File.separator+"management-agent.jar";

    // Attempt to load the JMX agent.

    vm.loadAgent (agent);

    // Once again, attempt to obtain the target virtual machine's
    // connector address.

    conAddr = vm.getAgentProperties ().getProperty (CON_ADDR);

    // Although the second attempt to obtain the connector address
    // should succeed, throw an exception if it does not.

    if (conAddr == null)
        throw new NullPointerException ("conAddr is null");
}

// Prior to connecting to the target virtual machine's connector
// server, the String-based connector address must be converted into a
// JMXServiceURL.

JMXServiceURL servURL = new JMXServiceURL (conAddr);

// Attempt to create a connector client that is connected to the
// connector server located at the specified URL.

JMXConnector con = JMXConnectorFactory.connect (servURL);

// Attempt to obtain an MBeanServerConnection that represents the
// remote JMX agent's MBean server.

MBeanServerConnection mbsc = con.getMBeanServerConnection ();

// Obtain object name for thread MBean, and use this name to obtain the
// name of the thread MBean that is controlled by the JMX agent's MBean
// server.

ObjectName thdName = new ObjectName (THREAD_MXBEAN_NAME);
Set<ObjectName> mbeans = mbsc.queryNames (thdName, null);
```

```java
// The for-each loop conveniently returns the name of the thread MBean.
// There should only be one iteration because there is only one thread
// MBean.

for (ObjectName name: mbeans)
{
    // Obtain a proxy for the ThreadMXBean interface that forwards its
    // method calls through the MBeanServerConnection identified by
    // mbsc.

    ThreadMXBean thdb;
    thdb = newPlatformMXBeanProxy (mbsc, name.toString (),
                                   ThreadMXBean.class);

    // Obtain and output thread information.

    System.out.println ("Threads presumably still alive...");

    long [] thdIDs = thdb.getAllThreadIds ();
    if (thdIDs != null) // safety check (possibly unnecessary)
        for (long thdID: thdIDs)
        {
            ThreadInfo thdi = thdb.getThreadInfo (thdID);
            System.out.println (" Name: "+thdi.getThreadName ());
            System.out.println (" State: "+thdi.getThreadState ());
        }

    // The information identifies any deadlocked threads...

    System.out.println ("Deadlocked threads...");

    thdIDs = thdb.findDeadlockedThreads ();
    if (thdIDs == null)
        System.out.println (" None");
    else
    {
        ThreadInfo [] thdsi = thdb.getThreadInfo (thdIDs);
        for (ThreadInfo thdi: thdsi)
            System.out.println (" Name: "+thdi.getThreadName ());
    }
}
}
}
```

ThreadInfoViewer demonstrates the kinds of things that a JMX client does to communicate with a target virtual machine's JMX agent. Notice the call to getAgentProperties(),
followed by a call to getProperty(), to determine if the com.sun.management.jmxremote.
localConnectorAddress property (as specified via constant CON_ADDR) is present. If this
property is not present, no JMX agent and connector server are running in the target.

You'll find Windows and Unix instructions for compiling ThreadInfoViewer.java near
the top of the source code. tools.jar must be in the classpath so the compiler can locate
the Attach API. Following a successful compilation, you'll need a suitable application to
try out this new JMX client. Consider the buggy threading application, whose source code
appears in Listing 7-2.

Listing 7-2. *BuggyThreads.java*

```
// BuggyThreads.java

public class BuggyThreads
{
   public static void main (String [] args)
   {
      System.out.println ("Starting Thread A");
      new ThreadA ("A").start ();
      System.out.println ("Starting Thread B");
      new ThreadB ("B").start ();

      System.out.println ("Entering infinite loop");
      while (true);
   }
}

class ThreadA extends Thread
{
   ThreadA (String name)
   {
      setName (name);
   }

   public void run ()
   {
      while (true)
      {
         synchronized ("A")
         {
```

```java
            System.out.println ("Thread A acquiring Lock A");
            synchronized ("B")
            {
               System.out.println ("Thread A acquiring Lock B");
               try
               {
                  Thread.sleep ((int) Math.random ()*100);
               }
               catch (InterruptedException e)
               {
               }
               System.out.println ("Thread A releasing Lock B");
            }
            System.out.println ("Thread A releasing Lock A");
         }
      }
   }
}

class ThreadB extends Thread
{
   ThreadB (String name)
   {
      setName (name);
   }

   public void run ()
   {
      while (true)
      {
         synchronized ("B")
         {
            System.out.println ("Thread B acquiring Lock B");
            synchronized ("A")
            {
               System.out.println ("Thread B acquiring Lock A");
               try
               {
                  Thread.sleep ((int) Math.random ()*100);
               }
               catch (InterruptedException e)
               {
               }
               System.out.println ("Thread B releasing Lock A");
```

```
            }
            System.out.println ("Thread B releasing Lock B");
        }
    }
  }
}
```

Compile the source code and run BuggyThreads in one command window (no extra libraries are required to run this application). Open a second command window and run jps to obtain the process identifier for BuggyThreads. Using this identifier, invoke ThreadInfoViewer (for example, java -cp %JAVA_HOME%/lib/tools.jar;. ThreadInfoViewer 1932). After a few moments, you should observe output similar to the following:

```
Threads presumably still alive...
  Name: JMX server connection timeout 15
  State: RUNNABLE
  Name: JMX server connection timeout 14
  State: TIMED_WAITING
  Name: RMI Scheduler(0)
  State: TIMED_WAITING
  Name: RMI TCP Connection(2)-xxx.xxx.xxx.xxx
  State: RUNNABLE
  Name: RMI TCP Accept-0
  State: RUNNABLE
  Name: B
  State: BLOCKED
  Name: A
  State: BLOCKED
  Name: Attach Listener
  State: RUNNABLE
  Name: Signal Dispatcher
  State: RUNNABLE
  Name: Finalizer
  State: WAITING
  Name: Reference Handler
  State: WAITING
  Name: main
  State: RUNNABLE
Deadlocked threads...
  Name: B
  Name: A
```

After reviewing the output, it comes as no surprise that the main thread is still running because it is in an infinite loop. It is also no surprise to discover that threads A and B are deadlocked. At some point in each thread's execution, the thread acquired a lock and then was forced to wait while attempting to acquire a second lock, which was already held by its counterpart thread.

Note Alan Bateman, Sun's specification lead on JSR 203: More New I/O APIs for the Java Platform, presents MemViewer as another example of a JMX client that works with the Attach API in his "Another piece of the tool puzzle" blog entry (http://blogs.sun.com/alanb/entry/another_piece_of_the_tool).

Using the Attach API with Your Own Java-Based Agent

You can also create your own Java-based agent and use the Attach API to load the agent into a target virtual machine. For example, consider a basic agent that does nothing more than output a message stating that it has been invoked, and a second message identifying options passed to the agent. Listing 7-3 presents the basic agent's source code.

Listing 7-3. *BasicAgent.java*

```java
// BasicAgent.java

import java.lang.instrument.*;

public class BasicAgent
{
    public static void agentmain (String agentArgs, Instrumentation inst)
    {
        System.out.println ("Basic agent invoked");
        System.out.println ();

        if (agentArgs == null)
        {
            System.out.println ("No options passed");
            return;
        }

        System.out.println ("Options...");
        String [] options = agentArgs.split (",");
```

```
    for (String option: options)
        System.out.println (option);
    }
}
```

The source code introduces `public static void agentmain(String agentArgs, Instrumentation inst)` as the entry point into the agent. According to the JDK 6 documentation for the `java.lang.instrument` package (introduced by Java 5), it is likely that an application will be running and its `public static void main(String [] args)` method will have been invoked before the virtual machine invokes `agentmain()`.

■Note According to the JDK documentation, the target virtual machine will attempt to locate and invoke a `public static void agentmain(String agentArgs)` method if it cannot locate `public static void agentmain(String agentArgs, Instrumentation inst)`. If it cannot find this fallback method, the target virtual machine and its application will keep running, without the agent running in the background. The target virtual machine/application will also keep running if either `agentmain()` method throws an exception; the uncaught exception is ignored.

The `agentmain()` method specifies a `String` parameter that identifies any arguments passed to this method. These arguments originate from the arguments string passed to `options` in `loadAgent(String agent, String options)` (described in Table 7-2). Because the arguments are combined into a single string, the agent is responsible for parsing them. `BasicAgent` refers to these arguments as options.

After compiling the agent's source code (`javac BasicAgent.java`), the resulting class file must be stored in a JAR file. As stated in the JDK documentation, this JAR file's manifest must contain an `Agent-Class` attribute that identifies the class containing an `agentmain()` method. Listing 7-4 presents a suitable manifest file with the `Agent-Class` attribute for the agent's JAR file.

Listing 7-4. *manifest.mf*

```
Agent-Class: BasicAgent
```

After creating a `basicAgent.jar` file via `jar cvfm basicAgent.jar manifest.mf BasicAgent.class` (or a similar command), you are almost ready to use the Attach API to load the JAR file's agent into a target virtual machine. To accomplish this task, I've created an attach application, whose source code appears in Listing 7-5.

Listing 7-5. *BasicAttach.java*

```
// BasicAttach.java

// Unix compile   : javac -cp $JAVA_HOME/lib/tools.jar BasicAttach.java
//
// Windows compile: javac -cp %JAVA_HOME%/lib/tools.jar BasicAttach.java

import java.io.*;

import java.util.*;

import com.sun.tools.attach.*;

public class BasicAttach
{
   public static void main (String [] args) throws Exception
   {
      if (args.length != 1)
      {
         System.err.println ("Unix usage   : "+
                             "java -cp $JAVA_HOME/lib/tools.jar:. "+
                             "BasicAttach appmainclassname");
         System.err.println ();
         System.err.println ("Windows usage: "+
                             "java -cp %JAVA_HOME%/lib/tools.jar;. "+
                             "BasicAttach appmainclassname");
         return;
      }

      // Return a list of running virtual machines to which we can potentially
      // attach.

      List<VirtualMachineDescriptor> vmds = VirtualMachine.list ();

      // Search this list for the virtual machine whose display name matches
      // the name passed to this application as a command-line argument.

      for (VirtualMachineDescriptor vmd: vmds)
          if (vmd.displayName ().equals (args [0]))
          {
              // Attempt to attach.
```

```
            VirtualMachine vm = VirtualMachine.attach (vmd.id ());

            // Identify the location and name of the agent JAR file to
            // load. The location is relative to the target virtual machine
            // -- not the virtual machine running BasicAttach. The location
            // and JAR name are passed to the target virtual machine, which
            // (in this case) is responsible for loading the basicAgent.jar
            // file from the location.

            String agent = vm.getSystemProperties ()
                             .getProperty ("java.home")+File.separator+
                             "lib"+File.separator+"basicAgent.jar";

            // Attempt to load the agent into the target virtual machine.

            vm.loadAgent (agent);

            // Detach.

            vm.detach ();

            // Attempt to attach.

            vm = VirtualMachine.attach (vm.id ());

            // Attempt to load the agent into the target virtual machine,
            // specifying a comma-separated list of options.

            vm.loadAgent (agent, "a=b,c=d,x=y");
            return;
        }

    System.out.println ("Unable to find target virtual machine");
    }
}
```

According to the source code, BasicAttach requires a single command-line argument that serves as the name of an application running on a target virtual machine. The application uses this argument to locate an appropriate VirtualMachineDescriptor so that it can obtain the target virtual machine identifier and then attach to the target virtual machine.

After attaching, BasicAttach needs to locate basicAgent.jar so that this JAR file can be loaded into the target virtual machine. It assumes that basicAgent.jar is placed in the same location as the JMX agent's management-agent.jar file. This location is the lib subdirectory of the target virtual machine's JRE home directory (%JAVA_HOME%\jre under Windows).

Open a command window and run the BuggyThreads application presented earlier (if it is not already running). In another command window, compile BasicAttach.java via the instructions near the top of the source code. To attach BuggyThreads on Windows systems, invoke the following:

```
java -cp %JAVA_HOME%/lib/tools.jar;. BasicAttach BuggyThreads
```

On Unix systems, invoke the following:

```
java -cp $JAVA_HOME/lib/tools.jar:. BasicAttach BuggyThreads
```

If all goes well, BasicAttach ends immediately, returning to the command prompt with no output. In contrast, the command window that shows the output from BuggyThreads will most likely intermingle BasicAgent's output with the BuggyThreads output. You might want to redirect the standard output device to a file when running BuggyThreads so that you can see the agent's output. Here's an abbreviated example of the output:

```
Starting Thread A
Starting Thread B
Entering infinite loop
Thread A acquiring Lock A
Thread A acquiring Lock B
Thread A releasing Lock B
Thread B acquiring Lock B
Thread A releasing Lock A
Thread B acquiring Lock A
...
Thread A releasing Lock A
Thread A acquiring Lock A
Thread A acquiring Lock B
Thread A releasing Lock B
Thread B acquiring Lock B
Thread A releasing Lock A
Thread B acquiring Lock A
Basic agent invoked
```

No options passed
```
Thread B releasing Lock A
Thread B releasing Lock B
Thread B acquiring Lock B
Thread B acquiring Lock A
Thread B releasing Lock A
Thread A acquiring Lock A
Thread B releasing Lock B
Thread A acquiring Lock B
```
Basic agent invoked

Options...
a=b
c=d
x=y
```
Thread A releasing Lock B
Thread A releasing Lock A
Thread A acquiring Lock A
Thread A acquiring Lock B
Thread A releasing Lock B
Thread B acquiring Lock B
...
```

Improved Instrumentation API

The instrumentation built into HotSpot and other virtual machines provides information about virtual machine resources, such as the number of running threads that are still alive, the peak usage of the heap memory pool since the virtual machine started, and so on. Collectively, this information is useful when you want to monitor an application's "health" and take corrective action if its health declines.

Although monitoring application health is important, you might prefer to instrument an application's classes (by adding bytecodes to their methods for the purpose of gathering statistics without modifying application state or behavior) to accomplish another goal. For example, you might be interested in creating a *coverage analyzer*, which systematically tests application code.

Note Steve Cornett's "Code Coverage Analysis" paper (http://www.bullseye.com/coverage.html) describes what a coverage analyzer does.

To support instrumentation for coverage analysis, event logging, and other non-health-related tasks, Java 5 introduced the java.lang.instrument package. This package's Instrumentation interface provides services needed to instrument classes, such as registering a *transformer* (a class that implements the java.lang.instrument. ClassFileTransformer interface) to take care of instrumentation.

Note Java 5's Instrumentation interface also provides services for redefining classes. In contrast to transformation, which focuses on changing classes from an instrumentation perspective, redefinition focuses on replacing a class's definition. For example, you might want to develop a tool that supports *fix-and-continue debugging*. This is an alternative to the traditional edit-compile-debug cycle, which lets you change a program from within the debugger and continue debugging without needing to leave the debugger, recompile, enter the debugger, and restart debugging from scratch. You would use redefinition to change the class's definition to include new class bytes resulting from compilation.

Instrumentation is one of the parameters in the two-parameter agentmain() method. Both overloaded versions of this method were added in Java SE 6. Instrumentation is also one of the parameters in the two-parameter premain() method, which was introduced by Java 5 and has a parameter list identical to that of agentmain(). Unlike premain(), which is always invoked before an application's main() method runs, agentmain() is often (but not necessarily) invoked after main() has run. Also, whereas agentmain() is invoked as a result of dynamic attach, premain() is invoked as a result of starting the virtual machine with the -javaagent option, which specifies an agent JAR file's path and name. When an Instrumentation instance is passed to either method, the method can access the instance's methods to transform/redefine classes.

Note According to Simone Bordet's "Attaching to a Mustang, explained" blog entry (http://bordet. blogspot.com/2005_11_01_archive.html), Java SE 6 also introduces a single-parameter premain() method to complement the single-parameter agentmain() method. As with agentmain(), this method's single parameter is also String agentArgs. Furthermore, it serves as a fallback to the two-parameter premain() method.

Retransformation Support

Java SE 6 adds four new methods to the `Instrumentation` interface to support retransformation:

- `void retransformClasses(Class<?>... classes)`

- `void addTransformer(ClassFileTransformer transformer, boolean canRetransform)`

- `boolean isModifiableClass(Class<?> theClass)`

- `boolean isRetransformClassesSupported()`

Agents use these methods to retransform previously loaded classes without needing to access their class files. Sun developer Sundar Athijegannathan demonstrates the first two of these methods in his class-dumper agent, presented as an example of a useful agent in his "Retrieving .class files from a running app" blog entry (http://blogs.sun.com/sundararajan/entry/retrieving_class_files_from_a). He passes `true` as `addTransformer()`'s `canRetransform` argument so that `retransformClasses()` invokes `transform()` for each candidate class. If `false` were passed, `transform()` would not be invoked.

The `isModifiableClass()` method returns true if a specific class can be modified via redefinition or retransformation. Java 5 made it possible to determine if the current virtual machine configuration supports redefinition via `boolean isRedefineClassesSupported()`. Java SE 6 complements this method with `boolean isRetransformClassesSupported()`, which returns true if retransformation is supported.

Note Java 5 provided a `Can-Redefine-Classes` attribute that had to be initialized to `true` in an agent's JAR manifest so that the agent could redefine classes. Java SE 6's new `Can-Retransform-Classes` attribute complements this other attribute. The agent can retransform classes only if `Can-Retransform-Classes` is initialized to `true` in its JAR manifest.

Native Method Support

Java SE 6 adds two new methods to the `Instrumentation` interface that agents can use to prepare native methods for instrumentation:

- `void setNativeMethodPrefix(ClassFileTransformer transformer, String prefix)`

- `boolean isNativeMethodPrefixSupported()`

Native methods cannot be directly instrumented because they have no bytecodes. According to the setNativeMethodPrefix() method's documentation, you can use a transformer to wrap a native method call inside a nonnative method, which can be instrumented. For example, consider native boolean foo(int x). To apply instrumentation, this method must be wrapped in a same-named nonnative method:

```
boolean foo (int x)
{
    ... record entry to foo ...
    // Specifying return foo (x); would result in recursion.
    return $$$myagent_wrapped_foo (x);
}


native boolean $$$myagent_wrapped_foo (int x);
```

A new problem arises in how to resolve the name of the called native method to the native method's implementation name. For example, suppose the original foo name for the native method resolves to Java_somePackage_someClass_foo. Because $$$myagent_wrapped_foo might correspond to Java_somePackage_someClass_$$$myagent_ wrapped_foo (which doesn't exist), resolution fails.

Invoking setNativeMethodPrefix() with $$$myagent_ as this method's prefix parameter value solves this problem. After unsuccessfully trying to resolve $$$myagent_wrapped_foo to Java_somePackage_someClass_$$$myagent_wrapped_foo, the virtual machine deletes the prefix from the native name and resolves $$$myagent_wrapped_foo to Java_somePackage_someClass_foo.

Note For an agent to set the native method prefix, the agent's JAR manifest must initialize Java SE 6's Can-Set-Native-Method-Prefix attribute to true. Call the isNativeMethodPrefixSupported() method to determine this attribute's value.

Support for Additional Instrumentation Classes

Finally, two more new Instrumentation methods can be used to make additional JAR files with instrumentation classes available to the bootstrap and system classloaders:

- void appendToBootstrapClassLoaderSearch(JarFile jarfile)

- void appendToSystemClassLoaderSearch(JarFile jarfile)

These methods allow you to specify JAR files containing instrumentation classes that are to be defined by the bootstrap or system classloaders. When the classloader's search for a class is unsuccessful, it will search a specified JAR file for the class. The JAR file must not contain any classes or resources other than those to be defined by the classloader for use in instrumentation.

Improved JVM Tool Interface

The Attach API's VirtualMachine class includes a pair of loadAgentLibrary() methods and a pair of loadAgentPath() methods. All four methods accomplish the same goal: they load a native agent library developed with the JVM Tool Interface. The loadAgentLibrary() methods require only the name of the library. The loadAgentPath() methods require the absolute path (including the name) of the library.

Java 5 introduced the JVM Tool Interface as a replacement for the JVM Debug Interface and JVM Profiler Interface, which were deprecated; JVM Debug is not present in Java SE 6. Java SE 6 cleans up and clarifies the JVM Tool Interface specification and offers the following new and improved features:

Support for class-file retransformation: A RetransformClasses() function has been added to facilitate the dynamic transformation of classes that have previously been loaded. Access to the original class file is no longer required to instrument a loaded class. Retransformation can easily remove an applied transformation, and retransformation is designed to work in a multiple-agent environment.

Support for enhanced heap traversal: The IterateThroughHeap() and FollowReferences() functions have been added to traverse objects in the heap. IterateThroughHeap() traverses all reachable and unreachable objects in the heap without reporting references between objects. FollowReferences() traverses objects directly and indirectly reachable from either a specified object or heap roots (the set of system classes, for example). These functions can be used to examine the primitive values in arrays, Strings, and fields via special callback functions. Various heap filter flags control which objects and primitive values are reported by the callbacks. For example, JVMTI_HEAP_FILTER_TAGGED excludes tagged objects.

Additional class information: GetConstantPool(), GetClassVersionNumbers(), and IsModifiableClass() functions have been added to return additional class information.

Support for instrumenting native methods: SetNativeMethodPrefix() and SetNativeMethodPrefixes() functions have been added to allow native methods to be instrumented via a virtual machine-aware mechanism for wrapping these methods in nonnative methods.

Enhanced support for instrumentation under the system classloader: An `AddToSystemClassLoaderSearch()` function allows the system classloader to define instrumentation support classes.

Support for early return from methods: "`ForceEarlyReturn`" functions, such as `ForceEarlyReturnObject()`, have been added to allow a debugger-like agent to force a method to return from any point during its execution.

Ability to access monitor stack-depth information: A `GetOwnedMonitorStackDepthInfo()` function has been added to obtain information about a thread's owned monitors and the depth of the stack frame when the monitors were locked.

Support for notification when a resource has been exhausted: A `ResourceExhausted()` function has been added to notify the virtual machine (via an event) when a critical resource, such as the heap, has been exhausted.

In addition to these enhancements, Java SE 6 introduces a new `JVMTI_ERROR_CLASS_LOADER_UNSUPPORTED` error code constant to indicate that the classloader does not support an operation. It also allows the `AddToBootstrapClassLoaderSearch()` function to be called during the *live phase* (the agent's execution phase between calls to `VMInit()` and `VMDeath()`).

Note For a JVM Tool Interface tutorial, check out "The JVM Tool Interface (JVM TI): How VM Agents Work" article (`http://java.sun.com/developer/technicalArticles/J2SE/jvm_ti/`) and the JVM Tool Interface demos (such as `heapViewer`) that are included in the JDK distribution.

Improved Management and JMX APIs

The Management API focuses on providing a variety of MXBean interfaces and their methods for accessing virtual machine instrumentation. The JMX API focuses on providing the infrastructure for the JMX agent and applications like JConsole that access the JMX agent.

Note For background on MXBeans, check out Sun JMX team leader Eamonn McManus's "What is an MXBean?" blog entry (`http://weblogs.java.net/blog/emcmanus/archive/ 2006/02/what_is_an_ mxbe.html`).

Management API Enhancements

Java SE 6 introduces several enhancements to the java.lang.management package. For starters, five new methods have been added to this API's ThreadMXBean interface. In addition to the new long [] findDeadlockedThreads() method, which returns an array of IDs for deadlocked threads (demonstrated in Listing 7-1), ThreadMXBean includes the four methods described in Table 7-3.

Table 7-3. *Additional New ThreadMXBean Methods*

Method	Description
ThreadInfo[] dumpAllThreads(boolean lockedMonitors, boolean lockedSynchronizers)	Returns thread information for all live threads. Pass true to lockedMonitors to include information on all locked monitors. Pass true to lockedSynchronizers to include information on all ownable synchronizers. An *ownable synchronizer* is a synchronizer that can be exclusively owned by a thread. Its synchronization property is implemented via a java.util.concurrent.locks. AbstractOwnableSynchronizer subclass.
ThreadInfo[] getThreadInfo(long[] ids, boolean lockedMonitors, boolean lockedSynchronizers)	Similar to the previous method, but restricts thread information to only those threads whose identifiers are stored in the ids array.
boolean isObjectMonitorUsageSupported()	Returns true if the monitoring of object monitor usage is supported. Because a virtual machine might not support this kind of monitoring, you will want to call isObjectMonitorUsageSupported() before passing true to lockedMonitors.
boolean isSynchronizerUsageSupported()	Returns true if the monitoring of ownable synchronizer usage is supported. Because a virtual machine might not support this kind of monitoring, you will want to call isSynchronizerUsageSupported() before passing true to lockedSynchronizers.

To support locked monitors, the ThreadInfo class includes a new public MonitorInfo[] getLockedMonitors() method that returns an array of MonitorInfo objects. To support ownable synchronizers, ThreadInfo has a new public java.lang.management.LockInfo[] getLockedSynchronizers() method that returns an array of LockInfo objects. MonitorInfo and LockInfo are new classes in Java SE 6.

Note `ThreadInfo` also includes a new `public LockInfo getLockInfo()` method that returns information related to a lock based on a built-in object monitor, as opposed to a lock based on an ownable synchronizer.

The `OperatingSystemMXBean` interface has been assigned a new `double getSystemLoadAverage()` method that returns the system load average for the last minute. (The *system load average* is the number of runnable entities queued to available processors, plus the number of runnable entities running on the available processors, averaged over a period of time.) The method returns a negative value if the load average is not available.

Note Sun offers `com.sun.management` as its platform extension to `java.lang.management`. This package's management interfaces provide access to platform-specific instrumentation. For example, the `UnixOperatingSystemMXBean` interface includes a `long getOpenFileDescriptorCount()` method that returns the number of open Unix file descriptors. Java SE 6 enhances `com.sun.management` by adding a new platform-neutral `VMOption` class and a `VMOption.Origin` enumeration to provide information about virtual machine options and their origins.

JMX API Enhancements

The two biggest enhancements that Java SE 6 brings to the JMX API have an impact on descriptors and MXBeans, and are as follows:

> *Attach arbitrary extra metadata to all kinds of MBeans*: The new `javax.management.`
> `DescriptorKey` annotation type lets you attach extra metadata to MBeans other than
> model MBeans. For more information, check out Eamonn McManus's "Adding
> Descriptors to MBeans in Mustang" blog entry (`http://weblogs.java.net/blog/`
> `emcmanus/archive/2005/10/adding_descript.html`).

> *Define your own MBeans*: The new `javax.management.MXBean` annotation type lets you
> explicitly mark an interface as being an MXBean interface or as not being an MXBean
> interface.

Additional enhancements include notification improvements, a convenient way to retrieve a `javax.management.remote.JMXServiceURL` from a `javax.management.remote.` `JMXConnector`, and the generification of the JMX API. To learn about these, check out Eamonn McManus's "Mustang Beta and the JMX API" blog entry (`http://weblogs.java.net/` `blog/emcmanus/archive/2006/02/mustang_beta_an.html`).

JConsole GUI Makeover

JConsole's GUI has been given an extensive makeover in Java SE 6. This makeover takes advantage of the system look and feel on Windows and GNOME desktops, which gives JConsole a more professional appearance. This professionalism is especially evident in the revamped connection dialog that appears when you start JConsole. As you can see from Figure 7-1, the biggest change to this dialog is the removal of its former tabbed interface. The GUI components previously located on the Local, Remote, and Advanced tabs have been merged into a more intelligent and simpler layout.

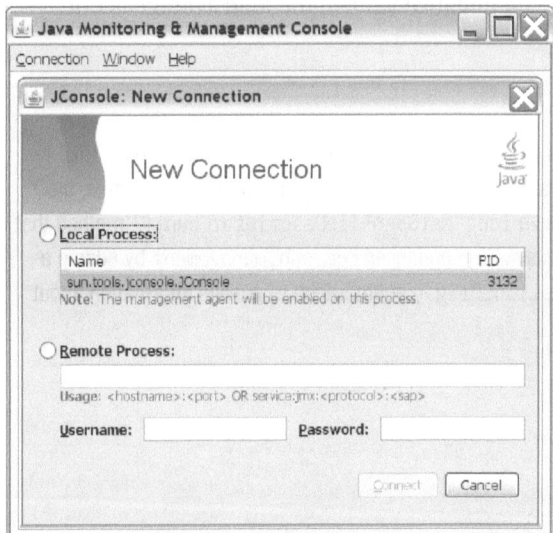

Figure 7-1. *The system look and feel gives the connection dialog a more professional appearance.*

JConsole's tabbed interface has also changed. The previous Summary and VM tabs have morphed into Overview and VM Summary tabs, as follows:

- The Overview tab is the equivalent of the previous Summary tab. However, unlike the Summary tab's textual display, the Overview tab presents live charts of heap memory usage, threads, classes, and CPU usage.

- The VM Summary tab is equivalent to the previous VM tab, but rearranges the VM tab's information. The Memory, Threads, Classes, and MBeans tabs are present in the new JConsole, although the MBeans tab has shifted position. Also, a convenient Detect Deadlock button has been added to the Threads tab.

Note Sun JMX team member Luis-Miguel Alventosa's "Changes to the MBeans tab look and feel in Mustang JConsole" blog entry (`http://blogs.sun.com/lmalventosa/entry/changes_to_the_mbeans_tab`) visually compares the Java 5 and Java SE 6 versions of JConsole's MBeans tab to reveal Java SE 6's structural changes to this tab.

JConsole Plug-ins and the JConsole API

In late 2004, Bug 6179281 "Provide a jconsole plug-in interface to allow loading user-defined tabs" was submitted to Sun's Bug Database, requesting that JConsole be extended with a plug-in API. This API would allow a developer to introduce new tabs to JConsole's user interface, for interacting with custom MBeans and performing other tasks. This request has been fulfilled in Java SE 6.

Java SE 6 supports JConsole plug-ins via the Sun-specific `com.sun.tools.jconsole` package (`http://java.sun.com/javase/6/docs/jdk/api/jconsole/spec/index.html`), which is stored in `jconsole.jar`. A plug-in must subclass this package's abstract `JConsolePlugin` class and implement the two methods listed in Table 7-4.

Table 7-4. *Methods for Adding JConsole Plug-ins*

Method	Description
`public abstract Map<String, JPanel>getTabs()`	Returns a java.util.Map of tabs to be added in the JConsole window. Each Map entry describes one tab, with the tab's name stored in a String and the tab's GUI components stored in a javax.swing.JPanel. An empty map is returned if this plug-in does not add any tabs. This method is called on the event-dispatching thread when a new connection is being made.
`public abstract SwingWorker<?, ?>newSwingWorker()`	Returns a javax.swing.SwingWorker that updates the plug-in's GUI, at the same interval as JConsole updates its GUI. jconsole's -interval command-line option specifies the interval (4 seconds is the default). This method is called at each update to obtain a new SwingWorker for the plug-in. It returns null if the plug-in schedules its own updates.

A Basic Plug-in

Consider a basic plug-in that adds a Basic tab to the JConsole window's list of tabs. When you select this tab, it will present the current date, updated once per interval. Because this plug-in also outputs various messages to the standard output device, JConsole will present another window that displays this output in real time. Listing 7-6 presents the basic plug-in's source code.

Listing 7-6. *BasicPlugin.java*

```
// BasicPlugin.java

// Unix compile   : javac -cp $JAVA_HOME/lib/jconsole.jar BasicPlugin.java
//
// Windows compile: javac -cp %JAVA_HOME%/lib/jconsole.jar BasicPlugin.java

import java.util.*;

import javax.swing.*;

import com.sun.tools.jconsole.*;

public class BasicPlugin extends JConsolePlugin
{
   private Map<String, JPanel> tabs = null;

   private BasicTab basicTab = null;

   public Map<String, JPanel> getTabs ()
   {
      System.out.println ("getTabs() called");

      if (tabs == null)
      {
         tabs = new LinkedHashMap<String, JPanel> ();

         basicTab = new BasicTab ();
         tabs.put ("Basic", basicTab);
      }
      return tabs;
   }
```

```java
   public SwingWorker<?, ?> newSwingWorker ()
   {
      System.out.println ("newSwingWorker() called");

      return new BasicTask (basicTab);
   }
}

class BasicTab extends JPanel
{
   private JLabel label = new JLabel ();

   BasicTab ()
   {
      add (label);
   }

   void refreshTab ()
   {
      label.setText (new Date ().toString ());
   }
}

class BasicTask extends SwingWorker<Void, Void>
{
   private BasicTab basicTab;

   BasicTask (BasicTab basicTab)
   {
      this.basicTab = basicTab;
   }

   @Override
   public Void doInBackground ()
   {
      System.out.println ("doInBackground() called");

      // Nothing needs to be done, but this method needs to be present.
      return null;
   }

   @Override
```

```
   public void done ()
   {
      System.out.println ("done() called");

      basicTab.refreshTab ();
   }
}
```

The plug-in consists of BasicPlugin, BasicTab, and BasicTask classes. The BasicPlugin class is the entry point into the plug-in. The BasicTab class describes a GUI container that contains a single label, which presents the current date. The BasicTask class describes a SwingWorker that refreshes the GUI component with the current date.

BasicPlugin's getTabs() method lazily initializes the tabs and basicTab fields to new java.util.LinkedHashMap (which stores the Basic tab's name and GUI) and BasicTab instances. Additional calls to getTabs() will not result in unnecessary LinkedHashMap and BasicTab instances being created. This method returns the solitary LinkedHashMap instance.

BasicPlugin's newSwingWorker() method, which is regularly called after getTabs() finishes, creates and returns a BasicTask SwingWorker object that stores the BasicTab instance. This instance is stored so that BasicTab's refreshTab() method can be called to update the label's text with the next current date when BasicTask's done() method is called.

Build and run this plug-in as follows:

1. Compile BasicPlugin.java as appropriate for Unix or Windows (see the comments near the top of the source code).

2. Create a META-INF/services directory structure. In the services directory, place a com.sun.tools.jconsole.JConsolePlugin text file whose single line specifies BasicPlugin.

3. Create the plug-in's JAR file by invoking this command:

   ```
   jar cvf basicPlugin.jar -C META-INF/ services *.class
   ```

The jconsole tool includes a new -pluginpath command-line option whose plugins argument lists directories or JAR files that are searched for JConsole plug-ins. As with a JAR file, a directory must contain a META-INF/services/com.sun.tools.jconsole. JConsolePlugin text file that identifies its plug-in entry-point classes, one per line.

To run JConsole with the basic plug-in, invoke jconsole -pluginpath basicplugin.jar. Figure 7-2 shows JConsole's GUI after a new connection has been made (via JConsole's New Connection dialog).

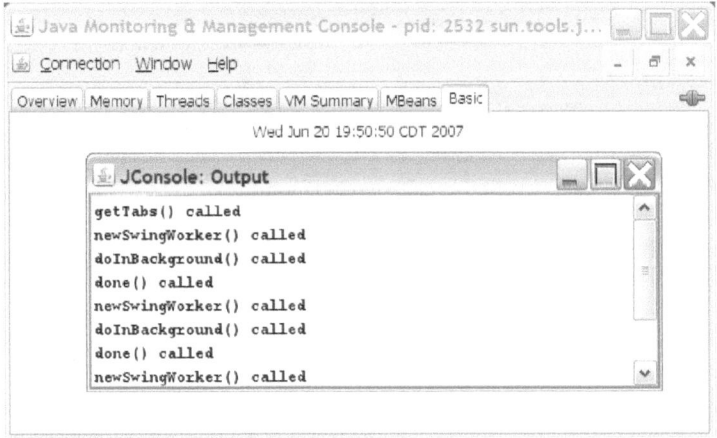

Figure 7-2. *The Basic plug-in tab added to the JConsole window. Notice that plug-in tabs appear to the right of the MBeans tab.*

In addition to showing a Basic tab with the current date (updated at the specified interval), the basic plug-in displays a console window that presents a real-time update of various messages sent to the standard output device. These messages help you to understand the behavior of the basic plug-in in terms of calls to its various methods and the order in which these calls occur.

Beyond the Basic Plug-in

After experimenting with the basic plug-in, you will want to try out more advanced plug-ins. Mandy Chung, a senior staff engineer at Sun, and Sundar Athijegannathan have created sample JConsole plug-ins, which are included with the JDK. Mandy's JTop plug-in is used to monitor the CPU usage of an application's threads; Sundar's script-shell plug-in demonstrates the power of using a scripting language with JMX technology. The following Windows-oriented command line runs JConsole with both plug-ins:

```
jconsole -pluginpath %JAVA_HOME%/demo/management/JTop/JTop.jar;
   %JAVA_HOME%/demo/scripting/jconsole-plugin/jconsole-plugin.jar
```

Invoke this command line (which must be specified as a single line; it is shown across two lines because of its length). In response, you should see the JTop and Script Shell tabs appear to the right of the MBeans tab. The JTop tab, shown in Figure 7-3, gives you more information about running threads. The Script Shell tab lets you interactively access the operations and attributes of MBeans via a scripting language.

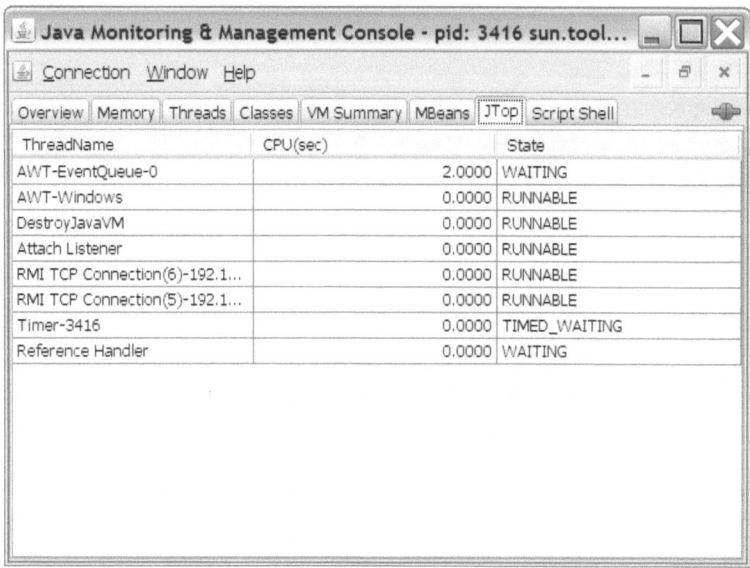

Figure 7-3. *Observe thread names, their CPU usages, and their current states on the JTop tab.*

You can learn how both of these plug-ins work by studying their source code, which is included in the JDK. To discover how JTop can run as a stand-alone JMX client, check out Alan Bateman's "Two fine demos" blog entry (http://blogs.sun.com/alanb/entry/two_fine_demos). To learn more about the script-shell plug-in, check out Sundar Athijegannathan's "Using script shell plugin with jconsole" blog entry (http://blogs.sun.com/sundararajan/entry/using_script_shell_plugin_with).

Note Blogger and Java developer Peter Doornbosch has created a top-threads JConsole plug-in as a replacement for JTop. You can learn about this plug-in, examine the Top threads tab's GUI, and download the plug-in's `topthreads.jar` file (source code does not appear to be available) from http://blog.luminis.nl/luminis/entry/top_threads_plugin_for_jconsole.

Another advanced plug-in is described by Luis-Miguel Alventosa in his "Per-thread CPU Usage JConsole Plugin" blog entry (http://blogs.sun.com/lmalventosa/entry/per_thread_cpu_usage_jconsole). This thread CPU usage JConsole plug-in graphs thread usage for multiple threads. According to Luis-Miguel, "The aim of this plugin is to show how easy it is to add a custom UI to JConsole based on the Java SE platform instrumentation MXBeans in conjunction with the JFreeChart chart library."

Summary

Java SE 6 enhances its support for monitoring and management by providing a new dynamic attach capability and the Attach API, an improved Instrumentation API, an improved JVM Tool Interface, improved Management and JMX APIs, a JConsole GUI makeover, and support for JConsole plug-ins via the new JConsole API.

The dynamic attach mechanism allows JConsole to connect to and start the JMX agent in a target virtual machine. JConsole and other Java applications take advantage of this mechanism by using the Attach API.

The Instrumentation API has been improved through the addition of eight new methods to the `Instrumentation` interface. Four of these methods support retransformation, two methods allow agents to prepare native methods for instrumentation, and two methods can be used to make additional JAR files with instrumentation classes available to the bootstrap and system classloaders.

Java SE 6 also cleans up and clarifies the JVM Tool Interface specification and offers a variety of new and improved features. These features provide support for class-file retransformation, enhanced heap traversal, instrumenting native methods, early return from methods, and notification when a resource has been exhausted. They also provide enhanced support for instrumentation under the system classloader, access to additional class information, and the ability to access monitor stack-depth information.

The Management API has been improved by introducing five new methods to this API's `ThreadMXBean` interface, new `ThreadInfo` methods for identifying locked monitors and ownable synchronizers, and a new `OperatingSystemMXBean` method for returning the system load average. Also, the JMX API has been improved, primarily through the ability to attach arbitrary extra metadata to all kinds of MBeans and the ability to define your own MBeans.

JConsole's GUI has been given a makeover, which takes advantage of the system look and feel on Windows and GNOME desktops. In addition to revamping the connection dialog, Java SE 6 reorganizes JConsole's tabbed interface.

Finally, Java SE 6 introduces a plug-in API for JConsole. The JConsole API allows developers to add new tabs to JConsole's user interface, for interacting with custom MBeans and performing other tasks.

Test Your Understanding

How well do you understand Java SE 6's new monitoring and management features? Test your understanding by answering the following questions and performing the following exercises. (The answers are presented in Appendix D.)

1. Describe local monitoring. Under Java SE 6, does the `com.sun.management.jmxremote` system property need to be specified when starting an application to be locally monitored?

2. What is the difference between class definition and transformation? Does redefinition cause a class's initializers to run? What steps are followed during retransformation?

3. What is the difference between `agentmain()` and `premain()`?

4. Create a `LoadAverageViewer` application modeled after `ThreadInfoViewer`. This new application will invoke `OperatingSystemMXBean`'s `getSystemLoadAverage()` method. If this method returns a negative value, output a message stating that the load average is not supported on this platform. Otherwise, repeatedly output the load average once per minute, for a specific number of minutes as determined by a command-line argument.

5. The JConsole API includes a `JConsoleContext` interface. What is the purpose of this interface?

6. `JConsolePlugin`'s `public final void addContextPropertyChangeListener (PropertyChangeListener listener)` method is used to add a `java.beans.PropertyChangeListener` to a plug-in's `JConsoleContext`. When is this listener invoked, and how does this benefit a plug-in?

CHAPTER 8

■ ■ ■

Networking

Have you ever needed a network interface's hardware address, but had to resort to executing an external program to obtain this information because Java did not provide the appropriate API? Java SE 6 addresses this need and more by adding a variety of new networking features to Java:

- CookieHandler implementation

- Internationalized domain names

- Lightweight HTTP server

- Network parameters

- SPNEGO HTTP authentication

CookieHandler Implementation

Server programs commonly use *cookies* (state objects) to persist small amounts of information on clients. For example, the identifiers of currently selected items in a shopping cart can be stored as cookies. It is preferable to store cookies on the client, rather than on the server, because of the potential for millions of cookies (depending on a web site's popularity). In that case, not only would a server require a massive amount of storage just for cookies, but also searching for and maintaining cookies would be time consuming.

Note Check out Netscape's "Persistent Client State: HTTP Cookies" preliminary specification (http://wp.netscape.com/newsref/std/cookie_spec.html) for a quick refresher on cookies.

A server program such as a web server sends a cookie to a client as part of an HTTP response. A client program such as a web browser sends a cookie to the server as part of an HTTP request. Prior to Java 5, applications worked with the `java.net.URLConnection` class (and its `java.net.HttpURLConnection` subclass) to get an HTTP response's cookies and to set an HTTP request's cookies. The `public String getHeaderFieldKey(int n)` and `public String getHeaderField(int n)` methods were used to access a response's Set-Cookie headers, and the `public void setRequestProperty(String key, String value)` method was used to create a request's Cookie header.

Note RFC 2109: HTTP State Management Mechanism (`http://www.ietf.org/rfc/rfc2109.txt`) describes the Set-Cookie and Cookie headers.

Java 5 introduced the abstract `java.net.CookieHandler` class as a callback mechanism that connects HTTP state management to an HTTP protocol handler (think `HttpURLConnection` subclass). An application installs a concrete `CookieHandler` subclass as the system-wide cookie handler via the `CookieHandler` class's `public static void setDefault(CookieHandler cHandler)` method. A companion `public static CookieHandler getDefault()` method returns this cookie handler, which is null if a system-wide cookie handler has not been installed. If a security manager has been installed and denies access, a `SecurityException` will be thrown when `setDefault()` or `getDefault()` is called.

An HTTP protocol handler accesses response and request headers. This handler invokes the system-wide cookie handler's `public void put(URI uri, Map<String,List<String>> responseHeaders)` method to store response cookies in a cookie cache, and the `public Map<String,List<String>> get(URI uri, Map<String,List<String>> requestHeaders)` method to fetch request cookies from this cache. Unlike Java 5, Java SE 6 provides a concrete implementation of `CookieHandler` so that HTTP protocol handlers and applications can work with cookies.

The concrete `java.net.CookieManager` class extends `CookieHandler` to manage cookies. A `CookieManager` object is initialized as follows:

- With a *cookie store* for storing cookies. The cookie store is based on the `java.net.CookieStore` interface.

- With a *cookie policy* for determining which cookies to accept for storage. The cookie policy is based on the `java.net.CookiePolicy` interface.

Create a cookie manager by calling either the `public CookieManager()` constructor or the `public CookieManager(CookieStore store, CookiePolicy policy)` constructor. The `public CookieManager()` constructor invokes the latter constructor with null arguments, using the default in-memory cookie store and the default accept-cookies-from-the-original-server-only cookie policy. Unless you plan to create your own `CookieStore` and `CookiePolicy` implementations, you will work with the default constructor. The following code fragment creates and establishes a new CookieManager as the system-wide cookie handler:

```
CookieHandler.setDefault (new CookieManager ());
```

Along with its constructors, CookieManager provides four methods, which Table 8-1 describes.

Table 8-1. *CookieManager Methods*

Method	Description
public Map<String, List<String>> get(URI uri, Map<String, List<String>> requestHeaders)	Returns an immutable map of Cookie and Cookie2 request headers for cookies obtained from the cookie store whose path matches the uri's path. Although requestHeaders is not used by the default implementation of this method, it can be used by subclasses. A java.io.IOException is thrown if an I/O error occurs.
public CookieStore getCookieStore()	Returns the cookie manager's cookie store. CookieManager currently works with CookieStore's void add(URI uri, HttpCookie cookie) and List<HttpCookie> get(URI uri) methods only. Other CookieStore methods are present to support more sophisticated implementations of CookieStore.
public void put(URI uri, Map<String, List<String>> responseHeaders)	Stores all applicable cookies whose Set-Cookie and Set-Cookie2 response headers were retrieved from the specified uri and placed (with all other response headers) in the immutable responseHeaders map in the cookie store. An IOException is thrown if an I/O error occurs.
public void setCookiePolicy(CookiePolicy cookiePolicy)	Sets the cookie manager's cookie policy to one of CookiePolicy.ACCEPT_ALL (accept all cookies), CookiePolicy.ACCEPT_NONE (accept no cookies), or CookiePolicy.ACCEPT_ORIGINAL_SERVER (accept cookies from original server only). Passing null to this method has no effect on the current policy.

In contrast to the get() and put() methods, which are called by HTTP protocol handlers, an application works with the getCookieStore() and setCookiePolicy() methods. Consider a command-line application that obtains and lists all cookies from its single domain-name argument. The source code appears in Listing 8-1.

Listing 8-1. *ListAllCookies.java*

```java
// ListAllCookies.java

import java.net.*;

import java.util.*;

public class ListAllCookies
{
    public static void main (String [] args) throws Exception
    {
        if (args.length != 1)
        {
            System.err.println ("usage: java ListAllCookies url");
            return;
        }

        CookieManager cm = new CookieManager ();
        cm.setCookiePolicy (CookiePolicy.ACCEPT_ALL);
        CookieHandler.setDefault (cm);

        new URL (args [0]).openConnection ().getContent ();

        List<HttpCookie> cookies = cm.getCookieStore ().getCookies ();
        for (HttpCookie cookie: cookies)
        {
            System.out.println ("Name = "+cookie.getName ());
            System.out.println ("Value = "+cookie.getValue ());
            System.out.println ("Lifetime (seconds) = "+cookie.getMaxAge ());
            System.out.println ("Path = "+cookie.getPath ());
            System.out.println ();
        }
    }
}
```

After creating a cookie manager and invoking setCookiePolicy() to set the cookie manager's policy to accept all cookies, the application installs the cookie manager as the system-wide cookie handler. It next connects to the domain identified by the command-line argument and reads the content. The cookie store is obtained via getCookieStore() and used to retrieve all nonexpired cookies via its List<HttpCookie> getCookies() method. For each of these java.net.HttpCookies, public String getName(), public String getValue(), and other HttpCookie methods are invoked to return cookie-specific information. The following output resulted from invoking java ListAllCookies http://apress.com:

```
Name = apress_visitedhomepage
Value = 1
Lifetime (seconds) = 83940
Path = null

Name = PHPSESSID
Value = f5938ccc43827a9e96b3c07be1edacf3
Lifetime (seconds) = -1
Path = /
```

Note For more information about cookie management, including examples that show you how to create your own `CookiePolicy` and `CookieStore` implementations, check out *The Java Tutorial*'s "Working With Cookies" lesson (`http://java.sun.com/docs/books/tutorial/networking/cookies/index.html`).

Internationalized Domain Names

The Internet's Domain Name System (DNS) is based on the American Standard Code for Information Interchange (ASCII), which restricts domain names to ASCII symbols. Because this is not fair to many of the world's users, who would like to register and access domain names using language-specific characters, the Internet Engineering Task Force's Network Working Group created RFC 3490: Internationalizing Domain Names in Applications (IDNA) (`http://www.ietf.org/rfc/rfc3490.txt`).

Rather than redesign the DNS infrastructure, RFC 3490 specifies how to translate between ASCII and non-ASCII domain names. Specifically, it presents the following algorithms that operate on individual domain name labels (`www`, `cnn`, and `com` are examples of individual labels for a domain name, as in `www.cnn.com`):

ToASCII: This algorithm modifies a label containing at least one non-ASCII character. It begins by applying the Nameprep algorithm to convert the label to lowercase and perform other normalization tasks. It next translates the result to ASCII by using the Punycode algorithm. ToASCII finishes by prepending `xn--` to the Punycode result. This four-character string is known as the ASCII Compatible Encoding (ACE) prefix. The ACE prefix distinguishes a Punycode label from an ASCII label. The ToASCII algorithm can fail for various reasons, including the resulting ACE-encoded ASCII label exceeding DNS's 63-character limit.

ToUnicode: This algorithm reverses the ToASCII algorithm by removing the ACE prefix and applying Punycode to the result. However, the Nameprep algorithm's processing is not undone, because its normalization of the label passed to ToASCII is irreversible. Unlike ToASCII, ToUnicode cannot fail; it returns its argument label if the label cannot be reversed (it does not begin with an ACE prefix, for example).

Note RFC 3491: Nameprep: A Stringprep Profile for Internationalized Domain Names (IDN) (`http://www.ietf.org/rfc/rfc3491.txt`) describes the Nameprep algorithm. RFC 3492: Punycode: A Bootstring encoding of Unicode for Internationalized Domain Names in Applications (IDNA) (`http://www.ietf.org/rfc/rfc3492.txt`) describes the Punycode algorithm.

Java SE 6 introduces a `java.net.IDN` utility class that presents two constants and four methods to handle ASCII/Unicode translation. The `ALLOW_UNASSIGNED` and `USE_STD3_ASCII_RULES` flag constants can be bitwise ORed together and passed as the `flag` argument to two of the methods:

- `ALLOW_UNASSIGNED`: Allows unassigned Unicode 3.2 code points to be processed. Exercise caution with this constant, because its use can ultimately lead to a spoofing attack, where one web site masquerades as another web site.

- `USE_STD3_ASCII_RULES`: Enforces restrictions on ASCII characters in hostnames. Characters are restricted to letters, digits, and the hyphen (minus sign). Furthermore, a hostname must not begin or end with a hyphen.

`IDN`'s methods are described in Table 8-2. Two of these methods are convenience methods that ignore `ALLOW_UNASSIGNED` and `USE_STD3_ASCII_RULES`.

Table 8-2. *java.net.IDN Methods*

Method	Description
`public static String toASCII(String input)`	Translates the `input` string from Unicode to ACE. An `IllegalArgumentException` is thrown if the input string does not conform to the RFC 3490 specification.
`public static String toASCII(String input, int flag)`	Translates the `input` string (a label or an entire domain name) from Unicode to ACE, taking the `flag` argument into consideration. (The previous method invokes this method, passing 0 to `flag`.) An `IllegalArgumentException` is thrown if `input` does not conform to RFC 3490.

Method	Description
public static String toUnicode(String input)	Translates the input string from ACE to Unicode. In case of error, the input string is returned with no changes.
public static String toUnicode(String input, int flag)	Translates the input string (a label or an entire domain name) from ACE to Unicode, taking the flag argument into consideration. (The previous method invokes this method, passing 0 to flag.) In case of error, input is returned with no changes.

An IDN Converter

Prior to submitting a domain name to the DNS, an IDNA-aware application invokes IDN.toASCII() to convert the domain name to ACE. Before showing a domain name to its user, the application would invoke IDN.toUnicode(). Listing 8-2 presents a converter application that lets you experiment with these conversions.

Listing 8-2. *IDNConverter.java*

```java
// IDNConverter.java

import java.awt.*;
import java.awt.event.*;

import java.net.*;

import javax.swing.*;

public class IDNConverter extends JFrame
{
   JTextField txtASCII, txtUnicode;

   public IDNConverter ()
   {
      super ("IDN Converter");
      setDefaultCloseOperation (EXIT_ON_CLOSE);

      getContentPane ().setLayout (new GridLayout (2, 1));

      JPanel pnl = new JPanel ();
      pnl.add (new JLabel ("Unicode name"));
      txtUnicode = new JTextField (30);
```

```
        pnl.add (txtUnicode);
        JButton btnToASCII = new JButton ("To ASCII");
        ActionListener al;
        al = new ActionListener ()
              {
                  public void actionPerformed (ActionEvent e)
                  {
                      txtASCII.setText (IDN.toASCII (txtUnicode.getText ()));
                  }
              };
        btnToASCII.addActionListener (al);
        pnl.add (btnToASCII);

        getContentPane ().add (pnl);

        pnl = new JPanel ();
        pnl.add (new JLabel ("ACE equivalent"));
        txtASCII = new JTextField (30);
        pnl.add (txtASCII);
        JButton btnToUnicode = new JButton ("To Unicode");
        al = new ActionListener ()
              {
                  public void actionPerformed (ActionEvent e)
                  {
                      txtUnicode.setText (IDN.toUnicode (txtASCII.getText ()));
                  }
              };
        btnToUnicode.addActionListener (al);
        pnl.add (btnToUnicode);

        getContentPane ().add (pnl);

        pack ();
        setVisible (true);
    }

    public static void main (String [] args)
    {
        Runnable r = new Runnable ()
                    {
                        public void run ()
                        {
                            new IDNConverter ();
                        }
```

```
        };
    EventQueue.invokeLater (r);
  }
}
```

For an example of what you can convert, consider the `.museum` top-level domain. According to `http://about.museum`, this domain "was created by and for the global museum community." The International Council of Museums (ICOM), which is an international organization of museums committed to the preservation of the world's natural and cultural heritage, provides native language ".museum" domain names to all of its national committees. One example is the domain name for the Cypriot National Committee (obtained from "The Internationalized Domain Names (IDN) in .museum – Orthographic issues" document at `http://about.museum/idn/issues.html`). This domain name and its ACE form appear in Figure 8-1.

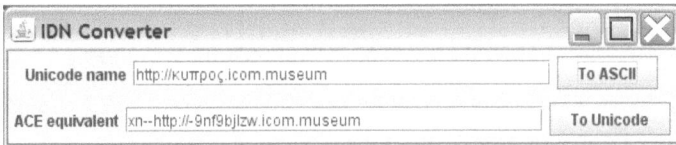

Figure 8-1. *Click the appropriate button to convert a domain name from its Unicode or ACE form to the other form.*

A Better Browser

Chapter 4 introduced two versions of a simple web browser application (see Listings 4-1 and 4-7). This application can be improved by adding support for internationalized domain names. Specifically, the action listener attached to the `txtURL` component can be changed from this:

```
Component c = tp.getSelectedComponent ();
JScrollPane sp = (JScrollPane) c;
c = sp.getViewport ().getView ();
JEditorPane ep = (JEditorPane) c;
ep.setPage (ae.getActionCommand ());
```

to this:

```
Component c = tp.getSelectedComponent ();
JScrollPane sp = (JScrollPane) c;
c = sp.getViewport ().getView ();
JEditorPane ep = (JEditorPane) c;
```

```
String url = ae.getActionCommand ().toLowerCase ();
if (url.startsWith ("http://"))
    url = url.substring (7);
ep.setPage ("http://"+IDN.toASCII (url));
```

The `if` statement is required to prevent `http://` from being included in the string passed to `IDN.toASCII()`. Although these methods can handle entire domain names, they are not designed to deal with the `http://` prefix. Figure 8-2 shows the IDNA-aware browser displaying part of a page retrieved from the `Bücher.ch` domain, where `Bücher` is the German word for books and `ch` is the country code for Switzerland.

Figure 8-2. *Because of the if statement, you can now specify addresses with or without http://.*

Unfortunately, the browser is not able to display a page for every valid IDN. For example, if you specify the second IDN in the list of two IDNs on *The Java Tutorial*'s Internationalized Domain Name page, at `http://java.sun.com/docs/books/tutorial/i18n/network/idn.html`, the server returns a 403 Forbidden message, and the browser displays an appropriate message in an error dialog.

Apparently, this site's server program checks the browser's User-Agent header to make sure that it recognizes the browser, and sends a 403 response to any browser it does not recognize. To prove that this is the case, I have created a small application that bypasses this error by impersonating the Firefox web browser. Its source code appears in Listing 8-3. The `www.xn--80a0addceeeh.com` value is the ACE equivalent of this second IDN.

Listing 8-3. *Bypass403.java*

```java
// Bypass403.java

import java.io.*;

import java.net.*;

import java.util.*;

class Bypass403
{
   public static void main (String [] args) throws Exception
   {
      URL url = new URL ("http://www.xn--80a0addceeeh.com");
      URLConnection urlc = url.openConnection ();
      urlc.setRequestProperty ("User-Agent", "Mozilla 5.0 (Windows; U; "+
                               "Windows NT 5.1; en-US; rv:1.8.0.11) "+
                               "Gecko/20070312 Firefox/1.5.0.11");

      InputStream is = urlc.getInputStream ();
      int c;
      while ((c = is.read ()) != -1)
         System.out.print ((char) c);
   }
}
```

The `urlc.setRequestProperty()` method call makes it possible to observe page contents instead of dealing with a thrown `IOException` when you run this application. Although it would be great to implement this solution for the simple web browser application, `javax.swing.JEditorPane`'s `setPage()` methods are not designed to impersonate different kinds of web browsers.

Note IDNs have raised concerns about spoofing. To learn about these concerns, check out the "Spoofing concerns" section of Wikipedia's Internationalized domain name entry (http://en.wikipedia.org/wiki/Internationalized_domain_name#Spoofing_concerns). Also see "Unicode Security Considerations" (http://www.unicode.org/reports/tr36/), a Unicode technical report from the Unicode Consortium.

Lightweight HTTP Server

Despite opposition (see Bug 6270015 "Support a light-weight HTTP server API"), Sun has included a lightweight HTTP server in Java SE 6. The server implementation supports the HTTP and HTTPS protocols. Its API can be used to embed an HTTP server in your own applications.

■Note Sun introduced the lightweight HTTP server to facilitate web service testing. Chapter 10 demonstrates this task.

Although Sun supports the lightweight HTTP server (see http://java.sun.com/javase/6/docs/jre/api/net/httpserver/spec/index.html), this server is not a formal part of Java SE 6, which means that it is not guaranteed to be available on non-Sun implementations of Java SE 6. Therefore, rather than packages such as java.net.httpserver and java.net.httpserver.spi, the HTTP server API is stored in the following packages:

- com.sun.net.httpserver: High-level HTTP server API for building embedded HTTP servers.

- com.sun.net.httpserver.spi: Pluggable service provider API for replacing HTTP server implementations with other implementations.

The com.sun.net.httpserver package contains an HttpHandler interface, which you must implement to handle HTTP request/response exchanges. This package also contains 17 classes; the 4 most important classes are described in Table 8-3.

Table 8-3. *Important Classes in com.sun.net.httpserver*

Class	Description
HttpServer	Implements a simple HTTP server that is bound to an IP address and a port number, and listens for incoming TCP connections from clients. One or more HttpHandlers are associated with HttpServer to process requests and create responses.
HttpsServer	A subclass that provides support for HTTPS. It must be associated with an HttpsConfigurator object to configure the HTTPS parameters for each incoming Secure Sockets Layer (SSL) connection.
HttpContext	Describes a mapping between a root Uniform Resource Identifier (URI) path and an HttpHandler that is invoked to handle those requests targeting the path.
HttpExchange	Encapsulates a single HTTP request and its response. An instance of this class is passed to HttpHandler's void handle(HttpExchange exchange) method to handle the specified request and generate an appropriate response.

Using a lightweight HTTP server consists of three tasks:

Create the server. The abstract `HttpServer` class provides a `public static HttpServer create(InetSocketAddress addr, int backlog)` method for creating a server that handles the HTTP protocol. This method's `addr` argument specifies a `java.net.InetSocketAddress` object containing an IP address and port number for the server's listening socket. The `backlog` argument specifies the maximum number of TCP connections that can be queued while waiting for acceptance by the server; a value less than or equal to zero causes a system default value to be used. Alternatively, you can invoke `HttpServer`'s `public static HttpServer create()` method to create a server not bound to an address/port. If you choose this alternative, you will need to invoke `HttpServer`'s `public abstract void bind(InetSocketAddress addr, int backlog)` method before you can use the server.

Create a context. After creating the server, you need to create at least one *context* that maps a root URI path to an implementation of `HTTPHandler`. Contexts help you organize the applications run by the server (via HTTP handlers) and are represented by the `HttpContext` class. (The `HttpServer` JDK documentation shows how incoming request URIs are mapped to `HttpContext` paths.) You create a context by invoking `HttpServer`'s `public abstract HttpContext createContext(String path, HttpHandler handler)` method, where `path` specifies the root URI path, and `handler` specifies the `HttpHandler` implementation that handles all requests that target this path. If you prefer, you can invoke `public abstract HttpContext createContext(String path)` without specifying an initial handler. You would later specify the handler via `HttpContext`'s `public abstract void setHandler(HttpHandler h)` method.

Start the server. After you have created both the server and at least one context (including a suitable handler), the final task is to start the server. This is accomplished by calling `HttpServer`'s `public abstract void start()` method.

To demonstrate these three tasks, I have created a minimal HTTP server application. This application's source code appears in Listing 8-4.

Listing 8-4. *MinimalHTTPServer.java*

```
// MinimalHTTPServer.java

import java.io.*;

import java.net.*;

import java.util.*;
```

```java
import com.sun.net.httpserver.*;

public class MinimalHTTPServer
{
    public static void main (String [] args) throws IOException
    {
        HttpServer server = HttpServer.create (new InetSocketAddress (8000), 0);
        server.createContext ("/echo", new Handler ());
        server.start ();
    }
}

class Handler implements HttpHandler
{
    public void handle (HttpExchange xchg) throws IOException
    {
        Headers headers = xchg.getRequestHeaders ();
        Set<Map.Entry<String, List<String>>> entries = headers.entrySet ();

        StringBuffer response = new StringBuffer ();
        for (Map.Entry<String, List<String>> entry: entries)
            response.append (entry.toString ()+"\n");

        xchg.sendResponseHeaders (200, response.length ());
        OutputStream os = xchg.getResponseBody ();
        os.write (response.toString ().getBytes ());
        os.close ();
    }
}
```

The handler demonstrates three HttpExchange methods:

- public abstract Headers getRequestHeaders() returns an immutable map of an HTTP request's headers.

- public abstract void sendResponseHeaders(int rCode, long responseLength) begins to send a response back to the client using the current set of response headers and the numeric code identified by rCode; 200 indicates success.

- public abstract OutputStream getResponseBody() returns an output stream to which the response's body is output. This method must be called after calling sendResponseHeaders().

Collectively, these methods are used to echo an incoming request's headers back to the client. Figure 8-3 shows these headers after `http://localhost:8000/echo` is sent to the server. Note that placing any path items before `echo` results in a 404 Not Found page.

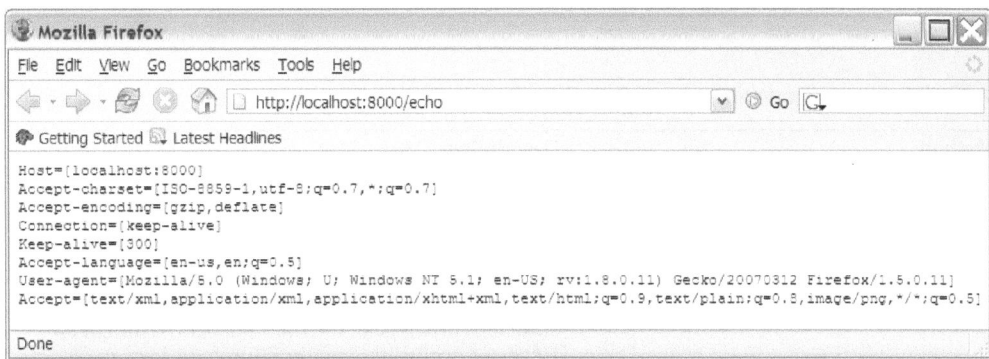

Figure 8-3. *Echoing an incoming request's headers back to the client*

Prior to invoking `start()`, you can specify a `java.util.concurrent.Executor` that handles all HTTP requests. This task is accomplished by calling `HttpServer`'s `public abstract void setExecutor(Executor executor)` method. You can also call `public abstract Executor getExecutor()` to return the current executor (the return value is null if no executor has been set). If you do not call `setExecutor()` prior to starting the server, or if you pass `null` to this method, a default implementation based on the thread created by `start()` is used.

You can stop a started server by invoking `HttpServer`'s `public abstract void stop(int delay)` method. This method closes the listening socket and prevents any queued exchanges from being processed. It then blocks until all current exchange handlers have finished or `delay` seconds have elapsed (whichever comes first). An `IllegalArgumentException` is thrown if `delay` is less than zero. Continuing, all open TCP connections are closed, and the thread created by the `start()` method finishes. A stopped `HttpServer` cannot be restarted.

Network Parameters

Java 1.4 introduced the `java.net.NetworkInterface` class to represent a *network interface* (a connection point between a computer and a network) in terms of a name (such as le0) and a list of IP addresses. Although a network interface is often implemented as a physical network interface card, it also can be implemented in software. For example, the *loopback interface* is a software-based network interface where outgoing data loops back as incoming data, which is useful for testing a client.

A physical network interface can be logically divided into multiple *virtual subinterfaces,* which are commonly used in routing and switching. These subinterfaces can be organized into a hierarchy where the physical network interface serves as the root. Java SE 6 adds new methods to NetworkInterface that let you access this hierarchy, along with additional network parameters. Table 8-4 describes these new methods.

Table 8-4. *New NetworkInterface Methods*

Method	Description
public byte[] getHardwareAddress()	Returns an array of bytes containing this network interface's hardware address, which is often referred to as the *media access control* (MAC) address. If the interface does not have a MAC address, or if the address cannot be accessed (perhaps the user does not have sufficient privileges), the method returns null. If an I/O error occurs, this method throws a java.net. SocketException.
public List<InterfaceAddress> getInterfaceAddresses()	Returns a list containing this network interface's interface addresses.
public int getMTU()	Returns this network interface's *maximum transmission unit* (MTU). This method throws a SocketException if an I/O error occurs.
public NetworkInterface getParent()	Returns this network interface's parent NetworkInterface if this network interface is a subinterface. If this network interface has no parent, or if it is a physical (nonvirtual) interface, this method returns null.
public Enumeration<NetworkInterface> getSubInterfaces()	Returns a java.util.Enumeration containing the subinterfaces that are attached to this network interface. For example, eth0:1 is a subinterface of eth0.
public boolean isLoopback()	Returns true if this network interface reflects outgoing data back to itself as incoming data. If an I/O error occurs, this method throws a SocketException.
public boolean isPointToPoint()	Returns true if this network interface is point-to-point (a PPP connection through a modem, for example). A SocketException is thrown from this method when an I/O error occurs.
public boolean isUp()	Returns true if this network interface is up (routing entries have been established) and running (system resources have been allocated). If an I/O error occurs while this method is executing, it will throw a SocketException.
public boolean isVirtual()	Returns true if this network interface is a virtual subinterface.
public boolean supportsMulticast()	Returns true if this network interface supports the ability to send the same message to multiple clients. This method throws a SocketException in response to an I/O error.

The getInterfaceAddresses() method returns a list of java.net.InterfaceAddress objects that contain a network interface's IP addresses, broadcast addresses (IPv4), and subnet masks (IPv4) or network prefix lengths (IPv6). For security reasons, this list does not contain InterfaceAddresses whose corresponding java.net.InetAddresses have been rejected by an installed security manager. Check out Table 8-5 for a complete list of InterfaceAddress methods.

Table 8-5. *InterfaceAddress Methods*

Method	Description
public boolean equals(Object obj)	Compares this InterfaceAddress with obj. Returns true if obj is also an InterfaceAddress, and if both objects contain the same InetAddress, the same subnet masks/network prefix lengths (depending on IPv4 or IPv6), and the same broadcast addresses.
public InetAddress getAddress()	Returns this InterfaceAddress's IP address as an InetAddress object.
public InetAddress getBroadcast()	Returns this InterfaceAddress's broadcast address (IPv4) or null (IPv6); IPv6 does not support broadcast addresses.
public short getNetworkPrefixLength()	Returns this InterfaceAddress's network prefix length (IPv6) or subnet mask (IPv4). The JDK documentation shows 128 (::1/128) and 10 (fe80::203:baff:fe27:1243/10) as typical IPv6 values. Typical IPv4 values are 8 (255.0.0.0), 16 (255.255.0.0), and 24 (255.255.255.0).
public int hashCode()	Returns this InterfaceAddress's hash code. The hash code is a combination of the InetAddress's hash code, the broadcast address (if present) hash code, and the network prefix length.
public String toString()	Returns a string representation of this InterfaceAddress. This representation has the form *InetAddress / network prefix length* [*broadcast address*].

You can employ these methods to gather useful information about your platform's network interfaces. For example, Listing 8-5 presents an application that iterates over all network interfaces, invoking the methods listed in Table 8-4 that determine if the network interface is a loopback interface, determine if the network interface is up and running, obtain the MTU, determine if the network interface supports multicasting, and enumerate all of the network interface's virtual subinterfaces.

Listing 8-5. *NetParms.java*

```java
// NetParms.java

import java.net.*;

import java.util.*;

public class NetParms
{
    public static void main (String [] args) throws SocketException
    {
        Enumeration<NetworkInterface> eni;
        eni = NetworkInterface.getNetworkInterfaces ();
        for (NetworkInterface ni: Collections.list (eni))
        {
            System.out.println ("Name = "+ni.getName ());
            System.out.println ("Display Name = "+ni.getDisplayName ());
            System.out.println ("Loopback = "+ni.isLoopback ());
            System.out.println ("Up and running = "+ni.isUp ());
            System.out.println ("MTU = "+ni.getMTU ());
            System.out.println ("Supports multicast = "+
                                ni.supportsMulticast ());
            System.out.println ("Sub-interfaces");
            Enumeration<NetworkInterface> eni2;
            eni2 = ni.getSubInterfaces ();
            for (NetworkInterface ni2: Collections.list (eni2))
                System.out.println ("   "+ni2);
            System.out.println ();
        }
    }
}
```

Compile the source code and run this application. You should observe output that is similar to the following (which shows that there are no virtual subinterfaces for my network interfaces):

```
Name = lo
Display Name = MS TCP Loopback interface
Loopback = true
Up and running = true
MTU = 1520
```

```
Supports multicast = true
Sub-interfaces

Name = eth0
Display Name = NVIDIA nForce Networking Controller - Packet Scheduler Miniport
Loopback = false
Up and running = true
MTU = 1500
Supports multicast = true
Sub-interfaces

Name = ppp0
Display Name = WAN (PPP/SLIP) Interface
Loopback = false
Up and running = true
MTU = 1480
Supports multicast = true
Sub-interfaces
```

The output reveals a different MTU size for each network interface. Each size represents the maximum length of a message that can fit into an *IP datagram* without needing to fragment the message into multiple IP datagrams. This fragmentation has performance implications, especially in the context of networked games. For this reason, the getMTU() method is a useful addition.

SPNEGO HTTP Authentication

Java SE 6 supports Microsoft's negotiate HTTP authentication scheme. This feature is referred to as SPNEGO in Bug 6260541 "SPNEGO HTTP authentication" (http://bugs.sun.com/bugdatabase/view_bug.do?bug_id=6260531), and is described in the "Http Authentication" section of the JDK documentation (http://java.sun.com/javase/6/docs/technotes/guides/net/http-auth.html). Although this documentation is fairly easy to follow if you already understand HTTP authentication, it might be somewhat obtuse if you are a newcomer to this topic. The following sections provide a brief review of HTTP authentication, which should help to clear up any confusion.

Challenge-Response Mechanism, Credentials, and Authentication Schemes

According to RFC 1945: Hypertext Transfer Protocol – HTTP/1.0 (http://www.ietf.org/rfc/rfc1945.txt), HTTP 1.0 provides a simple challenge-response mechanism that a server can use to challenge a client's request to access some resource. Furthermore, the client can use this mechanism to provide credentials (typically username and password) that prove the client's identity. If the supplied credentials satisfy the server, the user is then authorized to access the resource.

To challenge a client, the originating server issues a 401 Unauthorized message. This message includes a WWW-Authenticate header field that identifies an *authentication scheme* (the approach taken to achieve authentication) via a case-insensitive token. A comma-separated sequence of attribute/value pairs follows the token to supply scheme-specific parameters necessary for performing authentication. The client replies with an Authorization header field that provides the credentials.

Note HTTP 1.1 made it possible to authenticate a client with a proxy. To challenge a client, a proxy server issues a 407 Proxy Authentication Required message, which includes a Proxy-Authenticate header field. A client replies via a Proxy-Authorization field.

Basic Authentication Scheme and Authenticator Class

HTTP 1.0 introduced the *basic authentication scheme* by which a client identifies itself via a username and password. The basic authentication scheme works as follows:

- The WWW-Authenticate header specifies Basic as the token and a single realm="*quoted string*" pair that identifies the *realm* (a protected space to which a resource belongs, such as a specific group of web pages) referred to by the browser address.

- In response to this header, the browser displays a dialog box in which a username and password are entered.

- Once entered, the username and password are concatenated into a string (a colon is inserted between the username and password), the string is base64-encoded, and the result is placed in an Authorization request header that is sent back to the server. (To learn more about base64 encoding, check out Wikipedia's Base64 entry at http://en.wikipedia.org/wiki/Base64.)

- The server base64-decodes these credentials and compares them to values stored in its username/password database. If there is a match, the application is granted access to the resource (and any other resource belonging to the realm).

The Cornell University Library provides a site for testing basic authentication. If you specify `http://prism.library.cornell.edu/control/authBasic/authTest` in your browser, you will be challenged with a 401 response, as the application in Listing 8-6 demonstrates.

Listing 8-6. *BasicAuthNeeded.java*

```java
// BasicAuthNeeded.java

import java.net.*;

import java.util.*;

public class BasicAuthNeeded
{
   public static void main (String [] args) throws Exception
   {
      String s;
      s = "http://prism.library.cornell.edu/control/authBasic/authTest";
      URL url = new URL (s);

      URLConnection urlc = url.openConnection ();

      Map<String,List<String>> hf = urlc.getHeaderFields ();
      for (String key: hf.keySet ())
          System.out.println (key+": "+urlc.getHeaderField (key));

      System.out.println (((HttpURLConnection) urlc).getResponseCode ());
   }
}
```

This application connects to the testing address and outputs all header fields and the response code. After compiling its source code, run the application. You should see output that is similar to the following:

```
null: HTTP/1.1 401 Authorization Required
WWW-Authenticate: Basic realm="User: test Pass:"
Date: Wed, 02 May 2007 19:18:55 GMT
Transfer-Encoding: chunked
```

```
Keep-Alive: timeout=15, max=99
Connection: Keep-Alive
Content-Type: text/html; charset=iso-8859-1
Server: Apache/1.3.33 (Unix) DAV/1.0.3 PHP/4.3.10 mod_ssl/2.8.22 OpenSSL/0.9.7d
401
```

The WWW-Authenticate header's realm attribute reveals test as the username. Although not shown, the realm's password is this. In order to pass this username and password back to the HTTP server, the application must work with the java.net. Authenticator class, as Listing 8-7 demonstrates.

Listing 8-7. *BasicAuthGiven.java*

```java
// BasicAuthGiven.java

import java.net.*;

import java.util.*;

public class BasicAuthGiven
{
    final static String USERNAME = "test";
    final static String PASSWORD = "this";

    static class BasicAuthenticator extends Authenticator
    {
        public PasswordAuthentication getPasswordAuthentication ()
        {
            System.out.println ("Password requested from "+
                            getRequestingHost ()+" for authentication "+
                            "scheme "+getRequestingScheme ());
            return new PasswordAuthentication (USERNAME, PASSWORD.toCharArray());
        }
    }

    public static void main (String [] args) throws Exception
    {
        Authenticator.setDefault (new BasicAuthenticator ());

        String s;
        s = "http://prism.library.cornell.edu/control/authBasic/authTest";
```

```
    URL url = new URL (s);

    URLConnection urlc = url.openConnection ();

    Map<String,List<String>> hf = urlc.getHeaderFields ();
    for (String key: hf.keySet ())
        System.out.println (key+": "+urlc.getHeaderField (key));

    System.out.println (((HttpURLConnection) urlc).getResponseCode ());
  }
}
```

Because Authenticator is abstract, it must be subclassed. Its protected PasswordAuthentication getPasswordAuthentication() method must be overridden to return the username and password in a java.net.PasswordAuthentication object. Finally, the public static void setDefault(Authenticator a) method must be called to install an instance of the Authenticator subclass for the entire JVM.

After the authenticator has been installed, the JVM will invoke one of Authenticator's requestPasswordAuthentication() methods, which in turn invokes the overridden getPasswordAuthentication() method, when the HTTP server requires basic authentication. This can be seen in the following output, which proves that the server has granted access:

```
Password requested from prism.library.cornell.edu for authentication scheme
basic
Password requested from prism.library.cornell.edu for authentication scheme
basic
null: HTTP/1.1 200 OK
Date: Wed, 02 May 2007 19:20:49 GMT
Transfer-Encoding: chunked
Keep-Alive: timeout=15, max=100
Connection: Keep-Alive
Content-Type: text/html
Server: Apache/1.3.33 (Unix) DAV/1.0.3 PHP/4.3.10 mod_ssl/2.8.22 OpenSSL/0.9.7d
200
```

Digest Authentication

Because the basic authentication scheme assumes a secure and trusted connection between client and server, it transmits credentials in the clear (there is no encryption;

base64 can be readily decoded), making it is easy for eavesdroppers to access this information. HTTP 1.1, which is described in RFC 2616: Hypertext Transfer Protocol – HTTP/1.1 (`http://www.ietf.org/rfc/rfc2616.txt`), introduced the *digest authentication scheme* to deal with the basic authentication scheme's lack of security. The WWW-Authenticate header specifies `Digest` as the token. It also specifies the `realm="`*quoted string*`"` attribute pair.

The digest authentication scheme uses MD5, which is a one-way cryptographic hashing algorithm, to encrypt the password. It also uses server-generated one-time *nonces* (values that vary with time, such as timestamps and visitor counters) to prevent *replay* (also known as *man-in-the-middle*) attacks. Although the password is secure, the rest of the data is transferred in plain text, accessible to eavesdroppers. Also, there is no way for the client to determine that it is communicating with the appropriate server (there is no way for the server to authenticate itself).

The digest authentication scheme is not as widely supported by web browsers as is the basic authentication scheme.

NTLM and Kerberos Authentication

Microsoft developed a proprietary *NTLM authentication scheme*, which is based on its NT LAN Manager authentication protocol, to let clients access Internet Information Server (IIS) resources via their Windows credentials. This authentication scheme is often used in corporate environments where single sign-on to intranet sites is desired. The WWW-Authenticate header specifies `NTLM` as the token; there is no `realm="`*quoted string*`"` attribute pair. Unlike the previous two schemes, which are request-oriented, NTLM is connection-oriented.

In the 1980s, MIT developed Kerberos for authenticating users on large, distributed networks. This protocol is more flexible and efficient than NTLM. Furthermore, Kerberos is also considered to be more secure. Some of Kerberos's benefits over NTLM are more efficient authentication to servers, mutual authentication, and delegation of credentials to remote machines.

GSS-API, SPNEGO, and the Negotiate Authentication Scheme

Various security services have been developed to secure networked applications. These services include multiple versions of Kerberos, NTLM, and SESAME (an extension of Kerberos). Because it is difficult to rework an application to remove its dependence on some security service and place its dependence on another security service, the Generic Security Services Application Program Interface (GSS-API) was developed to provide a standard API for simplifying access to these services. A security service vendor typically provides an implementation of GSS-API as a set of libraries that are installed with the vendor's security software. Underlying a GSS-API implementation sits the actual Kerberos, NTLM, or other *mechanism* for providing credentials.

■**Note** Microsoft provides its own proprietary GSS-API variant, known as Security Service Provider Interface (SSPI), which is highly Windows-specific and somewhat interoperable with the GSS-API.

A pair of networked peers may have multiple installed GSS-API implementations from which to choose. As a result, the Simple and Protected GSS-API Negotiation (SPNEGO) pseudo-mechanism is used by these peers to identify shared GSS-API mechanisms, make an appropriate selection, and establish a security context based on this choice.

Microsoft's *negotiate authentication scheme* (introduced with Windows 2000) uses SPNEGO to select a GSS-API mechanism for HTTP authentication. This scheme currently supports only Kerberos and NTLM. Under Integrated Windows authentication (which was formerly known as NTLM authentication, and also known as Windows NT Challenge/Response authentication), if Internet Explorer tries to access a protected resource from IIS, IIS sends two WWW-Authenticate headers to this browser. The first header has Negotiate as the token; the second header has NTLM as the token. Because Negotiate is listed first, it has first crack at being recognized by Internet Explorer. If recognized, the browser returns both NTLM and Kerberos information to IIS. IIS uses Kerberos when the following are true:

- The client is Internet Explorer 5.0 or later.

- The server is IIS 5.0 or later.

- The operating system is Windows 2000 or later.

- Both the client and server are members of the same domain or trusted domains.

Otherwise, NTLM is used. If Internet Explorer does not recognize Negotiate, it returns NTLM information via the NTLM authentication scheme to IIS.

According to the JDK documentation's "Http Authentication" section, a client can provide an Authenticator subclass whose getPasswordAuthentication() method checks the scheme name returned from the protected final String getRequestingScheme() method to see if the current scheme is "negotiate". If this is the case, the method can then pass the username and password to the HTTP SPNEGO module (assuming that they are needed—no credential cache is available), as illustrated in the following code fragment:

```
class MyAuthenticator extends Authenticator
{
   public PasswordAuthentication getPasswordAuthentication ()
   {
      if (getRequestingScheme().equalsIgnoreCase("negotiate"))
      {
```

```
        String krb5user; // Assume Kerberos 5.
        char[] krb5pass;
        // get krb5user and krb5pass in your own way
        ...
        return (new PasswordAuthentication (krb5user, krb5pass));
    }
    else
    {
        ...
    }
  }
}
```

Summary

Java SE 6 introduces several new networking features, beginning with the CookieManager class. This class provides a concrete implementation of the CookieHandler class, and works with a cookie store and cookie policy so that HTTP protocol handlers and applications can handle cookies.

Because many of the world's users would like to register and access domain names using language-specific characters, the Internet Engineering Task Force's Network Working Group introduced support for internationalized domain names. This support consists of ToASCII and ToUnicode operations that specify how to translate between ASCII and non-ASCII domain names. Java SE 6 supports these operations via an IDN class and its methods.

Sun has included a lightweight HTTP server in Java SE 6, which is especially useful in testing web services. The server implementation supports the HTTP and HTTPS protocols. Its com.sun.net.httpserver package contains 17 classes, with HttpServer, HttpsServer, HttpContext, and HttpExchange being the 4 most important classes.

Java SE 6 adds new methods to the NetworkInterface class that let you access a physical network interface's hierarchy of multiple virtual subinterfaces, as well as other parameters such as the maximum transmission unit. NetworkInterface's getInterfaceAddresses() method returns a list of InterfaceAddress objects that contain a network interface's IP addresses, broadcast addresses (IPv4), and subnet masks (IPv4) or network prefix lengths (IPv6).

Finally, Java SE 6 supports Microsoft's negotiate HTTP authentication scheme. To understand this scheme, you first need to understand HTTP authentication basics. The basics begin with the challenge-response mechanism, credentials, and authentication schemes; continue with the basic, digest, NTLM, and Kerberos schemes; and conclude with GSS-API, SPNEGO, and the negotiate scheme.

Test Your Understanding

How well do you understand Java SE 6's new networking features? Test your understanding by answering the following questions and performing the following exercises. (The answers are presented in Appendix D.)

1. In Listing 8-1, what would happen if you placed new URL (args [0]). openConnection ().getContent (); before CookieManager cm = new CookieManager ();? Why would it happen?

2. Which pair of IDN methods—toASCII() or toUnicode()—throws IllegalArgumentException if the input string does not conform to RFC 3490?

3. Extend MinimalHTTPServer (Listing 8-4) with a second handler that is associated with the /date root URI. Whenever the user specifies http://localhost:8000/date, the server should return an HTML page that presents the current date bolded and centered. Assume the default locale.

4. Extend the network parameters application (Listing 8-5) to obtain all accessible InterfaceAddresses for each network interface. Output each InterfaceAddress's IP address, broadcast address, and network prefix length/subnet mask.

CHAPTER 9

■■■

Scripting

JavaScript, Ruby, PHP, and other scripting languages are popular choices for developing web-based (and other kinds of) applications. Java SE 6 recognizes their popularity by providing a new Scripting API, which lets you develop applications that are partly based on Java and partly based on scripting languages. This chapter explores the Scripting API via the following topics:

- Scripting API fundamentals

- The Scripting API and JEditorPane

- The Scripting API with JRuby and JavaFX Script

Note Wikipedia's Scripting language entry (http://en.wikipedia.org/wiki/Scripting_language) indicates that Ruby and PHP belong to the general-purpose dynamic languages category of scripting languages. To be consistent with the Scripting API's terminology, I refer to *scripting languages* instead of *dynamic languages* throughout this chapter.

Scripting API Fundamentals

The Scripting API was developed under JSR 223: Scripting for the Java Platform. The specification details page (http://www.jcp.org/en/jsr/detail?id=223) introduces a specification that "will describe mechanisms allowing scripting language programs to access information developed in the Java Platform and allowing scripting language pages to be used in Java Server-side Applications." You can download the latest version of this specification by first clicking the appropriate link on this page. Although JSR 223's Scripting API is usable for both web and non-web applications, this chapter focuses on the latter.

Note Early versions of the JSR 223 specification introduced the Web Scripting Framework for generating web content in any servlet container. Chaur Wu's "Speak your own programming language with Web script-ing" article (http://www.javaworld.com/javaworld/jw-05-2006/jw-0522-scripting.html) introduces this framework. As the specification became more generalized, the Web Scripting Framework was deemed optional; its javax.scripting.http package was not included in Java SE 6.

The Scripting API is assigned the javax.script package. This package contains six interfaces, five regular classes, and one exception class, which collectively define *script engines* (software components that execute programs specified as scripting-language-based source code) and provide a framework for using them in Java programs. Table 9-1 describes javax.script's classes and interfaces.

Table 9-1. *Scripting API Classes and Interfaces*

Class/Interface	Description
AbstractScriptEngine	A class that abstracts a script engine by providing several overloaded eval() methods.
Bindings	An interface that describes a mapping of key/value pairs, where keys are specified as Strings.
Compilable	An interface that describes a script engine that lets scripts be compiled to intermediate code. A script engine class optionally implements this interface.
CompiledScript	An abstract class extended by subclasses that store compilation results.
Invocable	An interface that describes a script engine that lets a script's global functions and object member functions be invoked directly from Java code. It also lets scripts implement Java interfaces and Java code invoke script functions through those interfaces. A script engine class optionally implements this interface.
ScriptContext	An interface used to connect script engines with scopes, which determine which script engines have access to various sets of key/value pairs. ScriptContext also exposes a reader and writers that script engines use for input/output operations.
ScriptEngine	An interface that represents a script engine. It provides methods to evaluate scripts, set and obtain script variables, and perform other tasks.
ScriptEngineFactory	An interface that describes and instantiates script engines. It provides methods that expose metadata about the script engine, such as the engine's version number.

Class/Interface	Description
ScriptEngineManager	A class that is the entry point into the Scripting API. It discovers and instantiates script engine factories, providing a method that lets an application enumerate these factories and retrieve a script engine that exposes the appropriate metadata (such as the correct language name and version number) from a factory. It also provides various methods for obtaining script engines by extension, MIME type, or short name. This class maintains a global scope; this scope's key/value pairs are available to all script engines created by the script engine manager.
ScriptException	A class that describes syntax errors and other problems that occur during script execution. Class members store the line number and column position where a problem occurred, and also the name of the file containing the script that was executing. The availability of this information depends on the context in which the problem occurred. For example, a ScriptException thrown from executing a script that is not based on a file is unlikely to record a filename.
SimpleBindings	A class that provides a simple implementation of Bindings, which is backed by some kind of java.util.Map implementation.
SimpleScriptContext	A class that provides a simple implementation of ScriptContext.

In addition to javax.script and its classes and interfaces, Java SE 6 includes a script engine that understands JavaScript. This script engine is based on the Mozilla Rhino JavaScript implementation. Check out Mozilla's Rhino: JavaScript for Java page (http://www.mozilla.org/rhino/) to learn about Rhino.

Note Mozilla Rhino version 1.6R2 is included with Java SE 6 build 105. This implementation includes most of Mozilla Rhino, except for JavaScript-to-bytecode compilation, Rhino's JavaAdapter for extending Java classes and implementing Java interfaces with JavaScript (Sun's JavaAdapter is used instead), ECMAScript for XML, and Rhino command-line tools. An experimental command-line tool, named jrunscript, is available. I discuss this tool in the "Playing with the Command-Line Script Shell" section later in this chapter, and also in Appendix B.

SCRIPTING API RESOURCES

I recommend several resources for learning more about the Scripting API after you've read this chapter:

- The JDK's script notepad Swing application, which is mostly implemented in JavaScript

- Sun developer Sundar Athijegannathan's useful and interesting Scripting API blog entries, such as "JavaScript debugging tips (for Mustang context)" (`http://blogs.sun.com/sundararajan/entry/javascript_debugging_tips_for_mustang`)

- John O'Conner's "Scripting for the Java Platform" article (`http://java.sun.com/developer/technicalArticles/J2SE/Desktop/scripting/`)

If you're interested in taking advantage of the Scripting API for web-based scripting, check out the following:

- Daniel López's "A Dynamic MVC Development Approach Using Java 6 Scripting, Groovy, and WebLEAF" article (`http://today.java.net/pub/a/today/2007/06/19/mvc-webappps-with-groovy-scripting-and-webleaf.html`)

- java.net's Project Phobos home page (`https://phobos.dev.java.net/`), which describes Phobos as "a lightweight, scripting-friendly, web application environment running on the Java platform"

Obtaining Script Engines from Factories via the Script Engine Manager

Prior to performing other scripting tasks, a Java program must obtain an appropriate script engine. A script engine exists as an instance of a class that implements the `ScriptEngine` interface or extends the `AbstractScriptEngine` class. The program begins this task by creating an instance of the `ScriptEngineManager` class via one of these constructors:

- The `public ScriptEngineManager()` constructor works with the calling thread's context classloader if one is available, or the bootstrap classloader otherwise, and a discovery mechanism to locate `ScriptEngineFactory` providers.

- The `public ScriptEngineManager(ClassLoader loader)` constructor works with the specified classloader and the discovery mechanism to locate `ScriptEngineFactory` providers. Passing `null` to `loader` is equivalent to calling the former constructor.

The program uses the ScriptEngineManager instance to obtain a list of factories via this class's public List<ScriptEngineFactory> getEngineFactories() method. For each factory, ScriptEngineFactory methods, such as String getEngineName(), return metadata describing the factory's script engine. Listing 9-1 presents an application that demonstrates most of the metadata methods.

Listing 9-1. *EnumerateScriptEngines.java*

```
// EnumerateScriptEngines.java

import java.util.*;

import javax.script.*;

public class EnumerateScriptEngines
{
   public static void main (String [] args)
   {
      ScriptEngineManager manager = new ScriptEngineManager ();

      List<ScriptEngineFactory> factories = manager.getEngineFactories ();
      for (ScriptEngineFactory factory: factories)
      {
         System.out.println ("Engine name (full): "+
                             factory.getEngineName ());
         System.out.println ("Engine version: "+
                             factory.getEngineVersion ());
         System.out.println ("Supported extensions:");
         List<String> extensions = factory.getExtensions ();
         for (String extension: extensions)
             System.out.println (" "+extension);
         System.out.println ("Language name: "+
                             factory.getLanguageName ());
         System.out.println ("Language version: "+
                             factory.getLanguageVersion ());
         System.out.println ("Supported MIME types:");
         List<String> mimetypes = factory.getMimeTypes ();
         for (String mimetype: mimetypes)
             System.out.println (" "+mimetype);
         System.out.println ("Supported short names:");
         List<String> shortnames = factory.getNames ();
         for (String shortname: shortnames)
```

```
                System.out.println ("  "+shortname);
            System.out.println ();
        }
    }
}
```

Assuming that no additional script engines have been installed, you should observe the following output when you run this application against Java SE 6 build 105:

```
Engine name (full): Mozilla Rhino
Engine version: 1.6 release 2
Supported extensions:
  js
Language name: ECMAScript
Language version: 1.6
Supported MIME types:
  application/javascript
  application/ecmascript
  text/javascript
  text/ecmascript
Supported short names:
  js
  rhino
  JavaScript
  javascript
  ECMAScript
  ecmascript
```

The output reveals that an engine can have both a full name (Mozilla Rhino) and multiple short names (rhino, for example). The short name is more useful than the full name, as you will see. It also shows that an engine can be associated with multiple extensions and multiple MIME types, and that the engine is associated with a scripting language.

ScriptEngineFactory's getEngineName() and a few other metadata methods defer to ScriptEngineFactory's Object getParameter(String key) method, which returns the script-engine-specific value associated with the argument passed to key, or null if the argument is not recognized.

Methods such as getEngineName() invoke getParameter() with key set to an appropriate ScriptEngine constant, such as ScriptEngine.ENGINE. As Listing 9-2 demonstrates, you can also pass "THREADING" as key, to identify a script engine's threading behavior, which you need to know if you plan to evaluate multiple scripts concurrently. getParameter()

returns null if the engine is not thread-safe, or one of "MULTITHREADED", "THREAD-ISOLATED", or "STATELESS", identifying specific threading behavior.

Listing 9-2. *ThreadingBehavior.java*

```java
// ThreadingBehavior.java

import java.util.*;

import javax.script.*;

public class ThreadingBehavior
{
   public static void main (String [] args)
   {
      ScriptEngineManager manager = new ScriptEngineManager ();

      List<ScriptEngineFactory> factories = manager.getEngineFactories ();
      for (ScriptEngineFactory factory: factories)
          System.out.println ("Threading behavior: "+
                              factory.getParameter ("THREADING"));
   }
}
```

Assuming that Mozilla Rhino 1.6 release 2 is the only installed script engine, ThreadingBehavior outputs Threading behavior: MULTITHREADED. Scripts can execute concurrently on different threads, although the effects of executing a script on one thread might be visible to threads executing on other threads. Check out the getParameter() section of ScriptEngineFactory's SDK documentation to learn more about threading behaviors.

After determining the appropriate script engine, the program can invoke ScriptEngineFactory's ScriptEngine getScriptEngine() method to return an instance of the script engine associated with the factory. Although new script engines are usually returned, a factory implementation is free to pool, reuse, or share implementations. The following code fragment shows how to accomplish this task:

```java
if (factory.getLanguageName ().equals ("ECMAScript"))
{
    engine = factory.getScriptEngine ();
    break;
}
```

Think of the code fragment as being part of Listing 9-1 or 9-2's for (`ScriptEngineFactory factory: factories`) loop; assume that the `ScriptEngine` variable engine already exists. If the scripting language hosted by the factory is ECMAScript (language version does not matter in this example), a script engine is obtained from the factory and the loop is terminated.

Because the previous approach to obtaining a script engine is cumbersome, `ScriptEngineManager` provides three convenience methods that take on this burden, listed in Table 9-2. These methods let you obtain a script engine based on file extension (possibly obtained via a dialog-selected script file), MIME type (possibly returned from a server), and short name (possibly chosen from a menu).

Table 9-2. *ScriptEngineManager Convenience Methods for Obtaining a Script Engine*

Method	Description
public ScriptEngine getEngineByExtension(String extension)	Creates and returns a script engine that corresponds to the given extension. If a script engine is not available, this method returns null. A NullPointerException is thrown if null is passed as extension.
public ScriptEngine getEngineByMimeType(String mimeType)	Creates and returns a script engine that corresponds to the given MIME type. If a script engine is not available, this method returns null. A NullPointerException is thrown if null is passed as mimeType.
public ScriptEngine getEngineByName(String shortName)	Creates and returns a script engine that corresponds to the given short name. If a script engine is not available, this method returns null. A NullPointerException is thrown if null is passed as shortName.

Listing 9-3 presents an application that invokes getEngineByExtension(), getEngineByMimeType(), and getEngineByName() to obtain a Rhino script engine instance. Behind the scenes, these methods take care of enumerating factories and invoking ScriptEngineFactory's getScriptEngine() method to create the script engine.

Listing 9-3. *ObtainScriptEngine.java*

```java
// ObtainScriptEngine.java

import javax.script.*;

public class ObtainScriptEngine
{
   public static void main (String [] args)
   {
      ScriptEngineManager manager = new ScriptEngineManager ();

      ScriptEngine engine1 = manager.getEngineByExtension ("js");
      System.out.println (engine1);

      ScriptEngine engine2 =
        manager.getEngineByMimeType ("application/javascript");
      System.out.println (engine2);

      ScriptEngine engine3 = manager.getEngineByName ("rhino");
      System.out.println (engine3);
   }
}
```

After compiling ObtainScriptEngine.java, running the application generates output that is similar to the following, indicating that different script engine instances are returned:

```
com.sun.script.javascript.RhinoScriptEngine@1f14ceb
com.sun.script.javascript.RhinoScriptEngine@f0eed6
com.sun.script.javascript.RhinoScriptEngine@691f36
```

Once a script engine has been obtained (via ScriptEngineFactory's getScriptEngine() method or one of ScriptEngineManager's three convenience methods), a program can access the engine's factory via ScriptEngine's convenient ScriptEngineFactory getFactory() method. The program can also invoke various ScriptEngine methods to evaluate scripts.

Note `ScriptEngineManager` provides `public void registerEngineExtension(String extension, ScriptEngineFactory factory)`, `public void registerEngineMimeType(String type, ScriptEngineFactory factory)`, and `public void registerEngineName(String name, ScriptEngineFactory factory)` methods that let Java programs dynamically register script engine factories with the script engine manager. Because these methods circumvent the discovery mechanism, you can replace an existing script engine factory and script engine with your own implementation, which is returned in subsequent calls to the "getEngine" methods.

Evaluating Scripts

After obtaining a script engine, a Java program can work with `ScriptEngine`'s six overloaded `eval()` methods to evaluate scripts. Each method throws a `ScriptException` if there is a problem with the script. Assuming successful script evaluation, an `eval()` method returns the script's result as some kind of `Object`, or null if the script does not return a value.

The simplest of the `eval()` methods are `Object eval(String script)` and `Object eval(Reader reader)`. The former method is invoked to evaluate a script expressed as a `String`; the latter method is invoked to read a script from some other source (such as a file) and evaluate the script. Each method throws a `NullPointerException` if its argument is `null`. Listing 9-4 demonstrates these methods.

Listing 9-4. *FuncEvaluator.java*

```java
// FuncEvaluator.java

import java.io.*;

import javax.script.*;

public class FuncEvaluator
{
   public static void main (String [] args)
   {
      if (args.length != 2)
      {
         System.err.println ("usage: java FuncEvaluator scriptfile "+
                             "script-exp");
         return;
      }
```

```
ScriptEngineManager manager = new ScriptEngineManager ();
ScriptEngine engine = manager.getEngineByName ("rhino");

try
{
    System.out.println (engine.eval (new FileReader (args [0])));
    System.out.println (engine.eval (args [1]));
}
catch (ScriptException se)
{
    System.err.println (se.getMessage ());
}
catch (IOException ioe)
{
    System.err.println (ioe.getMessage ());
}
    }
}
```

FuncEvaluator is designed to evaluate the functions in a Rhino-based script file via eval(Reader reader). It also uses eval(String script) to evaluate an expression that invokes one of the functions. Both the script file and script expression are passed to FuncEvaluator as command-line arguments. Listing 9-5 presents a sample script file.

Listing 9-5. *stats.js*

```
function combinations (n, r)
{
   return fact (n)/(fact (r)*fact (n-r))
}

function fact (n)
{
   if (n == 0)
       return 1;
   else
       return n*fact (n-1);
}
```

The stats.js file presents combinations(n, r) and fact(n) functions as part of a statistics package. The combinations(n, r) function works with the factorial function to calculate and return the number of different combinations of n items taken r items at a time. For example, how many different poker hands in five-card draw poker (where five cards are dealt to each player) can be dealt from a full card deck?

Invoke `java FuncEvaluator stats.js combinations(52,5)` to discover the answer. After outputting `null` on the first line (to indicate that `stats.js` does not return a value), `FuncEvaluator` outputs `2598960.0` on the line below. The `Double` value returned from `combinations(52,5)` indicates that there are 2,598,960 possible poker hands.

Note Wikipedia's Combination entry (`http://en.wikipedia.org/wiki/Combination`) introduces the statistical concept of combinations. Also, Wikipedia's Five-card draw entry (`http://en.wikipedia.org/wiki/Five-card_draw`) introduces the five-card draw poker variation.

Interacting with Java Classes and Interfaces from Scripts

The Scripting API is associated with *Java language bindings*, which are mechanisms that let scripts access Java classes and interfaces, create objects, and invoke methods according to the syntax of the scripting language. To access a Java class or interface, this type must be prefixed with its fully qualified package name. For example, in a Rhino-based script, you would specify `java.lang.Math.PI` to access the `PI` member in Java's `Math` class. In contrast, specifying `Math.PI` accesses the `PI` member in JavaScript's `Math` object.

To avoid needing to specify package names throughout a Rhino-based script, the script can employ the `importPackage()` and `importClass()` built-in functions to import an entire package of Java types or only a single type, respectively. For example, `importPackage(java.awt);` imports all of package `java.awt`'s types, and `importClass(java.awt.Frame);` imports only the `Frame` type from this package.

Note According to the *Java Scripting Programmer's Guide* (`http://java.sun.com/javase/6/docs/technotes/guides/scripting/programmer_guide/index.html`), java.lang is not imported by default, to prevent conflicts with same-named JavaScript types—Object, Math, Boolean, and so on.

The problem with `importPackage()` and `importClass()` is that they pollute JavaScript's global variable scope. Rhino overcomes this problem by providing a `JavaImporter` class that works with JavaScript's `with` statement to let you specify classes and interfaces without their package names from within this statement's scope. Listing 9-6's `swinggui.js` script demonstrates `JavaImporter`.

Listing 9-6. *swinggui.js*

```
// swinggui.js

function creategui ()
{
    var swinggui = new JavaImporter (java.awt, javax.swing);
    with (swinggui)
    {
        println ("Event-dispatching thread: "+EventQueue.isDispatchThread ());
        var r = new java.lang.Runnable ()
                {
                    run: function ()
                    {
                        println ("Event-dispatching thread: "+
                                    EventQueue.isDispatchThread ());

                        var frame = new JFrame ("Swing GUI");
                        frame.setDefaultCloseOperation (JFrame.EXIT_ON_CLOSE);

                        var label = new JLabel ("Hello from JavaScript",
                                        JLabel.CENTER);
                        label.setPreferredSize (new Dimension (300, 200));

                        frame. add (label);

                        frame.pack ();
                        frame.setVisible (true);
                    }
                };
        EventQueue.invokeLater (r);
    }
}
```

This script (which can be evaluated via java FuncEvaluator swinggui.js creategui())
creates a Swing GUI (consisting of a label) on the event-dispatching thread. The
JavaImporter class imports types from the java.awt and javax.swing packages, which
are accessible from the with statement's scope. Because JavaImporter does not import
java.lang's types, java.lang must be prepended to Runnable.

Note Listing 9-6 also demonstrates implementing Java's Runnable interface in JavaScript via a syntax similar to Java's anonymous inner class syntax. You can learn more about this and other Java-interaction features (such as creating and using Java arrays from JavaScript) from the *Java Scripting Programmer's Guide*.

Communicating with Scripts via Script Variables

Previously, you learned that eval() can return a script's result as an object. Additionally, the Scripting API lets Java programs pass objects to scripts via *script variables*, and obtain script variable values as objects. ScriptEngine provides void put(String key, Object value) and Object get(String key) methods for these tasks. Both methods throw NullPointerException if key is null, IllegalArgumentException if key is the empty string, and (according to the SimpleBindings.java source code) ClassCastException if key is not a String. Listing 9-7's application demonstrates put() and get().

Listing 9-7. *MonthlyPayment.java*

```java
// MonthlyPayment.java

import javax.script.*;

public class MonthlyPayment
{
   public static void main (String [] args)
   {
      ScriptEngineManager manager = new ScriptEngineManager ();
      ScriptEngine engine = manager.getEngineByExtension ("js");

      // Script variables intrate, principal, and months must be defined (via
      // the put() method) prior to evaluating this script.

      String calcMonthlyPaymentScript =
         "intrate = intrate/1200.0;"+
         "payment = principal*intrate*(Math.pow (1+intrate, months)/"+
         "                             (Math.pow (1+intrate,months)-1));";

      try
      {
         engine.put ("principal", 20000.0);
```

```
            System.out.println ("Principal = "+engine.get ("principal"));
            engine.put ("intrate", 6.0);
            System.out.println ("Interest Rate = "+engine.get ("intrate")+"%");
            engine.put ("months", 360);
            System.out.println ("Months = "+engine.get ("months"));
            engine.eval (calcMonthlyPaymentScript);
            System.out.printf ("Monthly Payment = %.2f\n",
                            engine.get ("payment"));
        }
        catch (ScriptException se)
        {
            System.err.println (se.getMessage ());
        }
    }
}
```

MonthlyPayment calculates the monthly payment on a loan via the formula $MP = P*I*(1+I)^N/(1+I)^N-1$, where MP is the monthly payment, P is the principal, I is the interest rate divided by 1200, and N is the number of monthly periods to amortize the loan. Running this application with P set to 20000, I set to 6%, and N set to 360 results in this output:

```
Principal = 20000.0
Interest Rate = 6.0%
Months = 360
Monthly Payment = 119.91
```

The script depends on the existence of script variables principal, intrate, and months. These variables (with their object values) are introduced to the script via the put() method—20000.0 and 6.0 are boxed into Doubles; 360 is boxed into an Integer. The calculation result is stored in the payment script variable. get() returns this Double's value to Java. The get() method returns null if key does not exist.

Java programs are free to choose any syntactically correct string-based key (based on scripting language syntax) for a script variable's name, except for those keys beginning with the javax.script prefix. The Scripting API reserves this prefix for special purposes. Table 9-3 lists several keys that begin with this prefix, together with their ScriptEngine constants.

Table 9-3. *Reserved Keys and Their Constants*

Key	Constant	Description
javax.script.argv	ARGV	An Object[] array of arguments
javax.script.engine	ENGINE	The full name of the script engine
javax.script.engine_version	ENGINE_VERSION	The script engine's version
javax.script.filename	FILENAME	The name of the script file being evaluated
javax.script.language	LANGUAGE	The name of the scripting language associated with the script engine
javax.script.language_version	LANGUAGE_VERSION	The version of the scripting language associated with the script engine
javax.script.name	NAME	The short name of the script engine

Apart from ARGV and FILENAME, ScriptEngineFactory methods such as getEngineName() pass these constants as arguments to the previously discussed getParameter(String key) method. A Java program typically passes ARGV and FILENAME variables to a script, as in the following examples:

```
engine.put (ScriptEngine.ARGV, new String [] { "arg1", "arg2" });
engine.put (ScriptEngine.FILENAME, "file.js");
```

Note The jrunscript tool employs engine.put("arguments", args) followed by engine.put(ScriptEngine.ARGV, args) to make its command-line arguments available to a script. It also uses engine.put(ScriptEngine.FILENAME, name) to make the name of the script file being evaluated available to a script. The jrunscript tool is discussed in the "Playing with the Command-Line Script Shell" section later in this chapter.

Understanding Bindings and Scopes

The put() and get() methods interact with an internal map that stores key/value pairs. They access this map via an object whose class implements the Bindings interface, such as SimpleBindings. To determine which *bindings* objects are accessible to script engines, the Scripting API associates a *scope* identifier with each bindings object:

- The `ScriptContext.ENGINE_SCOPE` constant identifies the engine scope. A bindings object that is associated with this identifier is visible to a specific script engine throughout the engine's lifetime; other script engines do not have access to this bindings object, unless you share it with them. `ScriptEngine`'s `put()` and `get()` methods always interact with bindings objects that are engine scoped.

- The `ScriptContext.GLOBAL_SCOPE` constant identifies the global scope. A bindings object that is associated with this identifier is visible to all script engines that are created with the same script engine manager. `ScriptEngineManager`'s `public void put(String key, Object value)` and `public Object get(String key)` methods always interact with bindings objects that are globally scoped.

A script engine's bindings object for either scope can be obtained via `ScriptEngine`'s `Bindings getBindings(int scope)` method, with `scope` set to the appropriate constant. This object can be replaced via the `void setBindings(Bindings bindings, int scope)` method. `ScriptEngineManager`'s `public Bindings getBindings()` and `public void setBindings(Bindings bindings)` methods obtain/replace global bindings.

■**Note** To share the global scope's bindings object with a newly created script engine, `ScriptEngineManager`'s `getEngineByExtension()`, `getEngineByMimeType()`, and `getEngineByName()` methods invoke `ScriptEngine`'s `setBindings()` method with `scope` set to `ScriptContext.GLOBAL_SCOPE`.

A Java program can create an empty `Bindings` object via `ScriptEngine`'s `Bindings createBindings()` method, and can temporarily replace a script engine's current bindings object with this new bindings object via `ScriptEngine`'s `getBindings()` and `setBindings()` methods. However, it is easier to pass this object to the `Object eval(String script, Bindings n)` and `Object eval(Reader reader, Bindings n)` methods, which also leave the current bindings unaffected. Listing 9-8 presents an application that uses this approach and demonstrates various binding-oriented methods.

Listing 9-8. *GetToKnowBindingsAndScopes.java*

```
// GetToKnowBindingsAndScopes.java

//import java.util.*;

import javax.script.*;

public class GetToKnowBindingsAndScopes
```

```
{
    public static void main (String [] args)
    {
        ScriptEngineManager manager = new ScriptEngineManager ();
        manager.put ("global", "global bindings");

        System.out.println ("INITIAL GLOBAL SCOPE BINDINGS");
        dumpBindings (manager.getBindings ());

        ScriptEngine engine = manager.getEngineByExtension ("js");
        engine.put ("engine", "engine bindings");

        System.out.println ("ENGINE'S GLOBAL SCOPE BINDINGS");
        dumpBindings (engine.getBindings (ScriptContext.GLOBAL_SCOPE));

        System.out.println ("ENGINE'S ENGINE SCOPE BINDINGS");
        dumpBindings (engine.getBindings (ScriptContext.ENGINE_SCOPE));

        try
        {
            Bindings bindings = engine.createBindings ();
            bindings.put ("engine", "overridden engine bindings");
            bindings.put ("app", new GetToKnowBindingsAndScopes ());
            bindings.put ("bindings", bindings);
            System.out.println ("ENGINE'S OVERRIDDEN ENGINE SCOPE BINDINGS");
            engine.eval ("app.dumpBindings (bindings);", bindings);
        }
        catch (ScriptException se)
        {
            System.err.println (se.getMessage ());
        }

        ScriptEngine engine2 = manager.getEngineByExtension ("js");
        engine2.put ("engine2", "engine2 bindings");

        System.out.println ("ENGINE2'S GLOBAL SCOPE BINDINGS");
        dumpBindings (engine2.getBindings (ScriptContext.GLOBAL_SCOPE));

        System.out.println ("ENGINE2'S ENGINE SCOPE BINDINGS");
        dumpBindings (engine2.getBindings (ScriptContext.ENGINE_SCOPE));

        System.out.println ("ENGINE'S ENGINE SCOPE BINDINGS");
```

```
        dumpBindings (engine.getBindings (ScriptContext.ENGINE_SCOPE));
    }

    public static void dumpBindings (Bindings bindings)
    {
        if (bindings == null)
            System.out.println ("  No bindings");
        else
            for (String key: bindings.keySet ())
                    System.out.println ("  "+key+": "+bindings.get (key));
        System.out.println ();
    }
}
```

Because the global bindings are initially empty, the application adds a single global entry to these bindings. It then creates a script engine and adds a single engine entry to the script engine's initial engine bindings. Next, an empty bindings object is created and populated with a new engine entry via the Bindings interface's Object put(String name, Object value) method. New app and bindings entries are also added so that the script can invoke the application's dumpBindings(Bindings bindings) method to reveal the passed Bindings object's entries. Finally, a second script engine is created, and an engine entry (with a value that differs from the first script engine's engine entry) is added to its default engine bindings. These tasks lead to output that is similar to the following:

```
INITIAL GLOBAL SCOPE BINDINGS
  global: global bindings

ENGINE'S GLOBAL SCOPE BINDINGS
  global: global bindings

ENGINE'S ENGINE SCOPE BINDINGS
  engine: engine bindings

ENGINE'S OVERRIDDEN ENGINE SCOPE BINDINGS
  app: GetToKnowBindingsAndScopes@1174b07
  println: sun.org.mozilla.javascript.internal.InterpretedFunction@3eca90
  engine: overridden engine bindings
  bindings: javax.script.SimpleBindings@64dc11
  context: javax.script.SimpleScriptContext@1ac1fe4
  print: sun.org.mozilla.javascript.internal.InterpretedFunction@161d36b

ENGINE2'S GLOBAL SCOPE BINDINGS
```

```
global: global bindings

ENGINE2'S ENGINE SCOPE BINDINGS
  engine2: engine2 bindings

ENGINE'S ENGINE SCOPE BINDINGS
  engine: engine bindings
```

The output shows that all script engines access the same global bindings, and that each engine has its own private engine bindings. It also reveals that passing a bindings object to a script via an eval() method does not affect the script's engine's current engine bindings. Finally, the output shows three interesting script variables—println, print, and context—which I discuss in the next section.

Tip The Bindings interface presents a void putAll(Map<? extends String,? extends Object> toMerge) method that is convenient for merging the contents of one bindings object with another bindings object.

Understanding Script Contexts

ScriptEngine's getBindings() and setBindings() methods ultimately defer to ScriptContext's equivalent methods of the same name. ScriptContext describes a *script context*, which connects a script engine to a Java program. It exposes the global and engine bindings objects, as well as a Reader and a pair of Writers that a script engine uses for input and output.

Every script engine has a default script context, which a script engine's constructor creates as an instance of SimpleScriptContext. The default script context is set as follows:

- The engine scope's set of bindings is initially empty.

- There is no global scope.

- A java.io.InputStreamReader that receives input from System.in is created as the reader.

- java.io.PrintWriters that send output to System.out and System.err are created as writers.

Note After each of ScriptEngineManager's three "getEngine" methods obtains a script engine from the engine's factory, the method stores a reference to the shared global scope in the engine's default script context.

The default script context can be accessed via ScriptEngine's ScriptContext getContext() method, and replaced via the companion void setContext(ScriptContext context) method. The eval(String script) and eval(Reader reader) methods invoke Object eval(String script, ScriptContext context) and Object eval(Reader reader, ScriptContext context) with the default script context as the argument.

In contrast, the eval(String script, Bindings n) and eval(Reader reader, Bindings n) methods first create a new temporary script context with engine bindings set to n, and with global bindings set to the default context's global bindings. These methods then invoke eval(String script, ScriptContext context) and eval(Reader reader, ScriptContext context) with the new script context as the argument.

Although you can create your own script context and pass it to eval(String script, ScriptContext context) or eval(Reader reader, ScriptContext context), you might choose to manipulate the default script context instead. For example, if you want to send a script's output to a GUI's text component, you might install a new writer into the default script context, as demonstrated in Listing 9-9.

Listing 9-9. *RedirectScriptOutputToGUI.java*

```java
// RedirectScriptOutputToGUI.java

import java.awt.*;
import java.awt.event.*;

import java.io.*;

import javax.script.*;

import javax.swing.*;

public class RedirectScriptOutputToGUI extends JFrame
{
   static ScriptEngine engine;

   public RedirectScriptOutputToGUI ()
   {
      super ("Redirect Script Output to GUI");
```

```java
        setDefaultCloseOperation (EXIT_ON_CLOSE);

        getContentPane ().add (createGUI ());

        pack ();
        setVisible (true);
    }

    JPanel createGUI ()
    {
        JPanel pnlGUI = new JPanel ();
        pnlGUI.setLayout (new BorderLayout ());

        JPanel pnl = new JPanel ();
        pnl.setLayout (new GridLayout (2, 1));

        final JTextArea txtScriptInput = new JTextArea (10, 60);
        pnl.add (new JScrollPane (txtScriptInput));

        final JTextArea txtScriptOutput = new JTextArea (10, 60);
        pnl.add (new JScrollPane (txtScriptOutput));

        pnlGUI.add (pnl, BorderLayout.NORTH);

        GUIWriter writer = new GUIWriter (txtScriptOutput);
        PrintWriter pw = new PrintWriter (writer, true);
        engine.getContext ().setWriter (pw);
        engine.getContext ().setErrorWriter (pw);

        pnl = new JPanel ();

        JButton btnEvaluate = new JButton ("Evaluate");
        ActionListener actionEvaluate;
        actionEvaluate = new ActionListener ()
                        {
                            public void actionPerformed (ActionEvent e)
                            {
                                try
                                {
                                    engine.eval (txtScriptInput.getText ());
                                    dumpBindings ();
                                }
```

```
                            catch (ScriptException se)
                            {
                                JFrame parent;
                                parent = RedirectScriptOutputToGUI.this;
                                JOptionPane.
                                    showMessageDialog (parent,
                                                        se.getMessage ());
                            }
                        }
                    };
        btnEvaluate.addActionListener (actionEvaluate);
        pnl.add (btnEvaluate);

        JButton btnClear = new JButton ("Clear");
        ActionListener actionClear;
        actionClear = new ActionListener ()
                    {
                        public void actionPerformed (ActionEvent e)
                        {
                            txtScriptInput.setText ("");
                            txtScriptOutput.setText ("");
                        }
                    };
        btnClear.addActionListener (actionClear);
        pnl.add (btnClear);

        pnlGUI.add (pnl, BorderLayout.SOUTH);

        return pnlGUI;
    }

    static void dumpBindings ()
    {
        System.out.println ("ENGINE BINDINGS");
        Bindings bindings = engine.getBindings (ScriptContext.ENGINE_SCOPE);
        if (bindings == null)
            System.out.println ("  No bindings");
        else
            for (String key: bindings.keySet ())
                System.out.println ("  "+key+": "+bindings.get (key));
        System.out.println ();
    }
```

```java
    public static void main (String [] args)
    {
        ScriptEngineManager manager = new ScriptEngineManager ();
        engine = manager.getEngineByName ("rhino");
        dumpBindings ();

        Runnable r = new Runnable ()
                    {
                        public void run ()
                        {
                            new RedirectScriptOutputToGUI ();
                        }
                    };
        EventQueue.invokeLater (r);
    }
}

class GUIWriter extends Writer
{
    private JTextArea txtOutput;

    GUIWriter (JTextArea txtOutput)
    {
        this.txtOutput = txtOutput;
    }

    public void close ()
    {
        System.out.println ("close");
    }

    public void flush ()
    {
        System.out.println ("flush");
    }

    public void write (char [] cbuf, int off, int len)
    {
        txtOutput.setText (txtOutput.getText ()+new String (cbuf, off, len));
    }
}
```

RedirectScriptOutputToGUI creates a Swing GUI with two text components and two buttons. After entering a Rhino-based script into the upper text component, click the Evaluate button to evaluate the script. If there is a problem with the script, a dialog appears with an error message. Otherwise, the script's output appears in the lower text component. Click the Clear button to erase the contents of both text components. Figure 9-1 shows the GUI.

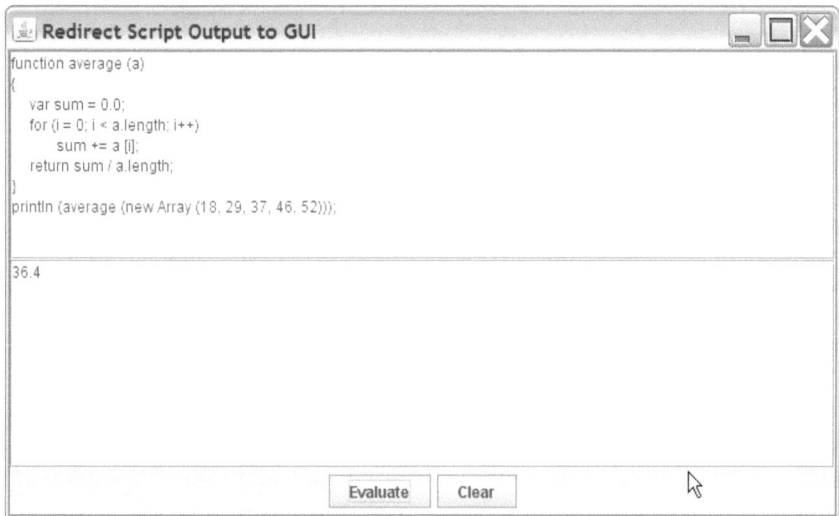

Figure 9-1. *By installing a new writer into the default script context, you can send a script's output to a GUI's text component.*

To redirect a script's output to the lower text component, RedirectScriptOutputToGUI creates an instance of GUIWriter and makes this instance available to the script engine via ScriptContext's void setWriter(Writer writer) and void setErrorWriter(Writer writer) methods. Although they are not used in the example, ScriptWriter also provides companion Writer getWriter() and Writer getErrorWriter() methods.

Note ScriptContext also provides a void setReader(Reader reader) method for changing a script's input source, and a Reader getReader() method for identifying the current input source.

In addition to displaying script output in the GUI, RedirectScriptOutputToGUI also outputs the engine scope's bindings to the console window when you start this program, and each time you click Evaluate. Initially, there are no bindings. However, after clicking Evaluate, you will discover context, print, and println script variables in the engine bindings.

The context script variable describes a SimpleScriptContext object that lets a script engine access the script context. The Rhino script engine needs to access the script context in order to implement the print() and println() functions. If you evaluate the println (println); script followed by the println (print); script, you will discover output similar to the following:

```
function println (str)
{
    print (str, true);
}

function print (str, newline)
{
    if (typeof (str) == "undefined")
    {
        str = "undefined";
    }
    else
    {
        if (str == null)
        {
            str = "null";
        }
    }
    var out = context.getWriter ();
    out.print (String (str));
    if (newline)
    {
        out.print ("\n");
    }
    out.flush ();
}
```

The output reveals that the context script variable is needed to access the current writer, which happens to be the GUIWriter in the RedirectScriptOutputToGUI application. This script variable can also be used to access arguments or the script's filename. For example, if this application invoked:

```
engine.put (ScriptEngine.ARGV, new String [] {"A", "B", "C"});
```

followed by:

```
engine.put (ScriptEngine.FILENAME, "script.js");
```

on a script engine referenced by the `ScriptEngine` variable engine, and you evaluated this script from the application's GUI:

```
println (context.getAttribute ("javax.script.filename"));
println (context.getAttribute ("javax.script.argv")[0]);
```

you would see `script.js` followed by A appear on separate lines in the lower text component.

Depending on your program, you might not want to "pollute" the default script context with new writers, bindings, and so on. Instead, you might want the same script to work in different contexts, leaving the default context untouched. To accomplish this task, create a `SimpleScriptContext` instance, populate its engine bindings via `ScriptContext`'s void `setAttribute(String name, Object value, int scope)` method, and invoke `eval(String script, ScriptContext context)` or `eval(Reader reader, ScriptContext context)` with this script context. For example, this instance:

```
ScriptContext context = new ScriptContext ();
context.setAttribute ("app", this, ScriptContext.ENGINE_SCOPE);
Object result = engine.eval (script, context);
```

allows the `script`-referenced script to access the engine bindings object app in a new context.

TIPS FOR WORKING WITH SCRIPT SCOPES AND CONTEXTS

The `setAttribute()` method is a convenient alternative to first accessing a scope's `Bindings` and then invoking its `put()` method. For example, `context.setAttribute ("app", this, ScriptContext.ENGINE_SCOPE);` is easier to express than `context.getBindings (ScriptContent.ENGINE_SCOPE).put ("app", this);`.

You will also find `ScriptContext`'s `Object getAttribute(String name, int scope)` and `Object removeAttribute(String name, int scope)` methods to be more convenient than the alternatives.

Finally, you will find the following to be useful in situations where there are more than engine and global scopes:

* `Object getAttribute(String name)` returns the named attribute from the lowest scope.

* `int getAttributesScope(String name)` returns the lowest scope in which an attribute is defined.

* `List<Integer> getScopes()` returns an immutable list of valid scopes for the script context.

It is possible to subclass `SimpleScriptContext` and define a new scope (perhaps for use by servlets) that coincides with this context, but this is beyond this chapter's scope (no pun intended).

Generating Scripts from Macros

Many applications benefit from *macros* (named sequences of commands/instructions that automate various tasks). For example, Word and other Microsoft Office products include a macro language called Visual Basic for Applications (VBA), which lets users create macros to automate editing, formatting, and other tasks.

■**Note** Check out Wikipedia's Macro entry (`http://en.wikipedia.org/wiki/Macro`) for a refresher on macros and macro languages.

A Java program that parses a macro generates an equivalent script in some scripting language. Because script syntax differs from one scripting language to another, it is important that the program be able to generate the script in a portable manner so that it can be easily adapted to various scripting languages. The `ScriptEngineFactory` interface provides three methods for this purpose, as listed in Table 9-4.

Table 9-4. *ScriptEngineFactory Methods for Generating Scripts from Macros*

Method	Description
`String getMethodCallSyntax(String obj, String m, String... args)`	Returns a `String` that can be used to invoke a Java object's method using a scripting language's syntax. Parameter `obj` identifies the object whose method is to be invoked, parameter `m` is the name of the method to be invoked, and parameter `args` identifies the names of the method's arguments. For example, invoking `getMethodCallSyntax ("x", "factorial", new String [] {"num"})` might return `"$x->factorial($num);"` for a PHP script engine. PHP variable names are prefixed with a dollar-sign character.
`String getOutputStatement(String toDisplay)`	Returns a `String` that can be used as a statement to output the argument passed to `toDisplay` using the scripting language's syntax. For example, invoking `getOutputStatement ("Hello")` might return `"echo(\"Hello\");"` for a PHP script engine, whereas it returns `"print(\"Hello\")"` for the Rhino JavaScript script engine.
`String getProgram(String... statements)`	Returns a `String` that organizes the specified statements into a valid script using the scripting language's syntax. For example, assuming that variable `factory` references a `ScriptEngineFactory`, invoking `factory.getProgram (factory.getOutputStatement (factory.getMethodCallSyntax ("x", "factorial", new String [] {"num"}))); ` might return `"<? echo($x->factorial($num)); ?>"` for a PHP script engine.

Do you notice a problem with `getOutputStatement()`? Although you might expect the Rhino script engine's `getOutputStatement()` method to be implemented as `return "print("+toDisplay+")";`, this method is implemented as `return "print(\""+toDisplay+"\")";`. In other words, anything passed in `toDisplay` is surrounded by double quotation marks. This is problematic when you want to pass a variable name to `getOutputStatement()`, and expect to obtain an output statement that outputs the variable's contents instead of its name. You can easily solve this problem by replacing the double quotation marks with spaces, assuming that `os` is a `String` variable holding `getOutputStatement()`'s result, `os = os.replace ('"', ' ');` replaces the double quotation marks with spaces. Because this problem might be addressed in a future version of the Rhino script engine, it's best to first verify the version number, as in:

```
if (factory.getEngineVersion ().equals ("1.6 release 2")) os = os.replace ('"', ' ');.
```

Compiling Scripts

Script engines tend to evaluate scripts via *interpreters*, which can be conceptualized as consisting of a *front end* for parsing source code and generating intermediate code, and a *back end* for executing the intermediate code. Every time a script is evaluated, the parsing and intermediate code-generation tasks are performed prior to execution, which tends to slow down script evaluation.

To hasten a script's evaluation, many script engines allow intermediate code to be stored and executed repeatedly. A script engine class that supports this *compilation* feature implements the optional `Compilable` interface. The `Compilable` interface's methods compile scripts into intermediate code and store results in `CompiledScript` subclass objects, whose `eval()` methods execute the intermediate code.

■ **Note** I refer to scripts as being *evaluated* instead of *executed*. After all, `ScriptEngine` specifies `eval()` methods, not `exec()` methods. In contrast, I refer to intermediate code as being *executed*, to be somewhat consistent with JSR 223.

A program must cast a script engine object to a `Compilable` before it can compile a script. Before doing this, the program should make sure that the engine's class implements the `Compilable` interface. Note that this is not necessary for the Rhino script engine, which supports `Compilable`. The following code fragment (which assumes the existence of an `engine` object) demonstrates this task:

```
Compilable compilable = null;
if (engine instanceof Compilable)
    compilable = (Compilable) engine;
```

The Compilable interface presents CompiledScript compile(String script) and CompiledScript compile(Reader script) methods for compiling a script and returning its intermediate code via a CompiledScript subclass object. Both methods throw a NullPointerException if the argument is null, and a ScriptException if there is a problem with the script.

The CompiledScript class includes public Object eval(), public Object eval(Bindings bindings), and public abstract Object eval(ScriptContext context) methods for executing the script's intermediate code. Each method throws a ScriptException if a script error occurs at runtime. CompiledScript also includes a public abstract ScriptEngine getEngine() method that provides access to the compiled script's engine.

What kind of speed improvement can you expect from compilation? To answer this question, I have created an application that presents a simple script consisting of a factorial function, evaluates this script 10,000 times, compiles the script, and executes the script's intermediate code 10,000 times. Each loop is timed to see how long it takes to run. The source code for this application appears in Listing 9-10.

Listing 9-10. *TestCompilationSpeed.java*

```java
// TestCompilationSpeed.java

import javax.script.*;

public class TestCompilationSpeed
{
   final static int MAX_ITERATIONS = 10000;

   public static void main (String [] args) throws Exception
   {
      ScriptEngineManager manager = new ScriptEngineManager ();
      ScriptEngine engine = manager.getEngineByName ("JavaScript");

      String fact = "function fact (n)"+
                    "{"+
                    "   if (n == 0)"+
                    "      return 1;"+
                    "   else"+
                    "      return n*fact (n-1);"+
                    "};";

      long time = System.currentTimeMillis ();
      for (int i = 0; i < MAX_ITERATIONS; i++)
```

```
        engine.eval (fact);
    System.out.println (System.currentTimeMillis ()-time);


    Compilable compilable = null;
    if (engine instanceof Compilable)
    {
        compilable = (Compilable) engine;
        CompiledScript script = compilable.compile (fact);

        time = System.currentTimeMillis ();
        for (int i = 0; i < MAX_ITERATIONS; i++)
            script.eval ();
        System.out.println (System.currentTimeMillis ()-time);
    }
  }
}
```

Each time you run this application, you will probably notice slightly different results. However, these results show a significant speed improvement. For example, you might see that the evaluated script took 1515 milliseconds and the compiled script took 782 milliseconds.

Note `TestCompilationSpeed` does not assume that `JavaScript` corresponds to the Mozilla Rhino 1.6 release 2 script engine. Recall that a script engine factory and its script engine can be overridden by any of `ScriptEngineManager`'s "registerEngine" methods. For this reason, `TestCompilationSpeed` verifies that the engine's class implements `Compilable`, even though Rhino's script engine class implements this interface.

Invoking Global, Object Member, and Interface-Implementing Functions

In contrast to compilation, which allows the intermediate code of entire scripts to be reexecuted, the Scripting API's support for *invocation* allows the intermediate code of only global functions and object member functions to be reexecuted. Furthermore, these functions can be invoked directly from Java code, which can pass object arguments to and return object results from these functions.

A script engine class that supports invocation implements the optional `Invocable` interface. A program must cast a script engine object to an `Invocable` instance before it can invoke global functions and object member functions. As with `Compilable`, your program should first verify that a script engine supports Invocable before casting. And again, this is not necessary for Rhino, which supports Invocable.

The Invocable interface provides an Object invokeFunction(String name, Object... args) method to invoke a global function. The global function's name is identified by name, and arguments to be passed to the global function are identified by args. If the global function is successful, this method returns its result as an Object. Otherwise, the method throws ScriptException if something goes wrong during the global function's invocation, NoSuchMethodException if the global function cannot be found, and NullPointerException if a null reference is passed to name. The following code fragment (which assumes the existence of a Rhino-based engine object) demonstrates invokeFunction():

```
// The script presents a global function that converts degrees
// Celsius to degrees Fahrenheit.

String script = "function c2f (degrees)"+
                "{"+
                "   return degrees*9.0/5.0+32;"+
                "}";

// First evaluate the script, to generate intermediate code.

engine.eval (script);

// Then invoke the script's c2f() global function with an argument
// that will be boxed into a Double. After passing the argument to
// the global function, its intermediate code will be executed, and
// a value will be returned to Java as a Double containing 212.0.

Invocable invocable = (Invocable) engine;
System.out.println (invocable.invokeFunction ("c2f", 100.0));
```

The Invocable interface provides an Object invokeMethod(Object thiz, String name, Object... args) method to invoke an object member function. The script object's reference (obtained after a previous script evaluation or via a prior invocation) is identified by thiz, the member function's name is identified by name, and arguments passed to the member function are identified by args. Upon success, the member function's result is returned as an Object. In addition to invokeFunction()'s exceptions, an IllegalArgumentException is thrown if either null or an Object reference not representing a script object is passed to thiz. The following code fragment demonstrates invokeMethod():

```
// The script presents an object with a member function that
// converts degrees Celsius to degrees Fahrenheit.
```

```
String script = "var obj = new Object();"+
                "obj.c2f = function (degrees)"+
                "{"+
                "   return degrees*9.0/5.0+32;"+
                "}";
```

```
// First evaluate the script, to generate intermediate code.
```

```
engine.eval (script);
```

```
// Then get script object whose member function is to be invoked.
```

Object obj = engine.get ("obj");

```
// Finally, invoke the c2f() member function with an argument that
// will be boxed into a Double. After passing the argument to the
// global function, its intermediate code will be executed, and
// a value will be returned to Java as a Double containing 98.6.
```

Invocable invocable = (Invocable) engine;
System.out.println (invocable.invokeMethod (obj, "c2f", 37.0));

Directly invoking a script's global and object member functions results in a Java program being strongly coupled to the script. As changes are made to function names and their parameter lists, the Java program must adapt. To minimize coupling, Invocable provides two methods that return Java interface objects, whose methods are implemented by a script's global and object member functions:

- <T> T getInterface(Class<T> clasz) returns an implementation of the clasz-identified interface, where the methods are implemented by a script's global functions.

- <T> T getInterface(Object thiz, Class<T> clasz) returns an implementation of the clasz-identified interface, where the methods are implemented by scripting object thiz's member functions.

Both methods return null if the requested interface is unavailable, because the intermediate code is missing one or more functions that implement interface methods. An IllegalArgumentException is thrown if null is passed to clasz, if clasz does not represent an interface, or if either null or an Object reference not representing a script object is passed to thiz.

The previous Java code fragments that demonstrated invokeFunction() and invokeMethod() worked directly with a c2f() global function. Because this function is coupled to the Java code, this code would need to be changed should c2f() be eliminated in favor of a more descriptive and generic global function, such as one that also converts to degrees Celsius. The generic global function's signature will not change, even if its implementation changes (it might start out calling c2f(), and later remove this function after integrating this other function's code into its implementation). As a result, the generic global function is a perfect choice for implementing a Java interface, as Listing 9-11 demonstrates.

Listing 9-11. *TemperatureConversion.java*

```java
// TemperatureConversion.java

import javax.script.*;

public class TemperatureConversion
{
   public static void main (String [] args) throws ScriptException
   {
      ScriptEngineManager manager = new ScriptEngineManager ();
      ScriptEngine engine = manager.getEngineByName ("rhino");

      String script = "function c2f(degrees)"+
                      "{"+
                      "   return degrees*9.0/5.0+32;"+
                      "}"+
                      " "+
                      "function f2c(degrees)"+
                      "{"+
                      "   return (degrees-32)*5.0/9.0;"+
                      "}"+
                      " "+
                      "function convertTemperature (degrees, toCelsius)"+
                      "{"+
                      "   if (toCelsius)"+
                      "      return f2c (degrees);"+
                      "   else"+
                      "      return c2f (degrees);"+
                      "}";
```

```
            engine.eval (script);
            Invocable invocable = (Invocable) engine;


            TempConversion tc = invocable.getInterface (TempConversion.class);
            if (tc == null)
                System.err.println ("Unable to obtain TempConversion interface");
            else
            {
                System.out.println ("37 degrees Celsius = "+
                                     tc.convertTemperature (37.0, false)+
                                     " degrees Fahrenheit");

                System.out.println ("212 degrees Fahrenheit = "+
                                     tc.convertTemperature (212.0, true)+
                                     " degrees Celsius");
            }
        }
}


interface TempConversion
{
    double convertTemperature (double degrees, boolean toCelsius);
}
```

The application provides a TempConversion interface whose double
convertTemperature(double degrees, boolean toCelsius) method corresponds to
a same-named global function in the script. Executing invocable.
getInterface(TempConversion.class) returns a TempConversion instance,
which can be used to invoke convertTemperature(). Here's the application's output:

```
37 degrees Celsius = 98.6 degrees Fahrenheit
212 degrees Fahrenheit = 100.0 degrees Celsius
```

Note The *Java Scripting Programmer's Guide*'s "Implementing Java Interfaces by Scripts" section
(http://java.sun.com/javase/6/docs/technotes/guides/scripting/programmer_guide/index.
html#interfaces) presents the source code for a pair of applications that further demonstrate the
getInterface() methods.

Playing with the Command-Line Script Shell

Java SE 6 provides jrunscript, an experimental command-line, script-shell tool for exploring scripting languages and their communication with Java. The SDK documentation's jrunscript - command line script shell page (http://java.sun.com/javase/6/docs/technotes/tools/share/jrunscript.html) offers a tool reference. Also, Appendix B presents a table of command-line options and four usage examples.

Although jrunscript can be used to evaluate file-based scripts or scripts that are specified on the command line, the easiest way to work with this tool is via interactive mode. In this mode, jrunscript prompts you to enter a line of code. It evaluates this code after you press the Enter key. To enter interactive mode, specify only jrunscript on the command line.

In response, you see the js> prompt. The js is a reminder that the default language is JavaScript (js is actually one of the short names for the Mozilla Rhino engine). At the js> prompt, you can enter Rhino JavaScript statements and expressions. When an expression is entered, its value will appear on the next line, as the following session demonstrates:

```
js> Math.PI // Access the PI member of JavaScript's Math object.
3.141592653589793
```

During its initialization, jrunscript introduces several built-in global functions to the Rhino script engine. These functions range from outputting the date in the current locale, to listing the files in the current directory and performing other file-system tasks, to working with XML. The following session demonstrates a few of these functions:

```
js> date()
July 12, 2007 2:11:00 PM CDT
js> ls()
-rw Jul 10    1043 swinggui.js
js> cat("swinggui.js", "frame")
16            :              var frame = new JFrame ("Swing GUI");
17            :              frame.setDefaultCloseOperation (JFrame.EXIT_ON_CLOSE);
23            :              frame.getContentPane ().add (label);
25            :              frame.pack ();
26            :              frame.setVisible (true);
js> load("swinggui.js")
js> creategui()
Event-dispatching thread: false
js> Event-dispatching thread: true
```

The example uses four jrunscript built-in functions:

- date() outputs the current date.

- ls() lists the current directory's files.

- cat() outputs part (based on a pattern match) or all of a file's contents.

- load() loads and evaluates a script file, such as swinggui.js.

After creategui() finishes, the Swing application's console output mixes with jrunscript's console output. Closing the GUI also closes jrunscript.

Note For a complete list of built-in functions, check out the "GLOBALS" section of the JavaScript built-ins documentation (http://java.sun.com/javase/6/docs/technotes/tools/share/jsdocs/index.html).

In addition to its utility functions, jrunscript provides jlist() and jmap() functions. jlist() allows you to access a java.util.List instance like an array with integer indexes. jmap() is for accessing a Map instance like a Perl-style associative array with string-based keys. A List or Map instance is passed to jlist() or jmap() as an argument. The functions return an object that provides the access, as the following session demonstrates:

```
js> var scriptlanguages = new java.util.ArrayList ()
js> scriptlanguages.add ('JavaScript')
true
js> scriptlanguages.add ('Ruby')
true
js> scriptlanguages.add ('Groovy')
true
js> var sl = jlist (scriptlanguages)
js> sl [1]
Ruby
js> sl.length
3
js> println (sl)
[JavaScript, Ruby, Groovy]
js> delete sl [1]
false
js> println (sl)
[JavaScript, Groovy]
```

```
js> sl.length
2
js> var properties = java.lang.System.getProperties ()
js> var props = jmap (properties)
js> props ['java.version']
1.6.0
js> props ['os.name']
Windows XP
js> delete props ['os.name']
true
js> props ['os.name']
js>
```

The session shows that ArrayList and System are prefixed with their java.util and java.lang package names, respectively. jrunscript does not import the java.util and java.lang packages by default, although it does import the java.io and java.net packages by default. This session also demonstrates the use of JavaScript's delete operator to delete list and map entries.

Note If you are wondering why delete sl [1] outputs false, whereas delete props ['os.name'] outputs true, the reason has to do with JavaScript's delete operator returning true only when the entry being deleted no longer exists. Ruby is removed from sl [1] by replacing sl [1]'s contents with Groovy. This implies that sl [2], which previously contained Groovy, no longer exists. Although delete sl [1] accomplished the objective of removing Ruby, sl [1] still exists and contains Groovy. Hence, delete sl [1] outputs false. If delete sl [2] had been specified, true would have been output because sl [2] would no longer exist—there is no sl [3] with a value to shift into sl [2].

The jrunscript tool introduces another built-in function to the Rhino script engine: JSInvoker(). As with jlist() and jmap(), this function returns a proxy object for a delegate object. JSInvoker()'s proxy is used to invoke the delegate's special invoke() member function via arbitrary member function names and argument lists. The following session provides a demonstration:

```
js> var x = { invoke: function (name, args) { println (name+" "+args.length); }};
js> var y = new JSInvoker (x);
js> y.run ("first", "second", "third");
run 3
js> y.doIt ();
doIt 0
js> y.doIt (10);
```

```
doIt 1
js>
```

Delegate object x specifies a single member function named invoke. This function's arguments are a string-based name and an array of object arguments. The second line employs JSInvoker() to create a proxy object that is assigned to y. By using this proxy object, you can call the delegate object's invoke() member function via an arbitrary name and number of arguments. Behind the scenes, y.run ("first", "second", "third") translates into x.invoke ('run', args), where args is an array containing "first", "second", and "third" as its three entries. Also, y.doIt () translates into x.invoke ('doIt', args), where args is an empty array. A similar translation is performed on y.doIt (10);.

If you were to print the contents of the jlist(), jmap(), and JSInvoker() functions via println (jlist), println (jmap), and println (JSInvoker), you would observe that these functions are implemented by JSAdapter, a java.lang.reflect.Proxy equivalent for JavaScript. JSAdapter lets you adapt property access (as in x.i), mutator (as in x.p = 10), and other simple JavaScript syntax on a proxy object to a delegate JavaScript object's member functions. For more information, check out JSAdapter.java (https://scripting. dev.java.net/source/browse/scripting/engines/javascript/src/com/sun/phobos/script/javascript/JSAdapter.java?rev=1.1.1.1&view=markup).

To terminate jrunscript after playing with this tool, specify the exit() function with or without an exit-code argument. For example, you can specify exit(0), or exit() by itself. When you specify exit() without an argument, 0 is chosen as the exit code. This code is returned from jrunscript for use in Windows batch files, Unix shell scripts, and so on. Alternatively, you can specify the quit() function, which is a synonym for exit().

The Scripting API and JEditorPane

The javax.swing.JEditorPane class and its HTML editor kit make it easy to present HTML documents. Because this editor kit's HTML support is limited (Java applets and JavaScript are not supported, for example), JEditorPane is not appropriate for implementing a web browser that can browse arbitrary web sites. However, this class is ideal for integrating web-based online help into Java applications (although you might prefer to work with the JavaHelp API).

Note Despite JEditorPane being inappropriate for implementing a generalized web browser, I used this class as the basis for two such web browser applications in Chapter 4 (Listings 4-1 and 4-7), for convenience. These applications demonstrated Java SE 6's "place arbitrary components on a tabbed pane's tab headers" and "print text component" features.

In an online-help scenario, an application's help documentation consists of web pages stored on a specific web site. It is easier to maintain help documentation in a single location than to update the documentation in many places. Because the application's editor pane is restricted to this web site, the pages' HTML can be limited to the features with which the editor pane can work.

The absence of JavaScript support makes it difficult to give the web pages a dynamic quality; for example, to change a link's color to some other color when the mouse pointer hovers over the link. Fortunately, it is possible to integrate JavaScript into the editor pane via the Scripting API and some editor pane knowledge.

To prove my point, I have developed a ScriptedEditorPane class that extends JEditorPane and evaluates a web page's JavaScript code via the Rhino script engine. I've also created an application that embeds the scripted editor pane component into its GUI, to demonstrate this component. Listing 9-12 presents this application.

Listing 9-12. *DemoScriptedEditorPane.java*

```java
// DemoScriptedEditorPane.java

import java.awt.*;

import java.io.*;

import javax.swing.*;
import javax.swing.border.*;
import javax.swing.event.*;

public class DemoScriptedEditorPane extends JFrame
    implements HyperlinkListener
{
    private JLabel lblStatus;

    DemoScriptedEditorPane ()
    {
        super ("Demo ScriptedEditorPane");
        setDefaultCloseOperation (EXIT_ON_CLOSE);

        ScriptedEditorPane pane = null;
        try
        {
            // Create a scripted editor pane component that loads the contents
            // of a test.html file, which is located in the current directory.

            pane = new ScriptedEditorPane ("file:///"+
```

```java
                                new File ("").getAbsolutePath ()+
                                "/demo.html");

         pane.setEditable (false);
         pane.setBorder (BorderFactory.createEtchedBorder ());
         pane.addHyperlinkListener (this);
      }
      catch (Exception e)
      {
         System.out.println (e.getMessage ());
         return;
      }
      getContentPane ().add (pane, BorderLayout.CENTER);

      lblStatus = new JLabel (" ");
      lblStatus.setBorder (BorderFactory.createEtchedBorder ());
      getContentPane ().add (lblStatus, BorderLayout.SOUTH);

      setSize (350, 250);
      setVisible (true);
   }

   public void hyperlinkUpdate (HyperlinkEvent hle)
   {
      HyperlinkEvent.EventType evtype = hle.getEventType ();

      if (evtype == HyperlinkEvent.EventType.ENTERED)
          lblStatus.setText (hle.getURL ().toString ());
      else
      if (evtype == HyperlinkEvent.EventType.EXITED)
          lblStatus.setText (" ");
   }

   public static void main (String [] args)
   {
      Runnable r = new Runnable ()
                  {
                       public void run ()
                       {
                          new DemoScriptedEditorPane ();
                       }
                  };
      EventQueue.invokeLater (r);
   }
}
```

The application's Swing GUI consists of a scripted editor pane and a status bar label. The editor pane displays the contents of a `demo.html` file, which must be located in the current directory. The status bar presents the URL that is associated with the link over which the mouse pointer is hovering. Move the mouse pointer over a link to change the link's color. Figure 9-2 shows this GUI.

Figure 9-2. *The scripted editor pane integrates JavaScript via the Scripting API.*

The `demo.html` file, shown in Listing 9-13, describes an HTML document that defines two JavaScript functions between one pair of `<script>` and `</script>` tags. (It is possible to specify multiple pairs of `<script>` and `</script>` tags.) It also specifies onmouseover and onmouseout attributes for each of its two anchor tags (`</a>`). Each attribute's JavaScript code invokes one of the defined functions.

Listing 9-13. *demo.html*

```
<html>
  <head>
    <script>
      function setColor(color)
      {
          document.linkcolor = color;
          println (document.linkcolor);
      }

      function revertToDefaultColor()
      {
          document.linkcolor = document.defaultlinkcolor;
      }
    </script>
  </head>
```

```
<body>
  <h1>demo.html</h1>

  Demonstrate JavaScript logic for changing link colors.

  <p>
  <a href="first.html" onmouseover="setColor (java.awt.Color.red);"
                        onmouseout="setColor (java.awt.Color.magenta);">
    first link</a>

  <p>
  <a href="second.html" onmouseover="setColor (java.awt.Color.green);"
                         onmouseout="revertToDefaultColor();">
    second link</a>

  <!-- I chose first.html and second.html to serve as example href values.
       The actual files do not exist; they are not needed. -->
  </body>
</html>
```

Listing 9-13 refers to a document object that is associated with the currently displayed HTML document. This object defines only linkcolor and defaultlinkcolor properties, whose values are java.awt.Color instances. The linkcolor property describes the color of the link being made active or inactive; it can be set or read. defaultlinkcolor is a read-only property that specifies the default color for all links.

Now that you are familiar with DemoScriptedEditorPane and demo.html, it should be somewhat easier to understand ScriptedEditorPane's implementation. This implementation consists of five private instance fields, two public constructors, one public method, and three private inner classes. Listing 9-14 shows the ScriptedEditorPane source code.

Listing 9-14. *ScriptedEditorPane.java*

```
// ScriptedEditorPane.java

import java.awt.*;

import java.io.*;

import java.net.*;

import java.util.*;
```

```
import javax.script.*;

import javax.swing.*;
import javax.swing.event.*;
import javax.swing.text.*;
import javax.swing.text.html.*;
import javax.swing.text.html.parser.*;

public class ScriptedEditorPane extends JEditorPane
{
    // The anchor element associated with the most recent hyperlink event. It
    // probably should be located in the ScriptEnvironment, where it is used.

    private javax.swing.text.Element currentAnchor;

    // The Rhino script engine.

    private ScriptEngine engine;

    // The Java environment corresponding to the JavaScript document object.

    private ScriptEnvironment env;

    // An initialization script that connects a JavaScript document object with
    // linkcolor and defaultlinkcolor properties, to an adapter with __get__()
    // and __put()__ member functions, which access the script environment.

    private String initScript =
        "var document = new JSAdapter ({"+
        "    __get__ : function (name)"+
        "             {"+
        "                 if (name == 'defaultlinkcolor')"+
        "                     return env.getDefaultLinkColor ();"+
        "                 else"+
        "                 if (name == 'linkcolor')"+
        "                     return env.getLinkColor ();"+
        "             },"+
        "    __put__ : function (name, value)"+
        "             {"+
        "                 if (name == 'linkcolor')"+
        "                     env.setLinkColor (value);"+
```

```
    "                  }"+
    "})";
```

```java
// The concatenated contents of all <script></script> sections in top-down
// order.

private String script;

// Create a scripted editor pane without an HTML document. A document can
// be subsequently added via a setPage() call.

public ScriptedEditorPane () throws ScriptException
{
    ScriptEngineManager manager = new ScriptEngineManager ();
    engine = manager.getEngineByName ("rhino");

    // For convenience, I throw a ScriptException instead of creating a new
    // exception class for this purpose.

    if (engine == null)
        throw new ScriptException ("no Rhino script engine");

    // Set up environment for JSAdapter and evaluate initialization script.

    env = new ScriptEnvironment ();
    engine.put ("env", env);
    engine.eval (initScript);

    addHyperlinkListener (new ScriptedLinkListener ());
}

// Create a scripted editor pane with the specified HTML document.

public ScriptedEditorPane (String pageUrl)
    throws IOException, ScriptException
{
    this ();
    setPage (pageUrl);
}

// Associate an HTML document with the scripted editor pane. Prior to the
// association, the document is parsed to extract the contents of all
```

```java
   // <script></script sections.

public void setPage (URL url) throws IOException
{
   InputStreamReader isr = new InputStreamReader (url.openStream ());
   BufferedReader reader;
   reader = new BufferedReader (isr);
   Callback cb = new Callback ();
   new ParserDelegator ().parse (reader, cb, true);
   reader.close ();
   script = cb.getScript ();

   super.setPage (url);
}


// Extract the contents of all <script> sections via this callback. Because
// the parser exposes these contents as if they were HTML comments, care is
// needed to differentiate them from actual HTML comments. Learn more about
// the parser from Jeff Heaton's "Parsing HTML with Swing" article
// (http://www.samspublishing.com/articles/article.asp?p=31059&seqNum=1).

private class Callback extends HTMLEditorKit.ParserCallback
{
   // A <script></script> section is being processed when this variable is
   // true. It defaults to false.

   private boolean inScript;

   // The contents of all <script></script> sections are stored in a
   // StringBuffer instead of a String to minimize String object creation.

   private StringBuffer scriptBuffer = new StringBuffer ();

   // Return the script.

   String getScript ()
   {
      return scriptBuffer.toString ();
   }

   // Only append the data to the string buffer if the parser has already
   // detected a <script> tag.
```

```java
   public void handleComment (char [] data, int pos)
   {
      if (inScript)
         scriptBuffer.append (data);
   }

   // Detect a <script> tag.

   public void handleStartTag (HTML.Tag t,
                               MutableAttributeSet a, int pos)
   {
      if (t == HTML.Tag.SCRIPT)
         inScript = true;
   }

   // Detect a </script> tag.

   public void handleEndTag (HTML.Tag t, int pos)
   {
      if (t == HTML.Tag.SCRIPT)
         inScript = false;
   }
}

// Provide the glue between document's properties and the Java environment
// in which the script runs.

private class ScriptEnvironment
{
   // The default color of an anchor tag's link text as determined by the
   // current CSS style sheet.

   private Color defaultLinkColor;

   // Create a script environment. Extract the default link color via the
   // current CSS style sheet.

   ScriptEnvironment ()
   {
      HTMLEditorKit kit;
      kit = (HTMLEditorKit) getEditorKitForContentType ("text/html");
```

```
        StyleSheet ss = kit.getStyleSheet ();
        Style style = ss.getRule ("a"); // Get rule for anchor tag.
        if (style != null)
        {
            Object o = style.getAttribute (CSS.Attribute.COLOR);
            defaultLinkColor = ss.stringToColor (o.toString ());
        }
    }


    // Return the default link color.

    public Color getDefaultLinkColor ()
    {
        return defaultLinkColor;
    }


    // Return the link color of the current anchor element.

    public Color getLinkColor ()
    {
        AttributeSet as = currentAnchor.getAttributes ();
        return StyleConstants.getForeground (as);
    }


    // Set the link color for the current anchor element.

    public void setLinkColor (Color color)
    {
        StyleContext sc = StyleContext.getDefaultStyleContext ();
        AttributeSet as = sc.addAttribute (SimpleAttributeSet.EMPTY,
                                    StyleConstants.Foreground,
                                    color);
        ((HTMLDocument) currentAnchor.getDocument ()).
            setCharacterAttributes (currentAnchor.getStartOffset (),
                                currentAnchor.getEndOffset ()-
                                currentAnchor.getStartOffset(), as,
                                false);
    }
}
```

```
// Provide a listener for identifying the current anchor element, detecting
// an onmouseover attribute (for an entered event) or an onmouseout element
// (for an exited event) that is associated with this element's <a> tag,
// and evaluating this attribute's JavaScript code.

private class ScriptedLinkListener implements HyperlinkListener
{
   // For convenience, this listener's hyperlinkUpdate() method ignores
   // HTML frames.

   public void hyperlinkUpdate (HyperlinkEvent he)
   {
      HyperlinkEvent.EventType type = he.getEventType ();

      if (type == HyperlinkEvent.EventType.ENTERED)
      {
         currentAnchor = he.getSourceElement ();
         AttributeSet as = currentAnchor.getAttributes ();
         AttributeSet asa = (AttributeSet) as.getAttribute (HTML.Tag.A);
         if (asa != null)
         {
            Enumeration<?> ean = asa.getAttributeNames ();
            while (ean.hasMoreElements ())
            {
               Object o = ean.nextElement ();
               if (o instanceof String)
               {
                  String attr = o.toString ();
                  if (attr.equalsIgnoreCase ("onmouseover"))
                  {
                     String value = (String) asa.getAttribute (o);
                     try
                     {
                        engine.eval (script+value);
                     }
                     catch (ScriptException se)
                     {
                        System.out.println (se);
                     }
                     break;
```

```
                    }
                }
            }
        }
    }
    else
    if (type == HyperlinkEvent.EventType.EXITED)
    {
        currentAnchor = he.getSourceElement ();
        AttributeSet as = currentAnchor.getAttributes ();
        AttributeSet asa = (AttributeSet) as.getAttribute (HTML.Tag.A);
        if (asa != null)
        {
            Enumeration<?> ean = asa.getAttributeNames ();
            while (ean.hasMoreElements ())
            {
                Object o = ean.nextElement ();
                if (o instanceof String)
                {
                    String attr = o.toString ();
                    if (attr.equalsIgnoreCase ("onmouseout"))
                    {
                        String value = (String) asa.getAttribute (o);
                        try
                        {
                            engine.eval (script+value);
                        }
                        catch (ScriptException se)
                        {
                            System.out.println (se);
                        }
                        break;
                    }
                }
            }
        }
    }
}
```

Despite its many comments, you will probably have a number of questions as you study Listing 9-14. The following points should answer at least some of those questions:

- I use JSAdapter (in an initially evaluated script) to connect the document object's linkcolor and defaultlinkcolor properties to a delegate's member function calls. It seems more natural to access document properties than to invoke document member functions. The __get()__ member function translates property reads into calls to ScriptEnvironment's public Color getLinkColor() and Color getDefaultLinkColor() methods. The __put()__ member function translates a property write on linkcolor into a call to the equivalent public void setLinkColor(Color color) method.

- I deliberately limit ScriptedEditorPane's document object model to ScriptEnvironment (perhaps I should have named this class ScriptDOM) and JSAdapter. Creating a sophisticated document object model is not a trivial undertaking. Among various considerations, you need to decide if this model should be external to the scripted editor pane component. This decision will impact how you access a status bar component from the model, for example.

- I override JEditorPane's public void setPage(URL url) method so that I can extract the content of each encountered <script> and </script> tag pair during an initial parsing operation. I cannot extract this content by depending on the HTML editor kit's internal parsing. Perhaps there is a way to extract this content and avoid the problem of parsing the url's content twice, but I have yet to find it.

- For simplicity, I do not work with the HTMLEditorKit.LinkController class, which can be used in situations where the mouse pointer hovers over an arbitrary HTML element (such as an image not associated with a link). Providing the custom editor kit necessary to work with LinkController would have added complexity to an otherwise simple example. In contrast, ScriptedLinkListener addresses only the limited scenarios of entering or exiting (or, if modified, activating) a link.

If you plan to modify the scripted editor pane component, or if you just want to gain a deeper understanding of the code within ScriptedLinkListener's public void hyperlinkUpdate(HyperlinkEvent he) method (not to mention the code within the ScriptEnvironment inner class), you will benefit from a book that extensively covers Swing's text components. One book that I have found to be very helpful in this regard is *Java Swing, Second Edition* by Marc Loy, Robert Eckstein, Dave Wood, James Elliott, and Brian Cole (O'Reilly, 2002).

Tip The authors of *Java Swing, Second Edition* created two sample PDF-based chapters on the HTML editor kit and HTML I/O, which can be downloaded from http://examples.oreilly.com/jswing2/ code/goodies/misc.html.

The Scripting API with JRuby and JavaFX Script

Because Java SE 6 comes with only the Rhino script engine, so far, this chapter has focused exclusively on JavaScript. In this section, you will learn how to use the Scripting API to interact with two other languages that also have script engines: JRuby and JavaFX Script. I chose JRuby because of the Ruby language's popularity. I chose JavaFX Script because it simplifies creating Swing GUIs.

Note An extensive list of available script engines and the languages that they support is located on java.net's scripting project home page (`https://scripting.dev.java.net/`).

JRuby and the Scripting API

JRuby is a Java implementation of the Ruby language syntax, as well as Ruby's core and standard libraries. JRuby was created by Jan Arne Petersen in 2001, and subsequently worked on by Charles Nutter, Thomas Enebo, Ola Bini, and Nick Seiger, among others. Recognizing the popularity of Ruby and JRuby, Sun hired Charles and Thomas (in September 2006) to work full time on JRuby.

Note Wikipedia's JRuby entry (`http://en.wikipedia.org/wiki/Jruby`) introduces JRuby. Wikipedia's Ruby (programming language) entry (`http://en.wikipedia.org/wiki/Ruby_programming_language`) introduces Ruby.

If JRuby is not installed on your platform, download the ZIP or TAR file for the latest version from the JRuby site (`http://dist.codehaus.org/jruby/`). I downloaded `jruby-bin-1.0.zip` because JRuby 1.0 happened to be the latest version while I wrote this chapter. Unarchive the ZIP or TAR file, and move its home directory to a suitable location. For example, I moved `c:\unzipped\JRUBY-~1.0\jruby-1.0` to the root directory on my C: drive, resulting in `c:\jruby-1.0` as the home directory. You should also add the home directory's `bin` subdirectory to your platform's PATH environment variable.

Caution JRuby requires that you set the JAVA_HOME environment variable to Java's home directory. Otherwise, JRuby script files (located in the `bin` subdirectory) will not run.

You can verify that JRuby has been installed by invoking the `jirb` (JRuby IRB) script to launch the Interactive Ruby tool at the command line. If all goes well, you should see an `irb(main):001:0>` prompt from which you can interact with JRuby. For example, type `puts "Hello, from Ruby"` and press Enter. In response, you should see `Hello, from Ruby` followed by `=> nil` (which indicates that `puts` does not return a value) on separate lines. When you are finished with Interactive Ruby, specify `exit` or `quit` to terminate this tool.

■ **Note** Although the `irb(main):001:0>` prompt looks complex, it is easy to understand. The `irb(main)` section identifies the location in a running JRuby application (typically invoked by the `jruby` script) where a breakpoint occurred, to drop the application into Interactive Ruby. `main` appears if Interactive Ruby is entered directly via `jirb`. The `:001` section identifies the number of lines of Ruby code that have been entered. Finally, the `:0` section identifies the current statement depth. Whenever a statement is opened, the depth increases by one; the depth decreases by one when the statement is closed. By the way, `jirb` replaces the `>` with an `*` when it detects that a statement is unfinished, such as when you have not yet specified `end` for an `if-else` statement.

Because JRuby is written in Java, it is easy to access Java classes and interfaces directly from a JRuby script. For example, assuming that Interactive Ruby is still running, enter `require 'java'` (on one line) followed by `puts java.lang.System.getProperty("java.version")` (on another line) to output the value of Java's `java.version` system property.

To access JRuby from a Java program, however, you will need to obtain a suitable script engine. Go to java.net's scripting project home page (`https://scripting.dev.java.net/`) and download either `jsr223-engines.tar.gz` (Unix/Linux) or `jsr223engines.zip` (Windows); each archive contains a group of JSR 223-compliant script engines packaged as JAR files. For JRuby, you will need to extract `jruby-engine.jar` from the archive.

■ **Tip** You might find it convenient to copy `jruby-engine.jar` to the JRuby home directory's `lib` subdirectory.

I have prepared an example that demonstrates accessing a JRuby script from a Java application. The script, shown in Listing 9-15, is a Ruby version of the temperature-conversion example shown earlier in this chapter (Listing 9-11). It consists of a `TempConverter` class and its two temperature-conversion methods, and a function that returns a `TempConverter` instance.

Listing 9-15. *TempConverter.rb*

```ruby
# TempConverter.rb

class TempConverter
  def c2f(degrees)
    degrees*9.0/5.0+32
  end

  def f2c(degrees)
    (degrees-32)*5.0/9.0
  end
end

def getTempConverter
  TempConverter.new
end
```

The application uses ScriptEngineManager's getEngineByName() method and the jruby short name to access JRuby's script engine. It loads and evaluates TempConverter.rb, invokes getTempConverter() to obtain a TempConverter instance, and uses this instance to invoke TempConverter's methods. The application is presented in Listing 9-16.

Listing 9-16. *WorkingWithJRuby.java*

```java
// WorkingWithJRuby.java

import java.io.*;

import javax.script.*;

public class WorkingWithJRuby
{
   public static void main (String [] args) throws Exception
   {
      ScriptEngineManager manager = new ScriptEngineManager ();

      // The JRuby script engine is accessed via the jruby short name.

      ScriptEngine engine = manager.getEngineByName ("jruby");

      // Evaluate TempConverter.rb to generate intermediate code.
```

```
engine.eval (new BufferedReader (new FileReader ("TempConverter.rb")));

Invocable invocable = (Invocable) engine;
Object tempconverter = invocable.invokeFunction ("getTempConverter");

double degreesCelsius;
degreesCelsius = (Double) invocable.invokeMethod (tempconverter, "f2c",
                                                  98.6);
System.out.println ("98.6 degrees Fahrenheit = "+degreesCelsius+
                    " degrees Celsius");

double degreesFahrenheit;
degreesFahrenheit = (Double) invocable.invokeMethod (tempconverter,
                                                     "c2f", 100.0);
System.out.println ("100.0 degrees Celsius = "+degreesFahrenheit+
                    " degrees Fahrenheit");
   }
}
```

To run this application, you will need to add jruby-engine.jar and jruby.jar (located in the JRuby home directory's lib subdirectory) to the classpath (via either the classpath environment variable or the java tool's -cp option). Here's an example for the Windows platform:

```
java -cp c:\jruby-1.0\lib\jruby.jar;c:\jruby-1.0\lib\jruby-engine.jar;.➥
WorkingWithJRuby
```

You should observe the following output:

```
98.6 degrees Fahrenheit = 37.0 degrees Celsius
100.0 degrees Celsius = 212.0 degrees Fahrenheit
```

If you want to play with JRuby via jrunscript, you will need to first copy all JAR files (including jruby-engine.jar) from the JRuby home directory's lib subdirectory to the JRE's lib\ext directory (or lib/ext, from the Unix perspective). Although you might be able to get away with copying only jruby.jar and a few other JARs, you will most likely receive a NoClassDefFoundError if a needed JAR file is missing when you try to access the script engine. After copying these files, jrunscript -l jruby will take you to jrunscript's jruby> prompt. From there, you can load and execute a Ruby script file, as in load "demo.rb". If you choose to copy all JAR files to the JRE's extensions directory, you will no longer need to add jruby-engine.jar and jruby.jar to the classpath before running WorkingWithJRuby.

JavaFX Script and the Scripting API

At its May 2007 JavaOne Conference, Sun introduced JavaFX, a family of products for creating rich Internet applications. Check out Wikipedia's JavaFX entry (`http://en.wikipedia.org/wiki/JavaFX`) for a brief introduction to JavaFX. This product family's scripting-language member is JavaFX Script, which is based on Chris Oliver's F3 (Form Follows Function) language.

Note Chris Oliver's "F3" blog entry (`http://blogs.sun.com/chrisoliver/entry/f3`) introduces F3. Also, Wikipedia's "JavaFX Script" entry (`http://en.wikipedia.org/wiki/JavaFX_Script`) introduces JavaFX Script.

JavaFX Script is maintained by java.net's OpenJFX project. According to this project's home page (`https://openjfx.dev.java.net/`):

> *Project OpenJFX is a project of the OpenJFX community for sharing early versions of the JavaFX Script language and for collaborating on its development. In the future, the JavaFX Script code will be open sourced. The governance, licensing, and community models will be worked out as the project evolves.*

For the latest information on the OpenJFX project, check out the home page's "What's New" section.

Caution Because Project OpenJFX is evolving, it is possible that some of this chapter's JavaFX Script content will no longer be correct when this book reaches bookstores.

The OpenJFX project's home page has this to say about the language: "JavaFX Script is a declarative, statically typed programming language. It has first-class functions, declarative syntax, list-comprehensions, and incremental dependency-based evaluation." *First-class functions* are functions that are treated as values. They might be used as function arguments, for example. Planet JFX's FAQ page (`http://jfx.wikia.com/wiki/FAQ`) defines declarative syntax, list comprehensions, and incremental dependency-based evaluation.

The OpenJFX project's home page goes on to say that JavaFX Script can make direct calls to the Java APIs that are located on the same platform. Also, its statically typed nature means that JavaFX Script "has the same code structuring, reuse, and encapsulation features (such as packages, classes, inheritance, and separate compilation and deployment units) [as Java] that make it possible to create and maintain very large programs using Java technology." Collectively, JavaFX Script's features allow you to quickly build "rich and compelling UIs leveraging Java Swing, Java 2D and Java 3D." For a detailed guide to the JavaFX Script language, check out OpenJFX's The JavaFX Script Programming Language page (`https://openjfx.dev.java.net/JavaFX_Programming_Language.html`).

Note Although JavaFX Script is statically typed, types can be omitted in many places because JavaFX Script can infer types from the contexts in which they are used. For an example, check out Sundar Athijegannathan's "JavaScript, JSON and JavaFX Script" blog entry (`http://blogs.sun.com/sundararajan/entry/javascript_json_and_javafx_script`).

The Downloads section of OpenJFX's home page provides a "via tar.gz or zip file" link that takes you to a page (`https://openjfx.dev.java.net/servlets/ProjectDocumentList`) where you can download the latest JavaFX script runtime, library source, and demos as either a ZIP file or a TAR file. When this chapter was written, `OpenJFX-200707201531.tar.gz` and `OpenJFX-200707201531.zip` were the latest files. Unarchiving this ZIP file results in an `openjfx-200707201531` home directory, whose `trunk` subdirectory contains various useful subdirectories.

Tip The Downloads section of OpenJFX's home page also provides links to plug-ins that let you work with JavaFX Script from within NetBeans IDE 5.5 and 6.0, and Eclipse 3.2. You might want to install the appropriate plug-in, so that you can explore JavaFX Script with your favorite IDE.

The `trunk` directory provides a `demos` subdirectory which contains programs that demonstrate the usefulness of JavaFX Script. To play with these demonstration programs, change to `demos` directory's `demo` subdirectory and launch `demo.bat` or `demo.sh`. After a moment, you should see a JavaFX Demos window that presents a JavaFX Demos tab with a list of demo names. Figure 9-3 shows the JavaFX Canvas Tutorial demo's introductory page.

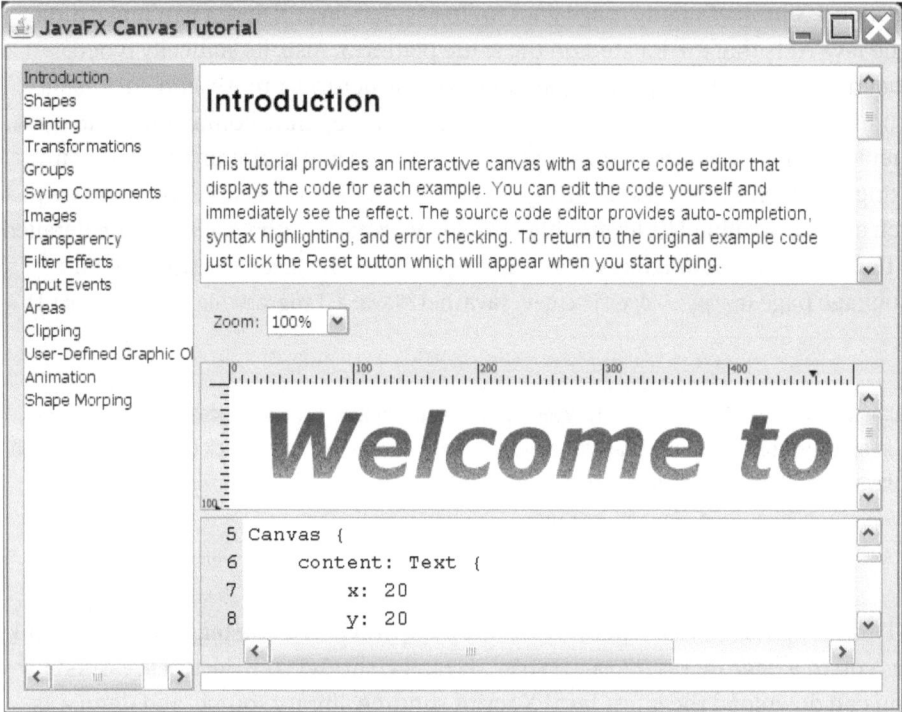

Figure 9-3. *JavaFX Canvas Tutorial lets you interactively explore JavaFX Script.*

The trunk directory also provides a lib subdirectory that contains Filters.jar, javafxrt.jar, and swing-layout.jar. These JAR files collectively implement JavaFX Script. javafxrt.jar contains JavaFXScriptEngine.class and JavaFXScriptEngineFactory.class, which serve as JavaFX Script's script engine. You can copy these JAR files to the JRE's extensions directory to access JavaFX Script from jrunscript (invoke jrunscript -1 FX, which takes you to this tool's FX> prompt), but you will not be able to accomplish anything. JavaFX Script's script engine keeps referring to script error: Invalid binding name 'javax.script.argv'. Must be of the form 'beanName:javaTypeFQN'. Obviously, jrunscript needs additional work before it can access JavaFX Script.

Fortunately, you can access JavaFX Script's script engine via the Scripting API. To prove this, I have prepared an example that demonstrates running a script via a Java application. This script presents a window that is centered on the screen. On a pale yellow background, it displays bluish text that is gradient-filled, noisy, glowing, and slightly blurred. Listing 9-17 presents this script.

Listing 9-17. *demo.fx*

```
// demo.fx

import javafx.ui.*;
import javafx.ui.canvas.*;
import javafx.ui.filter.*;

Frame
{
    width: 650
    height: 150
    title: "demo.fx"
    background: lightgoldenrodyellow
    centerOnScreen: true
    content: Canvas
    {
        content: Text
        {
            x: 15
            y: 20
            content: "{msg:<<java.lang.String>>}"
            font: Font { face: VERDANA, style: [ITALIC, BOLD], size: 80 }
            fill: LinearGradient
            {
                x1: 0, y1: 0, x2: 0, y2: 1

                stops:
                [
                    Stop
                    {
                        offset: 0
                        color: blue
                    },

                    Stop
                    {
                        offset: 0.5
                        color: dodgerblue
                    },

                    Stop
```

```
            {
               offset: 1
               color: blue
            }
         ]
      }

      filter: [MotionBlur { distance: 10.5 }, Glow {amount: 0.15},
               Noise {monochrome: false, distribution: 0}]
   }
  }
  visible: true
}
```

Listing 9-17 demonstrates JavaFX Script's declarative coding style, where values are assigned to GUI component properties (650 is assigned to the frame window's width property, for example) instead of invoking methods for this purpose. The {msg:<<java.lang.String>>} text is a placeholder for a String-based value, which is displayed in the window, and obtained from the application shown in Listing 9-18.

Listing 9-18. *WorkingWithJavaFXScript.java*

```
// WorkingWithJavaFXScript.java

import java.awt.*;

import java.io.*;

import javax.script.*;

public class WorkingWithJavaFXScript
{
   public static void main (String [] args)
   {
      ScriptEngineManager manager = new ScriptEngineManager ();

      // The JavaFX Script script engine is accessed via the FX short name.

      final ScriptEngine engine = manager.getEngineByName ("FX");

      engine.put ("msg:java.lang.String", "JavaFX Script");
```

```
    Runnable r = new Runnable ()
    {
        public void run ()
        {
            try
            {
                System.out.println ("EDT running: "+
                                     EventQueue.isDispatchThread ());
                engine.eval (new BufferedReader (new FileReader ("demo.fx")));
            }
            catch (Exception e)
            {
                e.printStackTrace ();
            }
        }
    };
    EventQueue.invokeLater (r);
  }
}
```

After obtaining JavaFX Script's script engine via the engine's FX short name, the application uses engine.put ("msg:java.lang.String", "JavaFX Script"); to pass a string value (to be displayed in the script's frame window) to the script. The script is then evaluated on the event-dispatching thread, because a Swing GUI is being created.

Run this application with Filters.jar, javafxrt.jar, and swing-layout.jar as part of the classpath. For example, assuming that these JAR files are located in \javafx, java -cp \javafx\Filters.jar;\javafx\swing-layout.jar;\javafx\javafxrt.jar;. WorkingWithJavaFXScript runs the application on a Windows platform. The application and script work together to generate the window that appears in Figure 9-4.

Figure 9-4. *This GUI created with JavaFX Script is initially centered on the screen.*

Furthermore, three messages are sent to the standard output device. The first message reports that the event-dispatching thread is running. The next two messages identify the thread that JavaFX Script's internal compiler uses to compile a script into intermediate code (to boost performance), and the amount of time that it takes to compile the script.

Because JVM class files offer better performance than intermediate code, java.net is hosting the OpenJFX Compiler project. According to this project's home page (https:// openjfx-compiler.dev.java.net/), the goal is to "focus on creating a JavaFX compiler to translate JavaFX scripts into JVM class files (bytecode)." Also, the new compiler will extend the standard Java compiler.

Note Chris Oliver provides a performance boost benchmark for an early version of this new compiler via his "First steps with the JavaFX Compiler" blog entry (http://blogs.sun.com/chrisoliver/ entry/first_steps_with_the_javafx).

Summary

Java SE 6 introduces the Scripting API so that servlets, applications, and other kinds of Java programs can work with Ruby, PHP, JavaScript, and other scripting languages.

The Scripting API was developed under JSR 223 and is provided in the javax.script package. Java SE 6 also includes the Rhino script engine.

Before you can benefit from this API, you need to master its fundamentals, including how to perform the following tasks:

- Obtain script engines from factories via the script engine manager

- Evaluate scripts

- Interact with Java classes and interfaces from scripts

- Communicate with scripts via script variables

- Use bindings, scopes, and script contexts

- Generate scripts from macros

- Compile scripts

- Invoke global, object member, and interface-implementing functions

- Use jrunscript

Integrating Rhino-based JavaScript into the `JEditorPane` component is a good example of what you can accomplish with the Scripting API. The resulting `ScriptedEditorPane` component lets you present an HTML document augmented with JavaScript so that the user can dynamically change the colors of the document's links when the mouse pointer moves over those links.

Although Rhino-based JavaScript is useful and fun to play with (especially via `jrunscript`), you will want to try the Scripting API with other scripting languages. This chapter presented examples of using the API with JRuby and JavaFX Script.

Test Your Understanding

How well do you understand Java SE 6's new Scripting API? Test your understanding by answering the following questions and performing the following exercises. (The answers are presented in Appendix D.)

1. What is the name of the package assigned to the Scripting API?

2. What is the difference between the `Compilable` interface and the `CompiledScript` abstract class?

3. Which scripting language is associated with Java SE 6's Rhino-based script engine?

4. What is the difference between `ScriptEngineFactory`'s `getEngineName()` and `getNames()` methods?

5. What does it mean for a script engine to exhibit the `MULTITHREADED` threading behavior?

6. Which of `ScriptEngineManager`'s three "getEngine" methods would be appropriate for obtaining a script engine after selecting the name of a script file via a dialog box?

7. How many `eval()` methods does `ScriptEngine` offer for evaluating scripts?

8. Why does the Rhino-based script engine not import the `java.lang` package by default?

9. What is the problem with `importPackage()` and `importClass()`, and how does Rhino overcome this problem?

10. How does a Java program communicate with a script?

11. How does `jrunscript` make command-line arguments available to a script?

12. What is a bindings object?

13. What is the difference between engine scope and global scope?

14. Although a program will have occasion to change a script engine's engine bindings, it is rather pointless to change the engine's global bindings. Why does ScriptEngine provide a setBindings(Bindings bindings, int scope) method that allows the global bindings to be replaced?

15. What does a script context do?

16. What is the difference between eval(String script, ScriptContext context) and eval(String script, Bindings n)?

17. What is the purpose of the context script variable? How would you output this variable's value in Rhino-based JavaScript and JRuby?

18. What is wrong with getOutputStatement()?

19. How do you compile a script?

20. What benefits does the Invocable interface provide?

21. What is jrunscript?

22. How would you discover the implementations for the jlist(), jmap(), and JSInvoker() functions?

23. What is JSAdapter?

24. If you were to modify demo.html's setColor(color) function to print document.linkcolor's value before and after setting this property to the color argument (as in function setColor(color) { println ("Before = "+document.linkcolor); document.linkcolor = color; println ("After = "+document.linkcolor); }), you would notice that the first time you move the mouse pointer over either of this document's two links, you get the output Before = java.awt.Color[r=0,g=0,b=0]. This output indicates that document.linkcolor's initial value is black (instead of blue, assuming the default setting). Why? How would you fix this so that the output is Before = java.awt.Color[r=0,g=0,b=255] (again, assuming the default blue style sheet setting)? Note that you will need to research the editor pane component to answer this question.

25. Modify WorkingWithJRuby (Listing 9-16) to invoke WorkingWithJavaFXScript (Listing 9-18). In the modified version, a Java program evaluates a Ruby script, which executes a Java program, which evaluates a JavaFX Script-based script.

CHAPTER 10

■■■

Security and Web Services

The JDK documentation itemizes Java SE 6's many security enhancements on its Java 6 Security Enhancements page (http://java.sun.com/javase/6/docs/technotes/guides/security/enhancements.html). This chapter discusses two new security APIs supplied with Java SE 6 for dealing with smart cards and digital signatures.

Prior to the release of Java SE 6, working with web services involved the use of enterprise Java APIs. Because Java SE 6 introduces several new web service and web-service-oriented APIs, such as the XML Digital Signature APIs, it is now considerably easier to develop web services and Java applications that interact with web services. This chapter describes Java SE 6's support for web services.

The following topics are covered in this chapter:

- Smart Card I/O API

- XML Digital Signature APIs

- Web services stack

Note Two security topics have been covered in previous chapters. Chapter 1 mentioned an enhancement involving Java SE 6's `jarsigner`, `keytool`, and `kinit` security tools. (Appendix B presents new `jarsigner` and `keytool` options.) Chapter 8 discussed SPNEGO HTTP authentication from the networking perspective.

Smart Card I/O API

Years ago, while working for a small software development company, I encountered an interesting device known as a *smart card*. As part of my job, I created a Java API to interact with smart cards via a smart card reader. This API detected card insertions and removals, and provided the means to acquire a user's credentials from an inserted smart card.

Note Check out Wikipedia's Smart card entry (http://en.wikipedia.org/wiki/Smart_card) for an introduction to smart cards.

Because the card reader's software consisted of Windows dynamic link libraries (DLLs), I used the Java Native Interface (JNI) to provide the bridge between Java and the native code that interacted with these DLLs—a messy business. My job would have been much easier if the version of Java that I worked with had provided an API for communicating with smart cards. Fortunately, Sun has finally addressed this situation by providing the Smart Card I/O API and the SunPCSC security provider in its Java SE 6 reference implementation.

■**Caution** Because the Smart Card I/O API and SunPCSC provider are not part of the Java SE 6 specification, they are only guaranteed to be available as part of Sun's reference implementation.

The Smart Card I/O API lets a Java application communicate with applications running on a smart card by exchanging ISO/IEC 7816-4 Application Protocol Data Units (APDUs). The SunPCSC security provider lets the API access the underlying platform's Personal Computer/Smart Card (PC/SC) stack (if available). SunPCSC accesses this stack via the libpcsclite.so library on Solaris and Linux platforms. On Windows platforms, SunPCSC accesses the stack via the winscard.dll library.

The Smart Card I/O API was developed according to JSR 268: Java Smart Card I/O API (http://jcp.org/en/jsr/detail?id=268). Although this JSR identifies javax.io.smartcard as the API's proposed package name, the API's official package name is javax.smartcardio. Table 10-1 describes this package's 12 classes, which are fully documented in the JDK at http://java.sun.com/javase/6/docs/jre/api/security/smartcardio/spec/. (Although these classes are documented in Sun's JDK documentation, they are not part of the Java SE 6 specification, and are only guaranteed to be part of Sun's reference implementation.)

Table 10-1. *javax.smartcardio Classes*

Class	Description
ATR	Stores a smart card's answer-to-reset bytes. A smart card sends these bytes to a *terminal* (a card reader slot) when the card is inserted into the terminal (which powers up the card), or when a command is sent to the terminal to explicitly reset the card. The answer-to-reset bytes are used to establish the basis for a communications session. If you are interested in the format of these bytes, see "Answer to Reset Explained" (http://www.cozmanova.com/content/view/18/34/).
Card	Describes a smart card with an associated connection. A Card is obtained by acquiring a CardTerminal instance and using this instance to invoke CardTerminal's public abstract Card connect(String protocol) method with the specified protocol.

Class	Description
CardChannel	Describes a logical channel to a smart card, which is used to exchange APDUs with the card. A CardChannel is obtained by invoking either of Card's public abstract CardChannel getBasicChannel() or public abstract CardChannel openLogicalChannel() methods via the Card instance.
CardException	Thrown when an error occurs during communication with the smart card or a smart card stack. In the future, it is possible that new smart card stacks will be introduced. PC/SC is the only stack currently available from Sun's reference implementation.
CardNotPresentException	Thrown when an application tries to establish a connection with a terminal and a card is not present in the terminal.
CardPermission	Describes the permission for smart card operations. This class identifies the name of the terminal to which the permission applies and the set of actions (connect, reset, and so on) that is valid for the terminal.
CardTerminal	Describes a card reader slot. A CardTerminal is obtained by invoking either of the CardTerminals class's list() methods and choosing a list entry, or by invoking the CardTerminals class's public CardTerminal getTerminal(String name) method with the vendor-specific name of the terminal.
CardTerminals	Describes the set of terminals supported by an instance of TerminalFactory. An application uses CardTerminals to enumerate available card terminals, obtain a specific card terminal, or wait for a card to be inserted or removed. The inner State enumeration describes various card terminal state constants, such as CardTerminals.State.CARD_PRESENT. A state constant is passed to CardTerminals's public abstract List<CardTerminal> list(CardTerminals.State state) method to return a list of all card terminals for which this state was detected during the most recent call to one of CardTerminals's two waitForChange() methods.
CommandAPDU	Stores an ISO/IEC 7816-4-structured command APDU, which consists of a 4-byte header (identifying an instruction's class, code, and parameters), followed by an optional body of variable length.
ResponseAPDU	Stores an ISO/IEC 7816-4-structured response APDU, which consists of an optional body followed by a 2-byte trailer. The trailer provides status information about the card's processing state following the command APDU's execution.
TerminalFactory	Entry point into the Smart Card I/O API. An application obtains a TerminalFactory instance by invoking this class's public static TerminalFactory getDefault() method to return the default terminal factory (which is always available, but might not provide any terminals). Alternatively, the application can call any of this class's three getInstance() methods to obtain a terminal factory based on some combination of a smart card stack type and a java.security. Provider implementation.
TerminalFactorySpi	Describes the service provider interface for introducing new smart card-oriented security providers. Applications do not interact with this class directly.

While writing this chapter, I did not have access to a smart card or a reader, which made it impossible to create a significant example. Instead, I opted for a limited example that demonstrates how to obtain the default terminal factory and a factory for the PC/SC stack. The example also shows how to enumerate a factory's card terminals. Listing 10-1 presents the source code.

Listing 10-1. *Terminals.java*

```java
// Terminals.java

import java.util.*;

import javax.smartcardio.*;

public class Terminals
{
    public static void main (String [] args) throws Exception
    {
        TerminalFactory factory = TerminalFactory.getDefault ();
        System.out.println ("Default factory: "+factory);
        dumpTerminals (factory);

        factory = TerminalFactory.getInstance ("PC/SC", null);
        System.out.println ("PC/SC factory: "+factory);
        dumpTerminals (factory);
    }

    static void dumpTerminals (TerminalFactory factory) throws Exception
    {
        List<CardTerminal> terminals = factory.terminals ().list ();
        for (CardTerminal terminal: terminals)
            System.out.println (terminal);
    }
}
```

After running Terminals on my Windows platform, the first line of output was as follows:

```
Default factory: TerminalFactory for type None from provider None
```

I also observed output related to a `java.security.NoSuchAlgorithmException`, which was thrown from `TerminalFactory.getInstance("PC/SC", null)`. I believe this exception was thrown because a card reader device was not present on my platform.

XML Digital Signature APIs

Web-based business transactions commonly involve a flow of XML documents that contain business data. Because these documents must remain private between their senders and recipients (you would not want just anyone to read your credit card data, for example), the business data within XML documents can be encrypted. Furthermore, various portions of these documents can be digitally signed, for the following reasons:

- To guarantee their *authenticity*: who sent the data?

- To guarantee *integrity*: was the data modified in transit?

- To provide *nonrepudiation*: senders cannot deny sending their documents.

Signing XML documents with an older digital signature standard such as RSA Security's Public Key Cryptography Standard (PKCS) #7 (`http://tools.ietf.org/html/rfc2315`) is challenging because older standards were not designed for XML. For example, a document might reference external data that needs to be signed. Also, several people might jointly develop a document, and they may want to sign only their part, to limit their liability.

Java SE 6's XML Digital Signature APIs make dealing with digital signatures easier. But before learning about those APIs, you should understand the fundamentals of digital signatures, as well as the digital signature standard that addresses XML's requirements, on which Java SE 6's XML Digital Signature APIs are based.

Digital Signature Fundamentals

Digitally signing a message, and later verifying its authenticity and integrity, involves *public-key cryptography* (see `http://en.wikipedia.org/wiki/Public_key_cryptography`). To sign a message, the sender first applies a mathematical transformation to the message, which results in a unique *hash* or *message digest*. The sender then encrypts the hash via the sender's private key. The encrypted hash is known as a *digital signature* (see `http://en.wikipedia.org/wiki/Digital_signature`).

After receiving the message, signature, and public key from the sender, the recipient performs verification by generating a hash of the message via the same mathematical transformation, by using the public key to decrypt the digital signature, and by comparing the generated and decrypted hashes. If the hashes are the same, the recipient can be confident of the message's authenticity and integrity. Because the recipient does not have the private key, nonrepudiation is also guaranteed.

Note Successful verification relies on knowing that the public key belongs to the sender. Otherwise, another person might claim to be the sender and substitute his public key in place of the actual key. To prevent this, a certificate vouching for the sender as owner of the public key, and issued by a certificate authority, is also sent to the recipient. For more information about certificates and certificate authorities, see the Wikipedia articles on these topics: http://en.wikipedia.org/wiki/Public_key_certificate and http://en.wikipedia.org/wiki/Certificate_authority.

XML Signatures Standard

Several years ago, the World Wide Web Consortium (W3C) and the Internet Engineering Task Force (IETF) jointly hammered out a digital signature standard for XML documents. Their XML Signatures standard is described by the W3C's "XML-Signature Syntax and Processing" document (http://www.w3.org/TR/2002/REC-xmldsig-core-20020212/) and the IETF's "(Extensible Markup Language) XML-Signature Syntax and Processing" document (http://www.ietf.org/rfc/rfc3275.txt).

Tip Because the W3C and IETF documents are somewhat difficult to read, you might want to check out the article titled "An Introduction to XML Digital Signatures" (http://www.xml.com/pub/a/2001/08/08/xmldsig.html). This article is written by XML security experts Ed Simon, Paul Madsen, and Carlisle Adams.

According to the XML Signatures standard, an *XML Signature* consists of a Signature element and contained elements that describe various aspects of the XML Signature. These elements are defined by the W3C namespace at http://www.w3.org/TR/2002/REC-xmldsig-core-20020212/xmldsig-core-schema.xsd, and are related by the following syntax specification, where * represents zero or more occurrences, + represents one or more occurrences, and ? represents zero or one occurrence.

```
<Signature Id?>
   <SignedInfo Id?>
      <CanonicalizationMethod Algorithm/>
      <SignatureMethod Algorithm/>
      (<Reference Id? URI? Type?>
         (<Transforms>
            (<Transform Algorithm/>)+
         </Transforms>)?
```

```
        <DigestMethod Algorithm/>
        <DigestValue>…</DigestValue>
    </Reference>)+
  </SignedInfo>
  <SignatureValue Id?>…</SignatureValue>
  (<KeyInfo Id?>…</KeyInfo>)?
  (<Object Id? MimeType? Encoding?>…</Object>)*
</Signature>
```

The Signature element is organized into SignedInfo, SignatureValue, KeyInfo (optional), and zero or more Object elements. The SignedInfo element is organized into CanonicalizationMethod, SignatureMethod, and one or more Reference elements. Each Reference element is organized into Transforms (optional), DigestMethod, and DigestValue elements. The Transforms element is organized into one or more Transform elements.

The SignedInfo element identifies that part of an XML document to be signed; all content within the SignedInfo section contributes to the signature. After *canonicalizing* this section via the algorithm identified by SignedInfo's CanonicalizationMethod element, an application signs the canonicalized content via the algorithm identified by SignedInfo's SignatureMethod element. (CanonicalizationMethod and SignatureMethod are part of SignedInfo to protect them from tampering.)

■Note Sean Mullan's "Programming With the Java XML Digital Signature API" article (http:// java.sun.com/developer/technicalArticles/xml/dig_signature_api/) describes canonicalization as follows: "*Canonicalization* is the process of converting XML content to a physical representation, called the canonical form, in order to eliminate subtle changes that can invalidate a signature over that data. Canonicalization is necessary due to the nature of XML and the way it is parsed by different processors and intermediaries, which can change the data in such a way that the signature is no longer valid but the signed data is still logically equivalent. Canonicalization eliminates these permissible syntactic variances by converting the XML to a canonical form before generating or validating the signature." Sean helped to bring XML Signatures to Java.

The SignedInfo element also includes a list of Reference elements. Each Reference element, which is part of the signature, identifies a *data object* (content that you want signed) to be digested via a URI. It also identifies an optional Transforms list of Transform elements to apply to the data object prior to digestion, the algorithm used to calculate the digest via the DigestMethod element, and the resulting digest value via the DigestValue element. Transform elements identify transformation algorithms that are used to process a data object prior to digestion. For example, if an XML Signature (that is, the Signature element and its contained elements) happens to be part of the data object being digested, you would not want the XML Signature to be included in the digest calculation. You could apply a transformation to remove the XML Signature from the calculation.

The final three elements contained within Signature work as follows:

- SignatureValue contains the actual digital signature value, which is encoded via the base64 algorithm.

- KeyInfo contains the public key information—keys, names, certificates, and other public-key management data such as key-agreement data—that a recipient needs to validate the signature (assuming that the public key is not otherwise known to the recipient).

- Object contains arbitrary data. This element may appear multiple times.

Note Learn more about the base64 algorithm by checking out RFC 2045: Multipurpose Internet Mail Extensions (MIME) Part One: Format of Internet Message Bodies (http://www.ietf.org/rfc/rfc2045.txt). For more information about key-agreement data, see Wikipedia's Password-authenticated key agreement entry (http://en.wikipedia.org/wiki/Password-authenticated_key_agreement).

Along with the XML Signature syntax specification, the "XML-Signature Syntax and Processing" document describes rules for generating and validating XML Signatures. These are summarized as follows:

Generating an XML Signature: First calculate a digest value over each Reference element's associated (and possibly transformed) data object, and then calculate the signature over the entire canonicalized contents of the SignedInfo element (including all Reference digest values).

Validating an XML Signature: First canonicalize the SignedInfo element and, for each Reference, digest the associated data object and compare the digest value with the Reference element's digest value (reference validation). The public key is then obtained from either the KeyInfo element or an external source, and used to confirm the SignatureValue over the SignedInfo element via the canonical form of the SignatureMethod (signature validation).

XML SIGNATURE TYPES

The "XML-Signature Syntax and Processing" document describes three types of XML Signatures, which are based on the relationship between a data object and its XML Signature:

- *Enveloping*: The signature is over data objects contained within the Signature element's Object elements (or subelements). Each Object or its subelement is identified via a Reference element (via a URI fragment identifier or a transformation).

- *Enveloped*: The signature is over the data object that contains the Signature element. The data object provides the root element of the XML document. The Signature element must be excluded from the data object's signature value calculation via a transformation.

- *Detached*: The signature is over data objects external to the XML Signature. Each object is identified by a Reference element (via a URI or transformation). Data objects can be located in external resources, or as sibling elements within the same XML document as Signature.

Java and the XML Signatures Standard

In 2001, Sean Mullan of Sun Microsystems and Anthony Nadalin of IBM jointly introduced JSR 105: XML Digital Signature APIs (http://www.jcp.org/en/jsr/detail?id=105) to support the XML Signatures standard in Java. According to this JSR's web page, it "defines and incorporates a standard set of high-level implementation-independent APIs for XML digital signatures services." JSR 105's APIs, which made it into Java SE 6, are implemented in terms of the six Java packages described in Table 10-2.

Table 10-2. *XML Digital Signature API Packages*

Package	Description
javax.xml.crypto	Common classes and interfaces for generating XML digital signatures, and for performing other XML cryptographic operations. For example, the KeySelector class is useful for obtaining an XML Signature's public key, for use in validating the signature.
javax.xml.crypto.dom	Document Object Model (DOM)-specific common classes and interfaces. Only developers who are using a DOM-based XML cryptographic implementation will need to work directly with this package.
javax.xml.crypto.dsig	Classes and interfaces for generating and validating XML Signatures. Various interfaces such as SignedInfo, CanonicalizationMethod, and SignatureMethod correspond to the equivalent W3C-defined elements.

Continued

Table 10-2. *Continued*

Package	Description
javax.xml.crypto.dsig.dom	DOM-specific classes and interfaces for generating and validating XML Signatures. Only developers who are using a DOM-based XML cryptographic implementation will need to work directly with this package.
javax.xml.crypto.dsig.keyinfo	Classes and interfaces for parsing and processing KeyInfo components and structures. KeyInfo corresponds to the equivalent W3C-defined KeyInfo element.
javax.xml.crypto.dsig.spec	Input parameter classes and interfaces for digest, signature, transform, or canonicalization algorithms that are used in XML digital signature processing. C14NmethodParameterSpec is an example.

The javax.xml.crypto.dsig.XMLSignatureFactory class is the entry point into these APIs. This class provides methods that do the following:

- Create an XML Signature's elements as objects.

- Create an instance of javax.xml.crypto.dsig.XMLSignature to contain these objects. XMLSignature and its signature are marshaled into an XML representation during a signing operation.

- Unmarshal an existing XML representation into an XMLSignature object before validating the signature.

However, before an application can accomplish these tasks, it needs to obtain an instance of XMLSignatureFactory. Accomplish this task by invoking one of XMLSignatureFactory's getInstance() methods, where each method returns an instance that supports a specific type of XML mechanism (such as DOM). The objects that this factory produces will be based on the XML mechanism type and abide by the type's interoperability requirements.

Note To discover DOM-interoperability requirements, check out the "Java XML Digital Signature API Specification (JSR 105)" Javadoc (http://java.sun.com/javase/6/docs/technotes/guides/security/xmldsig/overview.html).

I have created an example that demonstrates the XML Digital Signature APIs. The XMLSigDemo application, shown in Listing 10-2, provides the capabilities for signing an arbitrary XML document and for validating a signed document's XML Signature.

Listing 10-2. *XMLSigDemo.java*

```java
// XMLSigDemo.java

import java.io.*;

import java.security.*;

import java.util.*;

import javax.xml.crypto.*;
import javax.xml.crypto.dom.*;
import javax.xml.crypto.dsig.*;
import javax.xml.crypto.dsig.dom.*;
import javax.xml.crypto.dsig.keyinfo.*;
import javax.xml.crypto.dsig.spec.*;

import javax.xml.parsers.*;

import javax.xml.transform.*;
import javax.xml.transform.dom.*;
import javax.xml.transform.stream.*;

import org.w3c.dom.*;

public class XMLSigDemo
{
    public static void main (String [] args) throws Exception
    {
        boolean sign = true;

        if (args.length == 1)
            sign = false; // validate instead of sign
        else
        if (args.length != 2)
        {
            System.out.println ("usage: java XMLSigDemo inFile [outFile]");
            return;
        }

        if (sign)
            signDoc (args [0], args [1]);
```

```
        else
            validateSig (args [0]);
    }


    static void signDoc (String inFile, String outFile) throws Exception
    {
        // Obtain the default implementation of DocumentBuilderFactory to parse
        // the XML document that is to be signed.

        DocumentBuilderFactory dbf = DocumentBuilderFactory.newInstance ();

        // Because XML signatures use XML namespaces, the factory is told to be
        // namespace-aware.

        dbf.setNamespaceAware (true);

        // Use the factory to obtain a DocumentBuilder instance, which is used
        // to parse the document identified by inFile.

        Document doc = dbf.newDocumentBuilder ().parse (new File (inFile));

        // Generate a DSA KeyPair with a length of 512 bits. The private key is
        // used to generate the signature.

        KeyPairGenerator kpg = KeyPairGenerator.getInstance ("DSA");
        kpg.initialize (512);
        KeyPair kp = kpg.generateKeyPair ();

        // Create a DOM-specific XMLSignContext. This class contains context
        // information for generating XML Signatures. It is initialized with the
        // private key that will be used to sign the document and the root of
        // the document to be signed.

        DOMSignContext dsc = new DOMSignContext (kp.getPrivate (),
                                                 doc.getDocumentElement ());

        // The different parts of the Signature element are assembled into an
        // XMLSignature object. These objects are created and assembled using an
        // XMLSignatureFactory. Because DocumentBuilderFactory was used to parse
        // the XML document into a DOM object tree, a DOM implementation of
        // XMLSignatureFactory is obtained.
```

```
XMLSignatureFactory fac = XMLSignatureFactory.getInstance ("DOM");

// Create a Reference element to the content to be digested: An empty
// string URI ("") implies the document root. SHA1 is used as the digest
// method. A single enveloped Transform is required for an enveloped
// signature, so that the Signature element and contained elements are
// not included when calculating the signature.

Transform xfrm = fac.newTransform (Transform.ENVELOPED,
                                    (TransformParameterSpec) null);
Reference ref;
ref = fac.newReference ("",
                        fac.newDigestMethod (DigestMethod.SHA1, null),
                        Collections.singletonList (xfrm), null,
                        "MyRef");

// Create the SignedInfo object, which is the only object that is
// signed -- a Reference element's identified data object is digested,
// and it is the digest value that is part of the SignedInfo object that
// is included in the signature. The CanonicalizationMethod chosen is
// inclusive and preserves comments, the SignatureMethod is DSA, and the
// list of References contains only one Reference.

CanonicalizationMethod cm;
cm = fac.newCanonicalizationMethod (CanonicalizationMethod.
                                    INCLUSIVE_WITH_COMMENTS,
                                    (C14NMethodParameterSpec) null);
SignatureMethod sm;
sm = fac.newSignatureMethod (SignatureMethod.DSA_SHA1, null);
SignedInfo si;
si = fac.newSignedInfo (cm, sm, Collections.singletonList (ref));

// Create the KeyInfo object, which allows the recipient to find the
// public key needed to validate the signature.

KeyInfoFactory kif = fac.getKeyInfoFactory ();
KeyValue kv = kif.newKeyValue (kp.getPublic ());
KeyInfo ki = kif.newKeyInfo (Collections.singletonList (kv));

// Create the XMLSignature object, passing the SignedInfo and KeyInfo
// values as arguments.
```

```
    XMLSignature signature = fac.newXMLSignature (si, ki);

    // Generate the signature.

    signature.sign (dsc);

    System.out.println ("Signature generated!");
    System.out.println ("Outputting to "+outFile);

    // Transform the DOM-based XML content and Signature element into a
    // stream of content that is output to the file identified by outFile.

    TransformerFactory tf = TransformerFactory.newInstance ();
    Transformer trans = tf.newTransformer ();
    trans.transform (new DOMSource (doc),
                     new StreamResult (new FileOutputStream (outFile)));
}


@SuppressWarnings ("unchecked")
static void validateSig (String inFile) throws Exception
{
    // Obtain the default implementation of DocumentBuilderFactory to parse
    // the XML document that contains the signature.

    DocumentBuilderFactory dbf = DocumentBuilderFactory.newInstance ();

    // Because XML signatures use XML namespaces, the factory is told to be
    // namespace-aware.

    dbf.setNamespaceAware (true);

    // Use the factory to obtain a DocumentBuilder instance, which is used
    // to parse the document identified by inFile.

    Document doc = dbf.newDocumentBuilder ().parse (new File (inFile));

    // Return a list of all Signature element nodes in the DOM object tree.
    // There must be at least one Signature element -- the signDoc() method
    // results in exactly one Signature element.

    NodeList nl = doc.getElementsByTagNameNS (XMLSignature.XMLNS,
                                              "Signature");
```

```
if (nl.getLength () == 0)
    throw new Exception ("Missing Signature element");

// Create a DOM-specific XMLValidateContext. This class contains context
// information for validating XML Signatures. It is initialized with the
// public key that will be used to validate the document, and a
// reference to the Signature element to be validated. The public key
// will be obtained by invoking keyValueKeySelector's select() method
// (behind the scenes).

DOMValidateContext dvc;
dvc = new DOMValidateContext (new KeyValueKeySelector (), nl.item (0));

// The different parts of the Signature element are unmarshalled into an
// XMLSignature object. The Signature element is unmarshalled using an
// XMLSignatureFactory. Because DocumentBuilderFactory was used to parse
// the XML document (containing the Signature element) into a DOM object
// tree, a DOM implementation of XMLSignatureFactory is obtained.
```

XMLSignatureFactory fac = XMLSignatureFactory.getInstance ("DOM");

```
// Unmarshal the XML Signature from the DOM tree.
```

XMLSignature signature = fac.unmarshalXMLSignature (dvc);

```
// Validate the XML Signature.
```

boolean coreValidity = signature.validate (dvc);
```
if (coreValidity)
{
    System.out.println ("Signature is valid!");
    return;
}

System.out.println ("Signature is invalid!");

// Identify the cause or causes of failure.

System.out.println ("Checking Reference digest for validity...");

List<Reference> refs;
refs = (List<Reference>) signature.getSignedInfo ().getReferences ();
```

```
        for (Reference r: refs)
            System.out.println ("  Reference '"+r.getId ()+"' digest is "+
                                (r.validate (dvc) ? "" : "not ")+"valid");

        System.out.println ("Checking SignatureValue element for validity...");

        System.out.println ("  SignatureValue element's value is "+
                            (signature.getSignatureValue ().validate (dvc)
                            ? "" : "not ")+"valid");
    }


    private static class KeyValueKeySelector extends KeySelector
    {
        // Search the Signature element's KeyInfo element's KeyValue elements
        // for the public key that will be used for validation. No determination
        // is made if the key can be trusted.

        public KeySelectorResult select (KeyInfo keyInfo,
                                         KeySelector.Purpose purpose,
                                         AlgorithmMethod method,
                                         XMLCryptoContext context)
            throws KeySelectorException
        {
            if (keyInfo == null)
                throw new KeySelectorException ("Null KeyInfo object!");

            SignatureMethod sm = (SignatureMethod) method;
            List list = keyInfo.getContent ();

            for (int i = 0; i < list.size (); i++)
            {
                XMLStructure xmlStructure = (XMLStructure) list.get (i);
                if (xmlStructure instanceof KeyValue)
                {
                    PublicKey pk = null;
                    try
                    {
                        pk = ((KeyValue) xmlStructure).getPublicKey ();
                    }
                    catch (KeyException ke)
                    {
                        throw new KeySelectorException (ke);
```

```
            }

            // Make sure algorithm is compatible with signature method.

            if (algEquals (sm.getAlgorithm (), pk.getAlgorithm ()))
            {
                final PublicKey pk2 = pk;
                return new KeySelectorResult ()
                            {
                                public Key getKey ()
                                {
                                    return pk2;
                                }
                            };
            }
        }
    }

    throw new KeySelectorException ("No KeyValue element found!");
    }
}

static boolean algEquals (String algURI, String algName)
{
    if (algName.equalsIgnoreCase ("DSA") &&
        algURI.equalsIgnoreCase (SignatureMethod.DSA_SHA1))
        return true;

    if (algName.equalsIgnoreCase ("RSA") &&
        algURI.equalsIgnoreCase (SignatureMethod.RSA_SHA1))
        return true;

    return false;
    }
}
```

XMLSigDemo.java is based on the code found in the "XML Digital Signature API Examples" section of *The Java Web Services Tutorial* (http://java.sun.com/webservices/docs/2.0/tutorial/doc/XMLDigitalSignatureAPI8.html#wp511424). You will want to check out this resource for more information about how the code works.

Note *The Java Web Services Tutorial*'s influence is also evidenced by java.net author Young Yang in his "XML Signature with JSR-105 in Java SE 6" article (`http://today.java.net/pub/a/today/2006/11/21/xml-signature-with-jsr-105.html?page=1`). Young's `Sign` application demonstrates how to create an enveloping signature.

After compiling `XMLSigDemo.java`, you will need an XML document to sign. For example, you might want to try out `XMLSigDemo` with the simple purchase order document, `po.xml`, presented in Listing 10-3.

Listing 10-3. *po.xml*

```
<?xml version="1.0" encoding="UTF-8"?>
<po>
   <items>
     <item>
       <code>hw-1021</code>
       <desc>Hammer</desc>
       <qty>5</qty>
       <unitcost>11.99</unitcost>
     </item>
     <item>
       <code>hw-2103</code>
       <desc>Solar lights</desc>
       <qty>10</qty>
       <unitcost>24.99</unitcost>
     </item>
   </items>
</po>
```

To sign this purchase order, invoke the following:

```
java XMLSigDemo po.xml pos.xml
```

The *s* in `pos.xml` stands for *signed*. (You can choose your own name in place of `pos.xml`.) If all goes well, `XMLSigDemo` outputs the following:

```
Signature generated!
Outputting to pos.xml
```

Also, the signed document is stored in pos.xml. Its contents should be similar to Listing 10-4's contents.

Note Listing 10-4 has been reformatted for this book. The contents of pos.xml will vary from one signing operation to another, because XMLSigDemo generates a different public/private key pair for each run.

Listing 10-4. *pos.xml*

```
<?xml version="1.0" encoding="UTF-8" standalone="no"?>
  <po>
    <items>
      <item>
        <code>hw-1021</code>
        <desc>Hammer</desc>
        <qty>5</qty>
        <unitcost>11.99</unitcost>
      </item>
      <item>
        <code>hw-2103</code>
        <desc>Solar lights</desc>
        <qty>10</qty>
        <unitcost>24.99</unitcost>
      </item>
    </items>
    <Signature xmlns="http://www.w3.org/2000/09/xmldsig#">
      <SignedInfo>
        <CanonicalizationMethod Algorithm="http://www.w3.org/TR/2001/REC-xml-
                                  c14n-20010315#WithComments"/>
        <SignatureMethod Algorithm="http://www.w3.org/2000/09/xmldsig
                            #dsa-sha1"/>
        <Reference Id="MyRef" URI="">
          <Transforms>
            <Transform Algorithm="http://www.w3.org/2000/09/xmldsig#
                          enveloped-signature"/>
          </Transforms>
          <DigestMethod Algorithm="http://www.w3.org/2000/09/xmldsig#sha1"/>
          <DigestValue>nquYMOZPk5K6di76vnt63xvR1jI=</DigestValue>
        </Reference>
      </SignedInfo>
```

```
      <SignatureValue>ftXiy7gIDtU6O1BibABWfc+VteJw2O8xKMTALt14lmO91ATeU88+jA==
      </SignatureValue>
      <KeyInfo>
        <KeyValue>
          <DSAKeyValue>
            <P>/KaCzo4Syrom78z3EQ5SbbB4sF7ey8OetKII864WF64B81uRpH5t9jQTxeEuOIm
               bzRMqzVDZkVG9xD7nN1kuFw==</P>
            <Q>li7dzDacuo67Jg7mtqEm2TRuOMU=</Q>
            <G>Z4Rxsnqc9E7pGknFFH2xqaryRPBaQO1khpMdLRQnG541Awtx/XPaF5Bpsy4pNWM
               OHCBiNUONogpsQW5QvnlMpA==</G>
            <Y>ajryQOwA2H77GAt6LNhGwPALyGLMu/e7T7OytjObxpORQndX++ydqzKXW6POVZj
               1X9lRW3rVxEORBxp4yb7eMQ==</Y>
          </DSAKeyValue>
        </KeyValue>
      </KeyInfo>
    </Signature>
  </po>
```

Listing 10-4 reveals that XMLSigDemo created an enveloped signature. You can validate this signature by invoking java XMLSigDemo pos.xml. If the file has not been tampered with, XMLSigDemo will output Signature is valid!.

There are three ways to tamper with this file:

Modify the data object over which the digest value is created. For example, suppose you change the 5 to a 6 in the hammer item's quantity tag, and then invoke java XMLSigDemo pos.xml. XMLSigDemo responds with this output:

```
Signature is invalid!
Checking Reference digest for validity...
  Reference 'MyRef' digest is not valid
Checking SignatureValue element for validity...
  SignatureValue element's value is valid
```

Modify the signature value. For example, you might swap a couple of consecutive characters in the SignatureValue element. Assuming an exception is not thrown (because the signature is no longer base64-encoded), XMLSigDemo responds with this output:

```
Signature is invalid!
Checking Reference digest for validity...
  Reference 'MyRef' digest is valid
Checking SignatureValue element for validity...
  SignatureValue element's value is not valid
```

Modify both the digest value and the signature value. In this case, you would observe both `Reference 'MyRef' digest is not valid` and `SignatureValue element's value is not valid` messages.

■ **Tip** The XML Digital Signature APIs include extensive logging support that provides additional information to help you debug validation failures. Sean Mullan demonstrates how to take advantage of this support in the "Logging and Debugging" section of his "Programming With the Java XML Digital Signature API" article (`http://java.sun.com/developer/technicalArticles/xml/dig_signature_api/`).

Web Services Stack

One interesting feature that Java SE 6 brings to the Java platform is a web services stack. This stack allows you to create and locally test your own web services or access existing web services. When you locally test a web service, Java starts its lightweight HTTP server (another Java SE 6 feature, discussed in Chapter 8), which hosts the web service.

■ **Note** If you are new to web services, you might want to check out Dev2Dev's "Introduction to Web Services" article (`http://dev2dev.bea.com/pub/a/2004/02/introwebsvcs.html`) and Wikipedia's Web service entry (`http://en.wikipedia.org/wiki/Web_service`) for a brief introduction. You can then explore *The Java Web Services Tutorial* (`http://java.sun.com/webservices/docs/2.0/tutorial/doc/`) to learn about developing web services in the context of Sun's Java Web Services Developer's Pack version 2.0. Many of the APIs discussed in the tutorial are now present in Java SE 6.

In the Sun Developer Network article "Implementing High Performance Web Services Using JAX-WS 2.0" (`http://java.sun.com/developer/technicalArticles/WebServices/high_performance/index.html`), author Bharath Mundlapudi illustrates the web services stack's layered architecture, with JAX-WS 2.0 at the top, JAXB 2.0 in the middle, and StAX at the bottom. These APIs work as follows:

- *Java API for XML Web Services (JAX-WS)*: The API for building web services and clients (in Java) that communicate via XML. This API is assigned package `javax.xml.ws`. JAX-WS replaces the older JAX-RPC.

- *Java Architecture for XML Binding (JAXB)*: The API for accessing and processing XML data without needing to explicitly create a parser. This API is assigned package `javax.xml.bind` and various subpackages.

- *Streaming API for XML (StAX)*: Part of Java API for XML Processing (JAXP) 1.4, a parser API that addresses limitations with the Simple API for XML (SAX) and DOM parser APIs. This API is assigned the `javax.xml.transform.stax` package.

■Note You can learn more about JAXB by studying the technical article "Java Architecture for XML Binding (JAXB)" by Ed Ort and Bhakti Mehta (`http://java.sun.com/developer/technicalArticles/ WebServices/jaxb/`). You can learn more about StAX by checking out Wikipedia's StAX entry (`http://en. wikipedia.org/wiki/StAX`), and Elliotte Rusty Harold's "An Introduction to StAX" article (`http://www. xml.com/pub/a/2003/09/17/stax.html`). For an in-depth look at StAX, check out Anghel Leonard's "StAX and XSLT Transformations in J2SE 6.0 Mustang" article (`http://javaboutique.internet.com/ tutorials/staxxsl/`).

Along with JAX-WS, JAXB, and StAX, Java SE 6 introduces SOAP with Attachments API for Java (SAAJ) 1.3 (via the `javax.xml.soap` package). The *Java Web Services Tutorial* states that SAAJ "is used mainly for the SOAP [Service Oriented Architecture Protocol] messaging that goes on behind the scenes in JAX-WS handlers and JAXR [Java API for XML Registries] implementations."

■Note *The Java Web Services Tutorial* also reveals that you can use SAAJ "to write SOAP messaging applications directly rather than use JAX-WS." Tech writer Robert Eckstein provides an example in his "An Introduction to SAAJ" tech tip (`http://java.sun.com/developer/EJTechTips/2005/tt0425.html#1`). Also, Sun employee Ashutosh Shahi's "SAAJ 1.3" blog entry (`http://blogs.sun.com/ashutosh/ entry/saaj_1_3_br`) itemizes how SAAJ 1.3 differs from SAAJ 1.2.

In addition to bringing these four APIs to the Java platform, Java SE 6 introduces the Web Services Metadata API (via the `javax.jws` package), which consists of various annotation types such as `WebService` and `WebMethod`. These annotation types let you easily incorporate Java-to-Web Service Description Language (WSDL) mapping information into a web service's Java classes.

Note To learn more about the Web Services Metadata API, check out JSR 181: Web Services Metadata for the Java Platform (http://jcp.org/en/jsr/detail?id=181).

Creating and Testing Your Own Web Service

The web services stack is helpful for creating and testing your own web service. For example, you might create a web service that performs a variety of unit conversions (such as converting kilograms to pounds and pounds to kilograms). To keep this web service simple, you could confine it to a single class, such as the Converter class, whose source code is presented in Listing 10-5.

Listing 10-5. *Converter.java*

```java
// Converter.java

package wsdemo;

import javax.jws.WebService;

@WebService
public class Converter
{
   public double acresToSqMeters (double value)
   {
      return value*4046.8564224; // acres to square meters
   }

   public double sqMetersToAcres (double value)
   {
      return value/4046.8564224; // square meters to acres
   }

   public double lbsToKilos (double value)
   {
      return value*0.45359237; // pounds to kilograms
   }

   public double kilosToLbs (double value)
   {
      return value/0.45359237; // kilograms to pounds
   }
}
```

Converter is declared public and annotated with the @WebService annotation to identify its public methods (which cannot also be static) as web service operations. These
operations are available to client programs. Because @WebService-annotated classes are
stored in packages, Converter is assigned to the wsdemo package.

Tip Instead of using @WebService to identify all of a class's public methods as web service operations,
you can selectively identify public methods by annotating them with the @WebMethod annotation.

Converter must be published at a specific address to turn it into an active web
service. You can accomplish this task by invoking the javax.xml.ws.EndPoint class's public
static Endpoint publish(String address, Object implementor) method with the web
service's address URI and a Converter instance as arguments. Listing 10-6 presents the
source code to a RunConverter application that handles this task.

Listing 10-6. *RunConverter.java*

```
// RunConverter.java

package wsdemo;

import javax.xml.ws.Endpoint;

public class RunConverter
{
    public static void main (String [] args)
    {
        // Start the lightweight HTTP server and the Converter Web service.

        Endpoint.publish ("http://localhost:8080/WSDemo/Converter",
                          new Converter ());
    }
}
```

Before you can invoke RunConverter to start both the lightweight HTTP server and
web service, you need to create an appropriate package directory, compile Listings 10-5
and 10-6, and invoke the wsgen tool to generate web service artifacts that allow Converter
to be deployed as a web service. Complete the following steps to accomplish these tasks:

1. Within the current directory, create a wsdemo directory that corresponds to the
   wsdemo package. The Converter.java and RunConverter.java source files must be
   stored in this directory.

2. Assuming that the directory containing wsdemo is the current directory, invoke javac wsdemo/*.java to compile Converter.java and RunConverter.java. If all goes well, wsdemo should contain Converter.class and RunConverter.class. If a compiler error occurs, check the source code to make sure it matches Listings 10-5 and 10-6.

3. Assuming that the directory containing wsdemo is the current directory, invoke wsgen -cp . wsdemo.Converter to generate web service artifacts. The -cp option (with the period character argument representing the current directory) is necessary to ensure that Converter.class can be found. The artifacts' class files and source files are placed in a jaxws subdirectory of wsdemo.

4. Assuming that the directory containing wsdemo is the current directory, invoke java wsdemo.RunConverter to publish the Converter web service.

After completing these steps, you can verify that Converter has been published by starting your web browser and entering http://localhost:8080/WSDemo/Converter?wsdl into the browser's address field. In response, the browser should display the contents of Converter's WSDL file. Figure 10-1 shows a portion of this file.

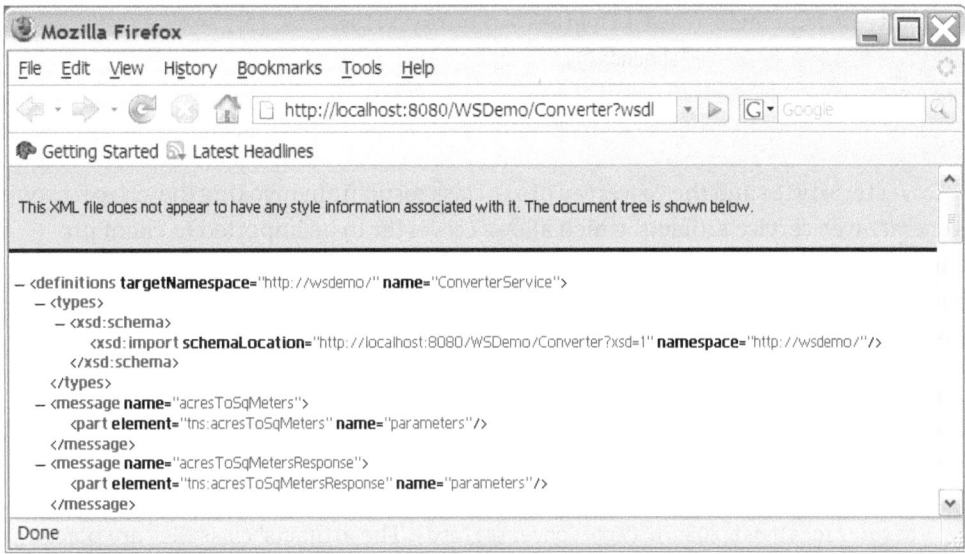

Figure 10-1. *Converter's WSDL file provides an XML-based description of this web service.*

Because a web service is no fun unless you can try it out, you need to create a client application that connects itself to Converter, obtains a Converter proxy object, and invokes Converter's methods via this proxy object. Listing 10-7 presents the source code to a sample TestConverter application that exercises the unit-conversion web service.

Listing 10-7. *TestConverter.java*

```
// TestConverter.java

import wsdemo.*;

public class TestConverter
{
    public static void main (String [] args)
    {
        ConverterService service = new ConverterService ();

        Converter proxy = service.getConverterPort ();

        System.out.println ("2.5 acres = "+proxy.acresToSqMeters (2.5)+
                            " square meters");
        System.out.println ("358 square meters = "+proxy.sqMetersToAcres (358)+
                            " acres");
        System.out.println ("6 pounds = "+proxy.lbsToKilos (6)+" kilograms");
        System.out.println ("2.7 kilograms = "+proxy.kilosToLbs (2.7)+
                            " pounds");
    }
}
```

ConverterService and the Converter proxy class result from invoking the wsimport tool
to generate web service artifacts, which allows Converter to be imported to client programs. Invoking this tool is one of several tasks that you need to take care of in order to
interact with this unit-conversion web service. Complete the following steps to accomplish these tasks:

1. Within the directory that contains wsdemo, create a TestConverter directory. The
   TestConverter directory must contain TestConverter.java.

2. Assuming that the TestConverter directory is the current directory, invoke wsimport
   http://localhost:8080/WSDemo/Converter?wsdl. The artifacts' class files are placed
   in a wsdemo subdirectory of TestConverter. If you want to keep the artifacts' source
   code for later study, include the -keep option, as in wsimport -keep http://
   localhost:8080/WSDemo/Converter?wsdl.

■**Note** wsimport's -keep option places artifact source code in the same directory as artifact class files.
You can choose another directory for the source code by specifying wsimport's -s option.

---

3. Assuming that the `TestConverter` directory is the current directory, invoke `javac` `TestConverter.java` to compile this client application's source code.

4. Assuming that the `TestConverter` directory is the current directory, invoke `java` `TestConverter` to interact with the web service. In response, you should observe the following output:

```
2.5 acres = 10117.141056 square meters
358 square meters = 0.08846372656524519 acres
6 pounds = 2.7215542200000002 kilograms
2.7 kilograms = 5.952481078991695 pounds
```

However, you might observe a thrown `java.net.ConnectionException` if the unit-conversion web service is not already running (via `RunConverter` and the lightweight HTTP server). If this is the case, invoke `java wsdemo.RunConverter` to publish the `Converter` web service, making sure the directory containing `wsdemo` is the current directory.

Accessing an Existing Web Service

The web services stack is also helpful for accessing an existing web service. For example, you might be interested in accessing a well-known web service from Amazon, eBay, Google, or another popular company. Alternatively, you might choose to access a lesser-known web service, such as one of the services listed on the XMethods directory site (`http://www.xmethods.net/ve2/index.po`).

Consider a `SkyView` application that obtains images from the image archive maintained by Sloan Digital Sky Survey (SDSS) (`http://www.sdss.org/`). Images are obtained via the Image Cutout web service, which is described by the WSDL file at `http://casjobs.sdss.org/ImgCutoutDR5/ImgCutout.asmx?wsdl`. Listing 10-8 presents `SkyView`'s source code.

Listing 10-8. *SkyView.java*

```java
// SkyView.java

import java.awt.*;
import java.awt.event.*;
import java.awt.image.*;

import java.io.*;
```

```java
import javax.imageio.*;

import javax.swing.*;

import org.sdss.skyserver.*;

public class SkyView extends JFrame
{
   final static int IMAGE_WIDTH = 300;
   final static int IMAGE_HEIGHT = 300;

   static ImgCutoutSoap imgcutoutsoap;

   public SkyView ()
   {
      super ("SkyView");
      setDefaultCloseOperation (EXIT_ON_CLOSE);

      setContentPane (createContentPane ());

      pack ();
      setResizable (false);
      setVisible (true);
   }

   JPanel createContentPane ()
   {
      JPanel pane = new JPanel (new BorderLayout (10, 10));
      pane.setBorder (BorderFactory.createEmptyBorder (10, 10, 10, 10));

      final JLabel lblImage = new JLabel ("", JLabel.CENTER);
      lblImage.setPreferredSize (new Dimension (IMAGE_WIDTH+9,
                                                IMAGE_HEIGHT+9));
      lblImage.setBorder (BorderFactory.createEtchedBorder ());

      pane.add (new JPanel () {{ add (lblImage); }}, BorderLayout.NORTH);

      JPanel form = new JPanel (new GridLayout (4, 1));

      final JLabel lblRA = new JLabel ("Right ascension:");
      int width = lblRA.getPreferredSize ().width+20;
```

```java
int height = lblRA.getPreferredSize ().height;
lblRA.setPreferredSize (new Dimension (width, height));
lblRA.setDisplayedMnemonic ('R');
final JTextField txtRA = new JTextField (25);
lblRA.setLabelFor (txtRA);

form.add (new JPanel ()
        {{ add (lblRA); add (txtRA);
            setLayout (new FlowLayout (FlowLayout.CENTER, 0, 5)); }});

final JLabel lblDec = new JLabel ("Declination:");
lblDec.setPreferredSize (new Dimension (width, height));
lblDec.setDisplayedMnemonic ('D');
final JTextField txtDec = new JTextField (25);
lblDec.setLabelFor (txtDec);

form.add (new JPanel ()
        {{ add (lblDec); add (txtDec);
            setLayout (new FlowLayout (FlowLayout.CENTER, 0, 5));}});

final JLabel lblScale = new JLabel ("Scale:");
lblScale.setPreferredSize (new Dimension (width, height));
lblScale.setDisplayedMnemonic ('S');
final JTextField txtScale = new JTextField (25);
lblScale.setLabelFor (txtScale);

form.add (new JPanel ()
        {{ add (lblScale); add (txtScale);
            setLayout (new FlowLayout (FlowLayout.CENTER, 0, 5));}});

final JLabel lblDO = new JLabel ("Drawing options:");
lblDO.setPreferredSize (new Dimension (width, height));
lblDO.setDisplayedMnemonic ('o');
final JTextField txtDO = new JTextField (25);
lblDO.setLabelFor (txtDO);

form.add (new JPanel ()
        {{ add (lblDO); add (txtDO);
            setLayout (new FlowLayout (FlowLayout.CENTER, 0, 5));}});

pane.add (form, BorderLayout.CENTER);
```

```
    final JButton btnGP = new JButton ("Get Picture");
    ActionListener al;
    al = new ActionListener ()
        {
            public void actionPerformed (ActionEvent e)
            {
                try
                {
                    double ra = Double.parseDouble (txtRA.getText ());
                    double dec = Double.parseDouble (txtDec.getText ());
                    double scale = Double.parseDouble (txtScale.getText ());
                    String dopt = txtDO.getText ().trim ();

                    byte [] image = imgcutoutsoap.getJpeg (ra, dec, scale,
                                                    IMAGE_WIDTH,
                                                    IMAGE_HEIGHT,
                                                    dopt);
                    lblImage.setIcon (new ImageIcon (image));
                }
                catch (Exception exc)
                {
                    JOptionPane.showMessageDialog (SkyView.this,
                                                exc.getMessage ());
                }
            }
        };
    btnGP.addActionListener (al);
    pane.add (new JPanel () {{ add (btnGP); }}, BorderLayout.SOUTH);

    return pane;
}

public static void main (String [] args) throws IOException
{
    ImgCutout imgcutout = new ImgCutout ();
    imgcutoutsoap = imgcutout.getImgCutoutSoap ();
```

```
        Runnable r = new Runnable ()
                    {
                        public void run ()
                        {
                            try
                            {
                                String lnf;
                                lnf = UIManager.
                                        getSystemLookAndFeelClassName ();
                                UIManager.setLookAndFeel (lnf);
                            }
                            catch (Exception e)
                            {
                            }
                            new SkyView ();
                        }
                    };
        EventQueue.invokeLater (r);
    }
}
```

Listing 10-8 is largely concerned with creating SkyView's user interface. If you are curious about new JPanel () {{ add (lblImage); }}, this code subclasses javax.swing.JPanel via an anonymous inner class, creates an instance of the subclass panel, adds the specified component to the instance via its object initializer, and returns the instance. (I find this and similar code to be a convenient shorthand.)

Listing 10-8 also refers to an org.sdss.skyserver package and its ImgCutout and ImgCutoutSoap member classes. This package is obtained by invoking the wsimport tool on the http://casjobs.sdss.org/ImgCutoutDR5/ImgCutout.asmx?wsdl URI to create the Image Cutout web service's artifacts. The following command line accomplishes this task:

```
wsimport -keep http://casjobs.sdss.org/ImgCutoutDR5/ImgCutout.asmx?wsdl
```

The wsimport tool creates an org directory within the current directory. This directory contains an sdss subdirectory, which has a skyserver subdirectory. In addition to the class files for accessing Image Cutout, skyserver contains the source files (thanks to the -keep option) that describe the artifacts for accessing this web service.

The ImgCutout.java source file shows that ImgCutout extends javax.xml.ws.Service, which provides a client view of a web service. ImgCutout's public ImgCutoutSoap getImgCutoutSoap() method invokes Service's public <T> T getPort(QName portName, Class<T> serviceEndpointInterface) method to return a stub for invoking web service operations via the stub's methods.

SkyView accesses ImgCutoutSoap's public byte[] getJpeg(double ra, double dec, double scale, int width, int height, String opt) method only. This method is invoked to return an array of bytes that describes a portion of the sky as a JPEG image. Its parameters are as follows:

- ra and dec: Specify the center coordinates of the image in terms of right ascension and declination values (each value is specified in degrees).

Note The astronomical terms *right ascension* and *declination* are described by Wikipedia's Right ascension (http://en.wikipedia.org/wiki/Right_ascension) and Declination (http://en.wikipedia.org/wiki/Declination) entries, respectively.

- scale: Specifies a scaling value, in terms of arcseconds per pixel. One arcsecond equals 1/1296000 of a circle.

- width and height: Identify the dimensions of the returned image.

- opt: Identifies a sequence of codes for drawing over the image. These are String codes such as the following:

  - G draws a grid over the image.

  - L labels the image.

  - I inverts the image.

The getJpeg() method never returns a null reference. If an error occurs, the method returns an image that presents the error message.

Assuming that the current directory contains both SkyView.java and the org subdirectory, invoke javac SkyView.java to compile this application's source code.

Following compilation, invoke java SkyView to run the application. Figure 10-2 shows what you will see when you specify the values that are shown in the figure's text fields.

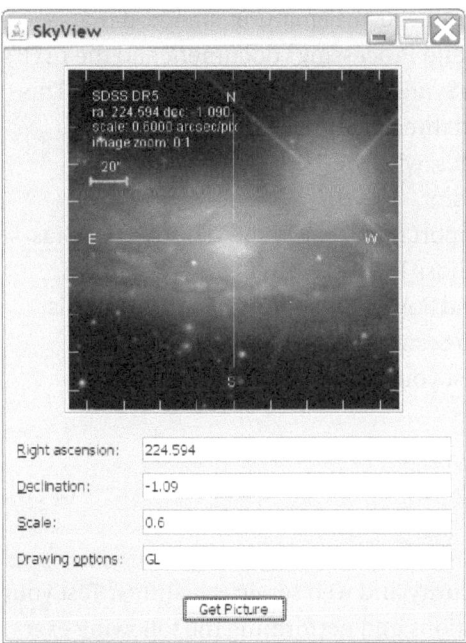

Figure 10-2. *Viewing an image of New Galatic Catalog (NGC) 5792, a spiral galaxy seen nearly edge-on. The bright red star is located in the Milky Way galaxy.*

Tip Check out the "Famous Places" section (http://cas.sdss.org/dr6/en/tools/places/) of the Sloan Digital Sky Survey/SkyServer site to obtain the right ascension/declination values for various astronomical images.

Summary

Java SE 6 provides various security enhancements. Two of these enhancements discussed in this chapter are the Smart Card I/O API and XML Digital Signature APIs.

Sun provides the Smart Card I/O API and the SunPCSC security provider in its Java SE 6 reference implementation. The API lets a Java application communicate with applications running on a smart card by exchanging ISO/IEC 7816-4 APDUs with them. The SunPCSC security provider lets the API access the underlying platform's PC/SC stack (if available). The javax.smartcardio.TerminalFactory class is the entry point into this API.

The XML Digital Signature APIs are based on the XML Signatures standard that is described by the W3C's "XML-Signature Syntax and Processing" document and the IETF's "(Extensible Markup Language) XML-Signature Syntax and Processing" document. This standard describes syntax, processing rules, and three kinds of XML Signatures. The APIs introduced by JSR 105 consist of six packages, with the `javax.xml.crypto.dsig.XMLSignatureFactory` class serving as the entry point.

This chapter also introduced Java SE 6's support for web services. This support has been made available via a web services stack, whose layered architecture consists of JAX-WS 2.0 at the top, JAXB 2.0 in the middle, and StAX at the bottom. Along with this stack, Java SE 6 introduces SAAJ 1.3 and the Web Services Metadata API. Collectively, these five APIs allow you to create and locally test your own web services and access existing web services.

Test Your Understanding

How well do you understand Java SE 6's new security and web services features? Test your understanding by answering the following questions and performing the following exercises. (The answers are provided in Appendix D.)

1. How does a Java application communicate with applications running on a smart card?

2. What package has been assigned to the Smart Card I/O API?

3. What is a terminal?

4. What do authenticity, integrity, and nonrepudiation mean?

5. What is a digital signature?

6. Assuming public-key cryptography, how does digitally signing a document differ from encrypting a document?

7. What is an XML Signature?

8. What does canonicalization accomplish?

9. Which algorithm is used to encode the `SignatureValue` element's signature in an XML document?

10. For which of the enveloping, enveloped, and detached XML Signature types is the `Signature` element excluded from the data object's signature value calculation?

11. Which class is the entry point into the XML Digital Signature APIs?

12. How does an application obtain an instance of the XML Digital Signature APIs entry-point class?

13. The web services stack's layered architecture is composed of which APIs?

14. What annotation is used to annotate a web service class?

15. How is a web service published?

16. Which tool is used to generate web service artifacts needed to deploy a web service?

17. Which tool is used to generate web service artifacts needed to import a web service to client programs?

18. The `SkyView` application's GUI becomes unresponsive whenever `byte [] image = Imgcutoutsoap.getJpeg (ra, dec, scale, IMAGE_WIDTH, IMAGE_HEIGHT, dopt);` takes a while to complete. Revise this application so that its GUI is always responsive.

APPENDIX A

███

New Annotation Types

Java 5's implementation of JSR 175: A Metadata Facility for the Java Programming Language (`http://www.jcp.org/en/jsr/detail?id=175`) brought *annotations* to the Java language. Annotations are a language feature that lets you associate *metadata* (data about data) with packages, classes, fields, methods, and other program elements. Prior to their use, annotations are defined as *annotation types* via an interface-like mechanism, such as `@interface Marker {}`. Because Java 5 limited itself to providing an annotations infrastructure, it introduced only seven annotation types that are important to this infrastructure: `java.lang.Deprecated`, `java.lang.Override`, `java.lang.SuppressWarnings`, `java.lang.annotation.Documented`, `java.lang.annotation.Inherited`, `java.lang.annotation.Retention`, and `java.lang.annotation.Target`. In contrast, Java SE 6 introduces a wide variety of annotation types, as discussed in this appendix.

Annotation Types for Annotation Processors

Without processing, annotations are useless. To spare you from having to write your own annotation-processing code, Java 5 introduced the nonstandard `apt` tool. Java SE 6 also lets you use `javac` to process annotations. Either command-line utility locates and executes *annotation processors*, which can process the annotations located in specified source files.

Annotation processing under Java 5 was not standardized; it was based on working with apt's `com.sun.mirror.apt`, `com.sun.mirror.declaration`, `com.sun.mirror.type`, and `com.sun.mirror.util` API packages. Java SE 6 addresses this lack of standardization by implementing JSR 269: Pluggable Annotation Processing API (`http://jcp.org/en/jsr/detail?id=269`). This implementation consists of the following:

- A new `javax.annotation.processing` package, whose API lets you declare annotation processors that can communicate with annotation tool environments

- A new `javax.lang.model` package and subpackages, whose interfaces model the Java language via methods that you can call during annotation processing to return information about various program elements

The `javax.annotation.processing` package introduces three annotation types that provide information about the annotation processor:

- `SupportedAnnotationTypes` identifies the annotation types supported by the annotation processor.

- `SupportedOptions` identifies the options supported by the annotation processor.

- `SupportedSourceVersion` identifies the latest source version supported by the annotation processor.

Each type is annotated `@Documented`, `@Retention(value=RUNTIME)`, and `@Target(value=ANNOTATION_TYPE)`.

For more information about Java SE 6 annotation processing, see Artima's interview summary, "Joe Darcy on Standardizing Annotation Processing" (`http://www.artima.com/forums/flat.jsp?forum=276&thread=179769`). This summary also includes an example that demonstrates `SupportedAnnotationTypes` and `SupportedSourceVersion`. Joe Darcy is a Sun engineer and specification lead for JSR 269. You can also check out the sample annotation processor presented in Appendix B of this book.

Common Annotations 1.0

Subsequent to Java 5's implementation of JSR 175, Sun expects future JSRs to introduce annotations that support their declarative programming needs. (As you will see in the next section of this appendix, various JSRs have already introduced new annotation types to Java SE 6.) Because JSRs might redundantly define annotations that support common concepts (such as annotations related to resource injection, where a container injects resources identified by annotations into an application during application initialization), Sun has developed JSR 250: Common Annotations for the Java Platform (`http://www.jcp.org/en/jsr/detail?id=250`) to promote a small set of annotations that other JSRs can use.

The final release of Sun's "Common Annotations for the Java Platform" document, which can be downloaded from `http://jcp.org/aboutJava/communityprocess/final/jsr250/index.html`, defines a few security-related common annotations specific to Java EE 5, as well as a handful of common annotations for use by future JSRs that target Java SE (and even future Java SE versions). Java SE 6 includes only the latter group of common annotations (in the `javax.annotation` package), as follows:

Generated: Marks source code generated by some tool. When the value element is specified, it must identify the (preferably fully qualified) name of the code generator. The date on which the code was generated is stored in the date element. All comments that the code generator is to include in the source code are stored in the placeholder comments element. This annotation type is annotated @Documented, @Retention(value=SOURCE), and @Target(value={PACKAGE,TYPE,ANNOTATION_TYPE, METHOD,CONSTRUCTOR,FIELD,LOCAL_VARIABLE,PARAMETER}).

PostConstruct: Marks a method (whose method signature follows @PostConstruct) that must be executed to perform initialization after dependency injection has occurred. This annotation type is annotated @Documented, @Retention(value=RUNTIME), and @Target(value=METHOD).

PreDestroy: Marks a method (whose method signature follows @PreDestroy) to serve as a callback notification signaling that an object is in the process of being removed from a container. This annotation type is annotated @Documented, @Retention(value=RUNTIME), and @Target(value=METHOD).

Resource: Declares a resource reference. This annotation type can be applied to an application component class, or to any of this class's methods or fields. When applied to a field or method, the container injects a resource instance into the component during the component's initialization. In contrast, an application looks up the resource at runtime if the annotation type is applied to the component class. The elements are as follows:

- The authenticationType element specifies the resource's authentication type.

- The description element describes the resource.

- The mappedName element specifies a product-specific name to which the resource should be mapped.

- The name element specifies the Java Naming and Directory Interface (JNDI) resource name.

- The shareable element indicates whether the component can be shared between this and other components.

- The type element specifies the resource's Java type.

This annotation type is annotated @Target(value={TYPE,FIELD,METHOD}) and @Retention(value=RUNTIME).

Resources: Acts as a container for multiple resource declarations. This annotation type exists because it is not possible to specify repeated Resource annotations. The value element serves as a container that stores multiple resource declarations. This annotation type is annotated @Documented, @Retention(value=RUNTIME), and @Target(value=TYPE).

The "Common Annotations for the Java Platform" document includes simple examples that demonstrate the use of these five annotation types.

More New Annotation Types

Java SE 6 introduces new annotation types to support the Java Architecture for XML Binding (JAXB), Java API for XML Web Services (JAX-WS), Java Web Service (JWS), Java Management Extensions (JMX), and JavaBeans APIs.

The JavaBeans API has just one annotation type, in the java.beans package: ConstructorProperties, which marks a constructor showing how its parameters correspond to a constructed object's getter methods. The annotation types for the other APIs are briefly described in Tables A-1 through A-4.

Table A-1 describes JAXB annotation types. Those types not prefixed with a package name are located in the javax.xml.bind.annotation package.

Table A-1. *JAXB Annotation Types*

Annotation Type	Description
XmlAccessorOrder	Controls the ordering of a class's fields and properties.
XmlAccessorType	Controls whether a class's fields and properties are serialized by default.
XmlAnyAttribute	In the context of an *open schema* (a schema that lets you include elements and attributes not formally defined in the schema), specifies that the parent element can contain XML attributes not formally defined in the schema.
XmlAnyElement	In the context of an open schema, specifies that the parent element can contain XML elements not formally defined in the schema.
XmlAttachmentRef	Marks a field or property whose XML representation is a Uniform Resource Identifier (URI) reference to Multipurpose Internet Mail Extensions (MIME) content.
XmlAttribute	Maps a property to an XML attribute.
XmlElement	Maps a property to an XML element that is derived from the property's name.
XmlElementDecl	Maps a factory method to an XML element.
XmlElementRef	Maps a property to an XML element that is derived from the property's type.

Annotation Type	Description
XmlElementRefs	Marks a property that refers to classes with XmlElement or JAXBElement.
XmlElements	Serves as a container for multiple @XmlElement annotations.
XmlElementWrapper	Generates a wrapper element around the XML representation of a collection.
XmlEnum	Maps an enumeration type to its XML representation.
XmlEnumValue	Maps an enumeration constant to its XML representation.
XmlID	Maps a property to an XML identifier.
XmlIDRef	Maps a property to an XML identifier reference.
XmlInlineBinaryData	Specifies not to use XML-binary Optimized Packaging (XOP) to encode data types (such as byte[]) that are bound to base64-encoded binary data when representing the data type (and its data) in XML.
XmlList	Maps a property of java.util.List<E> type to its XML representation.
XmlMimeType	Associates the MIME type that controls a property's XML representation with the property.
XmlMixed	Annotates a multivalued property to indicate that the property supports mixed content.
XmlNs	Associates a namespace prefix with an XML namespace URI.
XmlRegistry	Marks a class that contains XmlElementDecl annotations.
XmlRootElement	Maps a class or an enumeration type to an XML element.
XmlSchema	Maps a package name to an XML namespace.
XmlSchemaType	Maps a Java type to a simple schema type.
XmlSchemaTypes	Serves as a container for multiple @XmlSchemaType annotations.
XmlTransient	Prevents a property that does not participate in JAXB serialization/deserialization from being mapped to an XML representation.
XmlType	Maps a class or an enumeration type to an XML Schema type.
XmlValue	Enables the mapping of a class to an XML Schema complexType with nested simpleContent, or an XML Schema simpleType.
javax.xml.bind.annotation. adapters.XmlJavaTypeAdapter	Uses an adapter based on javax.xml.bind.annotation. adapters.XMLAdapter for custom marshaling.
javax.xml.bind.annotation. adapters.XmlJavaTypeAdapters	Serves as a container for multiple @XmlJavaTypeAdapter annotations.

Table A-2 describes JAX-WS annotation types. All of these types are located in the `javax.xml.ws` package.

Table A-2. *JAX-WS Annotation Types*

Annotation Type	Description
BindingType	Specifies the binding to use for a web service endpoint implementation class.
RequestWrapper	Annotates those methods in the Service Endpoint Interface (SEI) with the request wrapper bean that will be used at runtime.
ResponseWrapper	Annotates those methods in the SEI with the response wrapper bean that will be used at runtime.
ServiceMode	Indicates whether a `javax.xml.ws.Provider` implementation works with protocol messages in their entirety or just their payloads.
WebEndpoint	Annotates the get*PortName*() methods of a generated service interface.
WebFault	Annotates service-specific exception classes to customize to the local and namespace name of the fault element and the name of the fault bean.
WebServiceClient	Annotates a generated service interface.
WebServiceProvider	Annotates a `Provider` implementation class.
WebServiceRef	Defines a reference to a web service and (optionally) an injection target for the web service.
WebServiceRefs	Allows multiple web service references to be specified at the class level.

Table A-3 describes JWS annotation types. Those types not prefixed with a package name are located in the `javax.jws` package.

Table A-3. *JWS Annotation Types*

Annotation Type	Description
HandlerChain	Associates a web service with an external file that defines a handler chain.
OneWay	Indicates that a @WebMethod annotation has input parameters only; there is no return value.
WebMethod	Specifies that the method targeted by the @WebMethod annotation is exposed as a public operation of the web service.
WebParam	Customizes the mapping between the web service's operation input parameters and elements of the generated Web Services Description Language (WSDL) file. The @WebParam annotation is also used to specify parameter behavior.

Annotation Type	Description
WebResult	Customizes the mapping between the web service's operation return value and the corresponding element in the generated WSDL file.
WebService	Marks a Java class as implementing a web service, or a Java interface as defining a web service.
javax.jws.soap.InitParam	Deprecated as of JSR 181 version 2.0.
javax.jws.soap.SOAPBinding	Specifies the mapping of a web service onto SOAP (Service Oriented Architecture Protocol, also known as Simple Object Access Protocol).
javax.jws.soap.SOAPMessageHandler	Deprecated as of JSR 181 version 2.0.
javax.jws.soap.SOAPMessageHandlers	Deprecated as of JSR 181 version 2.0.

Table A-4 describes JMX annotation types. These types are located in the javax.management package.

Table A-4. *JMX Annotation Types*

Annotation Type	Description
DescriptorKey	Describes how an annotation element relates to a field in a javax.management.Descriptor.
MXBean	Explicitly marks an interface as being an MXBean interface or as not being an MXBean interface.

Because the JDK documentation's few annotation type examples are limited, you will want to search the Internet for additional (and more developed) examples. For starters, consider these two resources:

- Gautam Shah's JavaWorld article, "Mustang: The fast track to Web services" (http://www.javaworld.com/javaworld/jw-07-2006/jw-0703-mustang.html). This article discusses and illustrates various JWS annotation types.

- Sergey Malenkov's blog entry, "How to use the @ConstructorProperties annotation" (http://weblogs.java.net/blog/malenkov/archive/2007/03/how_to_use_the_1.html). This entry further develops the Point class example in the JDK's java.bean.ConstructorProperties documentation.

■ ■ ■

New and Improved Tools

Java SE 6 includes several new and improved command-line tools. A command-line script shell and tools for web services are examples of newly added tools. Tools that have been improved include the Java archivist and the Java language compiler. In addition to adding and improving various tools, Java SE 6 has enhanced its virtual machines and their associated runtime environment. This appendix briefly describes the new and improved Java SE 6 tools, as well as the virtual machine enhancements.

Basic Tools

The Java archivist (jar) and Java language compiler (javac) basic tools have been improved in Java SE 6. Improvements range from adding a single new option to the jar tool, to migrating the annotation-processing tool (apt) functionality into javac. (The apt tool most likely will be removed from Java SE 7.)

Note Java SE 6's Java SE Development Kit (JDK) tools documentation for the Java application launcher (java) basic tool now documents the version:*release* option, which was undocumented in Java 5. Also, the Java SE 6 documentation no longer presents the nonstandard -Xdebug and -Xrunhprof options; however, these options have not been removed from the java tool. For example, if you specify java -Xrunhprof *classname*, where *classname* represents some application starting class, the message Dumping Java heap ... allocation sites ... done will appear on the console. Also, the current directory will include a java.hprof.txt file.

Enhanced Java Archivist

A new -e option has been added to the jar tool. Use this option to identify the class that serves as the entry point into an application whose class files are bundled into an executable JAR file. This option creates or overrides the Main-Class attribute value in the JAR file's manifest file. It can be used when creating or updating the JAR file.

Listing B-1 presents source code that you can use to see how the new -e option works.

Listing B-1. *Classes.java*

```
// Classes.java

class ClassA
{
   public static void main (String [] args)
   {
      System.out.println ("This is class A.");
   }
}

class ClassB
{
   public static void main (String [] args)
   {
      System.out.println ("This is class B.");
   }
}
```

Follow these steps to try the example:

1. Compile the contents of Listing B-1:

   ```
   javac Classes.java
   ```

2. Bundle the resulting class files into a Classes.jar file, with ClassB as the main class:

   ```
   jar cfe Classes.jar ClassB *.class
   ```

3. Execute Classes.jar:

   ```
   java -jar Classes.jar
   ```

You should see this output:

```
This is class B
```

4. To switch the entry-point class to ClassA, combine -e with -u (update) and update the JAR file's class files (if their unarchived counterpart classes have changed) as well:

```
jar ufe Classes.jar ClassA *.class
```

This time, executing Classes.jar yields the following output:

```
This is class A
```

If you want to update the manifest without updating any classes, combine -e with -i (store index information, in the form of a META-INF/INDEX.LIST file, in the JAR file):

```
jar ie Classes.jar ClassA
```

The -e option is just one example of the many small but useful features that Java SE 6 introduces to make the developer's life easier. You no longer need to unpack and rebuild a JAR file when you want to update only the manifest's Main-Class attribute. Learn more about this option from the JDK's jar documentation (http://java.sun.com/javase/6/docs/technotes/tools/solaris/jar.html).

Enhanced Java Language Compiler

Java SE 6's version of the javac tool contains several enhancements. The biggest enhancement is the ability to process a source file's annotations, so that you no longer need to use the nonstandard apt tool. After creating an annotation and an annotation processor, invoke javac with the -processor option to load the processor, which processes all instances of the annotation prior to compiling the source file.

Consider a Java application whose source code is organized into many classes. This application is being built in an incremental fashion, where constructors and methods are partially or completely stubbed out until they need to be completely implemented. The @Stub marker annotation defined in Listing B-2 is used to identify those constructors and methods that are still a work in progress.

Listing B-2. *Stub.java*

```
// Stub.java

import java.lang.annotation.*;

@Target({ElementType.METHOD, ElementType.CONSTRUCTOR})
public @interface Stub
{
}
```

This annotation is to be used with an annotation processor that outputs the names of stubbed-out constructors and methods, as a reminder that there is still work to be done. Essentially, the annotation processor looks for constructor and method elements prefixed with the @Stub annotation, and outputs their names. Listing B-3 provides its source code.

Listing B-3. *StubAnnotationProcessor.java*

```
// StubAnnotationProcessor.java

import static javax.lang.model.SourceVersion.*;
import static javax.tools.Diagnostic.Kind.*;

import java.lang.annotation.*;

import java.util.*;

import javax.annotation.processing.*;

import javax.lang.model.element.*;

@SupportedAnnotationTypes("Stub")
@SupportedSourceVersion(RELEASE_6)
public class StubAnnotationProcessor extends AbstractProcessor
{
    // The javac tool invokes this method to process a set of annotation types
    // originating from the previous round of annotation processing. The method
    // returns a Boolean value indicating whether (true) or not (false) the
    // annotations are claimed. When annotations are claimed, they will not be
    // subsequently processed.
```

```
public boolean process (Set<? extends TypeElement> annotations,
                        RoundEnvironment roundEnv)
{
    // If types generated by this round of annotation processing are subject
    // to a subsequent round of annotation processing ...

    if (!roundEnv.processingOver ())
    {
        Set<? extends Element> elements;
        elements = roundEnv.getElementsAnnotatedWith (Stub.class);

        Iterator<? extends Element> it = elements.iterator ();
        while (it.hasNext ())
        {
            Element element = it.next ();
            String kind = element.getKind ().equals (ElementKind.METHOD)
                        ? "Method " : "Constructor ";
            String name = element.toString ();
            processingEnv.getMessager ().
              printMessage (NOTE, kind+name+ " needs to be fully implemented");
        }
    }

    return true; // Claim the annotations.
}
}
```

An annotation processor is required to implement the javax.annotation.processing. Processor interface, to register itself with javac. Various methods in the Processor interface inform javac about the annotation processor's capabilities. For example, Set<String> getSupportedAnnotationTypes() returns the names of annotation types supported by the annotation processor. For convenience, you can subclass the javax.annotation. processing.AbstractProcessor class instead of implementing Processor.

You need to implement the public abstract boolean process(Set<? extends TypeElement> annotations, RoundEnvironment roundEnv) method only in the AbstractProcessor subclass. javac invokes this method for each *round* of annotation processing, to process a set of annotation types (described by annotations) on element types that originated in the previous round.

The javax.annotation.processing.RoundEnvironment argument roundEnv provides a boolean processingOver() method that returns true if types generated by this round are not subject to another round of annotation processing. Its Set<? extends Element>

getElementsAnnotatedWith(Class<? extends Annotation> a) method returns elements annotated with the given annotation type.

StubAnnotationProcessor's process() method is called twice. Because processingOver() returns false for the first call, the set of all elements annotated with @Stub (Stub.class) is output via the processor's *messager* (an object that outputs messages to standard output, a window, or whatever destination is defined by a javax.annotation.processing.Messager implementation).

The process() method returns true to claim the annotations, which prevents these annotations from being processed by a subsequent processor, as in -processor StubAnnotationProcessor,StubAnnotationProcessor2. Because no types were generated in this round, the next call to process() results in processingOver() returning true, so no processing is performed.

Listing B-4 presents the source code for a Calculator application with a single stubbed-out constructor and single stubbed-out method.

Listing B-4. *Calculator.java*

```java
// Calculator.java

import javax.swing.*;

public class Calculator extends JFrame
{
    @Stub
    public Calculator ()
    {
        super ("Calculator");
        setDefaultCloseOperation (EXIT_ON_CLOSE);

        // ... To do.

        pack ();
        setVisible (true);
    }

    @Stub
    double doCalc (String expr)
    {
        return 0.0;
    }

    public static void main (String [] args)
```

```
{
    Runnable r = new Runnable ()
                    {
                        public void run ()
                        {
                            new Calculator ();
                        }
                    };
        java.awt.EventQueue.invokeLater (r);
    }
}
```

As an example of using `StubAnnotationProcessor`, compile Listings B-2 and B-3. Then invoke `javac -processor StubAnnotationProcessor Calculator.java` to load the `StubAnnotationProcessor` class, and have it process all instances of `@Stub` prior to compiling `Calculator.java`. You should observe the following output, which reveals the work that still needs to be done to complete this application.

```
Note: Constructor Calculator() needs to be fully implemented
Note: Method doCalc(java.lang.String) needs to be fully implemented
```

The `-processor` option is just one of several new `javac` options for processing annotations. Table B-1 describes all of these options.

Table B-1. *javac Annotation-Processing Options*

Option	Description
`-Akey[=value]`	Passes *key*–named options directly to annotation processors. The options are not interpreted by `javac`.
`-implicit:(class|none)`	Controls the generation of class files for implicitly loaded source files. A source file is implicitly loaded if it defines a searched-for type that is referenced from the source file being processed. Class files are generated if `-implicit:class` is specified. To prevent class files from being generated, specify `-implicit:none`. If this option is not specified, class files are automatically generated. Furthermore, the compiler presents a warning message stating that the implicitly found source file is not subject to annotation processing, if its equivalent class file is generated during annotation processing. This warning message is not issued if either `-implicit:class` or `-implicit:none` is specified.
`-proc:(none|only)`	Restricts the behavior of `javac` to compilation without annotation processing (`-proc:none`) or to annotation processing without compilation (`-proc:only`).

Continued

Table B-1. *Continued*

Option	Description
-processor *class1* [, *class2, class3*...]	Specifies a comma-separated list of annotation processors to load and run.
-processorpath *path*	Specifies the *path* location of annotation processors. By default, the classpath is searched.
-s *dir*	Specifies the *dir* location where generated source files are placed.
-Xprefer:(newer|source)	Determines which file to read when both a source file and a class file are found for a type. If the -Xprefer option is not specified, or if -Xprefer:newer is specified, the newer of the class file and source file is chosen. If -Xprefer:source is specified, the source file is always chosen.
-Xprint	Prints a textual representation of types to aid debugging. An example is javac -Xprint java.lang.String.
-XprintProcessorInfo	Prints information about annotation processors that have run and the annotations they have processed.
-XprintRounds	Prints information about each round of annotation processing.

A lesser-known javac enhancement is support for the @SuppressWarnings annotation, which tells the compiler to suppress various kinds of warnings. Although this annotation debuted in Java 5, it was left unsupported in the compiler. After supporting @SuppressWarnings in Java SE 6, Sun back-ported this support to Java 5, beginning with update 6.

The @SuppressWarnings annotation is especially useful for suppressing unchecked warnings, which indicate that the compiler cannot ensure type safety, and typically occur from mixing generic and raw types in legacy-code contexts. Casting to type parameters also results in unchecked warnings, as demonstrated in Listing B-5's trivial stack data-structure class.

Listing B-5. *Stack.java*

```java
// Stack.java

public class Stack<T>
{
   private T [] items;
   private int top;

   @SuppressWarnings("unchecked")
   public Stack (int size)
   {
      items = (T []) new Object [size];
```

```
      top = -1;
   }

   public void push (T item) throws Exception
   {
      if (top == items.length-1)
         throw new Exception ("Stack Full");
      items [++top] = item;
   }

   public T pop () throws Exception
   {
      if (top == -1)
         throw new Exception ("Stack Empty");
      return items [top--];
   }
}
```

The (T []) cast in items = (T []) new Object [size]; leads to an unchecked warning because of a mismatch between the static and dynamic parts of the cast. The "What is an 'unchecked' warning?" section in Angelika Langer's Java Generics FAQ (http://www. angelikalanger.com/GenericsFAQ/FAQSections/TechnicalDetails. html#What%20is%20an%20unchecked%20warning?) discusses this situation.

Because type safety has not been compromised, this warning is annoying. Fortunately, the warning can be suppressed by annotating the element where it occurs. With Java 5 update 6 and later versions, annotating Stack's constructor with @SuppressWarnings("unchecked") results in the unchecked warning message not appearing during compilation.

Command-Line Script Shell

Java SE 6 introduces jrunscript, an experimental command-line script shell tool to aid the exploration of Java-to-scripting language communication. Use this tool to evaluate one-line scripts, evaluate scripts interactively from standard input, or evaluate file-based scripts. Although jrunscript defaults to JavaScript, this tool can be used with any accessible scripting language. Table B-2 lists its options.

Table B-2. *jrunscript Options*

Option	Description
-classpath *path*	Identifies the *path* locations of the user's script-accessible class files.
-cp *path*	A synonym for -classpath.
-D*name*=*value*	Sets a Java system property identified by *name*.
-J*flag*	Passes *flag* to the underlying virtual machine.
-l *language*	Specifies an accessible scripting language to work with. JavaScript is the default language.
-e *script*	Evaluates a one-line script.
-encoding *encoding*	Specifies the character encoding of a script file.
-f *script-file*	Reads a script from a file and evaluates that script.
-f -	Reads a script on a line-by-line basis from standard input and evaluates each line.
-help	Outputs a help message and exits.
-?	A synonym for -help.
-q	Lists all available script engines and exits.

This tool's command-line syntax is jrunscript [*options*] [*arguments*...]. If options are passed to jrunscript, they must appear immediately after the command name. Any arguments are specified after the command name or after *options*. If you do not specify options or arguments, jrunscript executes in interactive mode:

```
jrunscript
js>Math.PI*20
62.83185307179586
js>cat("dumpargs.js")
for (i = 0; i < arguments.length; i++) println(arguments [i]);
```

If you specify at least one argument, and do not specify either the -e option or the -f option, the first argument identifies a script file, and the remaining arguments are passed to the script file. The file's script can access these arguments via the predefined arguments array engine variable, which is a String array:

```
jrunscript dumpargs.js arg1 arg2
arg1
arg2
```

If you specify -e (or -f) followed by the list of arguments, all arguments are passed to the script:

```
jrunscript -e "for (i = 0; i < arguments.length; i++) println(arguments [i]);" ➥
dumpargs.js arg1 arg2
dumpargs.js
arg1
arg2
```

Finally, it is possible to evaluate the contents of a script file and then enter interactive mode to continue evaluating scripts interactively:

```
jrunscript -f dumpargs.js -f - arg1 arg2
arg1
arg2
js>
```

You can learn more about jrunscript by reading Chapter 9 of this book and the JDK's jrunscript documentation (http://java.sun.com/javase/6/docs/technotes/tools/share/jrunscript.html).

Java Monitoring and Management Console

The Java monitoring and management console (JConsole) is a GUI-based application for monitoring and managing running applications on local or remote platforms. The jconsole command-line tool is used to launch JConsole.

Java SE 6 provides the ability to create custom JConsole plug-ins, such as the JTop example plug-in that is bundled with the JDK. (JTop is used to monitor the CPU usage of an application's threads.) Java SE 6 also updates jconsole with a new -pluginpath option, which specifies a list of directories and/or JAR files to be searched for plug-ins. (These plug-ins are subsequently loaded.)

Chapter 7 of this book provides a plug-in example. That chapter includes instructions for building the plug-in, packaging the plug-in into a JAR file, and running the plug-in with jconsole. Also, Chapter 2 discusses the ServiceLoader API, which jconsole uses to load the -pluginpath option's listed plug-ins.

Java Web Services Tools

By including a subset of the Java EE web services stack, Java SE 6 makes it easier for developers to create web services. In addition to the web services stack, Java SE 6 has introduced four new command-line tools for working with web services, as described in Table B-3.

Table B-3. *Tools for Web Services*

Tool	Description
schemagen	Java Architecture for XML Binding (JAXB) schema generator. This tool generates a schema file for each namespace that is referenced in your Java source files' classes. Check out the JDK documentation (http://java.sun.com/javase/6/docs/technotes/tools/share/schemagen.html) for more information.
wsgen	Web service generator. This tool is used with an end-point implementation class to generate web service artifacts that allow a web service to be deployed. It is further described in the JDK documentation (http://java.sun.com/javase/6/docs/technotes/tools/share/wsgen.html).
wsimport	Web service importer. This tool generates and compiles the web service artifacts needed to import a web service to a web client. Check out the JDK documentation (http://java.sun.com/javase/6/docs/technotes/tools/share/wsimport.html) to learn more about this tool.
xjc	JAXB schema binding compiler. This tool transforms (binds) a source XML schema to a set of JAXB content classes in the Java programming language. More information about this tool is available in the JDK documentation (http://java.sun.com/javase/6/docs/technotes/tools/share/xjc.html).

Chapter 10 of this book demonstrates wsgen and wsimport. Examples involving all four tools can be found in *The Java EE 5 Tutorial* (http://java.sun.com/javaee/5/docs/tutorial/doc/).

Java Web Start

Java Web Start (JWS), an implementation of Java Network Launching Protocol (JNLP), allows users to download and launch Java applications without the hassle of complicated installation procedures. From within a browser, the user runs an application by clicking a link whose .jnlp extension identifies a JNLP file. JWS first downloads the application if it is not cached.

This technology addresses security concerns by allowing only trusted applications to access various resources. It also lets users transparently run the latest application versions by automatically downloading these versions when users click their icons. If you are new to JWS, check out these two resources:

- *The Java Tutorial*'s "Java Web Start" lesson (http://java.sun.com/docs/books/tutorial/deployment/webstart/index.html) provides a good introduction to JWS.

- The JDK documentation's *Java Web Start Guide* (http://java.sun.com/javase/6/docs/technotes/guides/javaws/developersguide/contents.html) provides complete information about JWS.

Java SE 6 has made many improvements to JWS and its javaws launcher tool. Examples include enhanced icon support, and new <java> and <update> elements. Also, JNLPClassLoader has been rewritten to extend URLClassLoader. For a list of enhancements, see Sun's document "Java Web Start enhancements in version 6" (http://java.sun.com/javase/6/docs/technotes/guides/javaws/enhancements6.html).

Security Tools

Java SE 6 adds two new options to the keytool security tool, and two new options to the jarsigner security tool.

New keytool Options

The keytool tool allows you to manage a *keystore* database of trusted cryptographic keys, trusted certificates, and X.509 certificate chains. The following are the new keytool options:

- -genseckey: Generates a secret key (identified by an alias) and stores it in a keystore.

- -importkeystore: Imports one or all entries from a source keystore into a destination keystore.

Learn more about these options from the JDK's keytool documentation (http://java.sun.com/javase/6/docs/technotes/tools/solaris/keytool.html).

New jarsigner Options

The jarsigner tool generates digital signatures for JAR files, and verifies the signatures and integrity of signed JAR files. The following are the new jarsigner options:

- -digestalg: Overrides the message digest algorithm used when digesting a JAR file's entries. If -digestalg is not specified, the default SHA-1 message digest algorithm is used.

- -sigalg: Overrides the signature algorithm used to sign the JAR file. If -sigalg is not specified, the default SHA1withDSA or MD5withRSA algorithm (depending on the type of the private key) is used.

Learn more about these options from the JDK's `jarsigner` documentation (`http://java.sun.com/javase/6/docs/technotes/tools/solaris/jarsigner.html`).

Troubleshooting Tools

Deadlocks, memory leaks, and other problems can occur while developing Java applications. To aid the developer in determining the cause of these problems, Java provides a suite of experimental troubleshooting tools:

Java heap analysis tool (`jhat`): This tool was introduced by Java SE 6 to browse a heap dump. This snapshot is typically created by `jmap` or `jconsole`. It supports a built-in SQL-like Object Query Language (OQL) for querying heap dumps. It also includes built-in queries for examining classes, objects that are pending finalization, and more. Learn more about `jhat` from the JDK documentation (`http://java.sun.com/javase/6/docs/technotes/tools/share/jhat.html`).

Java configuration information (`jinfo`): This tool outputs configuration information (including Java system properties and virtual machine command-line flags) for a Java process. Java SE 6 introduces a new `-flag` option for setting a virtual machine option. For more information about `jinfo` and `-flag`, consult the JDK documentation (`http://java.sun.com/javase/6/docs/technotes/tools/share/jinfo.html`).

Memory map (`jmap`): This tool lets you obtain heap information for a Java process. Under Java SE 6, the Windows version of this tool now supports the `-dump` and `-histo` options. You can find more information about `jmap` and the new options in the JDK documentation (`http://java.sun.com/javase/6/docs/technotes/tools/share/jmap.html`).

Stack trace (`jstack`): This tool outputs a Java process's stack traces of all threads (Java and native) attached to the virtual machine, which is useful in detecting deadlocks. Starting with Java SE 6, `jstack` is supported on Windows. Check out the JDK documentation (`http://java.sun.com/javase/6/docs/technotes/tools/share/jstack.html`) to learn more about `jstack`.

It is great to finally have access to the `jstack` tool on Windows platforms, which makes it so much easier to find out where an application's threads have deadlocked. For example, compile Listing B-6's `Deadlock.java` source code and run the resulting application.

Listing B-6. *Deadlock.java*

```java
// Deadlock.java

public class Deadlock
{
   public static void main (String [] args)
   {
      new ThreadA ("A").start ();
      new ThreadB ("B").start ();
   }
}

class ThreadA extends Thread
{
   ThreadA (String name)
   {
      setName (name);
   }

   public void run ()
   {
      while (true)
      {
         synchronized ("A")
         {
            System.out.println ("Thread A acquiring Lock A");
            synchronized ("B")
            {
               System.out.println ("Thread A acquiring Lock B");
               try
               {
                  Thread.sleep ((int) Math.random ()*100);
               }
               catch (InterruptedException e)
               {
               }
               System.out.println ("Thread A releasing Lock B");
            }
            System.out.println ("Thread A releasing Lock A");
         }
      }
   }
}
```

```
class ThreadB extends Thread
{
   ThreadB (String name)
   {
      setName (name);
   }

   public void run ()
   {
      while (true)
      {
         synchronized ("B")
         {
            System.out.println ("Thread B acquiring Lock B");
            synchronized ("A")
            {
               System.out.println ("Thread B acquiring Lock A");
               try
               {
                  Thread.sleep ((int) Math.random ()*100);
               }
               catch (InterruptedException e)
               {
               }
               System.out.println ("Thread B releasing Lock A");
            }
            System.out.println ("Thread B releasing Lock B");
         }
      }
   }
}
```

Each thread will eventually acquire each other's lock and cannot proceed—the application is deadlocked. When this happens, open another command window and run the jps monitoring tool to obtain Deadlock's process ID. Pass this ID to jstack (as in jstack *pid*) to output stack traces:

```
2007-05-15 15:37:46
Full thread dump Java HotSpot(TM) Client VM (1.6.0-b105 mixed mode):

"DestroyJavaVM" prio=6 tid=0x00296000 nid=0xe68 waiting on condition [0x00000000..
0x0090fd4c]
```

```
        java.lang.Thread.State: RUNNABLE


"B" prio=6 tid=0x0aae3800 nid=0x9a8 waiting for monitor entry [0x0ae4f000..
0x0ae4fd14]
    java.lang.Thread.State: BLOCKED (on object monitor)
        at ThreadB.run(Deadlock.java:58)
        - waiting to lock <0x06b42948> (a java.lang.String)
        - locked <0x06b43200> (a java.lang.String)


"A" prio=6 tid=0x0aae2800 nid=0xb3c waiting for monitor entry [0x0adff000..
0x0adffd94]
    java.lang.Thread.State: BLOCKED (on object monitor)
        at ThreadA.run(Deadlock.java:26)
        - waiting to lock <0x06b43200> (a java.lang.String)
        - locked <0x06b42948> (a java.lang.String)


"Low Memory Detector" daemon prio=6 tid=0x0aabc800 nid=0xac0 runnable [0x00000000..
0x00000000]
    java.lang.Thread.State: RUNNABLE


"CompilerThread0" daemon prio=10 tid=0x0aab7c00 nid=0x628 waiting on condition
[0x00000000..0x0ad0f71c]
    java.lang.Thread.State: RUNNABLE


"Attach Listener" daemon prio=10 tid=0x0aab6800 nid=0xc24 waiting on condition
[0x00000000..0x00000000]
    java.lang.Thread.State: RUNNABLE


"Signal Dispatcher" daemon prio=10 tid=0x0aab5800 nid=0xad0 runnable [0x00000000..
0x00000000]
    java.lang.Thread.State: RUNNABLE


"Finalizer" daemon prio=8 tid=0x0aaa6800 nid=0x350 in Object.wait() [0x0ac1f000..
0x0ac1fc94]
    java.lang.Thread.State: WAITING (on object monitor)
        at java.lang.Object.wait(Native Method)
        - waiting on <0x02e80288> (a java.lang.ref.ReferenceQueue$Lock)
        at java.lang.ref.ReferenceQueue.remove(ReferenceQueue.java:116)
        - locked <0x02e80288> (a java.lang.ref.ReferenceQueue$Lock)
        at java.lang.ref.ReferenceQueue.remove(ReferenceQueue.java:132)
        at java.lang.ref.Finalizer$FinalizerThread.run(Finalizer.java:159)
```

```
"Reference Handler" daemon prio=10 tid=0x0aaa2000 nid=0xf5c in Object.wait()
[0x0abcf000.. 0x0abcfd14]
    java.lang.Thread.State: WAITING (on object monitor)
        at java.lang.Object.wait(Native Method)
        - waiting on <0x02e7bf40> (a java.lang.ref.Reference$Lock)
        at java.lang.Object.wait(Object.java:485)
        at java.lang.ref.Reference$ReferenceHandler.run(Reference.java:116)
        - locked <0x02e7bf40> (a java.lang.ref.Reference$Lock)


"VM Thread" prio=10 tid=0x0aa9f000 nid=0xe40 runnable

"VM Periodic Task Thread" prio=10 tid=0x0aabe000 nid=0xa5c waiting on condition

JNI global references: 624
```

Found one Java-level deadlock:
```
=============================
"B":
  waiting to lock monitor 0x0aaa32ec (object 0x06b42948, a java.lang.String),
  which is held by "A"
"A":
  waiting to lock monitor 0x0aaa3284 (object 0x06b43200, a java.lang.String),
  which is held by "B"

Java stack information for the threads listed above:
===================================================
"B":
        at ThreadB.run(Deadlock.java:58)
        - waiting to lock <0x06b42948> (a java.lang.String)
        - locked <0x06b43200> (a java.lang.String)
"A":
        at ThreadA.run(Deadlock.java:26)
        - waiting to lock <0x06b43200> (a java.lang.String)
        - locked <0x06b42948> (a java.lang.String)
```

Found 1 deadlock.

The output identifies a deadlock scenario during one execution of the `Deadlock` application. It reveals where this application's threads ran into trouble (the source lines are bolded in Listing B-6), which monitor each thread was waiting to lock, and which locked monitor was held by each thread.

Virtual Machine and Runtime Environment

In addition to providing new and improved tools, Java SE 6 enhances its virtual machines and their runtime environment. These consist of performance-related enhancements (identified in Appendix C), along with the following:

New classpath wildcards: A classpath entry can contain a wildcard character (*) to represent all files in the directory that end with the `.jar` or `.JAR` extension. Examine the JDK documentation for setting the classpath (`http://java.sun.com/javase/ 6/docs/technotes/tools/solaris/classpath.html`) to learn more about this enhancement.

Split verifier: According to JSR 202: Java Class File Specification Update (`http://www.jcp.org/en/jsr/detail?id=202`), the pre-Java SE 6 class verifier's algorithm for determining a class file's correctness has a memory overhead and impacts performance at runtime. Because these expenses are significant to small devices, Sun's Connected Limited Device Configuration (CLDC) team split verification into two phases: the compile-time phase adds extra `StackMap` attributes to the class file; the runtime phase uses these attributes to perform final verification. Because the "split verifier" causes classes to load faster (and has other benefits), Java SE 6 includes a split verifier that is partly implemented in the `javac` tool and partly implemented in the virtual machine. You can learn more about Java SE 6's split verifier by reading java.net's "New Java SE 6 Feature: Type Checking Verifier" (`https://jdk.dev. java.net/verifier.html`).

Better DTrace support: DTrace is Sun's dynamic tracing framework for tuning and troubleshooting Solaris-based applications. Java 5 introduced limited support for DTrace in the Solaris-based virtual machines; this support has been extended in Java SE 6. To learn more about the enhanced DTrace, read Jarod Jenson's "DTrace and Java: Exposing Performance Problems That Once Were Hidden" article (`http://www.devx. com/Java/Article/33943`) and the "Dynamic Tracing Support in the Java HotSpot Virtual Machine" white paper (`http://java.sun.com/j2se/reference/whitepapers/ java-dtrace-whitepaper.pdf`).

Improved Java Native Interface (JNI): Java SE 6 brings a few enhancements to the JNI. For starters, the `GetVersion()` function now returns `0x00010006` (the value of the constant defined by the new `JNI_VERSION_1_6` #define) to signify JDK/JRE 1.6. Also, a new `GetObjectRefType()` function has been added to return its `JObject` argument's type. This argument can be a local, global, or weak global reference. Finally, the deprecated `JDK1_1InitArgs` and `JDK1_1AttachArgs` structures have been removed; their `JavaVMInitArgs` and `JavaVMAttachArgs` replacements structures are to be used instead. Check out the JDK's Java Native Interface Specification (`http://java.sun.com/javase/6/docs/technotes/guides/jni/spec/jniTOC.html`) to learn more about these changes and the JNI in general.

Improved JVM Tool Interface (JVM TI): Java SE 6 improves the JVM TI. Its improvements are discussed in Chapter 7 of this book.

Improved Java Platform Debugger Architecture (JPDA): Java SE 6 enhances the JPDA. The biggest change is the removal of the Java Virtual Machine Debug Interface, which has been replaced by the JVM TI. (Because of the JVM TI, Java SE 6 also disables the Java Virtual Machine Profiler Interface, which will be removed in the next release; see Sun's Java SE 6 Release Notes Compatibility page, `http://java.sun.com/javase/6/webnotes/compatibility.html`.) A complete list of JPDA enhancements is available in the JDK documentation (`http://java.sun.com/javase/6/docs/technotes/guides/jpda/enhancements.html`).

Note Garbage collection has also been enhanced in Java SE 6. Parallel compaction has significant performance improvements (see `http://java.sun.com/javase/6/docs/technotes/guides/vm/par-compaction-6.html`). Also, the concurrent mark sweep collector has received several enhancements (see `http://java.sun.com/javase/6/docs/technotes/guides/vm/cms-6.html`).

APPENDIX C

■ ■ ■

Performance Enhancements

Each new release of the Java platform is expected to achieve better performance than its predecessor. Java SE 6 does not disappoint. A lot of work has gone into making this release perform better than Java 5. If you are having trouble convincing your management to transition to Java SE 6, it might help to point out the performance enhancements covered in this appendix.

A Fix for the Gray-Rect Problem

Java SE 6 fixes a long-standing problem with Swing. Prior to Java SE 6, exposing a Swing window after obscuring this window resulted in a noticeable delay between the moment when the window's background was erased and its contents were painted. This is known as the "gray-rect problem," which can be demonstrated by running the application in Listing C-1.

Listing C-1. *GrayRectDemo.java*

```
// GrayRectDemo.java

import java.awt.*;

import javax.swing.*;

public class GrayRectDemo extends JFrame
{
   public GrayRectDemo ()
   {
      super ("Gray Rect Demo");
      setDefaultCloseOperation (EXIT_ON_CLOSE);

      // Cover the main window with a component that delays after painting its
      // contents.
```

```java
        getContentPane ().add (new SlowPaintComponent ());

        setSize (300, 300);
        setVisible (true);
    }

    public static void main (String [] args)
    {
        Runnable r = new Runnable ()
                     {
                         public void run ()
                         {
                             new GrayRectDemo ();
                         }
                     };
        EventQueue.invokeLater (r);
    }
}

class SlowPaintComponent extends JLabel
{
    final static int DELAY = 1000;

    SlowPaintComponent ()
    {
        // This component will always paint its entire display area -- there are
        // no transparent areas.

        setOpaque (true);
    }

    public void paintComponent (Graphics g)
    {
        // Paint background.

        g.setColor (Color.white);
        g.fillRect (0, 0, getWidth (), getHeight ());

        // Paint foreground shape.

        g.setColor (Color.black);
```

```
      g.fillOval (0, 0, getWidth (), getHeight ());

      try
      {
         // Sleep for DELAY milliseconds so that the gray rect problem can be
         // demonstrated.

         Thread.sleep (DELAY);
      }
      catch (InterruptedException e)
      {
      }
   }
}
```

Compile this source code in a Java 5 context, and then run the application. Partially obscure the application's window by placing it under another window, and then select the application's window, bringing it to the front. You should briefly notice the window's unpainted region before this region is painted, as shown in Figure C-1.

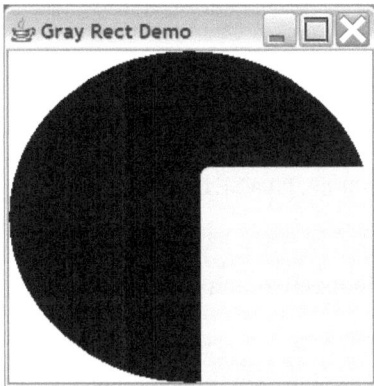

Figure C-1. *The unpainted region is filled in after a brief delay.*

If you perform the same experiment under Java SE 6, you will not see an unpainted region; the window will always appear fully painted. This is possible because true double-buffering support has been added to Swing. Each window is assigned an offscreen-image buffer, which is kept in sync with its onscreen image. When a window is exposed, its buffer's contents are quickly copied to the screen.

Ironically, Listing C-1's DELAY constant and the thread-sleep logic (which you can think of as representing time-consuming rendering code) are needed to view the unpainted region on fast machines. Without the delay (which you might need to increase if your machine is really fast), you probably would not be able to see the unpainted region.

For more information about the gray-rect fix, check out the following:

- Scott Violet's blog entry, "Swing Painting Improvements: No More Gray Rect!" (`http://weblogs.java.net/blog/zixle/archive/2005/04/no_more_gray_re_1.html`)

- Chet Haase's blog entry, "Swing Update: No More Gray Rect" (`http://weblogs.java.net/blog/chet/archive/2005/04/swing_update_no_1.html`)

- The "Gray Rect Fix" section of Sun's "New and Updated Desktop Features in Java SE 6, Part 1" technical article (`http://java.sun.com/developer/technicalArticles/javase/6_desktop_features/index.html`)

The "New and Updated Desktop Features in Java SE 6, Part 1" article includes a chart that compares the different NetBeans IDE window-validation speeds under JDK 1.4.2, JDK 1.5, and JDK 6. This chart is a definite asset for convincing the boss to commit to Java SE 6!

Better-Performing Image I/O

By avoiding finalization in Image I/O's `com.sun.imageio.plugins.jpeg.JPEGImageReader` plug-in class, the Java 5 desktop team achieved major gains in scalability and performance when reading JPEG images. After Java 5, they continued to study Image I/O's API and core plug-ins, looking for new ways to boost performance. Java SE 6 benefits from the team's fixes to these performance bugs:

- Bug 6299405 "ImageInputStreamImpl still uses a finalize() which causes java.lang.OutOfMemoryError"

- Bug 6347575 "FileImageInputStream.readInt() and similar methods are inefficient"

- Bug 6348744 "PNGImageReader should skip metadata if ignoreMetadata=true"

- Bug 6354056 "JPEGImageReader could be optimized"

- Bug 6354112 "Increase compiler optimization level for libjpeg to improve runtime performance"

The fix for Bug 6299405 improves performance by promptly disposing of native resources (such as `java.io.RandomAccessFile` file handles) via Java 2D Disposer (an internal mechanism that Java 2D uses to dispose of its graphics-related resources), instead of waiting for finalizers to run. As a result, applications experience smaller, less-frequent garbage collections where Image I/O is concerned.

To see how these performance enhancements have benefited Image I/O, review the Image I/O Improvements in Mustang chart in Chris Campbell's blog entry, "400 Horsepower: Image I/O Improvements in Mustang" (http://weblogs.java.net/blog/campbell/archive/2006/01/). This chart compares the performance (measured in pixels/millisecond) of PNG (vector art) and JPEG (photo) operations on 20-by-20-pixel images under JDK 1.4.2, JDK 1.5, JDK 6 (build 62), and JDK 6 (build 63).

Faster Java Virtual Machine

The performance boosts from the gray-rect problem fix (along with boosting perceived performance, this fix improves real performance by not erasing a window's background) and improved Image I/O are important reasons for switching to Java SE 6. However, information technology (IT) managers are more likely to be impressed with the fact that Java SE 6's HotSpot virtual machines are the fastest virtual machines (at least for Sun) to date.

This speed improvement is due to the newest client and server HotSpot virtual machines having been designed with out-of-box performance in mind. In other words, because these machines have been optimally configured to achieve the best possible performance for their environments, you no longer need to spend time adjusting tuning parameters to achieve the optimal configurations for your applications.

One could argue that part of this performance boost is due to numerous improvements made by Sun to the HotSpot compiler technology (for dynamically compiling Java bytecode instructions during execution). Improvements are documented in the bug database as bug entries 4850474, 5003419, 5004907, 5079711, 5101346, 6190413, 6191063, 6196383, 6196722, 6206844, 6211497, 6232485, 6233627, 6239807, 6245809, 6251002, and 6262235. For example, according to Bug 6239807, the HotSpot compiler now checks for various AMD features on 32-bit x86 architectures, including the presence of 3DNow! (see Wikipedia's 3DNow! entry at http://en.wikipedia.org/wiki/3DNow! for more information about this technology). Additionally, as mentioned in Appendix B, garbage-collection performance has also improved somewhat.

David Dagastine's blog entry, "Java 6 Leads Out of the Box Server Performance" (http://blogs.sun.com/dagastine/entry/java_6_leads_out_of) provides more information about the new out-of-box performance, and also provides charts that compare Java SE 6 virtual machine performance with the performance of various competitors.

Single-Threaded Rendering

Another Java SE 6 performance enhancement is *single-threaded rendering* (STR), where Java 2D's OpenGL rendering pipeline queues all rendering requests for execution by a single native thread. This improves rendering performance and reduces the likelihood of an OpenGL driver crash.

Because the OpenGL rendering pipeline is not enabled by default (due to various driver issues), you need to specify the unsupported `sun.java2d.opengl` property to take advantage of STR, as in this example:

```
java -Dsun.java2d.opengl=true -jar SwingSet2.jar
```

Learn more about STR by reading the "Single-Threaded Rendering" section of Sun's "New and Updated Desktop Features in Java SE 6, Part 1" technical article (`http://java.sun.com/developer/technicalArticles/javase/6_desktop_features/index.html`).

■Note To find out what else has been improved from a performance perspective, check out the various entries on Sun's Features and Enhancements page (`http://java.sun.com/javase/6/webnotes/features.html`). Also, the JDK 6 documentation includes a link to Sun's Java SE 6 Performance White Papers page (`http://java.sun.com/performance/reference/whitepapers/6_performance.html`), where you can download a white paper describing JDK 6 performance improvements. (This white paper was not available at the time of writing, but should be available when this book is published.)

Test Your Understanding Answers

Chapters 1 through 10 close with a "Test Your Understanding" section, which challenges your understanding of the chapter's material through questions and exercises. Answers to these questions and solutions to these exercises are presented in this appendix.

Note For brevity, this appendix presents only those portions of revised applications that differ from their same-named counterparts appearing elsewhere in this book. The complete source code is available with the rest of the book's code.

Chapter 1: Introducing Java SE 6

1. Sun refers to Java SE 6 instead of J2SE 6.0 because Sun's marketing team met with a group of its Java partners, and most agreed to simplify the Java 2 platform's naming convention to build brand awareness.

2. The themes of Java SE 6 are compatibility and stability; diagnosability, monitoring, and management; ease of development; enterprise desktop; XML and web services; and transparency.

3. Java SE 6 does not include internationalized resource identifiers.

4. The purpose of `Action`'s new `DISPLAYED_MNEMONIC_INDEX_KEY` constant is to identify the index in the `text` property (accessed via the `NAME` key) where a mnemonic decoration should be rendered.

5. You create a Swing program's GUI only on the event-dispatching thread because the Swing GUI toolkit is not multithreaded. The event-dispatching thread must not compete with other threads when creating and accessing Swing components.

6. You establish a window's minimum size by working with the `Window` class's `public void setMinimumSize(Dimension minimumSize)` method.

7. `NavigableSet<E>`'s closest-match methods include `public E ceiling(E e)`, `public E floor(E e)`, `public E higher(E e)`, and `public E lower(E e)`. The `ceiling()` method returns the least element in the set greater than or equal to the given element (or null if the element does not exist). The `floor()` method returns the greatest element in the set less than or equal to the given element (or null if the element does not exist). The `higher()` method returns the least element in the set strictly greater than the given element (or null if the element does not exist). Finally, the `lower()` method returns the greatest element in the set strictly less than the given element (or null if the element does not exist).

8. The `public JDialog(Frame owner)` constructor does not create a true ownerless window when `owner` is `null`. A shared hidden frame window is chosen as the owner of the dialog.

Chapter 2: Core Libraries

1. A cloned or serialized bitset is not trimmed if the bitset was created via `BitSet(int nbits)` and its implementation size has not changed since creation.

2. Invoking `close()` on the `Reader`/`PrintWriter` objects returned by the `Console` class's `reader()`/`writer()` methods will not close the underlying stream.

3. Listing D-1 presents a `ROW` application that lets you make a file or directory read-only or writable.

Listing D-1. *ROW.java*

```
// ROW.java

// Invoke java ROW filespec to show filespec's read-only/writable status.
//
// Invoke java ROW RO filespec to set filespec's status to read-only.
//
```

```java
// Invoke java ROW W filespec to set filespec's status to writable.

import java.io.File;

public class ROW
{
   public static void main (String [] args)
   {
      if (args.length != 1 && args.length != 2)
      {
         System.err.println ("usage: java ROW [RO | W] filespec");
         return;
      }

      String option = (args.length == 1) ? "" : args [0];
      File filespec = new File (args [(args.length == 1) ? 0 : 1]);

      if (option.equals ("RO"))
      {
         if (filespec.setWritable (false))
            System.out.println (filespec+" made read-only");
         else
            System.out.println ("Permission denied");
      }
      else
      if (option.equals ("W"))
      {
         if (filespec.setWritable (true))
            System.out.println (filespec+" made writable");
         else
            System.out.println ("Permission denied");
      }
      else
         System.out.println (filespec+" is currently "+
                              (filespec.canWrite ()
                               ? "writable" : "read-only"));
   }
}
```

4. The difference between Deque<E>'s void addFirst(E e) and boolean
offerFirst(E e) methods is their behavior if the element cannot be added
because of capacity restrictions. The former method throws an
IllegalStateException object, whereas the latter method returns false.

5. The following excerpt from the revised ProductDB application (see Listing 2-9
for the original application's source code) uses NavigableMap<K, V>'s K
higherKey(K key) and K lowerKey(K key) closest-match methods to output
the key higher than 2034 and the key lower than 2034.

```
System.out.println ("First key higher than 2034: "+db.higherKey (2034));
System.out.println ("First key lower than 2034: "+db.lowerKey (2034));
```

6. Listing D-2 presents a Copy application that uses a copyOf() method to copy an
array of Strings to a new CharSequence array.

Listing D-2. *Copy.java*

```java
// Copy.java

import java.util.*;

public class Copy
{
    public static void main (String [] args)
    {
        String [] sa = { "First", "Second", "Third" };
        CharSequence [] csa;
        csa = Arrays.copyOf (sa, sa.length, CharSequence[].class);
        for (int i = 0; i < csa.length; i++)
            System.out.println (csa [i].length ());
    }
}
```

7. ServiceLoader<S>'s iterator() method returns an Iterator<E> whose hasNext() and
next() methods are capable of throwing ServiceConfigurationError instead of an
exception. According to the JDK 6 documentation, this is because "a malformed
provider-configuration file, like a malformed class file, indicates a serious problem
with the way the Java virtual machine is configured or is being used. As such it is
preferable to throw an error rather than try to recover or, even worse, fail silently."

8. Whenever I execute `java -cp pcx.jar; EnumIO`, this application outputs `ca.mb.javajeff.pcx.PCXImageReaderSpi`. However, if I modify the code by passing `null` to `load()`, as in `ServiceLoader.load (ImageReaderSpi.class, null)`, and then invoke `for (ImageReaderSpi imageReader: imageReaders)`, a `ServiceConfigurationError` is thrown because `PCXImageReaderSpi` cannot be found. This class cannot be found because (as `ServiceLoader.java` and some deduction reveal) `Class.forName()` is used to load the class with the bootstrap (null) classloader, and the bootstrap classloader has no knowledge of classes other than the core system classes.

Although the JDK 6 documentation for `ServiceLoader`'s `public static <S> ServiceLoader<S> load(Class<S> service, ClassLoader loader)` method indicates that passing `null` to `loader` will first choose the system classloader, but delegate to the bootstrap classloader if the system classloader is not available, this is only partially true. According to `ServiceLoader.java`, a private `LazyIterator` class is used by the iterator that `ServiceLoader`'s `iterator()` method returns to the enhanced `for` statement. `LazyIterator`'s `hasNext()` method attempts to access the system classloader if `null` is passed to `loader`. In contrast, this class's `next()` method passes the `null` value specified in the `ServiceLoader.load()` call directly to `Class.forName()`, which automatically chooses the bootstrap classloader.

Chapter 3: GUI Toolkits: AWT

1. Listing D-3 presents a `LinkTest` application that displays a dialog with a custom link component when the user clicks the dialog's About button. When this link is clicked, `Desktop`'s `browse()` method is invoked to launch the default browser and display the page identified by the link.

Listing D-3. *LinkTest.java*

```
// LinkTest.java

import java.awt.*;
import java.awt.event.*;

import java.io.*;

import java.net.*;

import javax.swing.*;
```

```java
public class LinkTest extends JFrame
{
   public LinkTest ()
   {
      super ("Link Test");
      setDefaultCloseOperation (EXIT_ON_CLOSE);

      JButton btnAbout = new JButton ("About");
      ActionListener al;
      al = new ActionListener ()
              {
                 public void actionPerformed (ActionEvent e)
                 {
                    new About (LinkTest.this, "About LinkTest");
                 }
              };
      btnAbout.addActionListener (al);

      getContentPane ().add (btnAbout);

      setSize (175, 75);
      setVisible (true);
   }

   public static void main (String [] args)
   {
      Runnable r = new Runnable ()
                 {
                       public void run ()
                       {
                          new LinkTest ();
                       }
                 };
      EventQueue.invokeLater (r);
   }
}

class About extends JDialog
{
   About (JFrame frame, String title)
   {
      super (frame, "About", true);
```

```java
        getContentPane ().add (new Link ("Visit java.sun.com",
                                    "http://java.sun.com", Color.blue,
                                    Color.red), BorderLayout.NORTH);


      JPanel pnl = new JPanel ();
      JButton btnOk = new JButton ("Ok");
      btnOk.addActionListener (new ActionListener ()
                            {
                                public void actionPerformed (ActionEvent e)
                                {
                                    dispose ();
                                }
                            });
      pnl.add (btnOk);
      getContentPane ().add (pnl, BorderLayout.SOUTH);

      pack ();
      setResizable (false);
      setLocationRelativeTo (frame);
      setVisible (true); // This is a self-visible dialog; you don't need to
                       // make it visible.
   }
}

class Link extends JLabel
{
   private Desktop desktop;
   private String link;
   private Color textColor, activeColor;

   Link (String text, String link, Color textColor, Color activeColor)
   {
      super (text, JLabel.CENTER);

      this.link = link;
      this.textColor = textColor;
      this.activeColor = activeColor; // Link color when mouse button pressed.

      setForeground (textColor);

      if (Desktop.isDesktopSupported ())
```

```
        desktop = Desktop.getDesktop ();

    addMouseListener (new LinkListener ());
}

class LinkListener extends MouseAdapter
{
    private URI uri;

    public void mousePressed (MouseEvent e)
    {
        setForeground (activeColor);
    }

    public void mouseReleased (MouseEvent e)
    {
        setForeground (textColor);

        if (Link.this.contains (e.getX (), e.getY ()))
        {
            if (desktop != null &&
                desktop.isSupported (Desktop.Action.BROWSE))
                try
                {
                    if (uri == null)
                        uri = new URI (link);

                    // Although browse() is being invoked on the
                    // event-dispatching thread, this should not prove to be
                    // disruptive to the GUI because the call to launch the
                    // browser is not time-consuming.

                    desktop.browse (uri);
                }
                catch (Exception ex)
                {
                    JOptionPane.showMessageDialog (null, ex.getMessage ());
                }
        }
    }
}
```

For convenience, the link component is based on a JLabel. If you would prefer to base the component on a JButton, check out the Hyperlink class in my "Tools of the Trade: SwingX Meets Swing with New and Extended Components" article (http://www.informit.com/articles/article.asp?p=598024&seqNum=3&rl=1). I also present a third kind of link component in my "Java Fun and Games: Tips from the Java grab bag" article (http://www.javaworld.com/javaworld/jw-01-2007/jw-0102-games.html?page=2).

2. Changing from setModalExclusionType (Dialog.ModalExclusionType.APPLICATION_EXCLUDE); to frame.setModalExclusionType (Dialog.ModalExclusionType.APPLICATION_EXCLUDE); in the constructor of UnitsConverter.java's Help dialog class effectively excludes the frame window (and its child windows) from the new modality model. For this to happen, you must first click the Help button so the constructor can execute frame.setModalExclusionType (Dialog.ModalExclusionType.APPLICATION_EXCLUDE);.

3. When the -splash command-line option and the SplashScreen-Image manifest entry are specified together, -splash takes precedence.

4. The following excerpt from the revised QuickLaunch application (see Listing 3-5 for the original application's source code) boldfaces the default Launch Application menu item:

```
MenuItem miLaunch = new MenuItem ("Launch Application")
                    {
                        public void addNotify ()
                        {
                            super.addNotify ();
                            Font font = getFont ();
                            font = font.deriveFont (Font.BOLD);
                            setFont (font);
                        }
                    };
```

The excerpt is responsible for boldfacing the Launch Application menu item. The idea is simple: obtain the menu item's current font and invoke Font's deriveFont() method to derive a new font from the current font, with all the same properties except for the style, and then assign the derived font with its bold property set to the menu item. However, because the menu item has no current font until the menu item component has been made displayable (by connecting it to its native

menu peer resource), this change must be made after `MenuItem`'s `addNotify()`
method has been called. This is easy to accomplish by subclassing `MenuItem`,
overriding `addNotify()`, and placing the new font-modification code after a
`super.addNotify()` method call.

Caution The JDK documentation for `MenuComponent`'s `setFont()` method states, "Some platforms
may not support setting of all font attributes of a menu component; in such cases, calling `setFont` will have
no effect on the unsupported font attributes of this menu component."

Chapter 4: GUI Toolkits: Swing

1. If a tab is not associated with the `indexOfTabComponent()` method's `Component`
   argument, it returns –1.

2. `DropMode.USE_SELECTION` causes selected text to be temporarily deselected.

3. The following excerpt from the revised `PriceList1` application (see Listing 4-3 for
   the original application's source code) introduces a list selection listener to display
   the selected row's (view) index and model index (via `convertRowIndexToModel()`) via
   an option pane dialog. As you sort this table via different column headers and
   select different rows, you will notice that sorting affects only the view (and not the
   model).

```
table.setSelectionMode (ListSelectionModel.SINGLE_SELECTION);
ListSelectionListener lsl;
lsl = new ListSelectionListener ()
      {
          public void valueChanged (ListSelectionEvent lse)
          {
             int index = table.getSelectedRow ();
             if (index != -1)
             {
                 JOptionPane.showMessageDialog (PriceList1.this,
                                                "View index = "+index+
                                                ", Model index = "+
                                 table.convertRowIndexToModel (index));
             }
          }
      };
table.getSelectionModel ().addListSelectionListener (lsl);
```

4. It is necessary to have `SwingWorker<T, V>`'s `doInBackground()` method return a value, and then retrieve this value from within the `done()` method to properly communicate a computation's result from a worker thread to the event-dispatching thread. The worker thread invokes `doInBackground()` and stores its result in a future, and your code uses the event-dispatching thread to update the GUI after obtaining the result from the future. The computation cannot be performed on the event-dispatching thread because delaying this thread would result in a GUI that is slow at best and unresponsive at worst. The worker thread cannot update the GUI with the result because Swing is not thread-safe. Only the event-dispatching thread can safely update the GUI.

5. The following excerpt from the revised `BrowserWithPrint` application (see Listing 4-7 for the original application's source code) works with `javax.print.attribute.PrintRequestAttributeSet` to specify an initial ISO A4 paper size and print three copies:

```
PrintRequestAttributeSet set;
set =
 new HashPrintRequestAttributeSet ();
set.add (MediaSizeName.ISO_A4);
set.add (new Copies (3));
// Except for set, all of the
// arguments below are the default
// arguments passed when you call the
// no-argument print() method.
ep.print (null, null, true, null,
          set, true);
```

Chapter 5: Internationalization

1. The `Calendar.WEEK_OF_YEAR` and `Calendar.DAY_OF_YEAR` fields handle irregular rules in an imperial era's first year.

2. It is true that all canonically equivalent characters are also compatibility equivalent. Check out Wikipedia's Unicode equivalence entry (http://en.wikipedia.org/wiki/Canonical_equivalence) for more information.

3. Listing D-4 provides a `LocaleNameProviderImpl` subclass that extends the currency name provider example (see Listings 5-2 and 5-3) to also include a locale name provider for the `ti_ER` locale.

Listing D-4. *LocaleNameProviderImpl.java*

```java
// LocaleNameProviderImpl.java

import java.util.*;
import java.util.spi.*;

public class LocaleNameProviderImpl extends LocaleNameProvider
{
   final static Locale [] locales = new Locale [] { new Locale ("ti", "ER") };

   public Locale [] getAvailableLocales ()
   {
      return locales;
   }

   public String getDisplayCountry (String countryCode, Locale locale)
   {
      if (countryCode.equals ("ER"))
      {
         if (locale.equals (locales [0]))
             return "\u12a4\u122d\u1275\u122b";
         else
         if (locale.equals (Locale.ENGLISH))
             return "Eritrea";
      }

      return null;
   }

   public String getDisplayLanguage (String languageCode, Locale locale)
   {
      if (languageCode.equals ("ti"))
      {
         if (locale.equals (locales [0]))
             return "\u1275\u130d\u122d\u129b";
         else
         if (locale.equals (Locale.ENGLISH))
             return "Tigrinya";
      }

      return null;
```

```
   }

   public String getDisplayVariant (String variantCode, Locale locale)
   {
      return null;
   }
}
```

To prove that the contents of this example's tiER.jar file are correct, and that this
JAR file has been installed successfully, Listing D-5 presents a ShowLocaleInfo
application that invokes getDisplayCountry() and getDisplayLanguage() for the
ti_ER locale.

Listing D-5. *ShowLocaleInfo.java*

```
// ShowLocaleInfo.java

import java.util.*;

public class ShowLocaleInfo
{
   public static void main (String [] args)
   {
      Locale ti_ER = new Locale ("ti", "ER");

      String displayCountry = ti_ER.getDisplayCountry (Locale.ENGLISH);
      System.out.println (displayCountry);

      displayCountry = ti_ER.getDisplayCountry (ti_ER);
      for (int i = 0; i < displayCountry.length (); i++)
          System.out.print (Integer.toHexString (displayCountry.charAt (i))+
                            " ");
      System.out.println ();

      String displayLanguage = ti_ER.getDisplayLanguage (Locale.ENGLISH);
      System.out.println (displayLanguage);

      displayLanguage = ti_ER.getDisplayLanguage (ti_ER);
      for (int i = 0; i < displayLanguage.length (); i++)
          System.out.print (Integer.toHexString (displayLanguage.charAt (i))+
                            " ");
      System.out.println ();
```

```
            System.out.println (ti_ER.getDisplayVariant ());
       }
   }
```

4. Listing D-6 presents a ShowLocales application that is similar to ShowCurrencies (see Listing 5-3), where the Currency Code and Currency Symbol columns have been replaced with Country (Default Locale), Language (Default Locale), Country (Localized), and Language (Localized) columns.

Listing D-6. *ShowLocales.java*

```
// ShowLocales.java

import java.awt.*;

import java.util.*;

import javax.swing.*;
import javax.swing.table.*;

public class ShowLocales extends JFrame
{
   public ShowLocales ()
   {
      super ("Show Locales");
      setDefaultCloseOperation (EXIT_ON_CLOSE);

      final Locale [] locales = Locale.getAvailableLocales ();

      TableModel model = new AbstractTableModel ()
      {
         public int getColumnCount ()
         {
            return 5;
         }

         public String getColumnName (int column)
         {
            if (column == 0)
                return "Locale";
            else
```

```
    if (column == 1)
        return "Country (Default Locale)";
    else
    if (column == 2)
        return "Language (Default Locale)";
    else
    if (column == 3)
        return "Country (Localized)";
    else
        return "Language (Localized)";
}

public int getRowCount ()
{
    return locales.length;
}

public Object getValueAt (int row, int col)
{
    if (col == 0)
        return locales [row];
    else
        try
        {
            if (col == 1)
                return locales [row].getDisplayCountry ();
            else
            if (col == 2)
                return locales [row].getDisplayLanguage ();
            else
            if (col == 3)
                return locales [row].
                        getDisplayCountry (locales [row]);
            else
                return locales [row].
                        getDisplayLanguage (locales [row]);
        }
        catch (IllegalArgumentException iae)
        {
            return null;
        }
}
```

```
        };

        JTable table = new JTable (model);
        table.setPreferredScrollableViewportSize (new Dimension (750, 300));
        Renderer r = new Renderer ();
        table.getColumnModel ().getColumn (3).setCellRenderer (r);
        table.getColumnModel ().getColumn (4).setCellRenderer (r);
        getContentPane ().add (new JScrollPane (table));

        pack ();
        setVisible (true);
    }

    public static void main (String [] args)
    {
        Runnable r = new Runnable ()
                    {
                        public void run ()
                        {
                            new ShowLocales ();
                        }
                    };
        EventQueue.invokeLater (r);
    }
}


class Renderer extends JLabel implements TableCellRenderer
{
    Renderer ()
    {
        // Deactivate JLabel's use of the bold style.

        setFont (getFont ().deriveFont (Font.PLAIN));
    }

    public Component getTableCellRendererComponent (JTable table, Object value,
                                                    boolean isSelected,
                                                    boolean isFocus, int row,
                                                    int column)
    {
        String s = (String) value;
        if (s.equals ("\u12a4\u122d\u1275\u122b") ||
```

```
                s.equals ("\u1275\u130d\u122d\u129b"))
                setFont (new Font ("GF Zemen Unicode", Font.PLAIN, 12));

        setText (s);
        return this;
    }
}
```

Figure 5-3 (in Chapter 5) shows this application's GUI.

Chapter 6: Java Database Connectivity

1. To take advantage of automatic driver loading for MySQL Connector/J 5.1, start by creating a META-INF directory in the same directory as mysql-connector-java-5.1. 0-bin.jar. Next, create a services directory within META-INF. Continue by placing a java.sql.Driver text file containing com.mysql.jdbc.Driver in the services directory. Finally, assuming that the directory containing mysql-connector-java-5.1.0-bin.jar is current, execute jar -uf mysql-connector-java-5.1.0-bin.jar -C META-INF/ services to package the services directory and its contents in the JAR file.

2. The position where you will start writing to or reading from a BLOB or CLOB (via Blob's setBinaryStream() and new getBinaryStream() methods, and Clob's setCharacterStream() and new getCharacterStream() methods) is 1.

3. Connection's new setClientInfo() and getClientInfo() methods benefit connection management by making it possible to associate applications with connections. This allows a server-based monitoring tool to identify the application behind a JDBC connection that is hogging the CPU or otherwise bogging down the server.

4. A transient SQLException describes a failed operation that can be retried immediately. A nontransient SQLException describes a failed operation that cannot be retried without changing application source code or some aspect of the data source.

5. Listing D-7 presents a FuncSupported application that employs the isSupported() method presented in Chapter 6 to determine if a scalar function is supported by a data source.

Listing D-7. *FuncSupported.java*

```java
// FuncSupported.java

import java.sql.*;

public class FuncSupported
{
   public static void main (String [] args) throws SQLException
   {
      if (args.length != 2)
      {
         System.err.println ("usage: java FuncSupported jdbcURL funcname");
         return;
      }

      Connection con = DriverManager.getConnection (args [0]);

      System.out.println ("Function "+args [1]+
                          (isSupported (con, args[1]) ? " is supported" :
                          " is not supported"));

      if (con.getMetaData ().getDriverName ().equals ("Apache Derby "+
         "Embedded JDBC Driver"))
         try
         {
            DriverManager.getConnection ("jdbc:derby:;shutdown=true");
         }
         catch (SQLException sqlex)
         {
            System.out.println ("Database shut down normally");
         }
   }

   static boolean isSupported (Connection con, String func)
     throws SQLException
   {
      DatabaseMetaData dbmd = con.getMetaData ();

      if (func.equalsIgnoreCase ("CONVERT"))
         return dbmd.supportsConvert ();
```

```
      func = func.toUpperCase ();

      if (dbmd.getNumericFunctions ().toUpperCase ().indexOf (func) != -1)
          return true;

      if (dbmd.getStringFunctions ().toUpperCase ().indexOf (func) != -1)
          return true;

      if (dbmd.getSystemFunctions ().toUpperCase ().indexOf (func) != -1)
          return true;

      if (dbmd.getTimeDateFunctions ().toUpperCase ().indexOf (func) != -1)
          return true;

      return false;
   }
}
```

MySQL 5.1 does not support the EXTRACT function.

6. Listing D-8 presents a SQLROWIDSupported application that takes a single command-line argument, the JDBC URL to a data source, and outputs a message stating whether or not the data source supports the SQL ROWID data type.

Listing D-8. *SQLROWIDSupported.java*

```java
// SQLROWIDSupported.java

import java.sql.*;

public class SQLROWIDSupported
{
   public static void main (String [] args)
   {
      if (args.length != 1)
      {
          System.err.println ("usage: java SQLROWIDSupported jdbcURL");
          return;
      }

      try
      {
```

```
                Connection con;
                con = DriverManager.getConnection (args [0]);

                DatabaseMetaData dbmd = con.getMetaData ();
                if (dbmd.getRowIdLifetime () != RowIdLifetime.ROWID_UNSUPPORTED)
                    System.out.println ("SQL ROWID Data Type is supported");
                else
                    System.out.println ("SQL ROWID Data Type is not supported");

                if (con.getMetaData ().getDriverName ().equals ("Apache Derby "+
                    "Embedded JDBC Driver"))
                    try
                    {
                        DriverManager.getConnection ("jdbc:derby:;shutdown=true");
                    }
                    catch (SQLException sqlex)
                    {
                        System.out.println ("Database shut down normally");
                    }
            }
            catch (SQLException sqlex)
            {
                System.out.println (sqlex);
            }
        }
    }
```

Java DB version 10.2.1.7 does not support the SQL ROWID data type.

7. Listing D-9 presents a SQLXMLSupported application that takes a single command-line argument, the JDBC URL to a data source, and outputs a message stating whether or not the data source supports the SQL XML data type.

Listing D-9. *SQLXMLSupported.java*

```
// SQLXMLSupported.java

import java.sql.*;

public class SQLXMLSupported
{
    public static void main (String [] args)
```

```
{
    if (args.length != 1)
    {
        System.err.println ("usage: java SQLXMLSupported jdbcURL");
        return;
    }

    try
    {
        Connection con;
        con = DriverManager.getConnection (args [0]);

        DatabaseMetaData dbmd = con.getMetaData ();
        ResultSet rs = dbmd.getTypcInfo ();
        boolean found = false;
        while (rs.next ())
        {
            if (rs.getInt ("DATA_TYPE") == Types.SQLXML)
            {
                found = true;
                break;
            }
        }

        if (found)
                System.out.println ("SQL XML Data Type is supported");
            else
                System.out.println ("SQL XML Data Type is not supported");

        if (con.getMetaData ().getDriverName ().equals ("Apache Derby "+
            "Embedded JDBC Driver"))
            try
            {
                DriverManager.getConnection ("jdbc:derby:;shutdown=true");
            }
            catch (SQLException sqlex)
            {
                System.out.println ("Database shut down normally");
            }
    }
    catch (SQLException sqlex)
    {
```

```
            System.out.println (sqlex);
        }
    }
}
```

Java DB version 10.2.1.7 does not support the SQL XML data type.

8. The purpose of dblook's -z option is to limit DDL generation to a specific schema;
   only those database objects that belong to the schema will have their DDL statements generated. The purpose of dblook's -t option is to limit table-related DDL
   generation to those tables identified by this option. The purpose of dblook's -td
   option is to specify the DDL statement terminator (which is the semicolon character by default).

9. Listing D-10 presents a DumpSchemas application that takes a single command-line
   argument, the JDBC URL to a data source, and dumps the names of its schemas to
   the standard output.

Listing D-10. *DumpSchemas.java*

```
// DumpSchemas.java

import java.sql.*;

public class DumpSchemas
{
    public static void main (String [] args)
    {
        if (args.length != 1)
        {
            System.err.println ("usage: java DumpSchemas jdbcURL");
            return;
        }

        try
        {
            Connection con;
            con = DriverManager.getConnection (args [0]);
```

```
            DatabaseMetaData dbmd = con.getMetaData ();
            ResultSet rs = dbmd.getSchemas ();
            while (rs.next ())
                System.out.println (rs.getString (1));

            if (con.getMetaData ().getDriverName ().equals ("Apache Derby "+
                "Embedded JDBC Driver"))
                try
                {
                    DriverManager.getConnection ("jdbc:derby:;shutdown=true");
                }
                catch (SQLException sqlex)
                {
                    System.out.println ("Database shut down normally");
                }
        }
        catch (SQLException sqlex)
        {
            System.out.println (sqlex);
        }
    }
}
```

When you run this application against the EMPLOYEE database, the following schemas are identified:

```
APP
NULLID
SQLJ
SYS
SYSCAT
SYSCS_DIAG
SYSCS_UTIL
SYSFUN
SYSIBM
SYSPROC
SYSSTAT
```

Chapter 7: Monitoring and Management

1. Local monitoring refers to running JConsole (or any JMX client) on the same machine as the application being monitored. Both the application and JConsole must belong to the same user. You do not need to specify the com.sun.management. jmxremote system property when starting an application to be locally monitored under Java SE 6.

2. According to the JDK documentation for Class's protected final Class<?> defineClass(String name, byte[] b, int off, int len) method, *class definition* involves converting an array of bytes into an instance of class Class. In contrast, *transformation* involves changing the definition in some way, such as instrumenting the class through the addition of bytecodes to various methods. Redefinition does not cause a class's initializers to run. The retransform() method identifies these steps for retransformation:

   - Begin with the initial class-file bytes.

   - For each transformer added via void addTransformer(ClassFileTransformer transformer), or void addTransformer(ClassFileTransformer transformer, boolean canRetransform) where false is passed to canRetransform, the bytes returned by the transform() method during the last class load or redefinition are reused as the output of the transformation.

   - For each transformer that was added with true passed to canRetransform, the transform() method is called in these transformers.

   - The transformed class-file bytes are installed as the new definition of the class.

3. The agentmain() method is often (but not necessarily) invoked after an application's main() method has run. In contrast, premain() is always invoked before main() runs. Also, agentmain() is invoked as a result of dynamic attach, whereas premain() is invoked as a result of starting the virtual machine with the -javaagent option, which specifies an agent JAR file's path and name.

4. Listing D-11 presents a LoadAverageViewer application that invokes OperatingSystemMXBean's getSystemLoadAverage() method. If this method returns a negative value, the application outputs a message stating that the load average is not supported on this platform. Otherwise, it repeatedly outputs the load average once per minute, for a specific number of minutes as determined by a command-line argument.

Listing D-11. *LoadAverageViewer.java*

```java
// LoadAverageViewer.java;

// Unix compile   : javac -cp $JAVA_HOME/lib/tools.jar LoadAverageViewer.java
//
// Windows compile: javac -cp %JAVA_HOME%/lib/tools.jar LoadAverageViewer.java

import static java.lang.management.ManagementFactory.*;

import java.lang.management.*;

import java.io.*;

import java.util.*;

import javax.management.*;
import javax.management.remote.*;

import com.sun.tools.attach.*;

public class LoadAverageViewer
{
   static final String CON_ADDR =
     "com.sun.management.jmxremote.localConnectorAddress";

   static final int MIN_MINUTES = 2;
   static final int MAX_MINUTES = 10;

   public static void main (String [] args) throws Exception
   {
      int minutes = MIN_MINUTES;

      if (args.length != 2)
      {
         System.err.println ("Unix usage    : "+
                             "java -cp $JAVA_HOME/lib/tools.jar:. "+
                             "LoadAverageViewer pid minutes");
         System.err.println ();
         System.err.println ("Windows usage: "+
                             "java -cp %JAVA_HOME%/lib/tools.jar;. "+
                             "LoadAverageViewer pid minutes");
```

```
        return;
    }

    try
    {
        int min = Integer.parseInt (args [1]);
        if (min < MIN_MINUTES || min > MAX_MINUTES)
        {
            System.err.println (min+" out of range ["+MIN_MINUTES+", "+
                                      MAX_MINUTES+"]");
            return;
        }
        minutes = min;
    }
    catch (NumberFormatException nfe)
    {
        System.err.println ("Unable to parse "+args [1]+" as an integer.");
        System.err.println ("LoadAverageViewer will repeatedly check "+
                                " average (if available) every minute for "+
                                MIN_MINUTES+" minutes.");
    }

    // Attempt to attach to the target virtual machine whose identifier is
    // specified as a command-line argument.

    VirtualMachine vm = VirtualMachine.attach (args [0]);

    // Attempt to obtain the target virtual machine's connector address so
    // that this virtual machine can communicate with its connector server.

    String conAddr = vm.getAgentProperties ().getProperty (CON_ADDR);

    // If there is no connector address, a connector server and JMX agent
    // are not started in the target virtual machine. Therefore, load the
    // JMX agent into the target.

    if (conAddr == null)
    {
        // The JMX agent is stored in management-agent.jar. This JAR file
        // is located in the lib subdirectory of the JRE's home directory.

        String agent = vm.getSystemProperties ()
```

```
                            .getProperty ("java.home")+File.separator+
                            "lib"+File.separator+"management-agent.jar";

        // Attempt to load the JMX agent.

        vm.loadAgent (agent);

        // Once again, attempt to obtain the target virtual machine's
        // connector address.

        conAddr = vm.getAgentProperties ().getProperty (CON_ADDR);

        // Although the second attempt to obtain the connector address
        // should succeed, throw an exception if it does not.

        if (conAddr == null)
            throw new NullPointerException ("conAddr is null");
    }

    // Prior to connecting to the target virtual machine's connector
    // server, the String-based connector address must be converted into a
    // JMXServiceURL.

    JMXServiceURL servURL = new JMXServiceURL (conAddr);

    // Attempt to create a connector client that is connected to the
    // connector server located at the specified URL.

    JMXConnector con = JMXConnectorFactory.connect (servURL);

    // Attempt to obtain an MBeanServerConnection that represents the
    // remote JMX agent's MBean server.

    MBeanServerConnection mbsc = con.getMBeanServerConnection ();

    // Obtain object name for thread MBean, and use this name to obtain the
    // name of the OS MBean that is controlled by the JMX agent's MBean
    // server.

    ObjectName osName = new ObjectName (OPERATING_SYSTEM_MXBEAN_NAME);
    Set<ObjectName> mbeans = mbsc.queryNames (osName, null);
```

```java
// The for-each loop conveniently returns the name of the OS MBean.
// There should only be one iteration because there is only one OS
// MBean.

for (ObjectName name: mbeans)
{
    // Obtain a proxy for the OperatingSystemMXBean interface that
    // forwards its method calls through the MBeanServerConnection
    // identified by mbsc.

    OperatingSystemMXBean osb;
    osb = newPlatformMXBeanProxy (mbsc, name.toString (),
                                  OperatingSystemMXBean.class);

    double loadAverage = osb.getSystemLoadAverage ();
    if (loadAverage < 0)
    {   System.out.println (loadAverage);
        System.out.println ("Load average not supported on platform");
        return;
    }

    for (int i = 0; i < minutes; i++)
    {
        System.out.printf ("Load average: %f", loadAverage);
        System.out.println ();

        try
        {
            Thread.sleep (60000); // Sleep for about one minute.
        }
        catch (InterruptedException ie)
        {
        }

        loadAverage = osb.getSystemLoadAverage ();
    }

    break;
    }
    }
}
```

5. The purpose of the JConsole API's JConsoleContext interface is to represent a JConsole connection to an application running in a target virtual machine.

6. The java.beans.PropertyChangeListener is added to a plug-in's JConsoleContext via JConsolePlugin's public final void addContextPropertyChangeListener (PropertyChangeListener listener) method, or via a call to JConsolePlugin's public final JConsoleContext getContext() method followed by a call to JConsoleContext's void addPropertyChangeListener(PropertyChangeListener listener) method (assuming that getContext() does not return null). It is invoked when the connection state between JConsole and a target virtual machine changes. The JConsoleContext.ConnectionState enumeration's CONNECTED, CONNECTING, and DISCONNECTED constants identify the three connection states.

   This listener benefits a plug-in by providing a convenient place to obtain a new javax.management.MBeanServerConnection via JConsoleContext's MBeanServerConnection getMBeanServerConnection() method when the connection state becomes CONNECTED. The current MBeanServerConnection becomes invalid when the connection is disconnected. The sample JTop plug-in's jtopplugin. java source code (included in the JDK) shows how to implement PropertyChangeListener's void propertyChange(PropertyChangeEvent evt) method to restore the MBeanServerConnection.

Chapter 8: Networking

1. If you placed new URL (args [0]).openConnection ().getContent (); before CookieManager cm = new CookieManager (); in Listing 8-1, you would observe no cookie output. The HTTP protocol handler requires an implementation (the cookie manager, for example) of a system-wide cookie handler to be present before it executes. This is because the protocol handler invokes the system-wide cookie handler's public void put(URI uri, Map<String,List<String>> responseHeaders) method to store response cookies in a cookie cache. It cannot invoke this method to accomplish this task if a cookie handler implementation has not been installed.

2. IDN's toASCII() methods throw IllegalArgumentException if their input strings do not conform to RFC 3490.

3. The following excerpt from the revised `MinimalHTTPServer` application (see Listing 8-4 for the original application's source code) introduces a `DateHandler` class associated with the /date root URI. In addition to this excerpt, you need to add a `server.createContext ("/date", new DateHandler ());` method call in the `main()` method.

```
class DateHandler implements HttpHandler
{
   public void handle (HttpExchange xchg) throws IOException
   {
      xchg.sendResponseHeaders (200, 0);
      OutputStream os = xchg.getResponseBody ();
      DataOutputStream dos = new DataOutputStream (os);
      dos.writeBytes ("<html><head></head><body><center><b>"+
                         new Date ().toString ()+"</b></center></body></html>");
      dos.close ();
   }
}
```

4. The following excerpt from the revised `NetParms` application (see Listing 8-5 for the original application's source code) obtains all accessible `InterfaceAddresses` for each network interface, and outputs each `InterfaceAddress`'s IP address, broadcast address, and network prefix length/subnet mask:

```
List<InterfaceAddress> ias = ni.getInterfaceAddresses ();
for (InterfaceAddress ia: ias)
{
      // Because it is possible for getInterfaceAddresses() to
      // return a list consisting of a single null element -- I
      // found this to be the case for a WAN (PPP/SLIP) interface --
      // an if statement test is needed to prevent a
      // NullPointerException.

      if (ia == null)
         break;

      System.out.println ("Interface Address");
      System.out.println ("  Address: "+ia.getAddress ());
      System.out.println ("  Broadcast: "+ia.getBroadcast ());
      System.out.println ("  Prefix length/Subnet mask: "+
                         ia.getNetworkPrefixLength ());
}
```

Chapter 9: Scripting

1. The name of the package assigned to the Scripting API is javax.script.

2. The Compilable interface describes a script engine that lets scripts be compiled to intermediate code. The CompiledScript abstract class is extended by subclasses that store the results of compilations—the intermediate code, as it were.

3. The scripting language associated with Java SE 6's Rhino-based script engine is JavaScript.

4. ScriptEngineFactory's getEngineName() method returns an engine's full name (such as Mozilla Rhino). ScriptEngineFactory's getNames() method returns a list of engine short names (such as rhino). You can pass any short name to ScriptEngineManager's getEngineByName(String shortName) method.

5. For a script engine to exhibit the MULTITHREADED threading behavior, scripts can execute concurrently on different threads, although the effects of executing a script on one thread might be visible to threads executing on other threads.

6. ScriptEngineManager's getEngineByExtension(String extension) method would be appropriate for obtaining a script engine after selecting the name of a script file via a dialog box.

7. ScriptEngine offers six eval() methods for evaluating scripts.

8. The Rhino-based script engine does not import the java.lang package by default to prevent conflicts with same-named JavaScript types—Object, Math, Boolean, and so on.

9. The problem with importPackage() and importClass() is that they pollute JavaScript's global variable scope. Rhino overcomes this problem by providing a JavaImporter class that works with JavaScript's with statement to let you specify classes and interfaces without their package names from within this statement's scope.

10. A Java program communicates with a script by passing objects to the script via *script variables*, and by obtaining script variable values as objects. ScriptEngine provides void put(String key, Object value) and Object get(String key) methods for these tasks.

11. `jrunscript` makes command-line arguments available to a script by invoking `engine.put("arguments", args)` followed by `engine.put(ScriptEngine.ARGV, args)`, where `args` is the name of the `String` array passed to this tool's entry-point method.

12. A bindings object is a map that stores key/value pairs, where keys are expressed as `Strings`.

13. With engine scope, a bindings object is visible to a specific script engine through-out the engine's lifetime; other script engines do not have access to this bindings object (unless you share it with them). With global scope, a bindings object is visible to all script engines that are created with the same script engine manager.

14. `ScriptEngine` provides a `setBindings(Bindings bindings, int scope)` method that allows the global bindings to be replaced so that `ScriptEngineManager`'s `getEngineByExtension()`, `getEngineByMimeType()`, and `getEngineByName()` methods can share the global scope's bindings object with a newly created script engine.

15. A script context connects a script engine to a Java program. It exposes the global and engine bindings objects. It also exposes a reader and a pair of writers that a script engine uses for input and output.

16. `eval(String script, ScriptContext context)` evaluates a script with an explicitly specified script context. `eval(String script, Bindings n)` creates a new temporary script context (with engine bindings set to n, and with global bindings set to the default context's global bindings) before evaluating a script.

17. The purpose of the `context` script variable is to describe a `SimpleScriptContext` object that lets a script engine access the script context. You would output this variable's value in Rhino-based JavaScript via `println (context)`. You would output this variable's value in JRuby via `puts $context`.

18. Anything passed to the `getOutputStatement()` method's `toDisplay String` argument is quoted in the output statement returned by this method. This means that you cannot use `getOutputStatement()` to generate a statement for outputting a vari-able's value, unless you subsequently replace the quotation marks with spaces (as described in Chapter 9).

19. You compile a script by first making sure that its script engine instance imple-ments the `Compilable` interface. Next, cast the script engine instance to a `Compilable` instance. Finally, invoke one of `Compilable`'s `compile()` methods on this instance.

20. One benefit provided by the `Invocable` interface is performance. The `invokeFunction()` and `invokeMethod()` methods execute intermediate code. Unlike the `eval()` methods, they do not need to first parse a script into intermediate code, which can be time consuming. Another benefit of the `Invocable` interface is minimal coupling. The `getInterface()` methods return Java interface objects, whose methods are implemented by a script's global or object member functions. These objects minimize a Java program's exposure to the script.

21. `jrunscript` is an experimental command-line, script-shell tool for exploring scripting languages and their communication with Java.

22. You would discover the implementations for the `jlist()`, `jmap()`, and `JSInvoker()` functions by invoking `println (jlist)`, `println (jmap)`, and `println (JSInvoker)`.

23. `JSAdapter` is a `java.lang.reflect.Proxy` equivalent for JavaScript. `JSAdapter` lets you adapt property access (as in `x.i`), mutator (as in `x.p = 10`), and other simple JavaScript syntax on a proxy object to a delegate JavaScript object's member functions.

24. If you were to modify `demo.html`'s `setColor(color)` function to print `document.linkcolor`'s value before and after setting this property to the `color` argument (as in `function setColor(color) { println ("Before = "+document.linkcolor); document.linkcolor = color; println ("After = "+document.linkcolor); })`, you would notice that the first time you move the mouse pointer over either of this document's two links, `Before = java.awt.Color[r=0,g=0,b=0]` outputs. This output indicates that `document.linkcolor`'s initial value is black (instead of blue, assuming the default setting). The reason is that a link's text derives its foreground color (blue by default) from the document's style sheet, not from its foreground color attribute, which happens to be black.

To fix this to output `Before = java.awt.Color[r=0,g=0,b=255]` (again, assuming the default blue style sheet setting) instead, you would make the following changes to the `ScriptEnvironment` class:

- Add a `private boolean first = true;` field.

- Modify `getLinkColor()` to the following:

```
public Color getLinkColor ()
{
   if (first)
   {
       setLinksDefaultColorToCSS ();
       first = false;
```

```
        }

        AttributeSet as = currentAnchor.getAttributes ();
        return StyleConstants.getForeground (as);
    }
```

• Add the following setLinksDefaultColorToCSS() method:

```
public void setLinksDefaultColorToCSS ()
{
    HTMLDocument doc;
    doc = (HTMLDocument) ScriptedEditorPane.this.getDocument ();

    StyleContext sc = StyleContext.getDefaultStyleContext ();
    AttributeSet as = sc.addAttribute (SimpleAttributeSet.EMPTY,
                                       StyleConstants.Foreground,
                                       defaultLinkColor);

    HTMLDocument.Iterator itr = doc.getIterator (HTML.Tag.A);
    while (itr.isValid ())
    {
        doc.setCharacterAttributes (itr.getStartOffset (),
                                    itr.getEndOffset ()-
                                    itr.getStartOffset (), as, false);
        itr.next ();
    }
}
```

25. Listing D-12 presents a WorkingWithJRuby application that invokes
    WorkingWithJavaFXScript.

Listing D-12. *WorkingWithJRuby.java*

```
// WorkingWithJRuby.java

import javax.script.*;

public class WorkingWithJRuby
{
    public static void main (String [] args) throws Exception
    {
        ScriptEngineManager manager = new ScriptEngineManager ();
```

```
      // The JRuby script engine is accessed via the jruby short name.

      ScriptEngine engine = manager.getEngineByName ("jruby");

      engine.eval ("`java WorkingWithJavaFXScript`");
  }
}
```

Ruby invokes an external program by placing the command line between a pair of backtick (`) characters. In order for WorkingWithJavaFXScript to run properly, Filters.jar, javafxrt.jar, and swing-layout.jar must be part of the classpath.

Chapter 10: Security and Web Services

1. A Java application communicates with applications running on a smart card by exchanging ISO/IEC 7816-4 APDUs.

2. The package assigned to the Smart Card I/O API is javax.smartcardio.

3. A terminal is a card reader slot in which to insert a smart card.

4. Authenticity means that you can determine who sent the data. Integrity means that the data has not been modified in transit. Nonrepudiation means that senders cannot deny sending their documents.

5. A digital signature is an encrypted hash or message digest.

6. Assuming public-key cryptography, digitally signing a document requires the sender to use the sender's private key to sign the document (which results in an encrypted hash), and the recipient to use the sender's public key to decrypt the encrypted hash. In contrast, encrypting a document requires the sender to perform the encryption via the recipient's public key, and the recipient to perform the decryption via the recipient's private key.

7. An XML Signature is a Signature element and its contained elements, where the signature is calculated over the SignedInfo section and stored in the SignatureValue element.

8. Canonicalization converts XML content to a standardized physical representation, to eliminate subtle changes that can invalidate a signature over the XML content.

9. Base64 is the algorithm used to encode the SignatureValue element's signature in an XML document.

10. The Signature element is excluded from the data object's signature value calculation for the enveloped XML Signature type.

11. The XMLSignatureFactory class is the entry point into the XML Digital Signature APIs.

12. An application obtains an instance of the XML Digital Signature APIs entry-point class by invoking one of XMLSignatureFactory's getInstance() methods.

13. The web services stack's layered architecture is composed of the JAX-WS, JAXB, and StAX APIs. The stack also benefits from the SAAJ and Web Services Metadata APIs.

14. @WebService is used to annotate a web service class.

15. A web service is published by invoking the javax.xml.ws.EndPoint class's public static Endpoint publish(String address, Object implementor) method with the web service's address URI and an instance of the web service class as arguments.

16. The tool used to generate web service artifacts needed to deploy a web service is wsgen.

17. The tool used to generate web service artifacts needed to import a web service to client programs is wsimport.

18. Listing D-13 presents a revised SkyView application (shown in Listing 10-8) whose use of SwingWorker<T, V> ensures that the GUI is still responsive whenever byte [] image = Imgcutoutsoap.getJpeg (ra, dec, scale, IMAGE_WIDTH, IMAGE_HEIGHT, dopt); takes a while to complete. (Differences between Listing D-13 and Listing 10-8 are highlighted.)

Listing D-13. *SkyView.java*

```
// SkyView.java

import java.awt.*;
import java.awt.event.*;
import java.awt.image.*;

import java.io.*;
```

```java
import javax.imageio.*;

import javax.swing.*;

import org.sdss.skyserver.*;

public class SkyView extends JFrame
{
   final static int IMAGE_WIDTH = 300;
   final static int IMAGE_HEIGHT = 300;

   static ImgCutoutSoap imgcutoutsoap;

   double ra, dec, scale;
   String dopt;

   JLabel lblImage;

   public SkyView ()
   {
      super ("SkyView");
      setDefaultCloseOperation (EXIT_ON_CLOSE);

      setContentPane (createContentPane ());

      pack ();
      setResizable (false);
      setVisible (true);
   }

   JPanel createContentPane ()
   {
      JPanel pane = new JPanel (new BorderLayout (10, 10));
      pane.setBorder (BorderFactory.createEmptyBorder (10, 10, 10, 10));

      lblImage = new JLabel ("", JLabel.CENTER);
      lblImage.setPreferredSize (new Dimension (IMAGE_WIDTH+9,
                                                IMAGE_HEIGHT+9));
      lblImage.setBorder (BorderFactory.createEtchedBorder ());

      pane.add (new JPanel () {{ add (lblImage); }}, BorderLayout.NORTH);
```

```
JPanel form = new JPanel (new GridLayout (4, 1));

final JLabel lblRA = new JLabel ("Right ascension:");
int width = lblRA.getPreferredSize ().width+20;
int height = lblRA.getPreferredSize ().height;
lblRA.setPreferredSize (new Dimension (width, height));
lblRA.setDisplayedMnemonic ('R');
final JTextField txtRA = new JTextField (25);
lblRA.setLabelFor (txtRA);

form.add (new JPanel ()
        {{ add (lblRA); add (txtRA);
            setLayout (new FlowLayout (FlowLayout.CENTER, 0, 5)); }});

final JLabel lblDec = new JLabel ("Declination:");
lblDec.setPreferredSize (new Dimension (width, height));
lblDec.setDisplayedMnemonic ('D');
final JTextField txtDec = new JTextField (25);
lblDec.setLabelFor (txtDec);

form.add (new JPanel ()
        {{ add (lblDec); add (txtDec);
            setLayout (new FlowLayout (FlowLayout.CENTER, 0, 5));}});

final JLabel lblScale = new JLabel ("Scale:");
lblScale.setPreferredSize (new Dimension (width, height));
lblScale.setDisplayedMnemonic ('S');
final JTextField txtScale = new JTextField (25);
lblScale.setLabelFor (txtScale);

form.add (new JPanel ()
        {{ add (lblScale); add (txtScale);
            setLayout (new FlowLayout (FlowLayout.CENTER, 0, 5));}});

final JLabel lblDO = new JLabel ("Drawing options:");
lblDO.setPreferredSize (new Dimension (width, height));
lblDO.setDisplayedMnemonic ('o');
final JTextField txtDO = new JTextField (25);
lblDO.setLabelFor (txtDO);

form.add (new JPanel ()
        {{ add (lblDO); add (txtDO);
```

```
                         setLayout (new FlowLayout (FlowLayout.CENTER, 0, 5));}}});


    pane.add (form, BorderLayout.CENTER);


    final JButton btnGP = new JButton ("Get Picture");
    ActionListener al;
    al = new ActionListener ()
        {
            public void actionPerformed (ActionEvent e)
            {
              try
              {
                  ra = Double.parseDouble (txtRA.getText ());
                  dec = Double.parseDouble (txtDec.getText ());
                  scale = Double.parseDouble (txtScale.getText ());
                  dopt = txtDO.getText ().trim ();

                  new GetImageTask ().execute ();
              }
              catch (Exception exc)
              {
                  JOptionPane.showMessageDialog (SkyView.this,
                                                   exc.getMessage ());
              }
            }
        };
    btnGP.addActionListener (al);
    pane.add (new JPanel () {{ add (btnGP); }}, BorderLayout.SOUTH);

    return pane;
}


class GetImageTask extends SwingWorker<byte [], Void>
{
    @Override
    public byte [] doInBackground ()
    {
      return imgcutoutsoap.getJpeg (ra, dec, scale, IMAGE_WIDTH,
                                    IMAGE_HEIGHT, dopt);
    }


    @Override
```

```java
    public void done ()
    {
      try
      {
          lblImage.setIcon (new ImageIcon (get ()));
      }
      catch (Exception exc)
      {
          JOptionPane.showMessageDialog (SkyView.this,
                                      exc.getMessage ());
      }
    }
  }

  public static void main (String [] args) throws IOException
  {
    ImgCutout imgcutout = new ImgCutout ();
    imgcutoutsoap = imgcutout.getImgCutoutSoap ();

    Runnable r = new Runnable ()
                 {
                     public void run ()
                     {
                       try
                       {
                           String lnf;
                           lnf = UIManager.
                                   getSystemLookAndFeelClassName ();
                           UIManager.setLookAndFeel (lnf);
                       }
                       catch (Exception e)
                       {
                       }
                       new SkyView ();
                     }
                 };
    EventQueue.invokeLater (r);
  }
}
```

■ ■ ■

A Preview of Java SE 7

Approximately every two years, Sun Microsystems presents a new generation of the Java platform to the Java community. See the J2SE Code Names page (`http://java.sun.com/j2se/codenames.html`) for a list of official Java release dates. You can add a Java SE 6/Mustang/Dec 11, 2006 entry to this list. If Sun adheres to this pattern, the official release of the next generation, Java SE 7 (I assume that Sun will use this name; Java SE 7 is currently being referred to as Dolphin) should occur in mid-to-late 2008.

Work began on Java SE 7 before Java SE 6's official release. Danny Coward, the platform lead for Java SE, identifies a variety of features planned for Java SE 7 in his "What's coming in Java SE 7" document (`http://blogs.sun.com/dannycoward/resource/Java7Overview_Prague_JUG.pdf`) and in his "Channeling Java SE 7" blog entry (`http://blogs.sun.com/dannycoward/entry/channeling_java_se_7`).

This appendix discusses several features that are most likely to be part of Java SE 7.

■**Caution** Because Java SE 7 is a work in progress, some of the features discussed in this appendix may differ from those in the final release, or may not even be present.

Closures

Java 5 is largely remembered for introducing generics and other language features, including static imports, an enhanced `for` statement, auto-boxing, and type-safe enumerations. Java SE 7 will probably be remembered mainly for introducing *closures*, since language enhancements seem to make a bigger impact on Java developers than API enhancements.

You can find various definitions for the technical term *closure*. For example, Wikipedia's Closure (computer science) entry (http://en.wikipedia.org/wiki/ Closure_%28computer_science%29) defines *closure* as follows:

> *In computer science, a closure is a function that is evaluated in an environment containing one or more bound variables . . . In some languages, a closure may occur when a function is defined within another function, and the inner function refers to local variables of the outer function. At runtime, when the outer function executes, a closure is formed, consisting of the inner function's code and references to any variables of the outer function required by the closure.*

To demonstrate this definition, I have prepared a simple closure example. Listing E-1 provides this example's Rhino-based JavaScript source code.

Listing E-1. *counter.js*

```
// counter.js

var new_counter = function (current_count)
                {
                    return function (incr)
                    {
                        return current_count += incr;
                    };
                };
```

If you were to evaluate var c = new_counter (3), for example, the outer anonymous function would form a closure consisting of the inner anonymous function and a binding of current_count. Subsequently, evaluating println (c (4)) would result in the closure adding 4 to current_count's initial 3 value. The total (7) would then output.

How will this example look in Java SE 7? According to version 0.5 (the latest version when I wrote this appendix) of the closures specification, the example should look like this:

```
{ int => int } new_counter (int current_count)
{
    return { int incr => current_count += incr; }
}

{ int => int } counter = new_counter (3);
System.out.println (counter (4)); // Output 7.
```

The closures specification is accessible via a link on the Closures for the Java Programming Language page (http://www.javac.info/). Also available via a link on that page is a Google video with Neal Gafter, who is deeply involved in developing closures for Java. This video introduces closures and provides answers to various questions. Click the 2-hour talk with Q&A link (http://video.google.com/videoplay?docid=4051253555018153503) to view the video.

Note Although closures are bound to get most of the attention, other language enhancements are being considered for Java SE 7. Danny Coward's "What's coming in Java SE 7" document discusses enhancements related to performing arithmetic on big decimals, comparing enumerations, creating objects, specifying and accessing JavaBeans properties, and other tasks.

JMX 2.0 and Web Services Connector for JMX Agents

Java SE 7 could also benefit from work being done on Java Management Extensions (JMX). For example, JSR 255, which is headed by Eamonn McManus, introduces JMX version 2.0 (http://jcp.org/en/jsr/detail?id=255). According to Eamonn's "JMX API Maintenance Reviews" blog entry (http://weblogs.java.net/blog/emcmanus/archive/2006/03/jmx_api_mainten.html), JSR 255 merges the JMX and JMX Remote APIs into a single unified API.

Note JSR 255 refers to cascaded (federated) MBean Servers. Eamonn McManus explains this feature in his "Cascading: It's all done with mirrors" blog entry (http://weblogs.java.net/blog/emcmanus/archive/2007/02/cascading_its_a_1.html). Eamonn also discusses another JSR 255 feature, customizing the rules for mapping Java types to open types, in his "Custom types for MXBeans" blog entry (http://weblogs.java.net/blog/emcmanus/archive/2007/05/custom_types_fo.html).

In addition to JSR 255, Eamonn is the lead on JSR 262: Web Services Connector for Java Management Extensions (JMX) Agents (http://jcp.org/en/jsr/detail?id=262). This JSR seeks to define a JMX Remote API connector for making JMX instrumentation available to remote Java and non-Java clients via web services. For more information about JSR 262, check out Eamonn's "JMX Web Services Connector available in Early Access" blog entry (http://weblogs.java.net/blog/emcmanus/archive/2007/05/ web_services_co.html).

More Scripting Languages and invokedynamic

It is quite likely that Java SE 7 will introduce new scripting languages. Three possible candidates are JRuby, BeanShell, and Groovy. BeanShell is being standardized for the Java platform via JSR 274: The BeanShell Scripting Language (`http://jcp.org/en/jsr/detail?id=274`). Groovy is being developed under JSR 241: The Groovy Programming Language (`http://jcp.org/en/jsr/detail?id=241`).

■Note Sun employee Sundar Athijegannathan's "Java Integration: JavaScript, Groovy and JRuby" blog entry (`http://blogs.sun.com/sundararajan/entry/java_integration_javascript_groovy_and`) provides a nice side-by-side comparison of using JavaScript, Groovy, and JRuby to access various Java features. In Sundar's "Java Integration: BeanShell and Jython" blog entry (`http://blogs.sun.com/sundararajan/entry/java_integration_beanshell_and_jython`), he extends this side-by-side comparison to include BeanShell and Jython.

Also, Java SE 7 will probably add a new scripting-oriented instruction to the Java virtual machine. According to JSR 292: Supporting Dynamically Typed Languages on the Java Platform (`http://jcp.org/en/jsr/detail?id=292`), this instruction, which might be called `invokedynamic`, is designed to make it easier to create efficient scripting language implementations.

■Note In Gilad Bracha's "Invokedynamic" blog entry (`http://blogs.sun.com/gbracha/entry/invokedynamic`), he points out that `invokedynamic` will be similar to the `invokevirtual` instruction. However, the virtual machine's verifier will rely on dynamic checks (instead of static checks) for verifying the type of the method invocation's target, and that the types of the method's arguments match the method's signature. Gilad is a distinguished engineer whose bio (`http://bracha.org/Site/Bio.html`) indicates that he was formerly with Sun Microsystems. Sundar Athijegannathan's "invokespecialdynamic?" blog entry (`http://blogs.sun.com/sundararajan/entry/invokespecialdynamic`) provides additional insight into this instruction.

New I/O: The Next Generation

JSR 51 (`http://jcp.org/en/jsr/detail?id=51`) introduced a variety of new I/O APIs to version 1.4 of the Java platform. These APIs were for charset conversion, fast buffered binary and character I/O, and other features. Certain major components of this JSR were not addressed. For example, the new file system interface—with support for bulk access to file attributes (including MIME content types), escape to file system-specific APIs, and a service provider interface for pluggable file system implementations—was not realized for Java 1.4, Java 5, or Java SE 6. Other components were incompletely addressed. For example, the API for scalable I/O operations on files and sockets does not support asynchronous requests; only polling is supported.

▪**Note** Bulk access to file attributes seeks to address the performance problem in accessing the attributes of a large number of files; see Bug 6483858 "File attribute access is very slow (isDirectory, etc.)." It also seeks to overcome `java.io.File`'s limited file attribute support. You cannot obtain file permissions and access control lists, for example.

In 2003, JSR 203: More New I/O APIs for the Java Platform ("NIO.2") (`http://jcp.org/en/jsr/detail?id=203`) was introduced to address these and other limitations of the first NIO generation. There is a good chance that JSR 203 will make it into Java SE 7. This JSR's major components include JSR 51's file system interface, an API for performing asynchronous I/O operations on files and sockets, and finishing the socket channel functionality (supporting multicast datagrams, for example). To learn more about JSR 203, check out the "More New I/O APIs for Java" article (`http://www.artima.com/lejava/articles/more_new_io.html`), which documents an Artima interview with JSR 203 specification lead Alan Bateman.

Superpackages and the Java Module System

Most developers understand the notion of *modules*, which are self-contained subsystems with well-defined interfaces to other subsystems. Modules form the basis of many software systems, such as accounting packages.

As Gilad Bracha explains in his "Developing Modules for Development" blog entry (`http://blogs.sun.com/gbracha/entry/developing_modules_for_development`), Java packages are not very good at modularizing a software system. For example, consider a large system consisting of multiple subsystems, which interact with each other via a private API. If you want this API to stay private, you need to place all subsystems in the same package, which is inflexible. If you place each subsystem in its own package, the API must be publicly exposed, which violates information hiding. You currently are limited to either flexibility or information hiding (you cannot have both). JSR 294: Improved Modularity Support in the Java Programming Language (`http://jcp.org/en/jsr/detail?id=294`) has been introduced to address this situation.

JSR 294 intends to provide language extensions that support information hiding and separate compilation. Separate compilation (which, according to Gilad, is not as critical as information hiding) would allow you to compile a source file without requiring access to the source or binary code of imported packages: the compiler would need to access only a package's public declarations. To refer to the language extensions that make information hiding and separate compilation possible, the term *superpackage* is currently being used.

Andreas Sterbenz's blog entry "Superpackages in JSR 294" (http://blogs.sun.com/andreas/entry/superpackages_in_jsr_294) points out that this JSR focuses on modularity only at the language level. JSR 294 does not address the related topic of deployment modularity.

The current deployment solution of using JAR files to deploy Java applications has problems, such as JAR files being hard to distribute and version. JSR 277: Java Module System (http://jcp.org/en/jsr/detail?id=277) is being developed to provide a better alternative: the Java Module System (JMS). The JMS, which will rely on JSR 294's superpackages as its foundation, will provide the following:

- A distribution format involving Java modules as a unit of delivery

- A versioning scheme

- A repository for module storage and retrieval

- Runtime support in both the application launcher and classloaders for discovering, loading, and checking the integrity of modules

- A set of packaging and repository tools that support installing and removing modules

There is an excellent chance that superpackages and the JMS will be part of Java SE 7.

Note To download the JMS specification's PDF-based document, click the Download link on the JSR-000277 Java Module System page (http://jcp.org/aboutJava/communityprocess/edr/jsr277/index.html).

Swing Application Framework

The Swing Application Framework (SAF) is another feature that has potential for being included in Java SE 7. According to JSR 296 (http://jcp.org/en/jsr/detail?id=296), the SAF is designed to facilitate the development of Swing applications by providing an "infrastructure common to most desktop applications." This infrastructure is considered necessary because Java SE 6 and earlier versions do not include "any support for structuring [Swing] applications, and this often leaves new developers feeling a bit adrift, particularly when they're contemplating building an application whose scale goes well beyond the examples provided in the SE documentation."

Under the direction of specification lead Hans Muller, JSR 296 is being implemented as the appframework project (`https://appframework.dev.java.net/`). This project's An Introduction to the Swing Application Framework API (JSR-296) page (`https://appframework.dev.java.net/intro/index.html`) demonstrates this framework's goals, which include life-cycle management, actions, threading, localizable resources, and persistent session state. These goals are also demonstrated in Sun engineer John O'Conner's "Using the Swing Application Framework (JSR 296)" article (`http://java.sun.com/developer/technicalArticles/javase/swingappfr/`).

Rather than reinvent the wheel by revisiting the same material, I present my own example to demonstrate the SAF's usefulness. Because this example requires an implementation of the SAF, I downloaded `AppFramework-0.43.jar` from java.net's appframework: Documents & files page (`https://appframework.dev.java.net/servlets/ProjectDocumentList`). At the time of writing, 0.43 was the latest version of the SAF. I also chose to download `AppFramework-0.43-doc.zip` and `AppFramework-0.43-src.zip`, which contain the SAF's documentation and source code, respectively.

Because `AppFramework-0.43.jar` relies on code external to itself and Java SE 6, I also downloaded `swing-worker-1.1.jar` (`https://swingworker.dev.java.net/servlets/ProjectDocumentList`). Instead of importing Java SE 6's `javax.swing.SwingWorker` class and `javax.swing.SwingWorker.StateValue` enumeration, `AppFramework-0.43.jar`'s `Task` class imports `swing-worker-1.1.jar`'s `org.jdesktop.swingworker.SwingWorker` class and `org.jdesktop.swingworker.SwingWorker.StateValue` enumeration. This enumeration is also imported by `AppFramework-0.43.jar`'s `TaskMonitor` class.

My example provides an implementation of the WHOIS protocol (defined by RFC 3912: WHOIS Protocol Specification, `http://tools.ietf.org/html/rfc3912`). It consists of a `WhoIs` application that lets you enter an arbitrary domain name and obtain information about this domain name from a WHOIS server. Listing E-2 presents the source code.

Listing E-2. *WhoIs.java*

```
// WhoIs.java

import application.*;

import java.io.*;

import java.net.*;

import javax.swing.*;

public class WhoIs extends SingleFrameApplication
{
   final static int WHOIS_PORT = 43;
```

```java
    JButton btnGo;
    JTextArea txtInfo;
    JTextField txtDomain;

    String whoIsServer = "whois.geektools.com";

    @Override
    protected void initialize (String [] args)
    {
        if (args.length == 1)
            whoIsServer = args [0];
    }


    @Override
    protected void startup ()
    {
        show (makeContentPane ());
    }

    JPanel makeContentPane ()
    {
        JPanel pane = new JPanel ();
        GroupLayout layout = new GroupLayout (pane);
        pane.setLayout (layout);

        layout.setAutoCreateGaps (true);
        layout.setAutoCreateContainerGaps (true);

        JLabel lblDomain = new JLabel ();
        lblDomain.setName ("lblDomain");
        txtDomain = new JTextField (20);
        btnGo = new JButton ();
        txtInfo = new JTextArea (20, 50);
        JScrollPane spInfo = new JScrollPane (txtInfo);

        GroupLayout.Group group;
        group = layout.createParallelGroup (GroupLayout.Alignment.CENTER)
                .addGroup (layout.createSequentialGroup ()
                  .addComponent (lblDomain)
                  .addComponent (txtDomain)
                  .addComponent (btnGo))
                .addComponent (spInfo);
        layout.setHorizontalGroup (group);
```

```
   group = layout.createSequentialGroup ()
           .addGroup (layout.
                      createParallelGroup (GroupLayout.Alignment.BASELINE)
           .addComponent (lblDomain)
           .addComponent (txtDomain)
           .addComponent (btnGo))
           .addComponent (spInfo);
   layout.setVerticalGroup (group);

   ActionMap map = ApplicationContext.getInstance ().getActionMap (this);
   javax.swing.Action action = map.get ("retrieveInfo");
   btnGo.setAction (action);
   txtDomain.setAction (action);

   return pane;
}

@application.Action
public Task retrieveInfo ()
{
   return new WhoIsRetriever ();
}

public static void main (String [] args)
{
   Application.launch (WhoIs.class, args);
}

class WhoIsRetriever extends Task<String, Void>
{
   @Override
   protected String doInBackground () throws Exception
   {
      StringBuffer sb = new StringBuffer (1000);

      Socket s = new Socket (whoIsServer, WHOIS_PORT);

      PrintStream pso = new PrintStream (s.getOutputStream ());

      InputStreamReader isr = new InputStreamReader (s.getInputStream ());
      BufferedReader bri = new BufferedReader (isr);

      pso.print (txtDomain.getText ()+"\r\n");
      pso.flush ();
```

```
        String replyLine;
        while ((replyLine = bri.readLine ()) != null)
        {
            sb.append (replyLine);
            sb.append ('\n');
        }

        return sb.toString ();
    }

    @Override
    protected void succeeded (String info)
    {
        txtInfo.setText (info);
        txtInfo.setCaretPosition (0);
    }
  }
}
```

Because the SAF's main package is application, the source code begins by importing this package. One of the imported classes is SingleFrameApplication, which serves as the base class for simple GUIs that consist of one primary javax.swing.JFrame object. Behind the scenes, SingleFrameApplication creates this frame and also adds the capability to exit the application.

The public static void main(String [] args) method invokes Application's public static <T extends Application> void launch(Class<T> applicationClass, String [] args) method to start the application on the event-dispatching thread. Application is the superclass of SingleFrameApplication. This method's arguments are the name of the application class and the arguments passed to main().

■**Note** The architecture of the SAF reflects the importance of creating a Swing program's GUI on the event-dispatching thread. If you would like to learn more about the rationale for doing this, check out John Zukowski's "Swing threading and the event-dispatch thread" JavaWorld article (http://www.javaworld.com/javaworld/jw-08-2007/jw-08-swingthreading.html).

After internally creating an applicationClass instance and performing other tasks, launch() invokes the overridden protected void initialize(String [] args) method, which WhoIs uses to extract an optional server command-line argument. The WhoIs implementation of SingleFrameApplication's protected abstract void startup() method is then invoked to create and show the GUI.

The startup() method invokes JPanel makeContentPane() to create a panel containing the GUI. The panel relies on javax.swing.GroupLayout as its layout manager, which hierarchically groups components, from separate horizontal and vertical perspectives, in order to position them within a container. Refer to Chapter 1's discussion of GroupLayout for more information.

You will notice that makeContentPane() does not specify text for the lblDomain and btnGo components. Rather than hard-code this text in the source code, the text can be placed in a properties resource file, which makes the program easier to localize. The lblDomain.setName ("lblDomain"); statement connects the lblDomain component to its properties text.

In contrast to lblDomain, btnGo is linked to its properties text via its retrieveInfo action. This action is created via ActionMap map = ApplicationContext.getInstance ().getActionMap (this);, is obtained via map.get ("retrieveInfo"), and invokes public Task retrieveInfo (). The SAF requires this method to be annotated with @Action, and to have the same name as the string passed to map.get().

The retrieveInfo() method returns an instance of WhoIsRetriever, whose protected String doInBackground() method is invoked behind the scenes on a worker thread. When this method returns, the SAF invokes the overridden protected void succeeded(String info) method on the event-dispatching thread, which lets WhoIs update its GUI.

The directory containing the class files for the WhoIs application must also include a resources subdirectory that contains a WhoIs.properties file. In addition to providing localized text for the lblDomain and btnGo components, this properties file includes three special "Application" properties, as shown in Listing E-3.

Listing E-3. *WhoIs.properties*

```
Application.title = WhoIs
lblDomain.text = Domain:
retrieveInfo.Action.text = Go

Application.id = WhoIs
Application.vendorId = Jeff Friesen
```

The Application.title property specifies localized text that will appear on the frame window's title bar. Similarly, lblDomain.text and retrieveInfo.Action.text specify localized text for the lblDomain component and (via the retrieveInfo action) the btnGo component. This text is automatically injected into these components by the SAF.

Behind the scenes, the SAF manages the WhoIs application's session state (the size and position of its frame window, for example). It loads the session state when WhoIs starts running and saves this state when WhoIs exits. This state is stored in an XML file, whose path is determined by the user's home directory and the values of properties Application.id and Application.vendorId.

On my Windows XP platform, for example, the `c:\Documents and Settings\Jeff Friesen\Application Data\Jeff Friesen\WhoIs` directory stores the `WhoIs` application's `mainFrame.session.xml` file. The `Application.id` and `Application.vendorId` values are responsible for the final `Jeff Friesen\WhoIs` portion of the directory path.

Note If `Application.title` is not specified, the SAF defaults this property to `[Application.title not specified]`. If `Application.id` is not specified, the SAF defaults this property to the name of the application class, such as `WhoIs` in the example. If `Application.vendorId` is missing, the SAF chooses `UnknownApplicationVendor` as the default value.

Assuming that `AppFramework-0.43.jar` and `swing-worker-1.1.jar` are located in the same directory as `WhoIs.java` (and the `resources` subdirectory with its `WhoIs.properties` file), and assuming the Windows platform, `javac -cp AppFramework-0.43.jar;swing-worker-1.1.jar WhoIs.java` compiles this application's source code. `java -cp AppFramework-0.43.jar;swing-worker-1.1.jar;. WhoIs` runs this application with the default `whois.geektools.com` WHOIS server. (If you would like to use another server, simply specify the server's domain name via a command-line argument.) Figure E-1 shows the application's GUI.

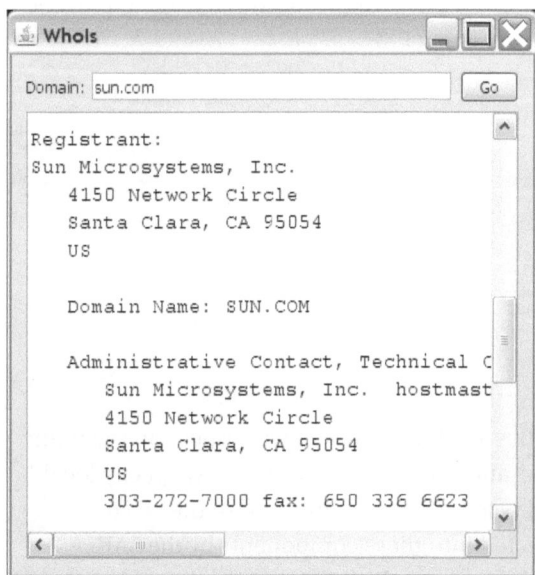

Figure E-1. *You can press the Enter key instead of clicking the Go button to obtain a domain's WHOIS information.*

Tip Although the system look and feel is the default, you can easily change to another look and feel by taking advantage of the `Application.lookAndFeel` property (described in the `Application` class's documentation). As an exercise, add `Application.lookAndFeel = default` to `WhoIs.properties`. What is the resulting look and feel?

Index

forums.apress.com

JOIN THE APRESS FORUMS AND BE PART OF OUR COMMUNITY. You'll find discussions that cover topics of interest to IT professionals, programmers, and enthusiasts just like you. If you post a query to one of our forums, you can expect that some of the best minds in the business—especially Apress authors, who all write with *The Expert's Voice*™—will chime in to help you. Why not aim to become one of our most valuable participants (MVPs) and win cool stuff? Here's a sampling of what you'll find:

DATABASES

Data drives everything.

Share information, exchange ideas, and discuss any database programming or administration issues.

PROGRAMMING/BUSINESS

Unfortunately, it is.

Talk about the Apress line of books that cover software methodology, best practices, and how programmers interact with the "suits."

INTERNET TECHNOLOGIES AND NETWORKING

Try living without plumbing (and eventually IPv6).

Talk about networking topics including protocols, design, administration, wireless, wired, storage, backup, certifications, trends, and new technologies.

WEB DEVELOPMENT/DESIGN

Ugly doesn't cut it anymore, and CGI is absurd.

Help is in sight for your site. Find design solutions for your projects and get ideas for building an interactive Web site.

JAVA

We've come a long way from the old Oak tree.

Hang out and discuss Java in whatever flavor you choose: J2SE, J2EE, J2ME, Jakarta, and so on.

SECURITY

Lots of bad guys out there—the good guys need help.

Discuss computer and network security issues here. Just don't let anyone else know the answers!

MAC OS X

All about the Zen of OS X.

OS X is both the present and the future for Mac apps. Make suggestions, offer up ideas, or boast about your new hardware.

TECHNOLOGY IN ACTION

Cool things. Fun things.

It's after hours. It's time to play. Whether you're into LEGO® MINDSTORMS™ or turning an old PC into a DVR, this is where technology turns into fun.

OPEN SOURCE

Source code is good; understanding (open) source is better.

Discuss open source technologies and related topics such as PHP, MySQL, Linux, Perl, Apache, Python, and more.

WINDOWS

No defenestration here.

Ask questions about all aspects of Windows programming, get help on Microsoft technologies covered in Apress books, or provide feedback on any Apress Windows book.

HOW TO PARTICIPATE:

Go to the Apress Forums site at **http://forums.apress.com/**.
Click the New User link.

FIND IT FAST
with the Apress *SuperIndex*™

You Need the Companion eBook

Your purchase of this book entitles you to buy the companion PDF-version eBook for only $10. Take the weightless companion with you anywhere.

We believe this Apress title will prove so indispensable that you'll want to carry it with you everywhere, which is why we are offering the companion eBook (in PDF format) for $10 to customers who purchase this book now. Convenient and fully searchable, the PDF version of any content-rich, page-heavy Apress book makes a valuable addition to your programming library. You can easily find and copy code—or perform examples by quickly toggling between instructions and the application. Even simultaneously tackling a donut, diet soda, and complex code becomes simplified with hands-free eBooks!

Once you purchase your book, getting the $10 companion eBook is simple:

❶ Visit **www.apress.com/promo/tendollars/**.

❷ Complete a basic registration form to receive a randomly generated question about this title.

❸ Answer the question correctly in 60 seconds, and you will receive a promotional code to redeem for the $10.00 eBook.

2855 TELEGRAPH AVENUE | SUITE 600 | BERKELEY, CA 94705

Offer valid through 5/19/08